My**S**KIN

SWAS MY

SIN The Progeny of
Africa in America

My Skin was My Sin

The Progeny of Africa in America

Quincy S. Smith

Diaspora Publishing

Published by: Diaspora Publishing

P.O. Box 21747
St. Petersburg, Florida 33742, USA

info@qssmith.com
www.qssmith.com

My Skin Was My Sin
Quincy S. Smith

Copyright © 2005 by Quincy S. Smith

Publisher's Cataloging-in-Publication Data
Smith, Quincy S.

> My skin was my sin : the progeny of Africa in America / Quincy S. Smith. -- Saint Petersburg, Fla. : Diaspora Publishing, 2005.

> p. ; cm.

> Includes index.
> ISBN: 0-9721078-9-4

> 1. Smith, Quincy S. 2. African American businesspeople--Biography. 3. African American young men--Social conditions--1975- 4. African Americans--Social conditions--1975 5. African Americans--Education. 6. Success--United States. 7. Success in business--United States. 8. African Americans--Study and teaching. I. Title.

E185.86 .S65 2005   2004097776
305.896/073--dc22   0502

Book Designer: Pamela Terry, Opus 1 Design
Illustrator: Steve Ferchaud
Printed in the United States of America

10 9 8 7 6 5 4 3 2 1

First Edition

Contents

The Prophecy 1

Ol'Time Religion 13

Orange Groves 23

School Days 37

Laura Street 47

Bobos 63

The Holy Ghost 69

Little White Lie 77

Cold Truth 83

Mis-Education 87

Gimmie 5, on the Black Hand Side 101

Lonely Teardrops 113

Rhythm of Africa 125

Beat Their Stringy Heads 137

Friends & Family 143

Eviction, Death, and The MVP 163

Big Man On Campus 171

Cracking Up 175

Hindsight; My Two, Me Too 193

Black Sounds & White Girls 209

Say It In My Face 225

How Ya Like Me Now 233

Stay In Your Place 253

No Compromise 259

Irony 267

Bet It Up. 281

What's The Charge. 293

Can You Play. 309

Chasing Pawns. 315

Déjà Vu 325

Barbershop Talk 335

Heart of Hearts. 347

Promise Fulfilled 355

Hit The Highway 363

The Joys of Learning 371

The New Phoenix. 381

Tennessee 397

Knowledge of Self 407

Black Jive 425

Weary. 443

Evidence of Things Not Seen 453

Index 467

"If there is no future for the Black ghetto, the future of all Negroes is diminished. What affects it, affects me, for I am a child of the ghetto"

Stanley Sanders,
"I'll Never Escape the Ghetto",
Black Voices (1971)

Why am I as I am? To understand that of any person, his whole life, from birth must be reviewed. All of our experiences fuse into our personality. Everything that ever happened to me is an ingredient.

Malcolm X,
The Autobiography of Malcolm X,
1965

I am not sure what *it* was exactly that made me write this book; but whatever *it* was, ordered me to the task. *It* did not overtake me all at once, but even upon the first thought of the undertaking, I knew that *it* would have the final say. So, I began to propitiate *it* on a fool's date of April 1, 2000 and I made my final sacrifice to *it* on March 19, 2001.

Quincy S. Smith
A late night in 2001

THE PROPHECY

During my early childhood, the story of my birth was something that I tried to avoid at all cost. As a small child, I can remember being embarrassed whenever I heard Grandma Dot tell "it". Grandma Dot was my maternal grandmother. She told the story numerous times to a countless number of friends and relatives. I thought that she added on another miracle with each recountal.

During many of her recitals, I was placed in a position in which I could not escape. Oftentimes, I was confined to a moving car or inside the house on a stormy night. I preferred to hear the story trapped in a car as opposed to hearing it cornered in the house on a stormy night.

A stormy night only added fuel to the fire for a more elaborate story. On the one hand, you had the miracle of nature and "God's work" going on outside. On the other hand, you had the miraculous story of my birth (which had to be God's work according to my grandmother) being told inside.

I can remember thinking on several occasions that it could not have been such a big deal if I were now such a normal child. I figured that if God had been so totally absorbed in making the events of my birth so miraculous, then He would have made me different at all stages of my life. I would have had a miraculous life too, not just a miraculous birth.

Besides, I didn't want my birth to be any more miraculous than any other child's birth; I was perfectly content in being a normal child. It seemed to me that I might have succeeded if it weren't for my grandmother's story. By her keeping the story alive, she forced people to do their best impression of Betty Wright: "Oh, yeah, now I remember". They would say: "That's right Dot, he wasn't supposed to make it."

Despite its obvious embellishments, the story carried a certain fascination that made most folks believe it. At first, I must admit that even I was spellbound with the way that my grandmother wove her tale. However, after hearing the new and improved version of the account so many times, I began to lose interest in the lore and skepticism replaced fascination.

I was much too young to even think that my grandmother would not tell the truth, but I wasn't convinced that she had not made a mistake in how she understood the whole thing. Perhaps that's why the latest report always contained a slightly different twist than the previous version. Nevertheless, in spite of the different twists, my grandmother's stories of my birth always ended with the same conclusion that I dreaded to hear: I was anything but a normal child—I was special.

I didn't want to be special. I wanted to be normal. That's why whenever I wasn't in a situation that I had to endure the story, I always chose to run for the hills; the hills were any place out of earshot of my grandmother. Still, by the age of four, I had heard the story so many times that I can tell you the complete saga of my birth from memory. That's something considering that I'm now twenty-six years old and I haven't heard "it" in nearly twenty years.

I was born on April 26, 1973 in Sarasota, Florida. I was born two months premature and weighed all of two pounds, nine ounces. My doctors did not know if I was going to live or die and told my family "not to get their hopes up".

Physicians are essentially pessimists when it comes to serious health issues because so many things can go wrong. That characteristic in medical doctors makes medical science an oxymoron profession. It's full of extremely bright people that prepare you for the worst while they work for the best.

Under that premise, the people with the white coats and the "glass is half-empty" outlook went to work on trying to ensure my survival. I was placed in an incubator until July of that same year.

While my doctors went to work on saving me according to the tradition of their training, another group of trained specialists also went to work on saving me according to the tradition of their training. I have no doubt that my doctors were very well trained in their profession, and I am sure that they understood the man made science of medicine. In contrast, the second group of trained specialists were not trained in any man made sciences; they were trained in that ol' time religion that believed in taking everything to God in prayer. Their faith forced them to believe that the glass was always half-full.

The members of the take everything to God in prayer group consisted of the friends and the family members of the two people who had brought me into the world. They had come to the hospital to pray for the child that wasn't supposed to make it. Unlike my doctors, they were eternal optimists that believed that in the end that hope would not disappoint. They believed that God could do anything but fail.

I didn't know it at the time, but the Black folks who came to that hospital to pray for me were a part of a long tradition of Black folks who bent their knees daily to thank God for His blessings. They were a continuation of the faith in the fact that prayer changed things. Sustained by their faith, they had grown accustomed to asking God to turn the impossible into the possible the same way that He turned water into wine.

In her never-ending stories, my grandmother acknowledged the prayers of all that came; but she told of the faith, prayers, and prophecies of Mama Cleo with special reverence. Mama Cleo was the mother of Charles Brooks, my Grandmother's second husband.

"Granddaddy Charles" was not my biological grandfather, but I never heard my grandmother refer to him any other way whenever she was in my presence. I don't remember too much about the man because he died when I was just a baby, but his mother remained in contact with my grandmother right up until the time of her death in 1999.

When Mama Cleo died many people believed that the Lord had truly called home to rest one of his most faithful and dutiful servants. Those people would not have been the least bit surprised if St. Peter himself had come down to escort her soul through the pearly gates.

In parts of Africa, it is a widely held view that it always rains when a great soul is called home to glory. It's not that God weeps; it's that the spirit of the great soul must be washed. If the African view is true and the stories of my grandmother are authentic, then surely there was a rain shower the day that Mama Cleo died.

In life, Mama Cleo had been afflicted with a condition that made it extremely difficult for her to walk and she rarely left the house unless for a church service. She was a woman respected for her strong faith and her belief in Jehovah Jireh. She was what is known in the church as an elder. Because of her difficulty walking, Mama Cleo couldn't make it to Sarasota Memorial; so she called on the telephone to pray for me when I was born. She used a conventional telephone to call the hospital, but those people who knew her best would tell you that her true call was placed through to that mainline to Jesus.

You can hear Black folks singing about that mainline to Jesus in a number of Black churches across the South on any given Sunday. Later on during my childhood, *"Jesus on the Mainline"* would become one of my favorite church songs. The refrain in the song would set my little hands to clapping and my little dangling feet to tapping while my little heart rejoiced in the Lord.

"Jesus on the mainline—tell him what you want"
"Jesus on the mainline—tell him what you want"

My grandmother told everybody that Mama Cleo rebuked those doctors who informed the family "not to get their hopes up" and said that God had told her that not only would I make it, but that I was "going to be a great man". Thus the prophecy was born.

I stayed in a hospital incubator for nearly three months before my doctors were convinced that I was going to make it. When the professionals who had prepared my family for the worst released me to go home in late July with a clean bill of health, the faithful Mama Cleo appeared to be dead on the money with her prophecy. I suppose my doctors' declarations of me being a healthy baby only added to the faith of the people that prayed for me. It added to their faith in God and it added to their belief in both parts of Mama Cleo's prophecy.

The second part of her prophecy claimed that I would one day be a great man. Throughout my childhood, I watched those who knew of my ordeal at birth watch me as they waited for signs of the second fulfillment. Their wait or expectancy isn't anything that I can explain; it was just something that I felt from time to time. Sometimes it blew over me in the form of a gentle breeze and other times as a strong and mighty wind; but no matter how it blew over me, it always felt like I had an obligation to do something more than what I was doing at the time. Sometimes I welcomed the challenge of trying to do that, but other times I wished that Mama Cleo had simply left off the part about being "a great man".

From the lack of stories between the trials and tribulations surrounding my birth and my first year of life, I can only infer that I had a normal infancy where I learned to walk and talk like normal babies. I'm confident that I would have heard otherwise if that were not the case; my grandmother was reared in the Black tradition of storytelling that kept an oral record of life events. That tradition can be traced all the way back to our African roots and the role of the Griot in different West African societies.

My grandmother was the official Griot in our family. She told me that I learned to walk at nine months of age and that I began to talk shortly after my first full year of life. I was returned to my doctors for follow-up visits that confirmed that I had made a wonderful recovery from any problems that I might have suffered from such an early birth. Life for the new baby boy was good, but it wouldn't stay that way. My period of typical infant development was soon broken by another life threatening situation.

At the age of two, I had to be rushed to the hospital for a very high temperature of 105 degrees. My doctors worked feverishly in an effort to reduce my temperature, but they could not determine its cause. They performed a CAT scan and a spinal tap on my tiny two-year-old body, but my grandmother was not satisfied with leaving my fate in the hands of men. Yet again, she had to get God and his faithful servant involved. She called Mama Cleo on the phone and Mama Cleo got on that mainline to Jesus one more time.

I suppose my grandmother figured that if it had worked once that two times wasn't too much to hope for when it came to her grandson. After Mama Cleo finished praying, she told my grandmother that I was going to be okay and not to worry. My grandmother said that my doctors came in within minutes of her getting off the phone with Mama Cleo and told her that they had isolated the germ that was responsible for my high fever. They claimed that if I had arrived five minutes later that I could have died.

As it turned out, I had suffered a fall that cracked my right hip, but no one knew it. The area had become infected and caused me to run a high temperature. I had an operation to repair the damage to my hip, but my doctors said that there was a chance that I may not walk again. They went on to add that if I did walk again, then I would always have problems with the hip.

As to be expected of a "miracle child", I recovered and I did indeed walk again—although I had to learn the skill all over at the age of two. I carry a scar in that area to this day from that operation. Every so often my hip gives me trouble when I try to stretch it further than it wants to go, but on the whole I consider myself to be a very blessed individual to be able to walk, run, and jump. Years can go by without me ever noticing it beyond the visual presence of the scar that my surgery left behind.

I still believe that my grandmother might have embellished a bit during my childhood when she told of my two brushes with death in my first two years of life, but I don't mind anymore. I know now that any embellishment that she may have done at the time was a result of her faith in God and her love for me. She, along with many others, believed that God had a direct hand in my survival during those early ordeals. I agree with them. Just the other day (4/7/2000), I was riding in my car thinking about that period of my life when I got stuck behind a truck that had one of the most powerful stickers that I have ever read on its bumper. The bumper sticker read: "I knew you before I formed you in the womb—God".

The funny thing was that just a minute or so before seeing that bumper sticker, I was pondering the prophecy made by Mama Cleo during my infancy. She said that I would become "a great man". I wondered if Mama Cleo's words were really messages that came to her from God … and if they were, what did they mean for my future? I wasn't feeling very "great" at the time, and I didn't see any greatness on the horizon. I knew enough by that time to know that many a Black male child had been prophesied for greatness in error.

I reckon I was close to considering my own prophecy an error. I wasn't a "great" anything. Right before I saw the bumper sticker, I was on the brink of concluding that God had never said anything about me to Mama Cleo.

Considering my state of mind, one can only imagine the impact that the bumper sticker had on me. I was already deep in thought about prophecies and the role of God in the first two years of my life. I read the sticker and I knew that it wasn't a coincidence. I felt that God had directly intervened in the conversation that had been going on within my mind. Even now as I am typing these words, my belief in the fact that God spoke with me that day is confirmed by something that I heard in the first hour of the new millennium.

The night of December 31, 1999 found me in church. I had never gone to church on New Year's Eve before, but the storms going on in my life at that time blew me right through the church doors. The words read by the preacher during the first hour of the new millennium were from Psalm 139 verses 1 - 13. They read:

O LORD, thou hast searched me, and known me.
Thou knowest my downsitting and my uprising,
Thou understandest my thoughts afar off.
Thou compassest my path and my lying down,
and art acquainted with all my ways.
For there is not a word in my tongue,
but, lo, O Lord, thou knowest it altogether.
Thou hast beset me behind and before,
and laid thy hand upon me.
Such knowledge is too wonderful for me;
it is high, I cannot attain unto it.
Whither shall I go from thy spirit?
Or whither shall I flee from thy presence?
If I ascend up into heaven thou art there:
if I make my bed in hell, behold thou art there.
If I take the wings of the morning,
and dwell in the uttermost parts of the sea;
Even there shall thy hand lead me,
and thy right hand shall hold me.
If I say, Surely the darkness shall cover me;
even the night shall be light about me.
Yea, the darkness hideth not from thee;
but the night shineth as the day:
the darkness and the light are both alike to thee.
For thou hast possessed my reins:
thou hast covered me in my mother's womb.

The passage suggests that there is no place that anyone can go to escape the presence of the Lord. It asserts that there is no thought that one can have of which the Lord is not already aware, and that there is no word that one can speak that the Lord has not already known before it was even formed by the tongue. It speaks of the inability of the human mind to even come close to the knowledge of God. Finally, it reveals the presence and protection of the Lord— even in the womb.

When I apply the facts of Psalm 139 verses 1-13 to the situation of getting stuck behind a truck with that particular bumper sticker, I can only believe. The random chance of everything happening the way that it did just as I was thinking about the credibility of Mama Cleo's prophecies and the role of God in my first two years of life is too small.

I can only believe that the Lord had direct intervention in the trials of my first two years of life through the intercessory prayers of Mama Cleo. I can only believe that there was direct intervention from God that morning in traffic when I saw that bumper sticker. I can only believe that there was direct intervention in both situations from a God who knew my thoughts before I had them. Direct intervention from a God who knew the words of my questions before I formed them. Direct intervention from a God who was and who is always with me. Direct intervention from a God who knew me and protected me—even in the womb.

The prophecies of Mama Cleo, while they were never something that I took lightly, are now very real to me and I trust that the Lord will lead me according to my purpose and His plan. I believe that I am here to take care of some business. As I once heard a famous preacher say, I have a supernatural assignment that my Father wants me to complete.

I have never taken an opportunity to thank Mama Cleo and the people who prayed and interceded unto the Lord on my behalf during those troubled times of my first two years of life. So, I would like to say a long overdue thank-you to those faithful who helped bring me through.

I know that I am either here to do a great thing in a big way or that I am here to do a small thing in a great way. I don't know which, but I know that His plan for me will be fulfilled. Nothing ever returns to God without fulfilling His plan for it—not even one drop of rain.

When I was a small child trying to escape the stories told by my grandmother, I rejected the fact that those prayers had any effect on the outcome of my survival. However, I began to realize some years later that if I were going to continue to reject the effectiveness of prayer, it would be at the price of rejecting the values and beliefs of those around me.

It seemed that religion was a constant thing in my childhood. It was either to be found lurking around the corner or right in my face. That statement is probably true for a lot of Black people who grew up in the South during the same time period in which I was raised. For me, it always seemed that the "ol' folks" were always talking about something or doing something that involved religion. I want to write a little about what I mean by that, but before I do, I want to share an e-mail that I received from a friend of mine.

The reason that I want to share this e-mail in this book is because we have all been caught in a situation where we've smelled the unique scent of rain. The next time that you smell that scent, I want you to think about this story and the greatness of God.

In an effort to protect the privacy of the family, I have purposefully omitted the surnames of the family members and not revealed the city in which they live. Here is the story of a little girl that was born premature just like I was. The e-mail is her family's testimony of the Lord's role in her birth. The title of the e-mail is *Smell of Rain*. It made me smile when the little girl's father told me that the child's grandmother wrote the story.

Smell of Rain

A cold March wind danced around the dead of night in Texas as the Doctor walked into the small hospital room of Diana. Still groggy from surgery, her husband David held her hand as they braced themselves for the latest news.

That afternoon of March 10, 1991, complications had forced Diana, only 24-weeks pregnant, to undergo an emergency cesarean to deliver the couple's new daughter, Danae. At 12 inches long and weighing only one pound and nine ounces, they already knew she was perilously premature.

9

Still, the doctor's soft words dropped like bombs. 'I don't think she's going to make it', he said, as kindly as he could.

'There's only a 10-percent chance she will live through the night, and even then, if by some slim chance she does make it, her future could be a very cruel one'.

Numb with disbelief, David and Diana listened as the doctor described the devastating problems Danae would likely face if she survived. She would never walk, she would never talk, she would probably be blind, and she would certainly be prone to other catastrophic conditions from cerebral palsy to complete mental retardation, and on and on.

No! No! was all Diana could say. She and David, with their 5-year-old son Dustin, had long dreamed of the day they would have a daughter to become a family of four. Now, within a matter of hours, that dream was slipping away. Through the dark hours of morning as Danae held onto life by the thinnest thread, Diana slipped in and out of sleep, growing more and more determined that their tiny daughter would live—and live to be a healthy, happy young girl.

But David, fully awake and listening to additional dire details of their daughter's chances of ever leaving the hospital alive, much less healthy, knew he must confront his wife with the inevitable.

David walked in and said that we needed to talk about making funeral arrangements. Diana remembers 'I felt so bad for him because he was doing everything, trying to include me in what was going on, but I just wouldn't listen, I couldn't listen.' I said, 'No, that is not going to happen, no way! I don't care what the doctors say; Danae is not going to die! One day she will be just fine, and she will be coming home with us!'

As if willed to live by Diana's determination, Danae clung to life hour after hour, with the help of every medical machine and marvel her miniature body could endure. But as those first days passed, a new agony set in for David and Diana. Because Danae's underdeveloped nervous system was essentially 'raw,' the lightest kiss or caress only intensified her discomfort, so they couldn't even cradle their tiny baby girl against their chests to offer the strength of their love. All they could do, as Danae struggled alone beneath the ultraviolet light in the tangle of tubes and wires, was to pray that God would stay close to their precious little girl.

There was never a moment when Danae suddenly grew stronger. But as the weeks went by, she did slowly gain an ounce of weight here and an ounce of strength there. At last, when Danae turned two months old, her parents were able to hold her in their arms for the very first time. And two months later-though doctors continued to gently but grimly warn that her chances of surviving, much less living any kind of normal life, were next to zero. Danae went home from the hospital, just as her mother had predicted.

Today, five years later, Danae is a petite but feisty young girl with glittering gray eyes and an unquenchable zest for life. She shows no signs, whatsoever, of any mental or physical impairment. Simply she is everything a little girl can be and more—but that happy ending is far from the end of her story.

One blistering afternoon in the summer of 1996 near her home in Texas, Danae was sitting in her mother's lap in the bleachers of a local ballpark where her brother Dustin's baseball team was practicing. As always, Danae was chattering non-stop with her mother and several other adults sitting nearby when she suddenly fell silent.

Hugging her arms across her chest, Danae asked, "Do you smell that?"

Smelling the air and detecting the approach of a thunderstorm, Diana replied, 'Yes, it smells like rain.'

Danae closed her eyes and again asked, 'Do you smell that?' Once again, her mother replied, 'Yes, I think we're about to get wet, it smells like rain.'

Still caught in the moment, Danae shook her head, patted her thin shoulders with her small hands and loudly announced, 'No, it smells like Him. It smells like God when you lay your head on His chest.'

Tears blurred Diana's eyes as Danae then happily hopped down to play with the other children. Before the rains came, her daughter's words confirmed what Diana and all the members of the extended family had known, at least in their hearts, all along. During those long days and nights of her first two months of her life, when her nerves were too sensitive for them to touch her, God was holding Danae on His chest and it is His loving scent that she remembers so well.

Isn't that a wonderful story! What a special little girl Danae must be. When I received her story, I knew that I had to share it in this book. I would like to say thank-you to the family for allowing me to reprint it in this form. I have only done so in an effort to glorify and magnify the name of the one Almighty who is most worthy to be praised.

OL' TIME RELIGION

I must have been around eight years old when I learned that religion was serious business for a lot of Black people. My paternal grandmother was one of those Black people. Her name was Mary and she believed that religion and prayer were things that were to be taken very seriously on a daily basis. Once or twice a week, she would attend special sessions that were strictly devoted to praying. In additions to those special sessions, she also prayed at home. There were numerous occasions that I stumbled upon her on her knees silently praying next to her bed.

During the special sessions that she attended once or twice a week, she prayed out loud with other people. She used to call those sessions prayer meetings. It was always super important to her that she go to her prayer meetings. She rushed around the kitchen to make sure that dinner was prepared before it was time to go. Once she was sure that we had what we needed to nourish our flesh, she dashed off to nourish her spirit. I can remember attending a few of those meetings with her; I wanted to go to find out why it was so important to her that she went so often.

Meetings usually took place at the church or at someone's house, and there was always a heavy concentration of older folks present. The ol' folks prayed for anybody or any situation that they thought required the special attention of the Lord. Despite my youth and my ignorance, it didn't take me long to realize that the ol' folks thought that everything and everybody required the special attention of the Lord. Thus, they prayed about everything and for everybody.

I thought that the Lord was going to get tired of them with all of their requests. Every other word out of their mouths was Lord this and Lord that. For each thing that they asked for, there was something else that they already had that they were thankful for. So after the Lord this and the Lord that; it was thank-you Lord for this and thank-you Lord for that. Lawd-ha-mercy, it was enough to drive a sinner holy!

Grandma Mary's prayer lists were always especially long because she was known as a person that had been blessed by the Lord with the ability to speak in tongues. Many people also believed that the Lord had blessed her with the ability to heal folks. People came from all over the county to have my grandmother pray for different sicknesses. Things that the doctors couldn't do anything for were brought to my grandmother. It didn't matter if you were saved or not, she never turned anyone away and she never charged one single cent for her healing. She was much like the great George Washington Carver in that sense. When explaining why he chose not to patent his many discoveries, Mr. Carver would simply say: "God gave them to me; how can I sell them to someone else?"

The prayers of those in attendance were a big part of the prayer meetings, but the part of those meetings that I liked the most was the singing that usually followed the prayers. Even at a young age, I could feel the power of the gospel when sang from pure hearts. I say the songs that they sang were from pure hearts because the people in those meetings were not wealthy people and they truly lived life one day at a time. They earnestly believed that the Lord would make a way out of no way. The multi-purpose cure for every problem, every ailment, or every grievance was to be found in the Lord. You were supposed to take it all to the Lord in prayer.

For the people in those meetings each new day had sufficient challenges of its own; and the challenges often required maximum physical, mental, and spiritual effort in order to be conquered. The experience of planning ahead and thinking about the problems of tomorrow and the problems of next week usually limits itself to a class of people who have enough money and security to easily handle the problems of the day at hand. The people in my grandmother's prayer meetings did not belong to that kind of class.

Many of the individuals were either around the same age or older than my grandmother which meant that they were either born in the 1920's, the 1930's, or the 1940's. They were Black people who had carried the yoke of oppression around their necks all of their lives while enduring the constant companionship of poverty.

A lot of the meetings were held at the home of my paternal great-grandparents (God bless their soul, they have both since passed from us) who were both but one generation removed from slavery. I never heard the story of how it happened, but my paternal great-grandfather was a blind man. By the time I was eight years old, he was in his eighties. He couldn't see me, but he knew my name and he always called me over to him so that he could examine my hands. He was never satisfied until he felt my hands. He did that with my cousins too.

I thought that he had some special powers to be able to tell who people were by shaking their hands. His wife was his perfect complement who he simply called Sister. That was something that I couldn't understand because I knew that my paternal great-grandmother was not his sister, but I didn't dare ask too many questions because of the old southern rule that said children should be seen and not heard. I wouldn't have been able to ask my great-grandmother anyway; she was very hard of hearing. Usually, she just nodded and smiled toward questions that were asked of her. If you really wanted to make sure that she heard you, then you had to repeat yourself real loud over and over. I wasn't about to do that either.

My great-grandparents, being in their seventies and eighties, were easily the oldest people in attendance at the prayer meetings held at their home, but the room also contained other ol' folks whose heads were already gray and tilted toward the grave. I didn't know it then, but I know now that those people had lived their whole lives sacrificing.

The lack of opportunities afforded to Black folks during their generations made doing without their standard method of operation. They did without for so long that they didn't even consider it as doing without. That was especially true when you consider the fact that some of those ol' folks in the prayer meetings had experienced being Black in America during the Great Depression of the 1930's. If that period was as bad as they say it was for white folks in America, then you know what it was for Black folks in America (If they caught a cold, we died from pneumonia).

I can recall the old rickety wooden frame house where my great-grandparents lived and the extremely modest dishes that we ate off when I ate Sunday dinner at their house. Many things in the house seemed to be as old as the two people that lived there, but I don't ever remember feeling embarrassed or saddened by the modest life of my great-grandparents. Perhaps I never felt those emotions because they never showed them.

All of the participants in the prayer meetings seemed to be very content with life. They were always thankful, despite the fact that they didn't seem to have many material possessions to show for their long years of struggle and strife. I don't recall very many of them arriving at my great-grandparents house in their own cars; it was just an accepted part of the meeting that the praying wouldn't start until so and so went to pick-up so and so, so and so, and so and so.

When I look back on those ol' Black folks in those prayer meetings, I know that being Black in America during their time severely limited their opportunities for material success. By contrast, I also know that their lack of material success enhanced their achievement of spiritual success. They couldn't depend on money or wealth to solve their problems. They had to depend on a mighty living God and each other in times of crisis. The fact that they repeatedly made it through tough times fortified their faith in God and their attachment to each other. Alaine Locke, the famous African-American philosopher, described their situation perfectly in *The New Negro* (1925) when he said:

> All classes of a people under social pressure are permeated with common experience; they are emotionally welded as others cannot be. With them, even ordinary living has epic depth and lyric intensity, and this their material handicap, is their spiritual advantage.

The spiritual advantage of the people in those prayer meetings was rooted in an inexhaustible faith in Jesus Christ. They had that mustard seed faith that moved mountains.

I was fortunate that I had an opportunity to see such faith as a small child. It has helped me to walk by faith and not by sight in the problem areas of my life that were too dark and too big for my human eyes to see beyond. I know that my ability to do that is a direct result of the tradition in which I was reared in as a child.

Our ancestors were, and our elders are, much more spiritual than my generation. We (my generation) have achieved more material wealth and success than the generations before us, but we lack the spiritual convictions of the past. I wish that I could say that I was an exception, but I'm not. Despite my remembrance of the old ways, I fail in comparison to the ol' folks when it comes to spiritual conviction.

The spiritual convictions of our ancestors and elders are being replaced with a materialism that threatens to destroy us from within. Black people have always been attacked from the outside, but now the core values of our people are no longer strong enough to withstand the market morality that is pervasive throughout American culture. New opportunities have diminished our remembrance of the old ways and our internal values are eroding.

We are setting ourselves up for an implosion. We, as a people, have survived in this country because we have always had a stronger morality than the mainstream society that surrounds us. Now, that survival is being threatened by a changing morality within our ranks that is becoming more in line with the morality of the mainstream society around us.

The mainstream society around us worships the almighty dollar and offers obeisance to the goods and services that can only be bought with currency. Where we were once a people spiritually motivated, we are fast becoming a people only currency motivated. *"Move on Up a Little Higher"* doesn't mean what it used to mean in Mahalia's day.

We can't afford to let our spirituality be bought and sold for the love of money. No amount of money or no amount of goods can compensate for the loss of our spirituality. Jesus asked the question, in Matthew 16:26: "For what is a man profited, if he shall gain the whole world, and lose his soul? or what shall a man give in exchange for his soul?". The answer is clear. There is nothing of this world that a man or woman can gain that will offset the loss of his or her soul. Our people have known the answer to that question for generations, but we now stand on the verge of bartering our souls in exchange for goods and services.

Our ancestors and elders taught us better than that and it is my hope that we can teach the next generation better than that; but if we are to accomplish that task, then we will have to reverse this terrible trend toward a market morality. And reverse it quickly!

Dr. Cornell West talked about market morality in his 1993 book, *Race Matters*. Dr. West is an African-American philosopher, theologian, activist, author, lecturer, and professor—a disseminator of knowledge. I am a tremendous fan of his keen intellect. He wrote:

Black people have always been in America's wilderness
in search of a promised land. Yet many black folk now
reside in a jungle ruled by a cutthroat market morality
devoid of any faith in deliverance or hope for freedom.

"Market morality" has pervaded many segments of current
African-American culture. It can be heard in our music. That's significant because the truest essence of the Black experience in America
has always been found in the music. That has been true from the
songs of the first slaves in this country to the songs of today's Black
artists. Evidence of market morality can be seen in our films and
our music videos. It has been embraced by some Black leaders and
by some Black organizations. It has grabbed some of our preachers
and religious leaders by the throats. Some are preaching from the
pulpit with Rolex watches with enough diamonds in them to blind
the congregation. Some, not all, are fleecing the flock.

We cannot afford this at a time when the need for leadership and
service from pure hearts is more important than ever before. We
have gotten caught up in the mainstream American definition of life
that was established early on in the history of this land. That definition has always placed profit above all else, and in the abhorrent
aftermath dared to ask the question: "what harm is a full purse?"
The United States of America is a country that has slaughtered a
countless number of Native Americans and enslaved a countless
number of Africans in order that it might achieve its "Manifest
Destiny". Despite its lofty claims of greatness, if no atonement is
made, that will be its most enduring legacy.

To justify its conscience against some of the most inhumane
crimes ever committed against humanity; the power structure of
America has often let the ends justify the means. The most important and enduring end for the hegemony of America has been the
divid "end".

Dr. W.E.B. Du Bois (the co-founder of the NAACP, writer, social
scientist, critic, and intellectual) did a superb job of summarizing the
definition of American life that I am referring to in his 1964 autobiography, *The Autobiography of W.E.B. Du Bois: A Soliloquy on Viewing
My Life from the Last Decade of Its First Century*. Dr. Du Bois wrote:

> The most extraordinary characteristic of current
> American life is the attempt to reduce life to buying and
> selling. Life is not love unless sex is bought and sold.

Life is not knowledge save knowledge of technique, of science for destruction. Life is not beauty except for beauty for sale. Life is not art unless its price is high and it is sold for profit. All life is production for profit, and for what is profit but for buying and selling again?

The deduction of life to the buying and selling of goods had previously been the domain of mainstream or white America. Historically, like so many other areas of mainstream American life, we were not invited to the party. We only watched from the outside looking in because we didn't have the economic clout or the economic opportunity to buy entry into the game. In a sense, the economic proscription that prevented us from buying entry into the game was a blessing, because now that some African-Americans have achieved a degree of economic success it has become very difficult to distinguish between their values and the values of mainstream America. They are mirror images of one another.

In far too many cases, there is no distinction and that is the underlying cause of the market morality that threatens to destroy our salvation as a people. If we sell-out to the idea that the dollar is all mighty, we can't possibly keep our faith grounded in the true Almighty. What's even more disturbing is the fact that the poorest of our people, who have long been the salt of the earth with their unwavering faith, have fallen victim to the lust for the dollar bill. Many of them are abandoning their faith for the love of money. At one point, we were bought and sold for the love of money, now we stand on the brink of selling-out to that same love.

The bible informs us of the evils associated with the love of money in I Timothy 6:10. It warns: "For the love of money is the root of all evil: which while some coveted after, they have erred from the faith, and pierced themselves through with many sorrows." If you believe in the words in I Timothy 6:10, then you know that we need to focus more on our faith accounts and less on our bank accounts. That is the philosophy that has brought our people this far. Our ancestors and elders did not spend all that time on their knees praying to God for us to go astray now. In these new and exciting times, we still need some of that "ol' time religion"; it was good enough for our ancestors and elders, and it is good enough for us. It's our time to get on our knees to thank the Lord for this and thank the Lord for that. We are providing the example for the generation that will follow us. Amen. Let us pray.

I don't want anybody to confuse my message when I write that we need to focus more on our faith accounts and less on our bank accounts. I recognize that it takes money to survive in this world that we live in today. It seems that everything has a price tag on it and the costs on those price tags are rising by the minute. I'm not suggesting that we ignore that fact of life or spend our time praying all day for something to feed our kids or a place to lay our heads at night. I am proposing that when we do pray, let us move our feet and go out and work for what we need in life. But while we are working hard, pray to the Lord and trust in the Lord to order our steps in helping us to meet the demands of our daily lives. When we do that we will find that all the things that we *need* will be provided unto us.

I'm not asking that you take my humble words as the gospel on this subject, I'm asking that you believe the words of the One who sits on high at the right hand of God with all power in His hand. In Matthew 6:33, Jesus said: "But seek ye first the kingdom of God, and his righteousness; and all these things shall be added unto you." Brothers and sisters I urge you to take heed to those words because: "It is written, Man shall not live by bread alone, but by every word that proceedeth out of the mouth of God." That's a testament from the old school (Deuteronomy 8:3).

I know that I have digressed a bit, but I will continue to do so throughout my story as particular experiences in my life lend themselves to providing insight into current problems facing African-Americans today. Therefore, I ask that you please tolerate my digressions on the grounds that I am only trying to bring relevant issues to the forefront for my people.

So far I have described the first two years of my life and recounted a fraction of my eighth year of life. I realize that there is a lot of life between two years of age and eight years of age, and I do not intend to leave ages three through seven out of the story. I thought it was important to establish right from the start the spirituality that has always been a part of my life and a part of the tradition of my people. Some of what I have written about my life up until this point has been based on what my maternal grandmother has told me, but beginning with the age of three I can recall the facts as they happened through my own eyes. So what you read from this point on will be based entirely on my own perspectives and my own perceptions.

Everything prior to this sentence has been from my memories as a twenty-six-year-old Black male. Everything following this sentence will be from my memories as a twenty-seven-year-old Black male. Today (4/26/00) is my twenty-seventh birthday. Another year; thank the Lord for that.

ORANGE GROVES

From three years of age until eight years of age, I spent most of my time in three different settings. I went back and forth between those settings quite frequently. It was nothing for me to go from one setting to another in the course of a few months. Because of that, I can't accurately give a simple chronological outline of the time spent in each setting. However, I can give a brief description of each environment, so that you will have a better understanding of each individual place.

The first environment was in Palmetto, Florida. Both sides of my family (paternal and maternal) had roots in Palmetto. I am sure that that was the place where my mother met my father. My family lived in an area of town that was called "Dirty Street". I have always taken the liberty to assume that our little neighborhood was called Dirty Street because none of the roads were paved. It seemed to me that it was common practice to name areas of that little community according to the attributes of the surrounding streets.

I remember when my friends and I would all go to ride our bikes in an area of the community referred to as the "Hard Road". That area was called the Hard Road due to the fact that the road was paved. We ventured to the Hard Road to enjoy our bikes on a smooth surface as opposed to contending with the bumps of the dirt roads.

In the back of Grandma Dot's house and across the railroad tracks there was a cluster of apartments called Overpass Apartments. The apartments were bordered on two sides by overpasses associated with U.S Highway 301.

The little tiny community defined by its streets where I grew up as a youngster in Palmetto was a community where I had family members virtually on every street that I have described with the exception of the Hard Road. Overpass Apartments was home to many of my blood uncles and cousins. If that wasn't bad enough, then add the fact that these people had an extensive network that included adopted relatives that had no consanguineous ties to me. Nearly every other apartment in Overpass had someone in it that was a part of the network. Dirty Street wasn't any better; I was related by blood to at least fifty percent of the people who lived there. Needless to say, there were very few places where I could misbehave without fear of consequence.

I can remember one of the worst beatings that I ever received at the hands of Grandma Dot was due to my use of profanity. Some person unknown to me had informed her that I was "in the streets cussing". The offense for which I was whipped did not trouble me because I was guilty. I had cussed up and down Overpass Apartments that entire day. I cussed until my heart was content and surely I deserved every stripe, so I knew that the beating was a justified beating.

The thing that did bother me was the fact that I did not know who the informant was or where he or she had heard me cussing. My ignorance of who snitched on me had the effect of eliminating my cussing habit altogether because I didn't know where I could indulge in the habit without fear of punishment. I was so mad about the whole thing that it took everything that I had not to ask my grandmother: "where in the hell did she get her damn information?" I was mad, but I wasn't stupid; I decided that it was best to just stop cussing everywhere.

The technique of community policing was used on a great number of the kids that I ran around with in that Palmetto neighborhood. It proved to be successful most of the time. Many of us would always weigh the consequences of our actions if we were caught before we engaged in inappropriate behaviors. We only did things when we thought that we were going to get away with them. With all the incognito spies, you never could be sure who was going to drop the dime on you.

The parents and guardians of the community strengthened the effectiveness of the community policing technique by verbally assuring us that there were eyes and ears everywhere. They told us that we were lucky because when they were growing up they used to receive a "whuppin" from anybody in the community who discovered them misbehaving which was usually followed up by a second whuppin when their parents found out about the inappropriate behavior. They considered the downgrade by the folks in the community from actual beating the children for what they had seen or heard to just reporting to the parents to be a stroke of luck for us.

I heard those stories long before I heard the famous African Proverb that claimed: "it takes a whole village to raise a child". When I did hear that proverb for the first time, I had a clear understanding of what it meant. It is sad for us that we are moving further and further away from that proverb as time passes.

I would be remiss if I didn't talk about the people of the community because the community contained an interesting diversity. As I remember them, the people of that little Palmetto community were a mixture of the working class poor, folks who received assistance from the state, and migrant workers.

The migrant workers were of particular interest to me because a great percentage of them were Mexican. Their presence was the only thing that stood in the way of that community being one hundred percent Black. I don't recall any white people in that community—not one single one.

The Mexican people brought with them their own language and their own culture, which provided a sharp contrast to the dominant Black culture of the area. Most of the Mexicans lived in Overpass Apartments. It was nothing to walk by one apartment and smell collard greens, macaroni and cheese, and fried chicken. In the very next apartment, you would smell burritos and enchiladas.

The second environment where I spent a good deal of my childhood was on the outskirts of Plant City, Florida. It took shape in a place that was referred to by all those in Plant City as "The Country". I found out recently that the official name of the locality was Bealsville, Florida. From my own memories, I can only infer that it was called The Country due to its rural qualities. Whenever we spent time in Bealsville, we lived in a trailer. A lot of the people that I knew in Bealsville lived in a trailer. The trailers weren't close together like some trailer parks; they were usually spread about over good portions of land.

The acreage of land supported many different kinds of fields, different kinds of animals, and orange groves. The particular tract of land where our trailer was staged boasted a strawberry field across the road from our front yard; an orange grove in the back yard; and a horse that remained tied to a tract on the side of our trailer.

The only time that I can remember that horse getting his freedom was when he took control of his own destiny and broke his chain. I don't remember anyone ever freeing him based on any sympathy for his plight or general concern for his happiness. I was always thrilled for him whenever he broke loose. Each time he got away, I secretly wished for them to never catch him. His long face was always so wistful whenever he was tied to that stake in the ground.

The people who lived in The Country seemed to be caught in a time warp. After my time in Bealsville, I saw movies that portrayed sharecroppers and the things that were involved in their day-to-day lives. Such portrayals always made me think that the little town was some sort of remainder of a sharecropping arrangement. I don't have any factual evidence to support such a claim, just a comparison of my memories as a child with the visual images of a sharecropper's lifestyle provided by television. Some of the similarities included: chicken coops and hog pens; we had to heat water on the stove in order to have hot water; and oftentimes things were hunted, shot, killed, skinned, cleaned, cooked, and eaten.

I can remember eating rabbit; it tasted just like chicken and was one of my favorites. I can remember eating possum. I don't recall what it tasted like, but I don't think that I enjoyed it very much. I can also remember eating raccoon—commonly referred to as "coon" in dem dar parts.

In contrast, there were two differences between what I saw in sharecropping movies and what I saw in Bealsville. The first difference was that most of the Black folks in Bealsville were landowners not tenants. The second difference was that I never saw anybody work in the fields that occupied the land immediately surrounding our community. I don't know, maybe we were never there during the picking seasons. Aside from those differences, the place was as sharecroppish and rural as sharecroppish and rural could be. If I had any ambitions of growing up to be a country boy, then Bealsville would have been the best environment for me to fulfill those dreams.

The third environment was very different from the two that I have already described. It was also my favorite during my early childhood. I write that despite the fact that it was the environment that gave birth to my troubled relationship with my mother. It, like Bealsville, was also in Plant City, Florida. It was in the city part of the town. Actually, I can't even say much about the town itself because the area that I had the most exposure to was only a street. Laura Street to be specific. Laura Street was home to Plant City's Black underground nightlife. My uncle's café/poolroom was my home on Laura St.

I called him my uncle, but I can't say that that title was established by consanguinity. I believe that the man known to me as "Uncle Hennisan" was actually Grandma Dot's first cousin; that would have made him my third cousin. My extended family was full of people who had titles that could not be substantiated through actual blood ties. Nonetheless, I thought of him as my uncle; I thought of his wife as my aunt; and I thought of their children as my cousins. Their children were my actual "real cousins" (when you grew up Black during my day you had real cousins and "play cousins"); they were just a little more distant than my suggested relationship to their mother and father would have led one to believe.

My uncle's place was one building that housed a pool hall, a restaurant (which we called the café), and a four-bedroom house. Considering the fact that my uncle and aunt slept in the same bed and each bedroom had multiple beds, the place actually slept ten people.

The café/poolroom did not open until very late afternoon and did not close down until the early morning hours. It was between those late afternoon hours and early morning hours that I learned lessons of a lifetime. Some lessons were good and some lessons were bad.

Laura Street was the environment where I was first exposed to drugs, gambling, violence, and the concept of sex (meaning I learned that a man was supposed "to stick his thing in a woman" and the more a man could "stick his thing in a woman" the better). It was also the place where my intense love for music developed. Music was a mainstay on the strip, and I became fully absorbed in the sound waves that permeated the night air.

My cousin Kary was two years behind me in age. He was also my uncle and aunt's youngest child. He and I would go to the cash register of the restaurant and grab all the quarters our little hands could hold and place them in the jukebox of the poolroom. We kept the place rocking for hours with all the latest hits of the time.

27

In addition to the beats that rocked my uncle's place were the beats of the other establishments on that street. The most notable of those establishments was the Laura St. Bar. That place ensured that my uncle's place had a steady stream of streetwise players as part of his clientele. Through the years I came to know many of them by name, and all of them by face. I guess that was something that I picked up from the hustlers; on the strip, being able to place a face was an important skill to possess. In order to keep up with what was what, you had to know who was who.

The guys that hung on the strip were larger than life for me. It seemed to me that they knew every answer in the world to every question that could be posed to a man. It didn't matter how simple or how complex the question was; the players knew the answer. And they were completely willing to share their knowledge. There was never a shortage of dialogue in the poolroom or in front of the café. I took advantage of every opportunity that I had to listen to them and learn from them.

I remember one late night rap session among those cool Laura St. players that really grabbed my interest. The conversation topic was centered on the topic of how to satisfy women. That topic led to all the players recounting past conquests. Some of the conquests were from long years ago and other conquests were from as recent as the previous night. I didn't understand everything that they were saying, but I understood enough of it to know that if I wanted to grow up to be a player that I needed the kind of power that makes a man a sexual conquistador. As I grew older and learned more about sex, I always referenced it against the words that I heard that night. (When I finally became a real man, I wished that my young, impressionable, and adulating ears had never heard that conversation.)

In looking back, it doesn't surprise me that the players' words stayed with me as long as they did. Their words had iron in them. They were strong words that were spoken with a strong power that I did not posses. Their power was the power that a person achieves when their words are supported by their actions on a daily basis. The rule of the streets was simply don't talk about it if you didn't live it. The guys on Laura St. understood and lived by that maxim.

The ability to deliver power in the spoken word form was at least half the source of the players' reputations, so they projected power through words clearly and consistently on every topic they discussed. The discussions were laced with the utmost authority on every topic. The kind of power that the players on Laura St. projected must not have been unique to my uncle's poolroom. I read a quote by Duke Ellington that described the same phenomenon. In his book, *Music is My Mistress* (1973), the great jazz musician and composer reported:

> The main thing about the poolroom, besides all the extraordinary talent, was the talk, ... [The] poolroom sounded as though the prime authorities on every subject had assembled there. Baseball, football, basketball, wrestling, racing, medicine, law, politics—everything was discussed with authority.

The Laura St. players became my pre-school teachers and the poolroom became my classroom. I learned what was cool and what wasn't cool—from a street perspective. So needless to say, the people who visited that street scene had a huge impact on me. But none of them had as big an impact on me as my mother.

My mother was a part of the Laura St. scene. The strip was home to my most significant exposure to my mother. I witnessed my mother use drugs, use alcohol, and generally behave in ways that I have never forgotten. I don't want to disillusion the reader by portraying a completely negative situation. I do recall nice memories of my mom in that environment.

I can recall feeling a special connection with my mom when she braided my hair. I remember feeling like I was somebody's child during those precious, but few, moments. It seemed that she twisted love and affection into each braid that she attached to my scalp. No matter how tight the braid, I felt the love through her fingers.

But those tender moments of love and affection were too few and too far between to compete with the number of times that I looked into my mother's eyes and found them red and glazed over from marijuana (we called it reefer) or alcohol. Those moments always shattered my heart into an infinite number of pieces.

When my mother was high or drunk, I felt like nobody's child. It made me so angry to see her in those states because I felt like she was choosing to be that way over loving me. Gradually, her behavior made me hate drugs, alcohol, and all of the negative things that came between us. I felt that those things were preventing me from having the natural relationship that I was supposed to have with my mother. My feelings were so strong that they have prevented me to this day from drinking alcohol or using any drugs.

I spent a lot of time during my childhood battling some of those early images that I received from my mom, but I never stopped loving her. It just became more and more difficult to express it. Later in life, I would have to pray very hard to see if I could ever fill the hollow where my love for her was supposed to live.

Palmetto, Florida; Bealsville, Florida; and Plant City, Florida were the places that I called home during the ages three to eight. (That's with the exception of a brief stint in Bradenton, Florida). I moved back and forth so much between those environments that my head started spinning as I tried to recall where I was during which age for this portion of this book.

In just dealing with the time from the age of five until the age of eight, I will have to explain how it came to be that I had already gone to seven different elementary schools. Nonetheless, I will dare to ask you to come along with me on this nomadic journey from my third year of life to my eighth year of life.

I know that I was three years old when I began to recall facts about my life because that's how old I was when Grandma Dot met Mr. Ceola Knighten. He was the man responsible for my exposure to Bealsville, Florida; the little country place was where he grew up as a kid. When my grandmother and I followed him back to his hometown, it was his family's land upon which we all lived. His family must have done reasonably well in a rural sort of way because they had nice tracts of land that seemed to be free and clear from any type of lien or mortgage situation.

Ceola, the farmboy, met my grandmother at Laura St. Bar. That was the bar across the street from my uncle's café in Plant City. Their romance began when I was three years old and they stayed together until I was ten years old.

Ceola Knighten was my most consistent male role model throughout that entire period of time. He taught me how to behave as a child without ever laying a punishing hand on me. I don't think that he ever felt comfortable punishing me physically because I was not his biological grandson; but short of that self-imposed limitation, he embraced me with all the love that one little boy could ever expect from any biological grandfather or father. I can remember how he would call me "Granboy" in his country slang; whenever he yelled to me from a distance, I ran with eagerness to do whatever he asked of me. I ran to him because I loved him, not because he called.

I wanted to be like Cee (that was his nickname) more than the kids today want to be like Mike. I admired him so much that it only took words from him to accomplish what could not be done through physical punishment from others. That even included Grandma Dot.

There was a potential whuppin in store for me from my grandmother anytime that we went to a public place and I did not behave like she thought I should. It was no secret. My grandmother didn't keep secrets when it came to what she was going to do to me if I didn't do what she expected of me.

There was one particular incident in a Quick Check grocery store (that's what the Black people around me called Winn Dixie when I was small) where I knew that I was going to receive a whuppin from my Grandmother. Either in the car or when we got home, I was going to get it. I knew that I was going to get it; I just didn't care. I was having too much fun "being bad". At the time, have fun now/get a whuppin later was an acceptable trade-off.

Granddaddy Cee pulled me to the side and talked to me about the situation. It was his custom to try to prevent me from being whupped as often as he could without suffering the wrath of my Grandmother himself. He explained to me that it was "ugly" to misbehave in public places and that I was not an "ugly" child. He explained to me that I should walk without running, look without touching, and speak without yelling. Those simple instructions and the reasons behind them were forever etched in my mind from that point forward and they saved me from a whuppin that night and guided my future behavior in grocery stores.

Even when I was in grocery stores without my grandmother and the threat of her belt, I wouldn't run, touch, or yell because I would hear his words telling me that it was acting "ugly". I don't know if it was the way that he explained the reasons why I shouldn't misbehave or the fact that the request not to act "ugly" had come from the all powerful, all knowing, Granddaddy Cee.

I loved Ceola Knighten, and I suspect that my memory of him will always reside in a special place in my heart. He was one of many who served in a chain of people who gave so much to me when the responsibility was not theirs to do what they did. They did not bear a responsibility through blood ties or through any other justifiable connections. I have come to view these people simply as Godsends. He was the first link, from my own memory, in my chain of many Godsends.

The valuable lessons and the deep love that I developed for Granddaddy Cee were not the only ways in which he impacted my life. The kind of work that he performed also had a tremendous influence on my early childhood. He was a seasonal fruit worker for the majority of the time that I knew him. He followed the crops in their different seasons in order to make money. He went from the tomato fields of Palmetto to the orange groves of Plant City. That was the migration pattern that contributed to me being exposed to Palmetto, Bealsville, and Plant City.

During the first two years of this period, I was too young to go to school so I went wherever my grandmother and Granddaddy Cee went. When I was three and four years old, I spent a lot of time in the orange groves with them and the other fruit pickers.

Those days in the groves were long days. The amount of hours in a day that we spent in the groves is better explained by an expression that I heard Malcolm X use on a CD than by the hands of a clock. When referencing the amount of hours our ancestors worked in the fields during slavery, Malcolm said: "they worked from sun up until sun down, from can't see in the morning until can't see at night." I read a quote from a slave that said it another way. The slave said: "We worked, in a manner of speaking, from can to can't, from the time they could see until they couldn't see". Either way, Malcolm's version or the slave's version, it was a very long day for the slaves. Grandaddy Cee and my grandmother weren't slaves, but the hours they put in were slave-like.

My grandmother woke me up during a time the "ol' folks" referred to as "foday in the morning" (translated as before daybreak in the morning in Standard English). I slept on the way to the groves and stayed sleep until the sun came beaming through the windows of the old brown Buick that Granddaddy Cee drove. By the time I woke up, my grandma and Granddaddy Cee were always well into the picking for the day.

The amount of fruit picked was far more important than the amount of time actually spent in the groves. The people were paid by the amount of fruit picked rather than the amount of time they worked. It was simple logic to get there early and to stay late. The longer you worked, the more fruit you could pick; the more fruit you could pick, the more you were paid.

Even to a four-year-old, it was clear that a person had to work hard and efficiently in the groves to earn enough to live. In spite of that fact, I was never made to pick one single orange. On the other hand, I wasn't discouraged either if I decided to pick a few. I did whatever I felt like doing at the time; the choice was totally mine. I passed the long days away with some work and some play. Sometimes I mixed the two together.

Every orange grove that I ever went to was full of long poles with hooks attached to them. They were called "pull poles". They were used to pull oranges down from the tops of the trees. For me, they were toys. I pretended that the oranges at the top of the trees were my enemies and the pull poles were my weapons. I yanked the oranges down only to pick them up and throw them in the bin— which served as a jail in my imaginary game.

I spent quite a bit of time going back and forth between work and play, but I also spent a great deal of time as the designated entertainer for the people who were seriously picking. One of my grandmother's favorite stories is how I set up the fruit buckets as a drum set and gave the pickers a free concert. My one-man show was highlighted by my own rendition of Wild Cherry's 1976 smash, "Play That Funky Music". When telling the story, my grandmother repeats the phrase:

Play that funky music white boy!

She says that over and over until she laughs hard enough to bring tears to her eyes.

Incidents like that concert were times when I was actually looking to be the entertainment. However, there were times when I wasn't looking to entertain anyone, but somehow I still found myself in the spotlight. For instance, there was the time when one of the dogs belonging to a picker decided that it wanted to play with me. There was only one problem, I was afraid of the dog. I was so afraid of the dog that I thought my heart was going to explode out of my chest.

As the playful pooch chased me up and down the rows of the grove, I ran with all the speed that my short legs could muster. Why the pickers thought the spectacle was so funny was a mystery to me; I was terrified!

I thought that my very life depended on me out running and out maneuvering that dog. But in thinking back, I'm sure it must have been a funny sight to see for those who could clearly see that the dog meant no harm. I felt that everybody in the grove had turned on me; out of the corner of my eye, I had even seen that both Grandma Dot and Granddaddy Cee had laughed. That was one of the days that I decided to go back to the car to take my optional mid-day nap. For that hour, I felt that the brown Buick was my only friend in the grove. When I awoke, both the fright and the dog were gone; I was back in love with the grove and its people.

When I reflect back on my grove days, it's very easy for me to see why I found enjoyment in them. Although I can't tell you the names of those individuals that my grandmother and Granddaddy Cee worked along side; I can tell you that I was among a special kind of people. I was among the kind of people that I would ultimately look toward for my own identity. Those people were the less fortunate of the world who toiled the hardest for the smallest piece of the pie; they also gave God the biggest praises for that piece of the pie. The less fortunate have a way of appreciating the smallest amount of anything. I guess that comes from being so close to having nothing at all.

I can still remember the men and women of the grove who gave thanks for a bologna sandwich during a fifteen-minute lunch break. The white bread of those sandwiches often bore the dirt fingerprints from hands that were not washed before eating. They believed in washing their hands before a meal. The fact that many of them didn't was more attributable to a lack of time than it was to a lack of belief. For them to go out of their way to find a place for such a thing would mean either less of the short lunch period or less time to pick the maximum amount for the maximum pay for that day.

I know that some might look back at those unclean hands and those black dirt fingerprints that the white bread of those bologna sandwiches bore and pronounce it as a crude or unrefined practice to eat a sandwich with dirty hands. I see it another way.

I look at the conditions that the people of the grove were subjected to and marvel at their meekness. At the end of each day, they were the people that society designated to receive the least amount of reward for the greatest toil; yet they returned before the sun came up the next day with the spirit of rich men and women. Their work was definitely hard, but I also remember an awful lot of storytelling and laughing throughout each day.

When I think about the essence of those workers, I place the emphasis not on their hands, but on their hearts. It wasn't the outside of their bodies that deserved attention, but the inside. That thought brings to mind something that I read in the New Testament. In Matthew chapter 15 verse 11, Jesus said: "Not that which goeth into the mouth that defileth a man; but that which cometh out of the mouth that defileth a man." Jesus went on to explain this parable to his disciples in Matthew chapter 15 verses 17-20. He said:

> Do not ye yet understand, that whatsoever entereth in at the mouth goeth into the belly, and is cast out into the draught? But those things that which proceeded out of the mouth come forth from the heart; and they defile a man. For out of the heart proceed evil thoughts, murders, adulteries, fornications, thefts, false witnesses, blasphemies: These are the things that defile a man: but to eat with unwashen hands defileth not a man.

Both then and now, my perception of the people of the grove has always been the same; I feel like the hearts of those people were cleaner than their hands ever were. For as long as I can remember, I have fought hard to keep the simple and humble values of the grove people as my foundation. I can't say that I have always been victorious in those battles. I will even go so far as to say that there have been times where I failed miserably. I have fallen prey to the materialism and the vices of this world on more than one occasion, but it has always been inside me that there was more to life than the material gumbo served to us as the daily course meal by the mainstream.

There was no way that I could have realized all the lessons that were standing in front of me on a daily basis as that three and four-year-old boy. However, as I grew older and my understanding of the world increased, I learned to draw from my memories of those times.

I am grateful for the exposure that I had to those people in the orange groves around Plant City. I am grateful because those people provided me with an identity. Because of their influence, my identity is rooted in the joy and the pain of those who endure the greatest toil for the smallest piece of the pie. In the groves, their spirit was all around me. It was a powerful thing.

For those of you who have never been around the poor, it would be hard for you to understand what I mean when I say their spirit was all around me. I think that Alice Walker, the Pulitzer Prize winning author of *The Color Purple* and other critically acclaimed works, does an excellent job in describing the spirit of the poor. In *Living by the Wind* (1985), Ms. Walker wrote: "The spirit of the poor people who have been ground down to a fine powder of humanity and yet who stand like rocks and refuse to be blown away." That is the spirit that I was first exposed to when I was among the fruit pickers. Their very lives were as movable as grains of sand blown by powerful and uncontrollable winds, but their spirits shouted in unison: "we shall not be moved"!

During that period of my life when I might have been in pre-school beginning to learn education of the head; I was in the groves, with Grandma Dot and Grandaddy Cee, learning education of the heart.

SCHOOL DAYS

My experiences with the grove people were cut off when I turned five years old and began to go to school. That period took me back to Palmetto, Florida—with the exception of a very short-lived stay with my mom and her new husband. At the age of twenty-one, my mom married a man that I met only a few days before her wedding.

The wedding was held on June 22, 1978 in a tiny little church in Palmetto called Miracle Hold. It seemed to me that every time I went to that little church where they would sing the old spiritual called *"Trouble In My Way"*. I guess it was only appropriate for my mom and her new husband to be married in a church known for its *"Trouble In My Way"* performances because their marriage was definitely headed for trouble.

My Granddaddy Cee gave my mother away and I was the ring bearer; Granddaddy Cee was even playing the part of my grandfather in my mom's wedding. I don't remember much about the wedding as far as how I felt about the situation, but I do remember what followed the wedding.

My mother and her new husband moved into a small wooden frame house in the back of his parents' house in Bradenton, FL. My grandmother told me that I was going to live with the newlyweds so I went. Everything was happening so fast that I couldn't make heads or tails of what I felt or thought. I suppose it didn't matter too much; no one had bothered to ask me anything anyway. The three of us, all strangers, moving into that house was the first time that I ever lived with my mom exclusively, but it wouldn't be the last time; I would live with my mom one more time for a brief period during my second grade school year. I can't say for sure if my mom planned to start her life over with that marriage or not, but it seemed that way to me.

I can remember her fixing my little room up with matching Incredible Hulk linen and drapes. My mom was very talented in a lot of areas; sewing was just one of her talents. She bought was she needed and made what she wanted on her sewing machine. She really seemed to be trying to make a life for herself.

Perhaps if my intuitive feelings had been more developed at the time, I would have known something was not right. You see, I loved the Incredible Hulk; but I don't remember any good vibes coming from that little room that my mom had worked so hard to fix up for me. I just remember being scared to go to sleep most of the time. But who was I going to tell? What was I going to do, go jump in between two strangers in a strange bed? I figured I'd be better off with the Incredible Hulk—at least we knew each other.

My mom and I had never been close. I didn't think a little pink house in Bradenton and a wedding ring on her finger was going to change that overnight. It was also obvious to me that the man who often walked out of the room with the large penis poking from his bikini briefs wanted me to stay in my room. Most of the nights that I spent in that little room were spent closing my eyes real tight trying to overcome fear and make myself fall asleep.

During the daytime, I remember my mom going to look for a job and dropping me off in Palmetto in her new husband's orange convertible VW Bug. My grandmother was so proud of her and I think that she was happy for me as well. Whenever my mom dropped me off, my grandma would smile from ear to ear. I smiled too, but I was just happy to be back in Palmetto with my grandmother. That's where I wanted to be all along, but I knew that if I said that it would have hurt my mom's feelings.

I still loved my mom a great deal, so I was willing to give her new start in life a fair chance to grow into something real. It seemed to me that she was doing the best that she knew how to do in order to make a life for her and for me. I honestly believe that my grandmother and my mother both invested a great deal of hope in the new arrangement. Although it was all so new and strange to me at the time, growing up in life has shown me that it was all so typical.

My mom was another Black woman hoping against hope that she would end up with a Black male who would be man enough to fulfill his wedding vows. Her new husband was a Black male hoping against hope that he would be able to be a man in a land that didn't plan on him ever being such a thing.

Shortly after we all moved into the wooden frame house, it was time for me to start school. I apologize to the reader because I cannot remember for certain the name of that school to save my life, but I think it was called Prine Elementary. However, even if that's not the name, it is of no great consequence because my stay with my mom and her new husband didn't last long and my time at Prine was over before it started.

I was a small child and I am sure that a great deal of the problems that my mother and her new husband had were hidden from me, but the fact that her so-called husband physically abused her was something that couldn't be kept behind close doors. I don't know how often it happened or if it happened more than once, but I do remember at least one occasion seeing my mom with a swollen black eye.

I never really knew my mom's new husband. I can't even recall any words that were ever exchanged between the two of us; however, I do remember feeling an incredible amount of anger toward him upon seeing my mother's eye. I wished with all my might that my little body was big enough to give him a swollen black eye along with a few extra bruises thrown in for GP (general purposes). To my mom's credit, she was smart enough to leave that cat. That's the way that our first family experience ended.

My mom's first and only marriage was her first attempt to keep me with her; but when it failed, we went our separate ways for awhile. I can tell you where my road took me, but I don't really know what happened to my mom during the next several months. I did appreciate her efforts to try to make a family for us and I did still love her very much during her temporary absence. Both she and my grandmother had hoped for so much, but they had received so little from their emotional investment in a male who did not know how to be a man. Perhaps his daddy was never a man, so maybe he never had anybody teach him how to be a man. Whatever his reasons for not being a man, he crushed the only serious attempt that I had seen where my mom was really trying to be a woman.

My next move was back to Grandma Dot in Palmetto. I had spent all of a month in my first elementary school, now it was time to enroll in my second elementary school. Granddaddy Cee wasn't with my grandmother during that time; he was in Beasville. He was a seasonal worker and that meant that he had to go where the work took him.

My Grandmother was living with a childhood friend of hers when things got bad between my mom and her husband, so that's where I went to live following my mom's break-up. I call it a break-up because I don't know if my mom ever got a divorce or not. I didn't think that a divorce was necessary, because it didn't seem to me that she had ever been married.

I knew my grandmother's childhood friend that we lived with as my Aunt Gene. I don't remember when I met Aunt Gene, but I can't remember a time where I didn't know who she was. She was not my aunt through blood or marriage. She was my aunt through the extended kinship system that Black people had used since the slave days. Her and my grandmother had known each other since they were children.

Extended kinship served Black folks well during slavery when traditional family structures were torn asunder by the greed and cruelty of the white slave master. Our ancestors were forced to adopt kinfolk in order to deal with the loss of real kin. A lady that had no blood or marriage ties with your biological parents might actually become your aunt. Oftentimes the relationship was just as strong or stronger than the more traditional kin relationship.

Extended kin was a tremendously valuable adaptation that Blacks made in an effort to survive. Under the lash of slavery, children lost their mothers and fathers forever at the whim of their slave masters; babies were ripped from their mothers' nursing bosoms without so much as a thought of the pain and injury being caused. Neither mother nor infant was spared from the separation anxiety. Sojourner Truth—the great African-American abolitionist, women's right advocate, religious visionary—proclaimed the following in her 1850 autobiography, *Narratives of Sojourner Truth, A Northern Slave*. Sojourner told the truth when she said: "I have borne thirteen children and seen them all sold into slavery, and when I cried out with all my mother's grief none but Jesus heard."

The confiscated children were taken to other plantations and cared for by the slaves of those plantations. Those slaves became the family—not by blood and not by marriage, but by necessity—for the displaced children. In the cases where the parents were sold away, their remaining children were taken in by the slaves remaining on the plantation. Sometimes the remaining slaves were blood relatives and sometimes they were not. In America, the plantation is where our history of extended kin and the extended family began, but it's definitely not where it ended.

There were various situations after slavery that continued to cause Blacks to rely on extended kin and extended family. I am not alone in my upbringing, which included both extended kin and extended family. My moving into my Aunt Gene's apartment with my Grandmother was just my first experience of living in the home of a person that was not related to me by blood or marriage (extended kin). However, it would not be my last.

My entire childhood, with the exception of two occasions, consisted of me living with actual family members who were not my parents (extended family). The majority of my childhood was spent going from one relative to another and one place to another. That may seem strange for people who are not familiar with or who do not understand the history of our people in this country. But to Black folks, this type of migratory living from place to place and family member to family member is something that has always been a part of our experience since we were brought to these shores. It's not that we value such a lifestyle, but sometimes circumstances prevail and the moves are in the best interest of the child or the children involved.

Bill Russell—1956 Olympic gold medal winner, eleven-time NBA champion, five-time NBA MVP, first African-American NBA head coach, and advocate of equal rights for African American athletes—said the following in his 1979 book, *Second Wind*. Russell said:

> Over many generations, all the way back to slavery, black families had developed customs for the sheltering and releasing of stray children. There seemed to be intricate rules about which relative would take what child under every circumstance. The taking in was to be done in the closest possible imitation of a natural family, and the giving up was to be done quickly with stoic smiles and a chorus of farewells that it was best for all.

The most important aspect of my life that I remember about living in Palmetto with my Aunt Gene was my first year of school.

My kindergarten year was spent at Orange Ridge Elementary in Bradenton, Florida. I was bused to Bradenton with a load of other kids that lived in Palmetto.

That school year was my introduction to a whole different world, a world outside of my culture and outside of my knowledge up until that point. I had some limited exposure to the Mexican children of the migrant workers who lived in Palmetto, but that was about the extent of my exposure to any group of people who were not Black. I don't remember any white children in Palmetto, in Bealsville, or on Laura St.; the closest thing to white that I had interacted with was a little mixed boy in Bealsville. His daddy was Granddaddy Cee's brother and his mama was white. His skin was kind of beige and his hair was fluffy and curly, but other than those things he didn't seem to be too much different than the other kids in Bealsville.

My kindergarten class provided me with my first significant exposure to white children and a couple of Vietnamese children. I had heard a lot of talk about white people. I had also seen them in various places and on television, but I didn't know them as real people. From what I had heard, I wasn't in a terrible hurry to meet any of them in order to get to know them. From what I could gather, white people were "craikas" ... and craikas didn't have anything better to do than to try to make life hard for "niggas".

I had never heard anything about Vietnamese people, so the two students in my class were very interesting to me. I don't remember any particular conversations with either of them, but I do remember watching them a lot. It's funny because one of those Vietnamese students in my kindergarten class would also turn up in my eighth grade social studies class. I never asked him if he remembered me from that kindergarten class, but I sure did remember him. The funny thing about him to me was his transformation—at least in my eyes it was a transformation.

My kindergarten memories of him versus what he had become by the time we reached eighth grade were totally different. In kindergarten he was a kid who either had some trouble with the language (English) or who did not talk very much, but in our eighth grade year he was easily one of the most popular kids in the entire school. If it were not for his physical features and his Asian last name, then you would not have been able to tell him apart from the stereotypical good old American white boy. His name in our kindergarten class was pronounced Sun; by the time I saw him again in the eighth grade, his name was Sonny.

My kindergarten year was also when I discovered that I was somewhat athletic. On the days that we went to physical education class, we always ran to and from a big tree at the start of class. Without fail, I always ended up in second place. There was a Black kid in my class that I just could not outrun no matter how hard I tried. Like the Vietnamese kid, the perennial first place kid would also appear again at a later time in my life. I would ultimately go on to play high school basketball with him; he could shoot three-point baskets from the left wing just as well as he could run to that big tree in kindergarten. In kindergarten his name was Julius, by the time that we hit high school, his name was Boogie.

My athletic talent was not the only thing that I remember discovering in my kindergarten class. I discovered the fact that people thought it was pretty important that we say the Pledge of Allegiance. It was a morning ritual that was to take place without exception everyday that we went to school.

The front office would come in through the intercom system and lead our class in the reciting of the Pledge of Allegiance. I had never been exposed to the Pledge of Allegiance before my kindergarten school year; but judging from the importance placed upon it by the school and the teachers I decided that it was something that was very important. I bring that fact up now in order to give you some idea about my initial feelings regarding the Pledge of Allegiance. I call them initial feelings because they would change later in my life. For me the salute to the Red, White, and the Blue would not always stay the thing to do.

The end of the 1978-79 school year brought a conclusion to my kindergarten school year and to our (my grandmother and myself) stay with my Aunt Gene. We moved from my aunt's apartment in Palmetto, Florida to Bealsville, Florida (the country) to join my Granddaddy Cee. I spent most of the summer months in Plant City at my uncle's café. That's when I got my first real taste of life on Laura St. Like a rookie, I watched all the veteran players on the strip and soaked up the game.

The beginning of the 1979-80 school year found me in Bealsville. I enrolled in a new school called Trapnell Elementary; it was my third elementary school in less than two years. In kindergarten, I discovered that I had at least some athletic talent. In first grade, I discovered that I had some intellectual potential as well.

There were two Black female teachers, Ms. Ford and Ms. Lee, in the first grade section of the school; I can remember those two teachers making me feel like I was a smart kid. I remember it because I had never experienced the feeling that their confidence in me inspired—at least not in a school setting. I validated their opinions by winning our spelling contest at the beginning of the year. I couldn't believe that the other finalist in the first grade couldn't spell the word: "Jar"; she spelled it with a G.

My small victory in the spelling contest was important for me. I had already established the fact that I was a pretty good athlete in kindergarten; the two Black teachers' confidence in me and the victory in the spelling contest made me believe that I was a pretty good student too. The concept of being a good athlete and a good student registered with me; it became something that I wanted to be. It wasn't a passion, but it did make me feel good.

For the most part, I would remain a student-athlete from my first grade school year through the end of my school days. I would always be a good athlete, but never the absolute best, only good enough to be around the best. However, in academics and on the intellectual side, I learned that I could be the absolute best among my peers if I applied myself to such a task. The application part was the issue for me. I would go through periods of my life where I would apply myself to the fullest, and at other times I would just seek to get by on the good sense that God gave me.

I am very happy and I feel blessed to be gifted in both areas; but as a child, if I had to choose between being smart and being a good athlete; I would have traded the intellectual side for the athletic side in a New York minute. I found that there was much more glory in being the best athlete than being the smartest kid in the classroom.

There were plenty of visual images of Black professional athletes to attest to the rewards of being the absolute best in sports. In contrast, I didn't see any successful visual images of the Black folks that made it as a result of being the best in the classroom. No one was teaching me about the scholars of Black America, so I didn't think that the race had any, wanted any, or needed any. I didn't have anybody in my family or my immediate surroundings to tell me any different. The culture that I grew up in held the sports industry and entertainment industry in the ultimate esteem. Those were industries where you could become a star and earn adoring adulation and real respect from Black folks.

I wanted to be a star; I was no different than any other Black child that I knew. I know that other children of other races want to grow up to be stars, but I think it is different in Black communities. I think that more emphasis and hope is placed on becoming a star in the athletic or entertainment industries. Those are two areas where Black people and their successes can be easily seen translating into the so-called American Dream. The emphasis and hope in the two areas only seems to intensify as you examine the communities of Black people toward the bottom of the economic ladder. Sports and entertainment are seen as the golden goose that lays the golden eggs.

I believe that the mentality amongst Black folk of placing an over-emphasis on achieving in the sports and entertainment world stems from the fact that for years and years those two industries were the greatest source of hope for our people as a whole. Our people were proud of Jack Johnson, Jessie Owens, Joe Louis, Marian Anderson, Mahalia Jackson, and Dorothy Dandridge. In some cases, those pioneers sang and danced their way into opportunities for a better life; in other cases, they ran and punched their way through. Their legacies were powerful and lasting among a people that seemed only to see hope as long as hope didn't see them first. We were a people who stole hope through sports and entertainment the way that Jackie Robinson stole home plate. That impact has survived and been passed down for generations.

My generation was no different. Without knowing my complete set of options, I started with the dream of becoming an entertainer or professional athlete that so many young Black males start with when they began from the same socioeconomic position from whence I came. My culture supported that I could become the next Michael Jackson, Tony Dorsett or Doug Williams (Doug Williams was looked upon almost like a god in the areas that I grew up in). However, my culture gave me little or no indication that I could become a doctor, a teacher (teachers should be paid more, what's more important than educating a child?), an engineer, a scientist, or a lawyer.

I read an interview in the April 22, 1991 issue of *Time* magazine. The interviewee was Dr. Henry Louis Gates Jr.—a Black man. Mr. Gates is currently (As of 5/28/00) serving as the Chairman of the Department of Afro-American Studies at Harvard University. He's the Michael Jordan in his area of expertise. In that interview, Mr. Gates discussed the aspect of Black culture that believes you have a better chance to be an athlete than a doctor or lawyer. He said:

> When I drive to my house and go through the black neighborhood that's between two white neighborhoods, I don't see black kids packing books at 5 o'clock. They have a basketball, and they're going down to the courts. We have to change the erroneous assumption that you have a better chance of being Magic Johnson than you do of being a brain surgeon. There are more black lawyers than professional athletes.

It is sad to say, but the great majority of Black culture when I was growing up as a kid perpetuated the myth that a little Black boy had a better chance of growing up to become an athlete or an entertainer than a doctor or a lawyer. What is even sadder is the fact that the myth is still perpetuated for far too many little Black boys in the year 2000. We all need to do a better job of instilling the full spectrum of possibilities that lies within the potential of our children.

A person once told me that urgent and important isn't always the same thing. Within the context in which he was talking he was right; but in the case of the Black community developing the full range of potential within Black children, I would have to say that the two words couldn't be paired any more appropriately. The full development of the potential within Black youth is urgent and important business for Black folks.

I have missed my opportunity for a childhood that cultivated and nurtured my potential as a child to do all and be all, but I can have an impact on those who have not missed their opportunity. It is my goal to do just that because we are losing a large number of our Black children to the pitfalls of crime, drugs, sub-standard academic achievement, and nihilism. We lose a lot of young Black children, especially males, to the pitfalls of life after their dreams of becoming a star athlete or big-time entertainer fall by the wayside. If we are to survive in this country, we can't continue to let those losses continue.

LAURA STREET

I finished my 1979-1980 first grade school year at Trapnell without serious incident, but the same could not be said about my grandmother. That was the time that my grandmother found out that she was a diabetic. If she had not been working two jobs, then it might have taken her a lot longer to discover her condition.

The 1979-80 school year found my grandmother and my Granddaddy Cee still working in the groves during the day while I attended school. Sometimes at night, my grandmother went to Plant City to work in the kitchen of my uncle's café. During the summer, I went with her to the café in order to play with my cousin Kary. On one of those nights, my cousin and I rushed into the kitchen to watch *The Dukes of Hazzard*. We rushed because it was our favorite television show. That in of itself was an interesting situation.

It was interesting because my favorite television show featured a car that showcased the Confederate flag during prime time on a major network. Now that was in 1979-1980. Twenty years later, in 1999-2000, the NAACP organized a boycott of South Carolina for their continued use and display of the Confederate flag. The fact that the General Lee displayed the Confederate flag had no impact on me as an ignorant child, and to be honest with you the fact that South Carolina flies the Confederate flag today has no impact on me as an educated adult.

The flag itself has no direct impact on our (African-Americans) day to day issues of poverty, education, health care, crime, broken homes, or lack of unity. The attitudes and behaviors of those who permit the display of the flag are more dangerous than the actual flag. I feel that we, as Black people, should be concentrating our immediate efforts on issues that have more of a direct impact on our day to day lives in not only South Carolina, but in all the states where Black people live. We could start with the states that have the highest percentage of Black folks first.

The display of the Confederate flag in South Carolina is a symptom of the disease; the fact that we don't have enough unity and power to remove the flag is the cause of the disease. I would rather focus on the cause and the cure of a disease than the symptom and the treatment of the disease.

Those people in power in South Carolina aren't taking our concerns about the removal of the flag seriously because they do not have to respect our power. On January 7, 1965, Malcolm X told us in his speech, *Prospects for Freedom in 1965*, that: "power never takes a step back—only in the face of more power".

The fact that the proposed resolution, as of May 24, 2000, will only move the flag from one location on Statehouse grounds to another location on Statehouse grounds shows that their power does not recognize or respect our power; they have definitely not taken a step backwards. If anything, they have merely sidestepped our concerns.

I don't want to sound like I am not in support of the NAACP or any other Black civil rights group because I am in favor of them all. I also believe that Mr. Kweisi Mfume is a keen mind among our people who is worthy of his African name (which translates to "conquering son of kings" in the African language spoken by the Ibgo). My statements are more assertions of my personal opinions than they are criticisms of the efforts of the NAACP. I firmly believe that we as Black people are in need of the efforts of the NAACP; I also know that we simply cannot afford to undermine the effectiveness of our leadership groups by not supporting one another.

However, I still feel that there are more important issues that need to be addressed in such a high profile manner. The removal of the Confederate flag or the relegating of the Confederate flag to a purely historical position is not going to feed, educate, or protect our children. Let's attack those issues that will feed, educate, and provide health care for our children in the same high profile manner in which we are trying to remove South Carolina's Confederate flag. We should spend one hundred percent of our energy addressing our important and urgent issues before we worry about what's flying over the capitol. I'll use the Confederate flag as a tablecloth, a bib, and a napkin if it meant that we could feed hungry Black children who are not eating in South Carolina or any other state.

Nevertheless, regardless of the differences of opinions or philosophies between individual Black people or Black leadership groups, we must stick together and work together to achieve the ultimate and common goal of freedom and equality. We have enough diversity among Black people to expect private disagreement, but we also have enough common problems among Black people to expect public unity.

I don't mean any disrespect toward the NAACP because I know that their efforts have opened several doors that I have passed through in my life. And as a Black male, I will be forever grateful for that. I just feel that our civil rights groups bear a huge burden to keep our *most* pressing issues right in the face of America at all times; I consider hunger, poverty, education, and healthcare to be pressing issues. Let us use the press on these issues. Let us boycott a state over hunger and poverty before we boycott over a flag. The today and the tomorrows of our children are at stake, and we can't afford to lose any time or resources in expending primary energy on secondary issues.

Arthur Ashe, the late great tennis champion and civil rights activist, said something that made me think about the role of our civil rights organizations. In the June 28, 1991 issue of *USA Weekend*, Mr. Ashe said: "You have not seen many civil rights groups marching for medical and nutrition rights for children." He's right; I have not seen many civil rights groups marching for those issues. The key words to me in Mr. Ashe's statement are "you have not seen". If they are taking place, which I'm sure they are, then let's keep those images in the media in our efforts to "rouse the conscious of a nation". Let's see and hear about those before we hear about the Confederate flag.

Once again, I have digressed. I was in the process of describing how 1979-80 was an uneventful school year for me, but a very significant year for my grandmother. My cousin and I were rushing into the kitchen of my uncle's café to watch *The Dukes of Hazzard* when my cousin accidentally knocked a heavy glass ashtray off the kitchen counter that landed on my grandmother's foot. The ashtray broke the skin of the foot and caused my grandmother's foot to swell. I don't remember if the foot was broken or not, but I do remember that the injury did require my grandmother to go to the hospital. She was placed on crutches and her foot eventually healed, but that visit left my grandmother with an illness that had no cure. It was during that hospital visit that my grandmother was diagnosed as a diabetic.

I don't remember my grandmother's daily life or my daily life changing that much at the time, but there would come a time when that diagnosis would play a big part in both of our lives. That's a story for another page and another chapter—perhaps, another book. The immediate story of the moment is to be found in the events of the summer of 1980.

I was out of school and my mother had moved back to Plant City from Palmetto. She was living with my uncle and aunt at their café. Her stay there gave me the perfect opportunity to make my pitch to my grandmother to leave Bealsville and to get back to Plant City. The nights at the café were electric; the nights in Bealsville were just dark. I moved in the electric night environment of the café with a great deal of freedom. The only moving I did in the dark nights of Bealsville was the tossing and turning associated with my early bedtime.

The freedom that I enjoyed at the café was a freedom that would have been considered liberal for a seventeen-year-old. Considering the more conventional restrictions that my real age of seven years old placed on my behavior, I was all for the liberating freedom of the seventeen-year-old. In a very real sense, I was allowed to act as grown as I dared on Laura St.

One could easily see why the decision of whether to spend the summer in Bealsville or on Laura Street was a very simple one for me. But what it was for me was one thing; what it was for my grandmother was another thing.

I knew that I had to tell my grandmother something different than what was really on my mind. I couldn't tell her that I wanted to run around cussing and acting like a knee-high player. I had to find an angle that she would approve. In the end, I got her to see it my way by telling her that I wanted to be around my mom a little more. For selfish reasons, I was happy that my mom was back in Plant City because that made the café an easy sell.

That easy sell to my grandmother was the first time that I realized that I had some degree of control over who I lived with and where I lived. I liked control. I also realized that, for the most part, I liked street life.

The summer of 1980 found me moving through the environment offered by Laura St. and the café like a veteran of the game. I knew all the players and hustlers, and they knew me. And if they knew me, then they also knew my cousin Kary. We moved together like we were joined at the hip. It was rare that you saw one of us and not the other.

We became players and hustlers in our own right. We were worse than monkey see monkey do. Whatever the cats on the strip did; we did, or at least we tried to do. Sometimes our limited access to cash prevented the exact replica of their authentic actions. They played 9-ball on the pool table for $10 and $20 bills; we played hi-lo ball on the pool table for $1 bills. They shot dice on the street and in the poolroom for $5, $10, and $20 bills; we pitched coins against the wall for nickels, dimes, and quarters. We considered ourselves too big-time for pitching pennies. They had girlfriends; we had girlfriends—at least in our minds.

We claimed ownership of our girlfriends by running up behind them and hitting them on their butts. If they smiled or laughed, then they were one of our girlfriends. The more that they would giggle; the more we smacked 'em on their butts to see their round rumps wiggle.

I don't ever remember getting a bad response from any of the women that we chose to claim in that manner; we had at least five different girlfriends. But that was cool too; some of the players on the strip had five different girlfriends.

There was this cat named Chris who looked like a girl. His hair was longer than a girl's hair and he had a soft kind of face. He was definitely a pretty boy; he might have taken too much after his mama. Anyway, I never saw him engaging in any hustles like shooting pool or craps. Chris only dealt in women. I guess he was a pimp. I mean I don't know if he had any women turning anything for him, but his women took care of him. I mean my man was always dressed sharp. He was so fly that he didn't have to talk too much. His game spoke for itself.

I think that he chose to deal in women because he was so pretty himself. He couldn't have the cats on the strip playing him for feminine because of his looks. He probably knew that it was hard to question the masculinity of cat that had so many women that wanted to be down for him.

I don't really know what Chris's reasons were; maybe he didn't have any. I'll tell you what I do know; he was one of the cats that Kary and I were trying to be like by having as many girlfriends as we could get away with.

The women that we claimed as our girlfriends were women that had super nice bodies with big butts. Some of them were pretty and some of them were just average as far as facial beauty. We really didn't put too much emphasis on their faces, for us, it was all about the booty. We were always on the lookout for Ms. Got the Booty. Sometimes we fell asleep talking about the butts of *our* women. Without fail, the thing that always perplexed us was the fact that sometimes their butts were hard and sometimes their butts were soft. Butts of the same women felt different on different nights. It never occurred to us that tight jeans had a different effect on the way a butt felt than a loose skirt on that very same butt. I didn't figure that out until years later.

Our girls/women were always much older than the two of us (Kary was four or five, and I was seven). They were probably in their late teens or early twenties—old enough to be stacked in the back, but young enough not to care about the two little mannish boys who grabbed their butts every time they turned around.

The super nice body with a big butt seemed to be the preferred body type of the realest players and hustlers. I am sure that's the reason why it became the preferred body type of Kary and I. Needless to say, we would sometimes (unknowingly at first) choose some of the same women that were already involved with one of the guys that we knew. Once we found out that the woman belonged to another player, we backed off. We did so because we viewed the friendships and relationships that we had with the guys on the street as more valuable than the relationships that we had with the women.

The guys on the streets were always looking out for us. For the most part they treated us like we were two of their jive-talking little brothers. For example, it was almost a nightly mission for us that we grab a few dollars from the café's cash register and try to get one of the guys on the strip to take us to one of the late night convenient stores that sold toys. No familiar player or hustler was immune from our "hey man, take us to da sto".

Sometimes it took longer than we wanted it to, but we always managed to find somebody to honor our request. Oftentimes, our most guaranteed assurance that we could get one of them to "take us to da sto" was the fact that many of them would promise to grant the request a few nights into the future if we let them slide on the night of the original question.

We asked more people than necessary just to build our "I promise I'll take y'all lil niggas tomorrow" bank. One might think that guys who broke laws as easily as the players on Laura St. did would easily break a promise to two little kids, but ninety-nine percent of them always kept their "I'll take y'all lil niggas tomorrow" promises. The strip was funny like that.

Because of the players' willingness to keep their promises, we had a pretty slick system of just cashing in on promises on any given night while making sure we always kept a positive balance in our promise account for future dates. That's just one example of how the guys on the Laura St. strip were down for us.

Another example was the time during that summer that Kary and I decided that we wanted to do something for his mom's birthday. Before I get to what we did for Kary's mom, who I called my "aunt", you must understand the all-around love and respect that that woman received from everybody on the strip.

Half of the reason that the people who visited Laura St. so universally loved her was the fact that she was a tremendously talented cook and her soul food was second to none. I refer to her food as soul food because it was so good that parts of her recipes must have included parts of her soul.

Her sweet potato pie was legendary; cats on the strip never had it so good. I never had pie so good. I can honestly say that every piece of sweet potato pie that I have ever eaten has been measured against the standard that she created in my mind as a small child; none has ever measured up.

The other half of the reason that my aunt was so universally loved was her heart. She was one of the sweetest people that I have ever known and she was a friend to all. She was one of those rare people who truly gave more to the world than she asked from the world.

On rare occasions, when you have the right pieces in place, a person like Kary's mom is shown just how well thought of and how truly loved she is. Her birthday, during that summer of 1980, had to be one of those times.

Kary and I wanted to do something nice for his mom's birthday. We also wanted it to be a surprise. That meant that we couldn't get the money from the café's register because we were always asked why we needed the money. In addition to that, our hands were always checked to make sure we didn't take more than what was required to satisfy our wants—which were usually nothing more than to fill-up the jukebox, to shoot pool, or to make a late night run to the store. None of those things required a lot of cash.

Considering our financing problems, it also didn't help our situation that we decided that we wanted to do something for her birthday ... on her birthday. We were caught in a bind where we had no money, no way to get any money, and a very short time interval before my aunt's birthday night was over—at least that was our initial perception of the situation. I say it was a perceived situation because it was true that we didn't have any money and a short time interval before her birthday night ended, but it was absolutely false that we did not have a way to get any money. We decided that we would do what we saw the players and hustlers do on a nightly basis when they needed money. We decided to get it from the streets.

The players that we saw getting money from the streets either gambled or sold nickel and dime bags of reefer. The nickel bags were short fat brownish yellow looking sacks that went for five dollars and the dime bags were longer skinnier brownish yellow looking sacks that went for ten dollars. We knew that there was usually some reefer in Kary's brother's bottom drawer; but we knew that we would be on his short list of suspects if it came up missing.

The gamble of choice was either shooting craps or shooting pool; but we didn't have the skills to beat any real hustlers in those areas. After we considered all of our hustle options, we knew that we couldn't steal Kary's brother reefer or out hustle the hustlers. We decided that it would be easier if we just asked the players and the hustlers for the money.

We came up with that strategy halfway through the night on the night of my aunt's birthday. We didn't even get the whole night to implement our plan, but the part of the night that we did solicit the strip was magical.

We decided that we had a good chance of collecting some money from the players and hustlers that we knew if we told them exactly why we needed the money. Even at our tender ages, we knew that it was best not to lie to a true player about his money. So we told the truth and began to collect money for my aunt's birthday.

The players who usually took us on our late night toy runs got hit up first. Instead of asking them to take us to the store, we asked them for a dollar. When they asked why we needed a dollar, we told them and they quickly reached into their pockets to comply with our wishes. The thing that really put us over the top was the fact that the players we asked made sure that the people they knew contributed. If we asked a player that we knew and he was with some people that we didn't know, then he made sure that those people broke us off a little something too. We were about three hours into the solicitations before we realized that we had accumulated a lot of bills, the empty PLANTERS CHEEZ BALLS can that we were using was starting to overflow with real cheddar.

The wad of bills told us that we had a small fortune; our street smarts told us that it was time to get off the streets. Even as junior players and hustlers, we knew that too much flash cash could be a dangerous thing on the strip. We took our money inside and told my mom and some of Kary's brothers and sisters what we did to collect money for my aunt's birthday.

By the time that they counted up all the bills, the total came up to three hundred and twenty-five dollars even—the players didn't deal in coins. We switched the money from the can to a nice hat and presented the hat to her at the end of the night. She was so happy and we were all (everybody who witnessed the presentation) happy that we could provide some happiness for one who provided happiness for so many.

Our take in rate was over a hundred dollars an hour—not bad for a couple of junior hustlers. But we couldn't take too much credit for our success. My aunt was known by all and respected by all who visited the strip. More importantly, she was loved by all. Once again, the strip was funny like that. Some of those dudes pimped women and would not have hesitated to pimp slap the taste out of a woman's mouth if she came short with his money, but they didn't hesitate to pull some money out of their pockets for my aunt.

The fact that different players would take time out of their nights to take two little kids to the store night after night without malice or mischief showed a kinder, softer, and caring side of the strip. The fact that we could collect so much money in such a short period of time for my aunt's birthday shows the love and compassion that we often found on the strip. However, those were not the only components of the personality of the strip. The only thing that I can say is that the strip had different personalities for different people at different times. That's what made it exciting and fun; but it also what made it dangerous.

During the 1980 summer, I saw something that I will always remember. The situation took place between two guys that I had seen on the strip from time to time, but I wouldn't say that I knew them really well. It would be a more accurate statement if I said that I knew of them. In looking back, I wouldn't have considered either of the two as a player or a hustler according to the rules of what a player or hustler was during that time. They were both lacking at least two requisites needed to be a player or a hustler—money and women.

One guy swept up the poolroom before my uncle's café opened for business when Red couldn't make it. We called Red's understudy Peewee. As his street name suggested, he was a small fellow compared to his peers. I didn't know the other guy all that much either, I knew even less about him than I did about Peewee. The only thing that I do remember about him was that his street name was Frog and that he was considered a tough guy by his peers.

Among his peer group, Frog was the most likely to be the first one to disrespect an older player if push ever came to shove. His peer group included guys in the late adolescent stage. I say late adolescent stage because they weren't boys and they weren't men. Despite their young ages, they were too old, had seen too much, and probably done too much to be told that they were boys. At the same time, I don't think they had enough street pre-requisites to make Laura St. refer them to as men.

Frog and Peewee were both members of the same peer group, but they did not like each other. I don't remember exactly why they didn't like each other, but I do know that Peewee was somewhat fearful of Frog; he was also angry about something that Frog had done. Peewee's situation with Frog made me realize that fear and anger was a dangerous combination on the strip.

One night outside of my uncle's café Peewee's fear and anger got the better of him and the results were bloody. Kary and I were on the strip that night doing our thing as we did every night. I had seen Peewee before I went out into the parking lot; he was inside the café shooting the breeze with Kary's brother Shaky. I had been in the parking lot for a couple of minutes when I saw Frog approaching the café from the other side of the street. I assumed that Peewee was still inside talking to Shaky; they were both a little off, so they spent a lot of time talking to each other. They also staged fake kung fu fights that were really funny. Shaky was fat and that made his moves even funnier than the sound effects that he and Peewee used during the mock battles.

From the conversations that I overheard Peewee engaged in earlier that day, I knew that there was about to be trouble. I had heard him say that Frog had disrespected him and that he couldn't let that go. Frog stopped outside to talk with someone in the parking lot of the café and that may have been his biggest mistake of the night because it diverted his attention. I'm not sure if Peewee saw him or if someone told Peewee that Frog was in the parking lot. In any event, I was standing a few feet away from Frog when Peewee charged Frog from his blind side. He came running around the corner with a long ax handle in his hand. Whack! The first blow from the solid piece of wood struck Frog right in the back of his head.

I heard the woosh sound that things make when they cut through the air; it was punctuated by the most violent pop that I had ever heard. I don't know what sounds Frog heard, but I know that he never saw Peewee coming. As he fell to the ground, blood splattered the parking lot. Peewee continued to hit him several more times before people intervened to stop the assault. Fortunately, he didn't get any more clean shots at Frog's skull. I just watched in amazement. I had never seen such a viscous attack on a person. I was glad that Frog had a small afro instead of a bald head.

I don't know if the ambulance or the police were called to the scene because some adult rushed Kary and I inside of the café and we had to remain inside for the rest of the night. I never heard any sirens, but that didn't matter. For all the stuff that went down on Laura Street, it was rare to hear sirens.

I didn't know why I had to stay inside; it was too late to protect me. My body was forced to stay inside, but my mind was still outside in the parking lot. I had witnessed my first real serious Black on Black violence. I played it over and over again as if my brain was a Betamax.

I went to bed that night thinking about it and I got up early the next day thinking about it. I remember going out to the parking lot to see if the blood was still there. It was ... along with the gin and juice cups, Hennesy bottles, and other remnants from the previous night.

People who didn't know the strip would have said that the parking lot was quiet that morning, but it wasn't quiet to me. The blood, the broken glass, the strong gin smell still left in the empty bottles were all telling the story of what had happened the night before. I couldn't get the scene out of my head and I was determined to find out exactly why the attack happened.

I bent my ear to all the conversations that might offer some clues as to why it happened. I did that for a whole week. Every time I thought that I might finally get an answer to my question of why it happened, the conversation that I was eavesdropping in on left me hanging in more suspense.

I overheard lots of opinions and recounts of the situation, but no real definite cause of the situation. I didn't need any recounts of the episode; I had seen it better than anybody else did. Still, I listened to all the recounts and all of the opinions; hoping that somebody would give me my answer.

Some people thought that Frog had gotten what he deserved and some people thought that the issue was unresolved and that there would be more trouble in the near future. Other people said that Peewee had better get a gun to keep Frog from whuppin his a**. That was the most informative comment that I overheard, because it let me know that Frog was at least still alive.

I understood all of the different opinions that I overheard, but I could not understand why nobody was talking about why the event had to happen at all. When it was all said and done, I never found out why such a viscous assault happened. The closest thing that I ever got to a specific answer was a general unassuming statement that a dude shooting pool said as he lined up special shots. When someone asked him about it, he said: "you know niggas gotta ack up in da summatime." For a minute, I wondered if that could have been the reason, then I dismissed it because it didn't make sense.

When it was all said and done, I never got a satisfactory answer as to why Peewee did what he did to Frog. I never forgot the lesson that not finding a legitimate reason taught me. It taught me that when I grew up that something that viscous and violent could happen to me without a clear and valid reason as to why if another Black male thought that I had disrespected him. The last thing that I had heard Peewee say about Frog before he hit him was that Frog had disrespected him and that he couldn't let that go.

Frog and Peewee were both Black and they were both males; by age seven, I was quite aware that that was the group to which I belonged. In one sense, that night in the parking lot was the end of innocence for me. I don't know if I was ever as innocent as a little kid my age should have been, but that scene pushed me over the edge of little kid mountain. Before that incident, I had never seen the raw emotion of anger or fear lead to such a beating, but after it happened I watched the streets more closely. I began to see signs everywhere that could have ended up as repeat performances of the brutality that characterized Peewee's attack on Frog.

I saw that little arguments and disagreements between the players and hustlers over gambling debts were possible sparks that could ignite the flame of violence. I saw the verbal disrespect of another Black male that sometimes erupted from the mouth of a Black male who had had a little too much to drink as a possible source of violence. I saw the roving eye of a Black male who looked at another Black male's girlfriend a bit too long as a potential cause of violence. The potential violence was everywhere on Laura St. I didn't know how I had never noticed any of it before; I guess I just didn't know what to look for.

Before Peewee stole Frog, I was only aware of the cool side of being a Black male. That was the only side that I had been exposed to and understood in a complete sense. I saw how each player had his own thing, but came together to show each other love. I saw how an older player or hustler would take time out to take me to the store to buy a toy or show me how to make the eight ball ride the rail to fall softly in the corner pocket in a game of pool. I saw the cool confidence that hustlers and players displayed in their walk. I heard the authority in their voice when they spoke to each other about issues, and I witnessed the respect that was given to each man's center of expertise.

I saw how a group of players came together and showed love for my aunt's birthday through their financial contributions. All those things made me want to grow up to be the kind of Black male that I perceived the guys on Laura St. to be, but the attack on Frog changed my perception forever.

I still loved a lot of things about being a Black male, but I also saw the other side of the game. I understood that any situation that produced the raw power of certain emotions could lead to physical violence within the ranks of the Black males on Laura Street. I saw the strong potential for violence in the majority of the Black males that I had been around all the time. They each had a part of them that was prone to the power of raw emotion that had provoked Peewee. I had always loved Black males because I only could see one side of them. But after that fateful night, I knew that it was also a time to fear a Black male.

As I studied the dudes on Laura St. more closely, I began to understand the types of situations that produced the raw power of emotion that could lead to splattered blood. I began to understand that the quickest way to make somebody feel that they had no other choice but to hurt you was to disrespect them. I understood that any misunderstanding could lead to hurt pride or challenged manhood.

Later on that summer, I realized that money and women were not far behind disrespect, injured pride, or challenged manhood in causing tempers to flare. When I *overstood* all of those things, my focused switched from trying to find out why situations took place to trying to make sure that I avoided them all together.

The summer of 1980 was the beginning of what would become a very rough relationship with my mother. I had been exposed to my mother prior to that point, but never in the type of environment that the strip provided. I had snowed my grandmother on the reason why I wanted to live in Plant City for the summer when I told her that I wanted to be with my mom. That wasn't exactly the whole truth; but when I actually got around my mom, it didn't feel like I had told my grandmother a whole lie. I loved my mom a great deal. I knew that. But being around her made me realize that I needed her to love me a great deal too.

Unfortunately, what I needed and what happened were two different things. The strip provided me with a full view of my mother participating in all the elements of street life. That summer my mother spent more time going to bars, dating guys, and partying with the crowd than she did with me. It was such a surreal experience for me because it was almost like we were not related at all, let alone mother and son. I often saw my mother high off reefer (marijuana) or tipsy from alcohol. As a matter of fact, the first and only time I puffed a joint was in the presence of my mother.

My cousin Kary and I found someone's stash of reefer, and we decided that we were going to get high. We had been around reefer the whole summer. We had seen people roll it up. We had seen people inhale it through their mouth and exhale it through their nose. We had seen people give shotguns— when someone placed the joint in their mouth with the lit portion actually inside their mouth and blew the smoke out of the other end into another person's nose. To make a long story short, we had already seen a lot when it came to reefer; so when we found that stash, we were ready to do a lot. We were ready to do everything that we had seen other people do. There was only one problem ... we couldn't find any reefer paper.

We came up with a solution to that problem. Our little minds reasoned that the reefer was far more important than the paper, so we figured we could substitute toilet paper for the normal reefer paper. The reefer rolled in the toilet paper almost looked like the reefer we had seen rolled in the thin white rolling paper, so we thought that they would smoke the same.

Thankfully, we would never get to find out how wrong we were. Before we finished rolling the joints, Kary's brother and my mom walked into the room. I didn't curse out loud in front of my mom like I did when Kary and I were by ourselves; but I remember thinking: "Uh oh, we gon get a good a** whuppin."

I was more wrong about that than I was about the toilet paper smoking the same as reefer paper. Our punishment was that we had to smoke some of the reefer. Needless to say, Kary and I were thrilled with our punishment. That's exactly what we had planned to do in the first place. They even re-rolled it in real reefer paper; we were all about to get high together.

At first, I thought to myself, what could be better than my mom letting me get high and I puffed the joint. But after that first puff, I thought to myself, moms aren't supposed to let children smoke reefer. I passed the joint and I didn't take it when it came back my way. I resented my mom for not acting like my mother in that situation. Suddenly, nothing about reefer seemed cool to me anymore. I didn't want to smoke anymore that night or ever again.

I coughed more than I really needed to and acted like I couldn't handle it. I had been around the second hand smoke so much that it wasn't like it was really my first time; I could have easily smoked through the coughing. I just didn't want to. Kary finished smoking the joint with them; they taught him how to swallow the smoke and make it come out through his nose. Later in life, I would think how backwards it was that he learned to do something like that before he even started elementary school.

Interactions like the reefer incident combined with the behaviors that I saw my mother engaged in on a nightly basis took their toll on me. They changed my perception that I had of my mom. I felt like she loved the things that she was doing more than she loved me, so I began to hate all the things that she was doing because I thought that they prevented her from loving me the way that I thought she should have been loving me. I hated to see her going to a bar; I hated to see her with a guy; but most of all, I hated to see my mother get high or drunk with everybody else. I always felt that she loved everything and everybody more than she loved me.

After that initial punishment of smoking the reefer, my cousin and I were sometimes invited into the smoke filled rooms where my mom was getting high with some of Kary's brothers and sisters. I suppose the "puff, puff, pass crew" found it entertaining to see the effects of the drug on two little kids. Maybe our reactions were funny to them; I don't know, but I do know that I didn't find anything funny about it. I went into the room when they called us in, but I didn't smoke and I didn't let anybody blow smoke into my face. I found the furthest corner away from the main smoke circle and watched my mom.

I didn't go into the room to get high. I went into the room to plead with my mother to stop getting high. I never opened my mouth. I just sat there. I cast my eyes upon her and pleaded with a sincerity that could only come from the pure heart of a child when seeking the love and affection of his or her mother. My eyes begged for her to see and feel how much she was hurting me, but I guess that her half-closed eyes could not see the pain on my face because she never stopped. She just kept smoking; she just kept coughing; she just kept laughing. I just kept hurting.

BOBOS

The long summer of 1980 finally ended, and it was time for me to go back to school. It had been some talk of me staying with my uncle and aunt at the café so that I could help my cousin Kary with his first year of school. I took advantage of the talk by expressing how much I would love to help my cousin with his all so important inaugural year. Everybody involved agreed that it would be O.K. for me to stay for that purpose, so it was decided that I would stay at the café and go to school with my cousin. They all felt that I would be a great help to the young lad since I was so smart.

I began my second grade school year at a school called Stonewall Jackson Elementary in Plant City. It was named for a white Confederate General who gained fame for his legendary stand at the Battles of Bull Run during the Civil War. Since he had fought so bravely to defend the South and slavery, I'm curious to know what he would have thought to have a little Black boy like me attending an institution of education bearing his name. I suppose it doesn't matter; by the time I went to his school, Stonewall was stone dead and that "peculiar institution" was dead right along with him.

My first day of school found me attending my fourth elementary school in three years. I spent the first half of my tenure at Stonewall Jackson living with my uncle and aunt at the café. I also lived up to my promise to help my younger cousin with his studies. In addition to helping him with the things that he needed to know, I can remember trying to teach him what I was learning as well. I used street concepts that I knew he would understand: counting and exchanging money, addition, subtraction, multiplication, and division. I exposed him to all those methods of mathematics in his kindergarten year. He responded better than average.

He easily came up with the right answer when I explained the problem to him in a manner that he could understand. What he understood was Laura Street. And money was one of the first things that you learned about on Laura Street, so I used money to teach him simple mathematics.

The math concepts were advanced for the kindergarten level, but because I approached the lessons in a manner that he could relate to without sacrificing the established principles of the math lessons he actually understood them. By writing that statement, I'm not suggesting that the school system should use a street based teaching philosophy. I am suggesting that the school system could embrace an approach of teaching from a perspective that places a value on who the child is and where the child is coming from in life.

The only thing that I did when teaching Kary math was to substitute the apples and the oranges in the math examples with dollars. I remembered I asked him how many dollars he would have if two players gave him two dollars. He knew that it was four, I just explained to him that that question was the same as asking him what 2 x 2 was. "Two" hustlers times "two" dollars equaled "four" dollars to go to the store with on any night of the week. Once again, I reiterate; I'm not suggesting that the school system use a street based teaching philosophy.

If American school systems embraced a modus operandi that included all backgrounds instead of strictly white curriculums, then they would have surprising results with kids that they are labeling unreachable. If the school systems made a conscious effort to incorporate the identity of the child into the teaching process, then they would succeed in unlocking the true potential of the child. When you approach teaching from that perspective, you don't force the child to choose between what you are teaching and who they are and what they know. Ralph Ellison, author of the classic novel *Invisible Man*, wrote these words in "What These Children Are Like," which appeared in *Going to the Territory*, 1986. He said:

> If you can show me how to cling to what is real to me, while teaching me a way into the larger society, then I will

not only drop my defenses and hostility, but I will sing your praises and I will help to make the desert bear fruit.

In referencing Mr. Ellison's quote, when you do not show the child that he or she can still cling to what is real to them while teaching them a way into larger society, you are going to run into problems. The problems are going to exist whether the child does well in the system or whether the child performs poorly in the system. That's especially true for the Black kid that grows up in school systems with curriculums that pay little or no attention to past or present Black culture.

Mainstream curriculums in the public school system normally ignore both the achievements and the failures of Black culture; in fact, it is quite the status quo for mainstream curriculums to ignore Black people period. Our culture is oftentimes the invisible culture. Some of our kids pick up on that on a conscious level; others absorb it on a subconscious level. Either way, they realize at an early age that Black is playing a subordinate position to white. That translates into less real achievements and more real failures for little Black boys and girls growing up in public education. It shouldn't be that way. We (Black people) should do something about that.

We are a people who put thirty thousand teachers in the South, wiped out illiteracy for the majority of the Black people of the South, and established institutions of higher education in less than a generation after slavery. That's quite an accomplishment when you consider that it was illegal for Blacks to learn to read during slavery.

Howard, Fisk, and Hampton were in existence just five short years after Lincoln issued the Emancipation Proclamation that legally freed the slaves. We are talking about 1868. Carter G. Woodson, son of a former slave, was a self-educated man who didn't start high school until he was twenty years old, but he went on to receive his Ph.D. from Harvard University in 1912. We have a history of achievement in education; it's just never taught in public schools. They are teaching our kids about Yankee Doodle and Patrick Henry while ignoring the slave songs and David Walker. That's a shame ... and *we* should do something about it.

There are two things that are distinct in my recollections of Stonewall Jackson Elementary. Early in the school year, the teacher told us that we would have to do all the problems of the chapter summary from each chapter by the end of the school year. I knew from experience that there was a good chance that I wouldn't be there at the end of the year. Still, I decided that I would do all the assignments over the course of a weekend.

I taught myself multiplication and division by using the principles of additions and subtraction that I had already learned. I applied practical street situations to the problems to gain a better understanding of the concepts. By the end of the weekend, I had taught myself both multiplication and division, and I had completed all the chapter summaries.

I didn't hang out on the strip that weekend; I was too focused on my self-imposed task. All of that studying went unnoticed by my mother; she was in her party mode. I didn't care. I was doing the work to prove to myself that I was smart enough to do it. I turned the completed assignments into my teacher and I can remember her being so impressed. She just automatically assumed that my parents had helped me complete the assignments, so I didn't try to tell her anything different.

The second thing that I remember is the fact that my teacher assigned me to be on a creative writing team. The team was made up of me and two classmates. We were given the task of writing a short story book. I really enjoyed the creativity of working with my two classmates on coming up with our own story. I always looked forward to our group sessions. We were supposed to finish the short story by the end of the school year, but I never had the opportunity to find out how the project turned out. The middle of the school year found me transferring to yet another elementary school.

My mother had been dating a guy for a few months when she decided that she and I would move in with him during the middle of my tenure at Stonewall Jackson. I'm not sure if my mother's hopes were as big for that situation as they were for her 1978 marriage. Regardless of whether they were or not, we both moved in with the guy. I don't remember saying very much to the guy. I felt the same way about him that I felt about the man that my mom had married; I really didn't know him, I really didn't care to know him. I didn't like him all that much because I could tell that he really didn't love my mother. He never said that much to me, so maybe he didn't really like me either. I didn't know and I didn't care. With all that said, I will be fair and say that he did do one thing for me that I did like.

While living with him, I needed a new pair of shoes for school. I remember him taking my mom and me down to the shoe store. I can recall thinking ... "I hope he doesn't buy me another pair of bobos". Bobos were cheap no-name brand sneakers that guaranteed that any kid in elementary school would be picked on. I had endured daily insults from the first day of school from two little Black kids who must've felt that it was their sole purpose in life to inform everybody in the world that I was not wearing name brand sneakers.

They informed the world that I was wearing bobos through joke and through song. Every time they did that, the rest of the kids would laugh their approval at my expense. It was something that I could deal with in class, but they would also do it at lunch where there were many more people. Everyday I tried to be as inconspicuous as possible, but nothing ever worked. The bobo song was bound to happen. That's why the result of the trip to the shoe store was so important to me.

The result of that trip would mean either an escape from the bobo jokes and the bobo song or the continuation of the daily insults. Every weekday since the school year begun, I had heard the song:

> He wearin' bobos
> How you know
> Cause I can see his toes
> He wearin' bobos

Man, I hated that song! Needless to say, I was absolutely thrilled that my mom's new boyfriend purchased me some name brand shoes. They were not the best or the most popular shoes, but I had seen some other kids wearing them without suffering the treatment that I was receiving. And that was enough for me. It was also enough to stop the jokes and the songs. I went to school the next day feeling good with my brand new shoes on my feet. I saw at least four or five other boys in my grade with the same shoes. I saw the two kids who picked on me before and they knew they couldn't sing their stupid song that day.

I was thankful that my mom's boyfriend did what he did. I had never told my mom about the bobo song, so I think that she would have been just as content with me getting another pair of bobos. Whatever the dude would buy would have been cool with her, so the whole thing was really up to him. That's how everything seemed while I was there ... like it was up to him.

One day I wanted to ask my mom why everything seemed to be always up to *him*, but I didn't know how to do it. I just didn't know my mom well enough to find a way to be able to talk to her like I wanted to. It might have been the same way for her, because we never talked to each other. She just talked at me by telling me to do this or do that. Even though we were now living in the same house with only three people, some things felt the same as before. Really, the only thing different that I learned about my mom from living with her was that she made some real good fried pork chops. I always ate two if I could get it ... but that seemed to be up to *him* too. If those pork chops weren't so good, then I would have never even asked for another one.

I didn't get to enjoy the joke free days for very long, because just as I escaped the verbal assaults of the two kids in my class, my mom and her boyfriend began to have problems. Their problems meant that it was time for me to move on again. I didn't mind it that much. Plant City just wasn't the same without me being able to be on the strip like I wanted to.

THE HOLY GHOST

Like a suitcase, I was packed up and sent on my way via a Greyhound bus. I bought a Whaler fish sandwich and a drink at the bus station with the ten dollars that I was given upon my departure. I put the change back in my pocket with the emergency information that I was supposed to use in case something happened.

I went to live with Grandma Dot. She was living in an apartment in Palmetto, FL. with my Aunt Gene, but it wasn't the same apartment that we had all lived in two years before. My Granddaddy Cee was out of town due to the seasonal nature of his job, but he and my Grandmother were still together. A lot of things had changed, but everything was still the same. Black people know how that goes.

I enrolled in Blackburn Elementary, but I don't remember anything about it because I wasn't there long enough for anything to happen. My Aunt Gene's apartment and my stay a Blackburn turned out to be more of a temporary placement than a legitimate relocation. The situation was not terribly bad, but it was one where I was an unexpected arrival and really had no place to fit in at the time.

I had grown accustomed to assessing my living arrangement options and steering the situation into the direction that I wanted it to go. That fact combined with Grandma Dot always wanting the best environment possible for her grandchild led me to Grandma Mary's house in Bradenton, FL. I enrolled in Manatee Elementary, my third elementary school of the 1980-1981 school year. In case you lost track, I was still in the second grade.

The change to another school had far less impact on me than the change to another living situation. Grandma Mary's house was very different from anywhere that I had lived up until that point in my life. It wasn't different from the aspect of the number people who lived in the house; I had lived in crowded conditions before. But it was different in the respect of how things were run in the house.

There were seven people who officially lived in a three-bedroom house: my grandmother and grandfather, my Uncle Willie, my Aunt Linda, my two cousins (Rhonda and Lynn were my Aunt Linda's two daughters) and me. Linda and Willie were just two of six of my grandparents' children. The names of all of their six children, from oldest to youngest, were John (my dad), Linda, Earnest, Michael, Jeffrey, and Willie.

At almost any given time John or Earnest made the count in the house an unofficial eight. Both of them always came with the same story of a temporary stay; I guess they looked at three and four month stints as temporary. However, no matter how many people were living in the house, it was clear that my grandfather was in charge. He was the biggest male in the family and he was the unchallenged and undisputed alpha male in the domicile.

My grandfather was a hardworking man who loved to go fishing, so his physical body was rarely at home; but that didn't matter, because his presence was always in the house. It was clear that there must always be enough food left on the stove and enough to drink left in the refrigerator for whenever my grandfather got home. It was also clear that his hard work provided most of the food and drink that was on the stove and in the refrigerator.

Every Friday my two cousins and I accompanied my grandparents first to the bank, and second to the grocery store. Every Friday was that one-two punch of bank and grocery store. That was a favorite activity of my cousins and I because we always got a lollipop from the bank and several different kinds of cereal that we wanted from the grocery store. We also got an allowance for different chores performed around the house like washing the dishes and mowing the lawn. My cousin Rhonda and I received $5 and Lynn received $2. Rhonda and I received more because we were the oldest; we were only ten days apart—with Rhonda being the eldest. That distinction not only made her my elder, but the elder of all of my grandparents' grandchildren. Lynn was a full five years behind the two of us having arrived on the scene in December of 1978.

No matter the differences in our ages, we all loved my grandfather. He used to always let us do things that the other adults would not let us do, and we knew that his approval was supreme over anybody else's disapproval. His word was the law ninety-nine percent of the time. He was the boss, and the boss let us get away with almost everything.

The only time where my grandfather's word did not mean diddlysquat was the exclusive domain of my grandmother. That domain was religion. My grandfather had a tremendously powerful influence on how the house was run, but you had to give my grandmother her due. She worked very hard cleaning white people's homes and she contributed to the general welfare of the household from an economic aspect, but her spiritual influence was clearly the area where she made the biggest impact.

There were several activities that were not allowed to go on either in my grandmother's house or in her presence. Cussing was one of those things. It seemed to me that it was something that was not even allowed within a one-mile radius of the house. No matter who you were, who you were not, how old you were, or how old you were not ... if my grandmother heard you cussing, you would have wished that she hadn't. Another thing that wasn't allowed in my grandmother's presence was dancing or listening to blues—blues was any type of music that wasn't gospel. She considered dancing and listening to blues to be devilish in nature.

My cousin Rhonda and I would sneak to watch BET on a really low volume after my grandmother went to bed for the night. My grandmother watched Frederick K. Price and Bobby Jones on BET, but Donnie Simpson was out of the question. If she heard Donnie's voice, she would yell for us "to turn dem blues off!" The next morning she made sure that she reaffirmed the connection between the blues and the red fiery pits of hell. Dancing received the same reaction as the blues. There was no such thing as learning any new dance in Grandma Mary's house unless you did it before she came home from work. Even then, you had to hope that one of your cousins didn't tell on you.

In contrast to all the things that couldn't be done in my grandmother's house, there was one thing that had to be done. You had to go to church. I had grown up hearing the only two things that I had to do was stay Black and die, but my grandmother modified that into stay Black … and die going to church. You were supposed to go to church from the cradle to the grave.

In her house, you had to go to church on Sundays. Not just one Sunday or a couple of Sundays out of the month, but every Sunday that you drew breath on God's green earth was a church going Sunday. I absolutely hated the fact that I was made to go to church every single Sunday. I wasn't accustomed to all that religion stuff. I still had the rhythm of Laura St. flowing through my blood. I went from hearing four-letter words used as standard nouns and verbs to no four-letter words within a one-mile radius of my grandmother's house. I went from the latest grooves on the street at deafening decibels to secretly watching their accompanying videos on BET at an almost whisper level.

For me the change was like going from one extreme to another, but it was no use in trying to circumvent my grandmother's religious rules. My grandmother was from the old school that still believed in raising children according to the words in Proverbs chapter 22 verse 6 that said: "Train up a child in the way that he should go: and when he is old, he will not depart from it." She was from the old school; but she, unlike my Grandma Dot, never laid a finger on me. After awhile, I realized that she never planned on laying a hand on me. I mainly did what she said because I didn't want to upset her or hurt her feelings, but never because I was afraid of what she might do to me if I disobeyed her wishes.

My grandmother had raised six kids of her own and maybe she was too tired or too worn down to take a belt to a child's backside by the time her sinning eight-year-old grandson became her responsibility. So when she dragged me to church, I did what any respectable eight-year-old sinner who had no real fear or no real home training would have done at church; I found the pew in the back of the church and went to sleep for as long as I could. My two cousins didn't have Laura St. pumping through their veins; they had spent their entire lives under my grandmother's strictness, so they never joined me in that back pew. Perhaps if I had been raised as they were and never seen such secular living, I would have had an easier time adapting to the preacher and his shouting. But I had seen serious secular living, and I understood players more than I understood preachers.

Religion was simply too hard for me to comprehend on my own, and nobody had ever really taken the time to try to break it down for my young intellect on a remedial level. Besides, the religion of the church always made me sleepy. No matter how early I went to bed the night before, just pulling up to the church made me drowsy. However, I always woke-up when the choir sang one of those songs like the gospel song that Shug Avery sang in Alice Walker's *The Color Purple*. It was like the Lord would send an angel down to wake me up as soon as it was singing time.

I learned more from the choir than I did from the preacher about Black folks and their spirituality. The choir always made people dance, shout, and catch the Holy Ghost. I had never really paid attention to the Holy Ghost. In fact, the only time that I heard about "It" was when I was on Laura St. listening to the Bar-Kays singing *"Holy Ghost"*. They would break through all that funky music and scream: "Your love is like the Holy Ghost". That song was funk on top of funk baby!

The Bar-Kays jam was the only time that I ever thought about the Holy Ghost … and it was only a fleeting thought then. But the more I went to church with my grandmother, the more I waited for the Holy Ghost to come and get somebody. I asked my grandmother what it all meant, but I never completely understood her explanations.

She told me that the Holy Ghost had the power to save people and make them do right. I asked her was it impossible for people to be saved and do right without the Holy Ghost; I didn't want to be made to do right, I only wanted to do right when I chose to do right. Sometimes doing bad was too much fun not to be done. She said that it was impossible to do right without the Holy Ghost, because you had to be touched by the Holy Spirit to be truly born again.

I asked her what was the Holy Spirit, and she said that it was the same as the Holy Ghost. I couldn't question her answers because I had never caught the Holy Ghost and I didn't know for sure what it did. She said it didn't matter for me until after I turned thirteen. I didn't understand that then and I still don't today … but I was glad that she said it because I was only eight and I had five more years of being able to do bad if I wanted to.

I didn't always understand everything that my grandmother told me, but the one thing that I did understand about the Holy Ghost was that it definitely had some kind of powers over some people. It seemed to me that the Holy Ghost could make the physically impaired dance and the speech impaired shout. Old ladies who limped in at the start of the church service became nimble in the knees when they caught the Holy Ghost and quiet people that I had never heard speak would start shouting at the top of their lungs with their arms flailing in the air.

When the choir got going real strong, you could bet your Sunday offering that someone was going to get up and catch the Holy Ghost. There were times that I wanted to dance and shout, but I didn't think that I was supposed to do that in church if I didn't have the Holy Ghost. That was okay because I enjoyed sitting back watching the adults do their Holy Ghost dances. Sometimes it was better than watching the Soul Train line.

The Holy Ghost people were something to see and the choir's music was something to hear. James Baldwin wrote about the uniqueness and excitement of a scene created in a church in relation to the music in his 1963 book, *The Fire Next Time*. Mr. Baldwin wrote:

> There is no music like that music, no drama like the drama of saints rejoicing, sinners moaning, the tambourines racing, and all those voices coming together and crying holy unto the Lord…. I have never seen anything equal the fire and excitement that sometimes, without warning, fill a church, causing the church, as Leadbelly and so many have testified, to "rock".

I want to testify that I too, like the "so many", have felt the church "rock"; and although I was not a big fan of the religion of the church at the time, I rocked right along with its music. The energy from the choir, the clapping from the congregation, and the folks filled with the Holy Ghost shook the building at its foundation. The songs sang in church were my most enjoyable introductions to the power of religion, but they were not my only introduction.

The requirements of a child living in my grandmother's house provided me with a myriad of opportunities to be exposed to religion. My cousins and I were in the church's Easter program, we were in the youth choir, we attended prayer meetings with my grandmother, and we watched her pray for folks and heal folks.

My grandmother's praying for folks and healing folks was something that made me very curious as a child. I would have to say that I was very skeptical about the effectiveness of someone praying for the removal of pain or illness and that pain or illness going away as a result of that prayer.

People who had various ailments came to see my grandmother and she prayed for all that came. She placed olive oil on their foreheads and then began to pray. As she moved further into her prayer, she always spoke in a manner where the words were no longer recognizable. I found out that that part was known as speaking in tongues. I was astute enough in my study of the religious world around me to catch on to the perception that maintained that only the truly righteous had the ability to speak in tongues.

Everybody I knew accepted without question that my grandmother healing powers were authentic, but it wasn't that easy for me. I knew that she was a good woman, but I wasn't one hundred percent ready to believe that anybody could be that good. I needed more information, so I asked a question every chance the opportunity presented itself.

Asking questions wasn't really considered a "child's place", I just got away with it more than most children would have gotten away with it when dealing with Grandma Mary. She gave me just a little more slack due to my persistent curiosity. It was just a part of my personality to ignore a "child's place" when I couldn't understand it. She seemed to understand that and I appreciated her for bending her rule of "stay in a child's place". I knew that I could bend it, but she wasn't going to let me break it.

In asking my questions, I discovered that the effectiveness of the prayers was based on whether or not you believed. Not a belief in my grandmother or a person, but a belief that underlies a faith in a mighty living God who had all power in His hands to do all things. While I didn't quite know what to think about that concept as an eight-year-old, I'm grateful that I was exposed to it.

I'm grateful because I can't tell you where I would be today without exposure to that kind of faith. Some of y'all reading this know what I'm talkin' 'bout when I say that faith has been the *"Ole Rickety Bridge"* that has brought me over. If you don't know, then go ask your grandmother; she'll tell you. If for some reason she can't tell you or you can't ask her, then go out and find a Dorothy Norwood CD.

I'm glad that I am a part of a people who have traditionally considered faith in a mighty living God to be sufficient in the face of all adversity. African-Americans should be proud to know that our people have expected and done the impossible through faith. We would be wise to study our history to see where our people have overcome major obstacles with little or no more resources than an unyielding faith in a mighty living God.

Mary McLeod Bethune—civil rights leader, government official, founder of the National Council of Negro Women, and founder of Bethune-Cookman College—would be a good place to start for such a study. In an article titled, "Faith That Moved a Dump Heap", which appeared in the June 1941 issue of WHO, Ms. Bethune talked about her initial resources when she started the school that would later become Bethune-Cookman College. She said:

> I opened the doors of my school ... with an enrollment of five little girls ... whose parents paid me fifty cents' weekly tuition ... Though I hadn't a penny left, I considered cash money as the smallest part of my resources. I had faith in a living God, faith in myself, and a desire to serve.

The words of Mary McCleod Bethune, the great educator, are just as relevant and practical today as they were in 1941. I once read somewhere that a great educator never dies. If we want to keep hope alive, then it is imperative that we do not let the legacies of our ancestors die. The words of our great educators should serve us daily as our people aspire to higher highs. We must look for the wisdom and instructions in their words under every rock and through every crevice of our history. To ensure that Mary McCleod Bethune never dies, we need to plant her comments regarding faith in God, faith in herself, and the desire to serve in the hearts and minds of our youth until they become the essence of their speech, their thoughts, and their actions.

LITTLE WHITE LIE

I ended my second grade year living with Grandma Mary and going to school at Manatee Elementary. As they must, all things come to an end, but most of the time endings are really never the end—they are really beginnings. It was the beginning of the summer of 1981 and a time of migration for me.

My Aunt Linda was always very fair to me and included me in everything that she did for her own children. I loved her dearly for that reason alone. She was moving in with a friend of hers and taking her children with her. Naturally, she said that I was welcome to come along. I wanted to be around other children, so I accepted. Considering that my two cousins were going and the fact that my aunt's friend had three children of her own, my goal was easily accomplished. The new apartment in east Bradenton's Sugg Projects would have six kids.

My aunt's friend just happened to live across the street from my absentee father, his girlfriend and their little girl—my half sister, Tonya. She was the same age as Lynn. It was hard for me to connect with her as my little sister because I never connected with my dad. Tonya didn't have the same problem as I did because I can honestly say that she really did love me in a major way and she probably still does to this day. I always felt bad that I couldn't feel the way that she did. I did care about her a great deal, but I think that the differences in our feelings resulted from the different feelings that we had for our dad.

She loved our dad in a way that I never did. I think to the degree where we differed in our feelings for our dad is the same degree to which we differed in our feelings for one another. She loved him dearly and therefore could love me dearly as her brother. I did not have particularly strong feelings for my dad and therefore it was hard for me to develop particularly strong feelings for her as my sister. Our dad was supposed to be our common bond of affection. Because we had different mothers, he was the only glue left to bond us together as siblings; I just never felt the bond with the man. She was his little girl, but I was never his little boy. Her daddy was the gap between us.

I remember having feelings for my dad, but they left me at an early age. Once they left, they never came back. I don't even think that the positive regard that I had when I was really small were natural feelings toward him as a person. My positive feelings for him were more directed at what a father was supposed to be and supposed to do. Once I realized that he was never going to be what he was supposed to be or do what he was supposed to do; I stopped thinking of him as my father. If he ever thought of me as his son, he never did anything to let me know about it.

Still, I didn't want to punish Tonya because of my dad, so I did the best that I could to be her big brother. But I was already old enough to know that doing your best wasn't always good enough. Despite all the trying, it just wasn't meant to be. Neither her love for me nor my best efforts to love her were good enough to cement our half sister/half brother relationship. Whenever I saw Tonya, I saw my so-called father.

I couldn't completely block him out as my father and still keep her as my little sister. I wished that things could have been different, but sometimes wishes don't come true—no matter how many shooting stars you see or how often you blow out all the candles on a birthday cake. That's the reality that separates real life from wishes.

It was weird living across the street from the man everybody called my dad, because I didn't know if people thought that I was supposed to be happy or feel grateful for his proximity. If anybody thought that, then it was a good thing that they didn't ask me how I felt about it. Sugg Projects were far away enough from both my grandmothers where I would have felt like it was okay to cuss. A question like that surely would have caused a few four-letter words to fly out of my mouth.

It didn't matter too much because I only lived across the street from the man for part of the 1981 summer. The time for me to be moving on from my aunt's friend's house came as quickly as a thief in the night. The thief came to the front door in the middle of the day in the form of a white insurance man.

One thing that must be made clear is that whether I actually lived with Grandma Dot or not, she was always a very integral part of my life. It seemed that she was always on the pulse of what was going on with me. During my stay with my Aunt Linda and her friend, my grandmother discovered that she did not like the pulse reading that she got one day when she found out that I had been punished.

I had received a whuppin for telling the "insurance man" that came around to collect premiums the truth. I told him that my aunt's friend was at home when she had specifically told all the kids to tell the white man with the black bag that she wasn't at home. But I was always an independent thinker, so I disregarded her instructions and did my own thing.

I knew that her motive in instructing us to tell a lie was to avoid making the premium payment. Perhaps I would not have had a problem with telling a lie if I had not been dragged to church all those Sunday mornings at the hands of my paternal grandma. Somewhere in between the choir songs and the sermons I had learned that it was a sin to lie. I didn't feel like wasting a sin on a lie that *she* wanted to be told. I felt that *her* lie should have been *her* sin, not mine.

It was on that maxim that I told the insurance agent the truth. I had not yet learned the difference between the little white lies that everybody tells and "real" lies. Maybe, I would have been better off if I had never learned the difference. Nevertheless, as a result of my failure to lie to the insurance man, I received a pretty good whuppin.

Somehow Grandma Dot found out about my punishment and asked me about the situation. I told her about it from the perspective of not wanting to tell a lie and she got very upset. She felt that I should not have been punished, while my aunt and her friend felt that I should have been punished. My aunt and her friend were coming from the popular perspective that maintained that kids were supposed to do what they were told, no matter what it was.

Normally, Grandma Dot agreed with that perspective and was not opposed to putting the belt on my backside, but not when I was only refusing to tell a lie. The two sides were not able to come to a consensus on the matter, but they all agreed that it was time for me to leave. My aunt and her friend said that I couldn't stay if they couldn't discipline me in a manner that they saw fit. My grandmother said that she would not let me stay if they were going to discipline me for telling the truth. My grandmother picked me up the next day, and I was on the road again.

Before I move on with my personal journey, I think it is interesting that I had such a prominent experience with that insurance man during the summer of 1981 in Bradenton, Florida. There was an article titled "Past Due" in the April 27, 2000 edition of the *Wall Street Journal* about insurance premiums that were collected from door to door for "burial insurance".

The article was written to highlight the higher premiums that Blacks were charged for industrial life insurance policies in the state of Florida. Those policies often involved very small payments that were collected on a weekly basis door to door by the type of agent that I lied to as an eight-year-old. Material in the article suggested that Blacks were charged premiums as much as twenty-five percent higher than the premiums that white folks paid for the same type of insurance.

The raced based premiums were common practice among many insurers up until the mid-1960s. It was during that period when companies began to receive pressure from the civil-rights movement that laws were adopted to end discriminatory pricing. But according to the Florida insurance department and lawyers representing Blacks in suits filed in 1999 against at least seven insurers, there were hundreds of thousands of Blacks who bought policies from the 1940s through the 1960s that were still paying higher rates.

The article went on to highlight the individual story of a man from Bradenton who had initiated a policy as late as 1972. As I read the article, I remembered that my early childhood memories were full of insurance men that came directly to the homes of many of the people who lived in Bradenton and Palmetto to collect insurance premiums. I wondered if any of those poor people had been victimized by the system of double standards and higher insurance premiums charged by their insurance companies and their agents.

Outside of that, the article reminded me of the almost endless amounts of injustices that Blacks have faced in this country from almost every angle. We have traditionally been the group that has carried the burden in this country that allows so many white people to live the quality of life that so many of them live. While that burden has diminished since its most obvious days of slavery when we did everything and white masters did little more than raise their penises to rape our women, it has not wholly disappeared.

In the case of the discriminatory insurance policies, we were the people who could least afford such pricing practices. Yet we were the ones that billion dollar insurance corporations chose to exploit; this country has always raped the Black race in order to get that green money. When I think about this it makes me wish to some degree that I had lied to that insurance agent—even if it was a sin.

The fact that I have such thoughts is a shame because I know that I should not sacrifice my moral position based on the injustices of which my group is a constant victim, but I do understand the temptation to do so. Lord knows my spirit is willing, but my flesh is weak. The white man in this country tests the endurance of my moral fiber on a daily basis.

It is very difficult for an individual or a group to maintain a moral and just position in life when they are the constant victims of immoral and unjust treatment. America has no problem discussing the moral shortcomings that exist among my people, but it has maintained a tight-lipped silence when it is time to discuss the unjust positions my people have been placed in by this society.

America has never openly admitted or atoned for its ugly record of slavery, prejudice, or discrimination. For hundreds of years America has lied to the rest of the world about the African in an effort to asuage its guilty conscious and justify her barbaric treatment of those Africans and their progeny within her borders.

> America has created a state of mood which is dangerous for the world. In order to buy and sell men like cattle, one had to pretend they were cattle. Being Christian, knowing it was wrong, they had to pretend it was not done to me but to animals. What has happened is that America, which used to buy and sell Black men, still isn't sure if they are animals or not. What I say ... applies to two-thirds of the globe. (James Baldwin, in "A Conversation with James Baldwin," Arts in Society, Summer 1966)

The atrocities contained in America's lies are only magnified by the fact that African contributions to antiquity have been snubbed out in all areas where it was feasable to do so. In all areas where it was infeasable to do so, the facts have been delibrately diminished.

> Pevious European schoalrship knew that the foundations of European civilization derived from classical Greek civilization. That scholarship further accepted what the Greeks had laid down as patently obvious: that classical Greek civilization derived in its religion, its philosophy, its mathematics and much else, from the ancient civilizations of Africa above all from Egypt of the Pharohs. To those 'founding fathers' in classical Greece, any notions that Africans were inferior, morally or intellectually, would have seemed silly. (Basil Davidson, *Africa in History*, 1991)

I know that I ultimately did the right thing in telling the insurance man the truth, but many of his kind had been lying and cheating my people for years by selling overpriced products. I wonder if the "insurance man" would have told me the truth if I would have asked him about his products and his industry's practice of discriminatory practices in Florida.

It doesn't matter, the law of you reap what you sow is a law that neither nation nor individual can escape. There's no insurance that any man/woman could buy to protect him/her from that. You best to believe that!

COLD TRUTH

My aunt, her friend, and my grandmother all agreed that it was time for me to leave after their disagreement about my punishment. It was the middle of the summer of 1981 and I was missing the action of the strip. I had long ago discovered that my opinion did count somewhat in where I went even if I had no say in when I went. I tested the waters with my grandmother to see if it was feasible for me to go back to Plant City for at least the rest of the summer and the waters proved to be favorable. She made the necessary arrangements with Kary's parents, and I was free once again to do what the players and hustlers did on Laura Street.

Grandma Mary's mandatory church services and strict religion were no match for the sin of the Laura Street strip, either the roots were not deep enough or the holy seeds had not yet germinated enough to drive the heathen out of me. I picked up right where I left off in my street game.

I could shoot pool like I never left. I grabbed the same butts of the same women as I did before I left. And most importantly, I was still down with the players and hustlers on the strip. There was one particular player that proved to be the key to a great finish to the 1981 summer. That player also proved to be the teacher who taught me a valuable lesson about my life that I would never forget.

His real name was Donell, but players were rarely called by their real names. The players on the strip called him Josey Whales. They gave him that name in the spirit of the Clint Eastwood character from the 1976 film, *The Outlaw Josey Wales*. He had a sterling reputation as a ladies man. Most women said that he looked like Michael

Jackson (the summer of 81 was before Michael's appearance began to change). Donell's off the wall good looks and I wanna rock with you talk game was the reason that he always had the baddest women on the strip working day and night to get his attention.

Donell was not an average player or hustler; he was a player's player and a hustler's hustler. He could shoot pool like it was part of his phenotype. I can remember watching him win large amounts of money from would be contenders on several occasions. He could do the same thing in craps, but pool was his preferred gamble. He was so automatic that most of the time it wasn't even a gamble. When he did lose in pool, it was usually due to him setting up some would be challenger for a big payday. He would do stuff like that; lose a couple of $20 games and then beat the same cat for a $100 the next time they played. Losing for him was more like an investment than actually losing.

In addition to his street rep, Donell must've enjoyed kids; he took up a great deal of time with Kary and me. Either that or he just liked spending time with his little brother, Kary.

Donell made it a point to take Kary and me to see professional wrestling and to other special events. One special event that he took us to in the summer of 1981 was a once in a lifetime experience that I probably would have never had if it were not for him. He took us to see the Jackson Five in concert at the Lakeland Civic Center.

I can remember being so excited at the thought of going to see Michael Jackson that I couldn't wait for the show. We had often pumped the jukebox of the poolroom with quarters in order to blast the hits from Michael's 1979 *Off the Wall* album. The soundwaves from the intro to *"Rock With You"* would break into the night air and make the atmosphere come alive. *"Don't Stop 'Til You Get Enough"* and *"Working Day And Night"* had similar effects on the night during that time. Michael's music was electric and it lit up Laura St.

Before we learned how the jukebox worked, we thought that whenever you put a quarter in the slot that small versions of the real singers were actually inside singing their songs. We thought they disappeared whenever you opened the top. Well, we knew better by the time that Donell told us that he was going to take us to the concert and we were ecstatic that we were going to see the real deal.

Donell used our excitement about going to the concert to his own advantage. He told us at least two weeks ahead of time that we had to be good all the way up until the concert or he was going to make us stay home. I took his word for his bond; I didn't even think about doing anything that would be considered as not being good.

I don't know if Kary took him as serious as I did because some of his behavior was questionable. I was aware that Kary and I were linked in the minds of all that knew us and I didn't want any word getting back to Donell that I was not being good as a result of Kary's individual behavior. Albeit it was behavior that I probably would have been a part of if I wasn't so concerned about jeopardizing my opportunity to go to the concert. So, I did the only thing that made sense to me at the time. If I had to be a snitch to go see the man that would set the world on fire just one year later, then I was just going to have to be a snitch.

I should've stuck to the street credo and just kept my mouth shut. But no, I couldn't do that. I told Donell myself that I had not been involved in any mischievous behavior that Kary might've been guilty of as an individual. After a few times of me informing Donell of those types of things, he offered me some information that I never forgot.

He told me that Kary was his brother and that if he was going to take me, then I should definitely know that he was going to take his little brother, his "blood" as he put it. The way that he said it was so serious and deep that I knew that he was telling me something more than the actual words coming out of his mouth.

After that, I didn't go to Donell with any more information about Kary's behavior. He ended up taking both of us to the concert and it was a great experience that I will never forget, but I also never forgot what he told me.

I realized that I had never enjoyed the type of relationship that existed between Kary and Donell. I realized that no matter how good I was, how smart I was, or how anything I was that I would never experience as a child the kind of unconditional bond that exists between parent and child or the unconditional bond that sometimes exists between siblings. After the comments from Donell, I was always aware that my presence always occupied a secondary role and I adjusted my behavior accordingly. I never asked or expected to receive the full measure of anything that was given among people who had those kinds of relationships. I never expected to go to a concert unless my cousin was going too. I knew that he could expect to go without me, but that I couldn't expect to go without him. That's what Donell was telling me.

He had made it so clear for me when he said: "you know that if I take you, then I'm going to take my little brother—my blood." I only came up with pain when I searched my own mind for the kind of relationships that were supposed to be responsible for giving me the kind of unconditional support that Donell was providing for Kary. I knew that I had none. I had just moved away from an apartment right across the street from the man who was supposed to be my dad. I was his "blood", but when I left my aunt's friend's house, neither one of us even bothered to say goodbye.

I realized that the people in my life who did things for me were not obligated to do them. I realized that a child in a situation like mine should just be happy to get whatever he got, because the people who did the most for me were not my parents or even my big brother or big sister. They were people not obligated to do anything for me; they were just being nice.

Donell's comments forever changed how I thought about my life. Joe Jackson's boys put on a hot show, but I took some cold truth with me to see that concert.

MIS-EDUCATION

At the conclusion of the 1981 summer, I went to live with Grandma Dot and Granddaddy Cee in Palmetto, FL. We lived in a house that belonged to my grandmother's grandmother; when Great Great-Grandma Carrie died, she left the house to Grandma Dot. The only thing that I can remember about Mama Carrie was that she was nice to me and that I popped the plastic bubbles on the seats in her car. The memory of popping the plastic on her car seats never made any sense to me until I got older and my grandmother told me that Mama Carrie drove a taxicab with plastic on the seats.

I spent the next two and a half years living in my deceased great great-grandmother's house. During that time, Grandma Dot was the only permanent fixture in the house. The first year, the living arrangements in the three-bedroom abode was made up of my grandmother and Granddaddy Cee occupying one room, my grandmother's younger brother (I guess he was my great uncle) and his girlfriend in one room, and her three children and me in the third room.

My great uncle's girlfriend had two girls and one boy. I slept in a twin bed with her son, and the two girls slept together in a separate twin bed. It was under those living arrangements that my whole world changed. It didn't change due to any particular conditions of the house; I was accustomed to living in crowded situations and with people who were not really related to me by blood. The thing that changed my whole world was my exposure to a world that I had never known. The strange world was brought into existence the first day that I started my third grade school year.

I lived in a school zone in Palmetto, FL that mandated that the kids in my neighborhood be bused to a school that was nearly forty-five minutes away in the west part of Bradenton. The name of the school was Stewart Elementary; it was the only elementary school where I spent consecutive years during my primary education.

I road the bus to Stewart Elementary from the beginning of my third grade school year until the second half of my fifth grade school year. During my forty-five minute bus ride, I went from one world that I knew very well to a completely different world that was occupied by strange people and strange things. The new world had huge houses, clean paved streets, and manicured lawns. I would soon find out that that was the world where rich white people lived.

I quickly noticed that all the white people in the third grade lived in the houses around the school, and all the Black people in third grade came on the two different buses from Palmetto. The lone exception was a little Black boy who had a father that played Major League Baseball. His family lived in the houses around the school too.

That little Black boy and I became friends almost right away. I missed him dearly when he left each year. His family lived in Bradenton during part of the school year and in Kansas City where his father played ball during the other part of the school year.

Whenever I heard my friend talk about his dad, it made me wish that I could have had a dad too. I didn't wish for a dad that played baseball for a professional team; I wished for a dad that would play baseball with me.

As I rode the bus from where I lived to Stewart, I noticed a lot of differences between the world of the rich white people and the world where I lived. The first difference that I noticed was very small. I noticed that many of the little white children did not have to get up as early as I did in order to get to school; I also noticed that they got home from school faster than I did. I knew that because the white children talked about cartoon television shows that came on after I left for school in the morning and cartoon television shows that came on before I got home from school in the afternoon.

That made me mad because I always had to make sure that I got out of the house in the morning before my favorite morning cartoon was over in order to avoid missing the bus. On the flip side, I would only catch the back end of my favorite afternoon cartoon if I hustled home from the bus after school. They watched the shows that I missed in their entirety with 20 or 30 minutes to spare.

After noticing their neighborhoods and how quickly they got to and from school, I began to notice all the other differences. I noticed that the white children pronounced their words differently than I did, and that sometimes they had no idea about the words or phrases that I used on a daily basis. For example, I can remember the white kids not understanding the question of: "way you stay at?" After a few seconds of puzzled and bewildered looks, they always translated the question to: "Are you asking me where do I live?"

Another thing that I began to notice was the fact that all the white children wore much nicer clothes than most of the Black children. In Plant City, I had been teased about my shoes, but now my whole body was clothed in garments that made me not fit in with the white children. But this time around, I wasn't the only one who didn't fit in. Unlike Plant City, I had a whole group of people to share the new experience of not fitting in because of the clothes on our bodies.

The name brands that the white children wore were Jordache, Calvin Klein, Sassoon, Izzod, Nike, Adidas, Lightning Bolt, and Ocean Pacific. The names stick in my mind as if I was in third grade just yesterday. None of the Black children, with the exception of the little Black boy whose father played professional baseball, had parents or guardians who could afford those types of brand name clothing. I knew that my grandma couldn't afford the high priced fashions, but that didn't make me feel any better or less embarrassed about not having those names on my body.

After Donell had stung me hard earlier in the summer by inadvertently making me aware that I should be thankful for anything that I got, I had grown somewhat thankful for even the little that I did have. But after being exposed to the nice clothes of the white kids on a daily basis, I forgot about Donell's lesson.

I began to want Izzod, Nike, and Ocean Pacific (OP) clothing; I wanted them bad. I'm sure that most of the Black kids felt the same way that I did. The fact that I didn't have the name brand clothing; and the fact that the white children did have them, made me feel like they were better than I was. Today, I know that clothes don't determine a person's worth, but I didn't know that at Stewart Elementary. At the time, it made perfect sense to me that the white children had better clothes than I did because they were better than I was. Why else would every thing they had be so much better than any thing I had?

When I compared the clothes of the white children with my own, I always felt dirty and ashamed. I wasn't actually dirty, my grandmother always made sure that I had clean clothes to wear; I just felt dirty. I think a lot of the white children looked at me as if I was dirty; I could tell that some of them thought that they were better than I was. They looked at me as if I wasn't there, almost like they were examining an inanimate object. I knew that they saw me, but I don't think that saw me as I was. Oftentimes, I felt that I was seen as some thing as opposed to being seen as a person. I didn't know it at the time, but I was in my infancy of becoming the *Invisible Man.*

There was this one boy named Kevin who made me feel like some Black trash on the street that he didn't want to let touch his Nike shoes. I hate that I ever gave anybody the consent to make me feel that way. But I shouldn't be too hard on myself; it would be a long time before I learned that no one could make you feel low without your permission.

My clothing was not the only thing that played into the fact that I started to feel like the white children were superior; there were other factors involved in the equation. I knew that they lived in nicer homes and their parents drove nicer cars. I could deal with those things, but at every new turn I found out that they had something that I didn't have. They had a better bicycle to ride, a pool to swim in at their house, and they had a regular lunch ticket instead of a free lunch ticket.

The lunch ticket comparison might seem a little petty now, but it wasn't to me as an eight-year-old third grader at Stewart Elementary. My ticket and the tickets of my friends who were bused in with me from Palmetto had big red writing on the front that let everyone know that we were on the free lunch program. Even though I hadn't read his words at that point, I had already felt the essence of what W.E. B. Du Bois wrote in his 1903 classic (*The Souls of Black Folk*). Dr. Dubois wrote: "To be a poor man is hard, but to be a poor race in a land of dollars is the very bottom of hardships."

I really hated using that free lunch ticket. I tried to keep it out of sight until the very last minute so that the cafeteria lady would be the only one to see it. I didn't want her to see it either, but I didn't see how I could pull that off and still get some food. I think that if I had a choice in the matter, I would've skipped lunch and waited until I got home to eat.

Despite my best efforts to hide my ticket from the world, the cafeteria lady always hole punched the ticket so that everybody saw that big embarrassing red writing. It seemed like the white children had their tickets out and ready to present from the time that we left our classroom until the time they handed it over to the ticket lady. Conversely, I always clutched my ticket in the secrecy of my own shame until I had no other option left but to hand it to the lady.

In a way, I felt that many of the white children were aware of my shame regarding the ticket. I often thought that they only paraded their tickets so openly because they wanted to pour salt into my wound. But there was no way that I could say for sure, because I never made eye contact with anyone while that ticket was crumpled in my tiny little fist. By the end of the week, I had crumpled it so many times that it was probably the worst looking ticket in the whole school. Still, no matter how bad it looked, it always looked better than I felt.

That third grade school year at Stewart Elementary really did a number on my psyche. I was no longer satisfied with the things that I had because the things that I had were never as good as what the white children had. I wanted a lunch ticket like the one that the white children had. I wanted to wear nice clothes like the white children wore. I wanted a bicycle like the white children rode. I wanted to live in a nice house like the houses where the white children lived. I wanted a pool in my backyard at my nice house like a lot of the white children had in their backyards. After a while, I think I just wanted to be white.

I was no longer satisfied with being Black because Black was beginning to mean that I could not have nice things. I had forgotten all the joy that I got out of my Black experience up until that point. I forgot all about the players and hustlers on Laura Street. I forgot about the people in the orange groves and all the fun I had when I was around them. I forgot all about the goodness of being Black because it was overshadowed by my new intimate exposure to the white world that I saw at Stewart Elementary.

There was one thing that happened during that 1981-1982 school year that brought me back to the reality of being a Black male in the ghetto. Grandma Dot's youngest brother, Dennis, was shot and killed at Bird's Bar in Palmetto by another Black male. I can't say that I knew Dennis all that well, but I did have some exposure to him. That exposure came from the few times when I was with my mom and he was around.

During those times, I can remember thinking how much he reminded me of the players and hustlers on Laura Street. The night that I found out that he had been killed was on a Thursday night. I was in the backroom of the house with all of my uncle's stepchildren watching the television show *Gimme a Break*. We watched that show every Thursday night. I found out that Dennis had been killed on February 18, 1982. My mom remembered the exact date.

Immediately, I connected Dennis's death to the night in 1980 when Peewee attacked Frog in the parking lot of my uncle's café. I was not there when Dennis was killed, but I just knew that it was just as senseless as Peewee's attack on Frog. Unlike the situation with Peewee and Frog, I didn't spend any time trying to make sense out of the senseless with Dennis's death. I didn't hang around the adults to see if I could gain a clue as to the cause of the incident. I didn't have to do that to find out what prior experience had already taught me. The lessons that I learned from the summer of 1980 were sufficient in providing me with all the answers that I needed in respect to why Dennis was dead.

I knew that he was killed because somebody felt that he had disrespected him according to some street rule. Some rule that only made real sense in the world of the street. It was a ninety-nine percent chance that Dennis's killer thought that Dennis had challenged his manhood, messed with his money, or messed with his woman. Every question that I had was answered with the same conclusion: it was a senseless act of violence. Nothing could have made me change my mind about that conclusion then, and nothing can make me change my mind about it now. Even if Dennis had done any one of those three things, it didn't mean that the dude had to make the get-back so permanent and fatally final.

In my mind, I knew all of the answers as to why Dennis died at Bird's Bar at the hands of another Black male. Still, I found more questions to ask myself when I attended his funeral with my grandmother. I asked myself why were all those people in the church screaming and crying over a death that didn't have to happen. Why didn't they scream and cry over the conditions that preceded his death? I asked myself why was I a member of a group that had what seemed to me to be a penchant for hurting one another. I asked myself was his little girl, who I had met, going to remember anything about her daddy. I didn't know the answers to any of those questions, but I did know that the whole thing was senseless. I prayed for Dennis's soul, and I prayed that what happened to him would not happen to me. I asked God to not let me be killed by another Black male. I prayed the way that my paternal grandmother taught me to pray, I asked God in Jesus name to protect me from challenging another Black male's manhood, from messing with his woman, and from messing with his money. I prayed that prayer because I was what Peewee was, I was what Frog was, and I was what Dennis was ... a Black male in danger.

After Dennis's funeral, the school year continued on for me as it had before he died. I wasn't feeling very good about who I was and I still wanted to have the kind of things and the kind of life that the white children who went to Stewart had. There was no blurring of the lines between the races at Stewart Elementary. Ninety-nine percent of the Black children who went to Stewart were bused in from poor areas of Palmetto and ninety-nine percent of the white children who went to Stewart were coming from upper middle class or rich families. Those realities really painted a very polarized picture of Black and white for me. White came to symbolize rich and Black came to symbolize poor. The white children were also impacted by the polarization of the races. It was clear to me that some of them treated us Blacks like we were not as good as they were.

The white students' prejudices against us weren't anything really blatant, but the prejudices were there. It was just an overall feeling that I felt, and I think that the white children felt it too. We felt the same feeling, but it made me feel inferior and made them feel superior. It is a hard thing to describe in words, but maybe a quote by Marian Anderson might help describe the kind of prejudice that I felt during that third grade school year. Marion Anderson was the first African-American singer to perform at the Metropolitan Opera in 1955. In describing prejudice, she said:

Prejudice is like a hair across your cheek. You can't see it, you can't find it with your fingers, but you keep brushing at it because the feel of it is irritating.

That's what it was like for me—something that I could not touch, but definitely something that I could feel.

The feel of the prejudice that I felt coming from the white children combined with all of my observed differences of life for Blacks and life for whites added up. The sum total of everything not only made me wish that I was white, but it caused me to doubt my self-worth as an individual. I received all sorts of messages from everywhere that said that I was not as good as a white person. To make matters worse, I wasn't getting any counter messages that told me that as a Black male that I was worth something. Those desperately needed counter messages were not coming from school, and they definitely were not coming from home.

My home life left a lot to be desired in the way of installation of self-worth and Black pride. Don't misunderstand me; Grandma Dot and Granddaddy Cee loved me very much and they did all that they could for me, but most of their time was spent making sure that I had enough food to eat, clean clothes to wear, and somewhere warm to sleep. But those things were not enough to keep up with the constant messages of Black inferiority that I was receiving on a daily basis as I attended Stewart Elementary. I needed a direct and clear message that I belonged to a race of people who were just as good as any other race of people. I needed a direct and clear message that said that I was just as good as anybody else.

The third grade curriculum was no better help than the school environment in which it was taught. As a matter of fact it was probably worse. The reading textbooks did not contain any images of Black people. The teacher did not talk about anything that related to my culture or my experiences. The stories that were read to the class were stories grounded in the mainstream white culture. It is safe to say that I was being taught in a curriculum that did not include anything that contributed to a positive Black image for an African-American child during that entire school year. It makes me sick to write such an atrocious statement.

It makes me sick because any approved curriculum that does not embrace positive images in relation to all the people that it will serve to teach is a racist curriculum. I read something by Malcolm X that described the attributes of my third grade curriculum as well as anything that I have ever read. In *Malcolm X Speaks* (1965), Malcolm said:

> Regardless of where or when one attends school in America, he receives along with legitimate educational experiences, a dose of pure unadulterated racism. Since the earliest days of this nation's history, students attending its schools have achieved competence in the four, not three, "Rs," Reading, Riting, Rithmetic, and Racism.

Malcolm's words were definitely true of my third grade school year. I learned the traditional three "Rs" quite well, but that learning definitely had its price. That price was the detrimental effects of a racist curriculum on my mind and my self-image.

The white children paid a price for the biased curriculum as well. It gave them an inflated sense of self at the expense of the Black and Mexican children who attended Stewart (some of the children of the migrant workers in Palmetto were bused in with us). Some of the white children walked around like they were the best thing to happen since sliced bread. That by itself wasn't so bad; I didn't mind that the white kids were feeling good about themselves. There isn't anything inherently wrong with teaching a child in a manner that will teach that child to have a positive self-image. But there is an inherent danger when that teaching is done in a vacuum and at the expense of teaching that child about the positive attributes and contribution of others.

That's what happened at Stewart Elementary. White students' self-esteem was purchased at the expense of the self-esteem of little Black boys and girls. That's a shame and it should never happen. It is only the racism interwoven into the fabric of this country that permits such a thing.

The one-sided teaching and racist curriculum taught at Stewart Elementary created an attitude in some of the white kids that they, and those who looked like them, were superior to those who did not look like them. I call the curriculum racist because it was strictly grounded in the Eurocentric version of history where white Europeans did everything that was ever worth doing. A white child growing up in that curriculum only believes what he or she is taught. That child believes, consciously or subconsciously, that the people of their race are the only folks that have ever done anything worthwhile.

With some white folks, I suspect that that kind of early biased teaching is how the color of an individual's skin becomes more important than the content of an individual's character. That type of attitude inspires a blind color prejudice that those white people often accept without even realizing it. Needless to say, the effects of the blind color prejudice manifests itself in various degrees from one white person to the next and not all prejudiced whites fit the same mold. Some white folks will say that they could never be friends with any Black person ever and some will say that some of their best friends are Black; but neither one will want their son or daughter marrying someone Black. It's just different degrees of the same thing—their unwillingness to accept the full humanity of Black folks. (Mom, Dad ... guess who's coming to dinner?)

It is almost one hundred percent accurate to say that those individuals who posses the attitude that they are superior and others are inferior will not be able participate in a comprehensive model of diversity that celebrates the value that is to be found in differences. The key word in the last sentence is "celebrates". Those individuals will not genuinely feel like there is anything worthy to celebrate about those who do not look like them because they will not know anything about anybody else other than the members of their own group. That is what happens to a lot of white people as they grow up. The only stuff that they know about Black folks is what they see in the mass media.

They are taught in a historical context that only celebrates the achievements of Europeans (Conquerors write history), and that evolves into a teaching that only celebrates the achievements of white Americans. That is why the average white American today knows so little about the other cultures and achievements of the other groups who occupy this country. That is not simply true of white folks who are straight-out racists, but it is also true of a great number of white folks who consider themselves to be diverse individuals. The international term "ugly American" really means "ugly white man" because it is the white man who has the international reputation for not respecting other people and their cultures or practices.

The American school systems raises white children everyday in a curriculum that fosters ignorance of all other groups; and then society expects white children to grow up to be adult members of society who embrace diversity ... or is that the lie that America wants me to believe? I am inclined to think that that is simply the lie that America wants me to believe. But I don't believe it; even if I was born yesterday, I stayed up all night to play catch-up on that one.

I say that America and its school systems aren't interested in any real diversity at all. The only way that I would believe that the American school systems was interested in any real diversity with the type of curriculums that they use was if farmers could sow corn and expect to reap wheat. To expect that is to admit illogical thinking. It's an absolute unreasonable expectation and it doesn't happen. All whites can easily admit to the illogical thinking in the corn/ wheat hypothetical, but few will be willing to admit the illogical thinking in expecting racist school curriculums to yield a diverse society. Why would there be a difference in willingness to admit identical illogical thinking?

The reason for the difference is because there is an implied expectation by white people in America that all other groups that are not white are expected to conform to the customs and norms of the mainstream white culture when it comes to high priority issues. To expect that in a world where there are so many other groups is not only arrogant, but racist as well. Yet, the curriculums of our schools continue to embrace educational practices that don't adequately include the history and accomplishments of others.

Despite the injuries that biased curriculums cause to little white children and without regard to the crippling effects that they have on little Black children, schools continue to teach with such curriculums. Black children are growing up with a feeling that Black people have never achieved anything worthy of inclusion into the curriculums. When the heat gets too hot in the kitchen from a few Black folks complaining, then the school boards throw in a little tokenism on Dr. King and the like as if our experience in this country began with the Montgomery Bus Boycott. They even introduce that in such a watered-down way that it becomes an insult to what really happened.

As a result of the no-inclusion and tokenism inclusion, little Black children conclude that whites have done everything worth while, and that leads them to believe that white people are superior to Black people. It makes a lot of little Black children wish that they were white because they associate white with achievement. They don't realize that we belong to a group of prolific achievers. Nimrod "began to be a mighty one in the earth" in Genesis chapter 10 verse 8; he was a descendant of Ham as he was begat by Cush.

You can change the C to a K, but Kush is still Cush and the advanced civilizations achieved in Ethiopia (a Greek term taken from a Greek expression meaning "burnt faces". A term once used by the Greeks for all of Africa) cannot be ignored forever. The progeny of Ethiopia will awake! The complete history of the African in the world is very profound; that profundity is only enhanced by the complete history of the African in America.

In the American school system, some Black children actually become ashamed of their Blackness. That's what happened to me as a third grader at Stewart Elementary in 1981-82. The real shame is that it is still happening today with many Black children in the year 2000. We have known about the effects of biased curriculums on both whites and Blacks for a long time now and little or nothing has been done to change them with the exception of a token gesture here or there. We don't want any token gestures; we need major reform. If this country can send a man to the moon, explore space, and develop enough weapons of mass destruction to destroy the world a million times over, then it is definitely capable of major reform in public education. Let's not get it twisted!

Major reform in the education system should be an open and shut case, but it isn't because this country still turns its head to the historical contributions of the African. Carter G. Woodson, the famous historian and educator, documented the concept of the experience that I had as a third grader at Stewart Elementary in his 1933 book, *The Mis-Education of the Negro.* Woodson wrote:

> The same educational process which inspires and stimulates the oppressor with the thought that he is every-
> thing and has accomplished everything worth while,
> depresses and crushes at the same time the spark of

genius in the Negro by making him feel that his race does not amount to much and never will measure up to the standards of other people.

The message that I got at Stewart Elementary over and over was that I was not good enough. My clothes were not good enough. My English was not good enough (if the white man had left my ancestors in Africa, then he wouldn't have to worry about my English). My house was not good enough. In my mind, there were just so many areas that I did not measure up to my white counterparts.

Thank God there was at least one area where I was clearly their equal and often their superior. That area was the three "Rs" and that is where the curriculum proved to be a positive. There was some bias in reading and science, but math was exact and left little room for race biased.

I could read, write, add, subtract, multiply, and divide just as well as, if not better than, anyone in my class. I took advantage of every opportunity that I had to show it. Whenever we played games that related to the three "Rs" or broke into our small reading groups I always made sure that I was up to the challenge. I made sure that if anybody beat me in the games or read better than me in the small reading groups that it was due to their superior knowledge; not my own deficiency.

My competency in the academic arena was my best bulwark against a total negative self-image. I thank God for the intelligence that he put in my head and in the heads of other Black children. Otherwise, we would all be left totally vulnerable to a brutal system that ignores the historical contributions of Black people to the world ... unless it is some contribution that supports the status quo images that the world now deems acceptable.

GIMME 5, ON THE BLACK HAND SIDE

The summer of 1982 finally came and I was ecstatic. I was happy for all the normal reasons that would make any child my age happy, but I was also happy for reasons that were totally unique to me. I was glad that I didn't have to go to school and feel like I wasn't as good as white kids.

I spent the summer in Palmetto and the only kids in Palmetto that I saw were either Black or Mexican. I thought that I might try to get back to Plant City, but I couldn't think of an angle, so I resigned myself to having a blast with my friends. I knew that having a blast in Palmetto was different than having a blast in Plant City.

In Palmetto, life was more concentrated into daytime hours. In Plant City, the night was just the beginning of the party. In Palmetto, the approaching of the night meant that it was time for me to get my butt in the house. Grandma Dot had already laid down the ground rule that I better not let the streetlights catch me. She meant that when the streetlights came on that I needed to be in the house or else she would catch me with her switch. Grandma Dot and a switch were a combination that I tried to avoid at all cost.

The streetlights always made a buzzing sound when they first started to come on, that buzzing noise meant that I had about five minutes before they were all the way on. Whenever I heard that buzz, I broke into a dead sprint for the house no matter what I was doing. I wasn't the only one. The first flicker of the streetlights would cause many kids to break into their fastest gear in order to make it home in time. If I was at the Palmetto Youth Center, I jumped on Grandaddy Cee's bicycle and peddled until even the wind couldn't keep up with me.

That summer proved to be very different than any other summer that I had ever experienced in my life. The night sky was off limits unless I was looking up at it from inside the house, but the choice of how I spent my days was totally up to me. Grandma Dot spent the days working and so did Granddaddy Cee. The best thing about that was that my grandmother always made sure that I had either some money or a food stamp in my pocket to get something to eat or something to drink. Sometimes she gave me money just so that I wouldn't be broke. She had a thing about me being what she called "dead broke".

My grandmother giving me money was a tremendous advantage that I had over a lot of my friends that summer. The money that she gave me was enough for me, but it wasn't enough for all of my "dead broke" friends to get something to eat too. That harsh reality meant that what "we" were going to eat became a serious priority for the group on some days.

Most of the time, we were pretty resourceful in getting around the hunger problem. In the best case scenario everybody went home to get something to eat. That was always an option for me, but on the majority of the days that was not an option for at least one kid in our group. Sometimes that kid tagged along with me to my house and we each made a sandwich to eat, but I knew that I could not do that everyday because my grandmother had made it clear that she did not want anyone in the house when she wasn't at home.

In the event that we all couldn't satisfy our hunger within the circle of our houses, we did have other options. There were two places in our neighborhood that offered a free lunch program for the neighborhood kids. One place was the local Head Start and the other one was the Palmetto Youth Center. Those two places saved the day on many occasions, and life was a beautiful thing for forty-five minutes when we got those free lunches that consisted of a sandwich, a snack, and something cold to drink.

The funny thing about that was that I never felt embarrassed about the free lunches at the Head Start or the Youth Center. The free lunches in Palmetto were nothing but a showcase for the free-masonry among poor Black kids from poor Black families that only had each other.

On those days where we all ate a free lunch, we went to the store to spend the money that my grandmother gave me to eat with for that day. Every now and then someone else would have some money too; we put everything we had together to see what we could get. If there wasn't enough money for everybody to get their own thing we found other ways to make sure everyone was included. One of the most common ways was the use of the phrase "save me some". For example, if there was one soda and two people, then one person would say "save me some" and it was almost like an obligation for the other person to save some of the soda for the person who would have normally gone without. You couldn't be "stingy" about it either.

I think we just automatically, through osmosis, picked up on the customs of our elders who often sent children in the neighborhood to Sister So and So house to borrow "a cup of milk", "a few slices of bread", or "a cup of sugar". If the person had it, inconsequential of how much or how little they had, then the request was always granted with a smile. If the grown-up wasn't home and a child answered the door, then they either gave it to you or suffered the wrath of their parent or guardian later. That's how it was in the old school—Black folks used to look out for one another. I think that we had to be that way because nobody had a pot to piss in or a window to throw it out of. You never knew when it was going to be your turn to borrow something.

Years after I was a part of that type of sharing, I was watching a nature show on a species of the bat. All of the bats would go out for their nightly feeding; the successful ones were obligated by some social custom of the group to regurgitate some of their food to the ones that weren't successful. That tripped me out; the bats had a system of "save me some". The narrator of the show speculated that they even had a system of identification for those bats that were stingy.

But as I was saying, our trips to the store were more frequent when we benefited from the free lunch programs. The only problem with the free lunch programs was that they were not permanent and did not last the entire summer. That meant that there were some days where our backs were against the wall with our empty stomachs at stake. On those days we went our separate ways and did the best we could.

That wasn't so bad for me because my grandmother always made sure that I had something to eat, but for some of the others it was rough and I can't say that everybody always ate. I guess you could call those days of hunger the famine days, but we also had some feast days.

There were times where either our caretakers gave us a few bucks or we collected enough soda bottles to raise enough money for the entire group to eat out. When the money came from the collection of glass soda bottles, the effort was tremendous and usually took a couple of days. We went all over our neighborhood and a few surrounding neighborhoods collecting empty soda bottles to be redeemed for either a dime or twenty cents. The sixteen-ounce bottles were good for a dime and the thirty-two-ounce bottles were good for twenty cents. We collected until we had enough money to go to a favorite eatery of ours.

The fare to ride the bus was only twenty-five cents during the summer; an extra bottle or two easily paid for our fare. We took the route two city bus to Bradenton and transferred to route nine to get to Duffs Smorgasbord. We got there early enough to take advantage of the lunch rates and stayed well into the dinner shift.

Our street sense, hunger pains, and poverty told us to pay the cheaper lunch price and stay until dinner was served! We ate until we got full. After the initial gorging, we laughed and talked until we were able to eat some more and get full again. Most people went to a place like that and stayed for an hour or so; we stayed for three and four hours.

Thinking back to how much food we ate, I guess James Baldwin was right in his 1955 classic, *Notes of a Native Son*, when he said: "It's impossible to eat enough if you're worried about the next meal". That quote was the reality for most of my friends, I simply went along with the summer gorging for the choice of foods involved and because it was fun.

My friends were always cool to me, but they were even cooler to me when we were eating at Duff's. Their whole personalities changed with the abundance of food beckoning us to eat as much as we wanted. I wondered if their personalities would have been like that all the time if they had more food on a daily basis. I think that the lack of food in their daily lives was the reason that many of my friends weren't good students during the school year. It's a very real possibility that they were too busy thinking about lunch to pay attention in class.

Their jokes were always funnier at Duff's than they were at any other time because we had plenty of good food to eat, so we laughed loud. The loud laughter combined with the fact that we often stayed for hours caused the staff to look at us with a bit of contempt, but we didn't care; we were "happy to be escaping poverty ... however brief". We were determined to get every penny's worth of our money and then some before we returned to the regular routine of those hot summer days of worrying if our whole crew would eat lunch that day.

Duff's wasn't the only place of business that we used to fit our needs. Sometimes, we rode our bikes to the Holiday Inn across the bridge that connected Palmetto to Bradenton by spanning the banks of the Manatee River. I can see now that it was a very dangerous thing to do, but during that time we either scoffed at danger or simply didn't recognize it.

We used the Holiday Inn's pool just like paying customers until someone came to kick us out. That usually took at least thirty minutes. If we were really lucky, then we were able to swim for an hour before someone informed us that the pool was only for hotel guest and asked us to leave. We simply got our stuff and left. We knew that we weren't supposed to be there, but we didn't care. Our parents and guardians had no idea what we did while they were at work. We were also out of the reach of the informal network of the neighborhood watch of older adults who lived in our neighborhood. The last place you were going to find them was at the Holiday Inn Resort.

In between the excursions to Duff's and the pool getaways to the Holiday Inn, we thought up all kinds of crazy things to do in our own neighborhood. In the name of adventure and exploration, we chopped our way through heavy brush filled with snakes. We used screens from windows to catch crawdads and minnows out of the ditch that ran underneath the railroad tracks. We walked the railroad tracks until we found freight cars to play on; we examined the funny looking rocks that one could only find on the railroad tracks. We tried to time when the train was going to go by so that we could place a penny or nickel on the tracks to be flattened into a hot thin piece of metal. We didn't do that too often because we understood that money was precious. Besides, once you saw one locomotive flattened coin, you've seen them all.

When the things that we did required extra bravery, things like jumping from rooftops, we would run to the edge and yell

"Geronimo!" We yelled that to summon up the extra courage that we needed to perform the deed. We thought that by screaming the name of the great Native American Chiricahua Apache Chief that we would be protected against any and all danger. I had no idea why we thought that or where it came from because I don't believe that any of us really knew who or what Geronimo was all about; but we thought it and believed it enough to do almost any deed.

We also did more mainstream things in our neighborhood. We organized softball, soccer, and football games that matched the neighborhood Black kids against the neighborhood Mexican kids. You could have had a microcosm of any African nation versus Mexico in any given sport on any given day. We referred to the Mexican kids as "migos". Don't ask me where that term came from because I couldn't tell you. My best guess is that it was a shortened version of amigo, the Spanish word for friend, but that's only a guess.

In any event, those athletic contests gave me a little reputation for being a good athlete. I wasn't the very best, but I was far from the worst. I was usually a second or third pick. Sometimes if the person that was picking the team was a little weak-minded, I could stare at him hard enough to make him pick me first. Being a first pick was a sign of respect, and everybody wanted to be respected. But being picked first also meant that you had to play well, so I always tried extra hard when I was picked first.

My athletic status combined with the leadership position that I occupied within our little group left me feeling pretty good. I felt good about me, and I felt good about being Black again. The freemasonry of that little Palmetto neighborhood let me know that being Black was hard when it came to not having, but it also taught me that being Black was more about a feeling than anything else ... and the feeling was good.

When the feeling felt real good my friends and I slapped each other five. It was just an automatic thing. We would say:

Gimme 5
On the Black hand side
Stick it in the hole
You got soul.

I guess it was all about a soul thing ... a Black soul thing. It was something that we did whenever we felt real good about being Black. We grew up watching the older Black guys slapping palms in the neighborhood; I had also seen it on Laura Street. Cats would be all excited when Doug Williams threw a touchdown pass or when Magic Johnson threw a no-look pass. You see Doug could throw like that because he was Black; Magic had so much flair because he was Black. Their extra skills were a Black thing.

The next big thing that brothers were going to be slapping palms about in 1982 was some cat named Moses Malone who was supposed to take the Philadelphia 76ers to the "promised land". The brothers were going to slap hands for that because they knew that if he did it, then it was going to be just like he was taking Black people to the "promised land" ... at least that was the case for Philly fans. And chances were that if you were Black in 1982 and you liked basketball, then you were either a Philly fan or a Laker fan.

With all that Black feel good stuff running through my body, there was no way that I was going to let my upcoming fourth grade school year have the same impact on me as my third grade school year did. I went back to Stewart Elementary with an attitude that I was just as good as anybody else and I wasn't going to let anybody tell me anything different. I was ready to flip things over to the Black hand side; I still didn't have any money, but I had soul.

The environment at Stewart was the same as it was the previous school year. Ninety-nine percent of the Blacks that went to the school were still poor and bused in from Palmetto and ninety-nine percent of the whites that went to the school still lived in surrounding areas and came from upper middle class or rich families. The curriculum did not include any more positive images of Blacks than it did the year before. I was still on free lunch and the lunch ticket still had the huge red writing. I still didn't have the clothes or things that the majority of the white children had. The environment was still very much the same, but the difference was in my mind. I discovered that that was the only difference that I really needed!

My different mindset was my greatest advantage against all the elements of the past school year that had made me feel inferior and ashamed to be Black. The mind is the greatest weapon that any Black person can possibly have in an oppressive environment where he or she is made to feel inferior. Whoever controls the human mind has all the power that he or she needs to control human speech, thought, and action. Therefore, if you are in control of your own mind, you are in control over yourself and the way in which you let things impact you.

My summer experiences combined with my own God given intelligence would not let me feel the way I did during my third grade school year. I still thought that there were problems at Stewart; I just knew that I wasn't a part of those problems.

One of the biggest problems was that some of the white folks at the school treated us like we were some second hand item with no real value. I knew that I wasn't making that feeling up because I felt it even when I tried to pretend it wasn't there. I stopped looking at myself as the cause of that problem. I started to look at those white people to try to find the reason why things were the way that they were. I didn't have any problems with white people; white people had a problem with me. I didn't realize it then, but I had come to a conclusion at nine years old that would play itself out throughout the rest of my life.

It seemed to me that the white people didn't just have a problem with me, but they also had a problem with all of my Black friends that were bused in with me. I began to try to figure out what white people thought that Black people had done that was so terrible to make them have such a problem with us. I always thought about that on the long bus rides to and from school, but I never came up with anything that made any sense. I also couldn't come up with anything in my mind on why there was so much inequity between the two races. Everyday that I went to that school: "why did white people have nicer things than Black people?" I never came up with a satisfactory answer.

There were other questions that I couldn't answer, but I did know that how I was treated by white children during my third grade year was wrong. Once I determined that the treatment was wrong, I took my first available opportunity to say that it was wrong. That opportunity presented itself in the form of my very first speech that I was asked to write.

Everybody in the fourth grade had to write a speech in order to participate in the 4-H Public Speaking Program. We were not given any requirements on the topic, but it did have to be a certain time limit. I knew right away that I was going to write about the prejudice that existed in the school from some of the whites towards the Blacks.

I ran into three slight problems when trying to write about the prejudice. The first problem was that it was really hard for me to convey the prejudice in written form because it wasn't always an easy thing to put into words. The second problem that I encountered was that I did not want to make it seem like it was all the white people in the school that treated Blacks unfairly; there were a few white people who were always nice to me. The third problem that I faced was that I was afraid to directly accuse anybody.

Despite all those problems, I was persistent in my desire to want to write my speech on the unfair treatment that the Black children sometimes received at the school. That desire was soon filled as my solution to all three problems soon presented itself to me while I was watching one of my favorite Saturday morning cartoons—*The Smurfs.*

I enjoyed watching *The Smurfs* because they always had a lesson at the end of the show on how one should behave or what one should do or not do in a particular situation. I don't know if the kids that I went to school with enjoyed the show for the same reasons that I did, but I do know that it was a school favorite. Many of the white children collected little figurines of the tiny blue cartoon characters. They lined up the figurines on their desks and talked about their favorite smurf—most of the girls chose Smurfette as their favorite.

The little blue characters had solved my problems by giving me the perfect opportunity to write about prejudice while avoiding my three snags. I decided that I would use the characters and their village to simulate our school and the people in our school. I had to make color a factor in my story so I left all the Smurfs in my story blue, just as they appeared on the television show, with the exception of one lone Smurf. I made that smurf Black. He was the main character in my story, so the title of my speech became *The Black Smurf.* That speech was my first time writing about prejudice and being Black. I was a nine-year-old fourth grader at Stewart Elementary during the 1982-1983 school year.

My speech described many injustices and ill-treatments that the Black Smurf had to endure at the hands of his blue counterparts. He was made to wear less smurfy clothes, he ate less smurfy food, he lived in a less smurfy house, he wasn't considered to be as smart as the other Smurfs, and he was made to work harder than the other Smurfs. In my speech, I made the color of his skin the sole basis for the less than smurfy treatment that he received.

After describing how the Black Smurf was treated and why he was treated that way, I shifted gears in the speech to describe a situation that placed the whole entire Smurf village in danger. The entire village would have been destroyed if it weren't for the heroic deeds and quick thinking of the Black Smurf. After the Black Smurf saved the village, every other blue Smurf realized that they had treated the Black Smurf unfairly and promised to never treat him in a less than smurfy way again. He was given smurfy clothes to wear, he was given smurfy food to eat, he was given a smurfy house to live in, he wasn't treated as if he wasn't as smart as the blue Smurfs, and he didn't have to work harder than the other smurfs anymore. They all lived smufily ever after.

I was really excited about my speech, I thought that I had done quite well; I even remember telling my grandmother about it. That was unusual for me because I rarely talked about school projects with anybody. Talking about what was going on at school was a habit that I never developed in moving from place to place all the time. I guess I didn't really want to bother anyone with what I was doing in school. Since no one really seemed to be particularly interested in the day to day issues of what happened to me in school, I just assumed that I would be bothering them if I brought them up.

The big day came for me to deliver my speech in front of my classmates, and I did a really good job. I didn't even have to read all of it from the index cards like most of my classmates. I had memorized most of it over the previous two days. The top three speeches in my class were selected to compete against the rest of the fourth grade classes. I must have finished second or third in my class because I didn't win, but I did compete against the other fourth grade classes.

The winner out of the entire fourth grade group would represent our school in the Manatee County competition. I thought that I might be able to win the whole fourth grade contest; the winner of each grade would read his or her speech in the library before going on to county competition. I was looking forward to the library more than the county competition. The people that I wanted to hear my speech the most were at Stewart Elementary.

It didn't matter in the end; my speech didn't win our entire fourth grade competition. A little white girl from another class who wrote about how she and her mother baked cookies was chosen as the speech that would represent our school. I listened to her read her speech in the library; no one outside of the fourth grade ever heard my speech. After hearing her speech, I thought that it was good, but I was a little disappointed because I thought mine was better.

I suppose that my reaction was only natural. I didn't remember when the last time that I saw my mother, and she and I had never baked any cookies. I just couldn't appreciate the depth of her speech coming from a background like mine. However, even though I was little disappointed that I didn't win, I was happy that I had a chance to express how I felt about an issue that always seemed to be on my mind.

My fourth grade school year proved to be a period where I could express what was on my mind, but it was also a time where I could express my athletic talent. I found out that I was good enough to represent our school in the nine-year-old and under category in the county track meet. I performed well in most of the events at my school, but the only one that I was the best in the school was the High Jump.

The High Jump was probably the most unusual event for me to be so successful in because every year I was always one of the shortest kids in my class. My P.E. coach kept telling me to jump again just to make sure it wasn't fluke. After I did it over and over, Coach Banks was convinced; I was the highest jumper in our school in my age group, and I got a chance to compete against the best from the other schools in the county track meet.

To the dismay of a lot of people I'm sure, I went on to finish second in the county track meet to another kid that I knew from the Palmetto Youth Center named Howard. I finished second again the following year to Howard and a kid named Brian. They were both so much taller than I was that it seemed that I was David engaged in battle with two Goliaths for the county championship. I didn't beat those two, but I beat all of the other competitors from the other schools for two years in a row.

My success at the county track meet gave me the confidence that I needed to never let my size or lack of size become an issue for me in anything that I did. I had jumped higher than any kid in my age group in Manatee County with the exception of two. The confidence that that achievement gave me would really prove to be a valuable asset for my future.

LONELY TEARDROPS

The fourth grade school year passed on and it was time for the 1983 summer. By that time Michael Jackson had taken over the world with his moonwalk on Motown 25 and some significant changes had taken place regarding who lived in my grandmother's house.

My grandmother's brother and his family were now gone. He had been arrested earlier in the year for shooting another Black male. It was the same old story, some dude had challenged his manhood and he had to prove how much of a man he was by shooting him. With him in jail, his girlfriend and her three children found another place to live. The vacancies they left gave me my own room for a very short period of time, but that was quickly changed by my mom moving in with her new boyfriend and my uncle (my mom's brother) moving in with his new girlfriend who just happened to be white. She and my uncle had a little boy who had been born in September of 1982.

The baby brought a lot of good excitement to the house; his favorite thing to do when he learned to run was to sprint by the bathroom and throw things in the toilet. He wouldn't even wait to see if he made it or not; he'd just wait for the splash sound to let him know if he had scored or not. If he hit, he would laugh like it was the funniest thing in the world. As long as it wasn't anything of mine, I laughed right along with him.

The residents of the house were now three couples consisting of: my grandmother and Granddaddy Cee, my mom and her new boyfriend, and my uncle and his new girlfriend. My baby cousin and I were the odd people out. He was still young enough to sleep in a baby bed; I was relocated to the couch. I actually didn't mind the new arrangement because the house was a little more peaceful without my grandmother's brother. He was a man with a volatile temperament. My grandmother said that his disposition had a lot to do with the fact that he served in the Vietnam War. She said that people were just never the same after they came from Vietnam.

As a child growing up I didn't have much sympathy for what my grandmother's brother went through by serving in Vietnam, but now I feel sorry for any victim of war. I say victim because that's all you can be when it comes to war, no matter what side you are fighting for in a war you are a victim and there are never any real winners or real gains. The only things that are real are the losses and the deaths.

I spent the summer of 1983 doing a lot of the same things that I had done in the summer of 1982 and it passed away with little fanfare. In the fall of 1983, I was ten years old and ready to start my fifth grade school year at Stewart Elementary. It was a year that was set to mark unprecedented territory for me as an elementary school student. I was about to embark on a third consecutive school year in which I would be attending the same school and living in the same place.

When I actually started my fifth grade year at Stewart, I asked myself: "what's going on here"? I had been at Stewart for two whole years and it was about to be three whole years. As I thought about the unusualness of that reality, my mind reminded me that I had not stood up and introduced myself to a new class in a long time. I actually enjoyed the normalcy of not being the new kid.

But my instincts should have told me that something was wrong with my life for something to actually be going halfway right and semi-normal. It seemed that no sooner than I was having those thoughts that things in my world changed again.

The changes came about as the composition of my household began to change. The first change took place when my mom's brother, his girlfriend, and their son moved into their own apartment. The second and most significant change was when my beloved Granddaddy Cee separated from my grandmother and moved back to Plant City. He and my grandmother had been having problems for awhile, when another woman entered into the picture to make the problems worse for them.

My grandmother was devastated by the separation. I sensed that she really wished that they could have stayed together. I think that she hoped for a long time that they would get back together. I was hurt too. I loved Granddaddy Cee as much as my grandma did. I am sure that we both loved him for much different reasons; but the amount of love was probably the same. I let my hopes for their reunion live in my heart for a long time ... but it never happened.

I had grown up watching the love that they had between them go through good times and bad times. I had seen them both struggle through the hardships of extremely long workdays only to find comfort in each other's arms at night. I watched them laugh at almost nothing until everything seemed funny. My grandmother was his "Sugar Baby"; I couldn't tell who enjoyed that nickname more. I didn't know if he enjoyed saying it more or if she enjoyed hearing it more. I had seen my grandmother use all her powers as a woman to try to hold a certain position only to watch him use their love and all his powers as a man to change that position.

I laughed when I recently heard a commercial that said it was a woman's prerogative to change her mind, but it was a man's prerogative to change it back. I laughed because I had witnessed that to be true in their love. But after he moved out, they were to be together never more.

When their love was good it was really something to behold, but it also had its bad times. But what love doesn't? The only thing that one could hope for in love is to grow together through the bad times and that there are more good times than bad times. But in their case, I knew that the last bad time was different than any other bad than I had ever seen between the two of them. I knew in my heart that it was over between them. Upon that realization my heart broke into an infinite number of tiny pieces right along with my grandmother's heart.

Granddaddy Cee had been there for me and done more things for me than any other man had at that point in my life. I loved him dearly. In my heart, whatever faults he had as a man were clearly overshadowed by the love that he gave me as a grandfather. And for that ... I will always consider him to be one of the true Godsends in my life.

He took me fishing, he took me hunting, he taught me responsibility, he taught me how to behave and how not to behave, and most important of all he took time with me. I knew that I would miss him a great deal, but I had to put all those feelings aside in that moment that he left because my grandmother needed me. When human spirits are truly crushed they need something with warm blood running through its veins to love them. Although I was only ten years old, I had warm blood running through my veins and my grandma cried in my arms like a baby.

I felt power in my little ten-year-old heart and strength in my eternal soul that told me that I had to take care of my grandmother. The fact that I couldn't even take care of myself at the time didn't cross my mind. I looked at my grandmother and with a strength that must have come straight down from the Almighty, I said: "Everything's gonna be alright. I'm uh take care of you." From that day up until the very moment that I typed these keystrokes I have always moved with a purpose to do just that.

I have raced against time itself with the hope that I might be able to one day fulfill that promise that I made to my grandmother as that ten-year-old boy. I would consider it to be among the greatest successes that I could ever achieve in this life to see her truly happy without worry. If I could only see her smile for a minute without first crying for an hour or if I could only see her experience an ounce of joy without first enduring a pound of heartache, then I would be a very happy person.

All the changes in my grandmother's household created a lot of uncertainty and it was decided that it was time for me to move again. I weighed my options and realized that there weren't too many. My paternal grandparents' house was really the only place that provided me with more stability than continuing to live with Grandma Dot, my mom, and my mom's new boyfriend. So I cast my vote to go live with my paternal grandparents. Grandma Dot went to plead my case and it was done.

Very shortly after, I found myself standing in a new classroom introducing myself as the new kid at Wakeland Elementary. It wasn't too hard to do; it was something that I could do with my eyes closed because of all the moves that I had gone through up until that point. By 1983, I had attended eight different elementary schools since I started school in 1978. I hoped that Wakeland would be my final stop on my elementary school tour.

With all the changes that I had been through, it was nice to see that not much had changed about living with my paternal grandparents. My grandmother was still very religious and the rules of the house regarding religion had not changed all that much. You still had to go to church every Sunday and it was still a very "for as me in my house we shall serve the Lord" type of environment. My grandfather presence was just as strong, and he still had the final say so in all non-religious matters.

I shared a room with my dad's youngest brother who was about nine years older than me. He was a tremendous athlete; he had been a star football player at Southeast High. He was sort of my athletic hero. He had a lot of trophies around the house that I looked at all the time. Looking at those trophies one day, I decided that I wanted some orange and blue trophies of my own from Southeast High.

I fantasized that I would be just like my dad's youngest brother; I would be a football star and collect a lot of trophies along the way too. I had played organized football in Palmetto before all the changes at Grandma Dot's house, but the move to Bradenton caused me to have to quit the team. Before the move I had played in two organized games and scored two touchdowns; one as a running back and one on a kick-off return. My dad's youngest brother had even seen the kick-off return for a touchdown. He tried to act like he wasn't impressed, but I knew that he was. I just knew that I could be a football star if I tried really hard.

I am glad that I had that feeling, because it served as a basis to teach me that sometimes trying really hard is not enough in life. Once I left Palmetto and Grandma Dot's, I never played organized football again. My two touchdowns as a Palmetto Eagle would be the only two touchdowns that I would ever score on a football field during an organized game. Nevertheless, the move back to my paternal grandparents' house found me exploring my athletic potential on another kind of field.

I signed up to play organized baseball at the 24th Street Ballpark because it was only a few blocks up the street from the house. I had never played fast pitch baseball in my life, but I was a good athlete. I could field and throw like I had been playing as long as the other kids; but I couldn't hit the ball to save my life. Before we actually played any games, we had some practices at my coach's house. He lived in the part of east Bradenton that was too east and too rich for Black folks.

My coach was a Veterinarian and the name of our team was Suncoast Animal Clinic; I don't know if he owned the place or simply worked there, but our team was named after the animal hospital. His house was as nice as the houses that I rode by on the school bus on the way to Stewart Elementary in west Bradenton. The only difference was the land; my coach's house seemed to be a mile away from any other houses.

My coach had two sons that played baseball and one of them was on my team. I was awestruck by all the things that his children had, but nothing impressed me more than the Kawasaki motorbikes that they both had. I asked myself: "how did they get to be that lucky as kids"?

My coach had made part of his yard into a baseball diamond and the team practiced on that field for a year. He took me to and from practice because I didn't have anybody else to take me or pick me up. Occasionally he picked up and took another kid home, but I was the only one he picked up and took home every practice. I didn't like being the only one that he did that for, but it was the only way that I was going to be able to play.

The fact that he took me to and from every practice wasn't the only differences between the rest of my teammates and me. The first difference that I immediately noticed was that I was the only Black kid on my team. The second difference was that most of the other kids had tremendous family support when it came to their baseball activities. The third difference was that the majority of them, with the exception of maybe two, came from families who did well financially. The last and final thing that I noticed was that they could all hit the ball better than I could. Soon everybody who came to our games noticed that too.

Not being able to hit the baseball was a major source of embarrassment for me because I had considered myself to be a pretty good athlete up until that point. The people who cheered for the other team would yell: "he can't hit, he's too scared to even swing!" They were right. I was scared to swing, but I swung anyway just to try to prove them wrong.

That usually only made it worse because I usually missed the ball. Whenever I struck out, the people cheering for my team always said: "that's alright Quincy maybe next time." They said that a lot over the course of the season. I hated it because the other people cheering for the other team would learn my name; they always used my name when they really wanted me to miss the ball: "C'mon 'Quincy', give us that out we need … swing!" Damned if I did swing and damned if I didn't swing; I swung! Even at that early age, it was a part of my personality to go out swinging. The ump yelled: "strike three, you're out!"

The other team's fans cheered wildly because I had come through for them ... again. I walked back to the dugout with my head down and my pride broken. My teammates tried to act like it was alright ... only because coach made them act that way, but I knew that they were tired of me either striking out or praying for a walk each time I went to bat. I didn't blame them; I was even tired of me not being able to shut the other team's fans up with some kind of contact with the ball.

I was really ashamed of my inability to hit the ball. However the thing that embarrassed me the most was the fact that after the night games I didn't have a ride home. My mom and her boyfriend drove from Palmetto to see a few games and when they did, they gave me a ride back to my grandmother's house. But they didn't come to see that many games. So when they didn't come to see the game, I didn't have a ride back to my grandmother's house. That became a problem for me.

The problem was not the distance that I had to walk to my grandmother's house because she only lived about five blocks from the park. The problem was the fact that it was nighttime and many of the people often asked me if I needed a ride home. I said no because I had become self-conscious over the years about not being part of a "normal family". I knew that if I were a part of a "normal family" I would have had a ride home. I knew that if I accepted a ride from the people at the park, then they would ask me questions that I didn't want to be asked or look at me in a way that I didn't want to be looked at.

I didn't want people to ask me why there was nobody there to pick me up from the game and I didn't want people to look at me with those eyes people look through when they feel sorry for someone. So I held my head high and when someone asked if I needed a ride home I always said no. I looked at them with a fake smile and lied. I told them that I could walk because I only lived right across the street.

But truth be told, it was really starting to bother me that I didn't have anybody that I could count on for a ride home from the game. I didn't want to get a ride with my coach since he was already going out of his way by picking me up for practice and taking me home after practice. The fact that I didn't have a "normal" relationship with either of my parents left a huge void in my life as far as the little support that a child needs in life. Whether it was a ride to and from a game or someone to say it was wrong for a ten-year-old child to be walking alone in the dark, I was looking for some support.

The issue of getting home after the night games surpassed my not being able to hit the ball as my biggest concern about playing baseball. I couldn't keep using my "I live right across the street" excuse because sometimes the person who I gave that line to the night before would see me four blocks away from the field the very next game. So in order to get around that problem, I started waiting in some deserted part of the park until all the cars cleared out—which only added to the danger of walking home alone in the dark.

When all the people left, I started my journey back to my grandmother's house. By doing that, I didn't have to answer any questions and nobody saw me walking along the street. I also avoided being looked at like an object of pity through the eyes of those tender souls that only wanted to help. I knew that they were only trying to help, but I didn't want to accept their help. I didn't want to share the pain that I felt from not having any parents with total strangers. I didn't want to share my pain of being a tiny little soul all alone in a big scary world. The trouble with that was that the whole world seemed to be made up of total strangers ... it was just me, myself, and I.

On many of those walks from the ballpark to my grandmother's house, I cried all the way up until the time that I walked into my grandmother's front door. I never cried about whether we won or lost the game or if I did or didn't hit the ball. I cried because it hurt not to be a part of a family situation where I could assert my natural rights as a child to be loved and supported in the little ways by the two people who were responsible for bringing me into the world.

The fact of not having a ride from the game was just one more thing on a long list of things that grew over the years from essentially being a child without parents; I was hurting deep down in my soul. I never felt so alone as I did when I was hiding in those dugouts waiting for everybody to leave the park; my only companions of those tearful journeys home were pain and sorrow.

I realized that the people who were doing things for me were not the people who should have been doing things for me, Donnell had taught me that. As a result of that lesson, I was just happy to be where ever I was, no matter how marginal my existence. I didn't want to let how I felt about not having any parents make me appear ungrateful to the people who were taking care of me. I knew that I was not their child and that I was not their top priority, so I didn't ask for much and I didn't expect much.

For example, I was sad that I didn't have a ride from the games, but I was grateful that Grandma Mary had a clean uniform ready for me for every game. It made me feel good when she asked me when my next game was so that she could have my "suit" (old Black people never called things what they were) ready. It made me feel good because I knew that she didn't have to do that. I really appreciated everything that was done, but they couldn't add up to the feeling you get when you know you are the most important person in the world to someone.

I would have gone through my entire childhood never feeling like I was the most important person in the world to anybody if it had not been for my Grandma Dot. She was the only person who ever made me her number one priority, but it wasn't always possible for me to be where she was for many different reasons. She did the best that she could and I loved her dearly for her efforts.

If she couldn't give me what I needed on her own; then she would literally beg for it or borrow it. When she found out that I needed something, then she made sure that I had it. But when she didn't find out about a particular need, I usually missed out. As a result, a lot of that little support that a child needs wasn't there for me during my childhood.

I gave up asking for it at a very early age. I thank God that I had people who made sure that I received the big support that comes in the form of food, clothing, and shelter. My needs for the little support fell through the cracks most of the time. The little support like a ride to baseball practice, a ride to and from a baseball game that was being played five blocks away, or someone saying: "no ten-year-old child, you are not walking home after dark by yourself".

After baseball season ended, I began to dabble on the basketball court at a neighbor's house across the street from my grandparents' house. At first, I would shoot by myself; then I began to play with a friend of mine who was also a fifth grader at Wakeland. Our games took place before the middle school boys came to the courts and they stopped immediately after they arrived.

The middle school boys wouldn't let me play with them because I wasn't good enough and I was too small. However, a fortuitous thing happened on one of those days that they came to take over the court. They needed one more person to make it an even run and I was the only one around. It was truly a case of the kind of luck that many have defined as a thing that happens when preparation meets opportunity.

The trash talkin' middle school boys didn't know that I took it personally when they kicked me off the court every day. They didn't know that I practiced hard everyday before they got there so that there would be one day where they couldn't kick me off anymore. I played a few games with the big boys until another boy their age showed up and they dismissed me for the day, but they did not dismiss before paying a little respect to my skills as a "shorty".

The respect that I got that day from the older boys made me a valuable substitute anytime one of their regulars didn't show up and I took advantage of the opportunities. It was during the games with the big boys in my neighbor's back yard that I fell in love with basketball. The highlight of my day was whenever I made a bigger boy look stupid for getting "took to da hole" by a kid in elementary school. If I did something that somebody on the other team thought that I wasn't supposed to do, then they jumped all over the bigger kid that was guarding me. I always acted like I just got lucky in those situations, but I actually I went to bed thinking about how I was going to make that happen again the next time that I played with the big boys.

As the fifth grade school year went on, I adjusted to my new school very nicely. I met a boy named Michael Jermaine Williams. He became my first lifelong friend—he always liked to say his whole name (His mom must've been a big Jackson 5 fan). I was selected to receive the citizen of the month award during one month and I was also chosen to be a patrol. A patrol was a person who was given authority to make sure that the other kids were following the rules.

I was doing well in school and my grades were a reflection of that fact, but grades were like an after thought for me because there was nobody around to praise me for good grades or admonish me for bad grades. Many kids were happy or sad because of the consequences they received as a result of good grades or bad grades, but

I was really indifferent either way about my grades from a consequence standpoint.

I basically made good grades because it was easy for me and I didn't want anybody to think that I was not as smart as they were. The latter reason was a result of my third grade experience at Stewart Elementary. Once I satisfied myself, I really didn't have anybody to answer to about school performance.

I was supposed to get my report card signed by my parents in order to bring it back to my teacher; but I never got my report card signed. I never even brought it back to my teacher because it was rare that I even showed it to anyone at home. My teacher was more concerned about the people who didn't do well bringing their report cards back, so she didn't sweat me too much when I didn't return mine. I usually had all A's and B's with a C in handwriting. I probably deserved a D in handwriting, but I guess it was hard to put a D for handwriting on a report card full of A's and B's.

The 1983-1984 school year had begun kind of rocky, but it had actually turned out to be a good year for me. Still, after it was over, I felt bothered the whole summer about having to leave Grandma Dot. I had really meant what I told her after my Granddaddy Cee left when I said that I would take care of her. I wanted to be there for her in a most desperate way. So the end of the 1984 summer found me engineering a move back to Palmetto to live with Grandma Dot.

The end of the '84 summer was also the time for my coach to reconvene baseball practices for our team. Despite my poor hitting performance, our team had made it all the way to the championship series the previous season. There were two differences my second time around.

The first difference was that I could really hit the ball now. I mean not just sometimes, but all the time. I worked extra hard in every hitting drill that we had during practice. I was driven by the images that I stored in my head of me striking out to the wild cheers of the opposing fans. Apparently the hard work had paid off; my coach changed me from batting ninth to the leadoff hitter. After learning how to hit the ball and actually getting on base; I became the best base stealer on our team.

The second difference was that I was living in Palmetto. The one thing that stayed the same was the fact that I still didn't have a ride to or from practice. My coach insisted on picking me up from Palmetto to take me to practice and bringing me home after practice, but I felt bad that he had to do that. Palmetto was quite a bit out of his way; every time that we crossed the bridge that connected Palmetto to Bradenton, my heart sank like a rock dropped into the river below. I also revisited the awful feeling of not having someone who could take me back and forth. My mom and her boyfriend were living in the house with my grandmother, but there was still a lack of support for something like me playing baseball in Bradenton. In a situation like that you are talking about resources that just weren't available in an abundant supply—mainly gas money and time. So, just as my baseball skills were developing, I told my coach that I would have to stop playing. I told him that he didn't have to drive so far to pick me up anymore. He tried to convince me otherwise, but I had made up my mind on the way home from my last practice with the team.

I was having fun playing baseball, and I was getting better with each practice. Ironically, during my last practice with the team, I had hit the ball farther than I had ever hit it before. It wasn't baseball that I wasn't enjoying; it was all the other stuff that went in to me trying to play baseball. I just didn't want to deal with the situation anymore. I definitely couldn't hide in the dugout and walk home from Bradenton to Palmetto.

RHYTHM OF AFRICA

My move back to Grandma Dot's house meant that I was not going to play baseball that year (as it turns out I never played baseball again). It also meant that I was now living in the same school district that I lived in when I attended Stewart Elementary. I was about to go to another new school, but so was every other fifth grader in the state of Florida who was being promoted to the sixth grade. My elementary school days were over. I was about to become a middle school kid. The 1984-85 school year found me enrolling in Martha B. King Middle School.

King Middle School was less than a mile away from Stewart Elementary. They must have been sister schools. The proximity wasn't the only way the two schools were close. The racial composition of King Middle was very similar, if not identical, to the racial composition of Stewart Elementary. The socio-economic status of the Blacks and whites who attended King was pretty much the same as the Blacks and whites who attended Stewart.

Basically, I was going to school with the same well-to-do white children that I had met during my days at Stewart. I was being bused in with the same poor Black kids from Palmetto that I rode the bus with two and three years earlier. I was hit with the same polarized race picture that I received such a heavy dose of while attending Stewart. That wasn't the only thing that I was being hit with on the race front. The race issue was about to take on a whole new twist for me. Some of my questions about race were about to be answered—at least in my mind.

My mom had collected some literature from a local religious group that told the story of slavery and the historical mistreatment

125

that Blacks in the U.S. had suffered at the hands of whites. On top of that, my mom's boyfriend rented a VCR and *Roots*. Before he brought those tapes home, the only thing that I had heard about roots was from old Black folks who claimed that roots on a person made people do things that they wouldn't have ordinarily done. I once heard an old Black lady tell another old Black lady that her daughter's boyfriend had left her daughter for another woman because the other woman had put roots on the man. I thought that the man left because the other woman had a better body and bigger booty. I didn't believe in the roots that ol' folks talked about.

Roots, the video series, was a collection of six videotapes that were based on the 1977 epic written by, writer and journalist, Alex Haley. I devoured my mom's literature and I watched *Roots* volume one through six without interruption all by myself. As I read through the literature and watched the VHS tapes, I became very angry. I felt that I had been robbed, lied to, and outright cheated by white people.

Denzel Washington, in his portrayal of Malcolm X in Spike Lee's motion picture titled *Malcolm X* (1992), gave the best description that I've heard to date on how I felt during the moments when I found out the truth about my people's history and the role that white people played in that history. In addressing a group of Black people in Harlem, Denzel (as Malcolm) announced to the people that they had been deceived for hundreds of years by the white man. He screamed: "Ah I say and I say it again! You've been had; you've been took; you've been hoodwinked, bamboozled, led astray, run amok!" Malcolm's words expressed exactly how I felt as that eleven-year-old boy reading that literature and watching those tapes.

I felt that I had been betrayed into thinking that Black folks' alleged inferiority was responsible for our second class citizenship in this country. When in reality, it had been an unyielding and systematic racist effort by many whites to keep us in a subordinate position in society. This was all done for their own benefit and material prosperity. That, more than anything else, was to blame for the conditions of Black lives in the United States. I had been had; I had been took; I had been hoodwinked, bamboozled, led astray, run amok!

From the very beginning, we (Black people) were not meant to share in the opportunities that this nation was supposed to bring into existence for all of its citizenry, but then again we were not brought here as citizens. We were brought here as slaves with the intention that we would always be slaves. Nothing else! We, unlike any other group that came to this land we call America, were brought over in chains in the filthy hulls of ships. While other groups made the voyage across the Atlantic to America with the hope of a new start on a new life, we endured the dreadful "Middle Passage". The Middle Passage was a term used to describe the transatlantic slave voyages between Africa and the Americas that claimed the lives of approximately 1.8 million slaves over a period of about 350 years (many believe, myself included, that that figure is *grossly* underestimated).

We were brought to this country in chains with an expectation from the white people of America that we would never be their equal in their "land of the free". The Rev. C.L. Franklin, the renowned Baptist preacher, described the differences in the expectations of the groups of Europeans who came to this country and the expectations of the Africans who were brought to this country. He said:

> When the Europeans came to this country, embarked upon these shores, America to them was a land of promise, was a mountaintop of possibilities. But to the Negro, when he embarked upon these shores, America to him was a valley of slave huts, a valley of slavery and oppression, a valley of sorrow. (C.L. Franklin, "The Prophet and Dry Bones in the Valley," c. 1957)

After watching *Roots* and reading my mom's literature, my eleven-year-old mind began to rethink my third, fourth, and fifth grade experiences at Stewart Elementary. I began to rethink a lot of things that I had not been able to understand before I knew the truth about how my people arrived in this country.

I've watched *Roots* many times since I watched it for the first time as that eleven-year-old boy. Every time that I have watched it since that time, I've always had the urge to watch it all the way through from volume one through six. Each volume of the collection captivates my interest for different reasons.

In volume two, the businessmen that were involved in the slave trade gave their economic justification for the enslavement of my people as if it were a brand new business model. The character known as

John Carrington described the slave trade as a triangle of commerce that included tobacco from America to London, goods from London to the Guinea coast, and slaves from the areas surrounding the Gambia River on the West Coast of Africa to America. In that so-called "triangle of commerce", Mr. Carrington declared that it was all for profit and none was the loser as a result. He then went on to ask with deplorable impunity: "what harm is a full purse I liked to know?"

Mr. Carrington's attitude and question echoed the sentiment that prevailed in the minds of most Europeans involved in the transatlantic slave trade; they asked what harm was a full purse as my people were being stripped of their heritage, their religions, their languages, their customs, and their self-esteem. What harm is a full purse? They didn't see the problem with our women being raped and robbed of their virtue as our men were forced to become helpless bystanders (Maya Angelou referred to our men who witnessed such things as "muscles without memory" because they couldn't fight to help or protect our women).

I guess in Mr. Carrington's view, things like loss of heritage, religion, language, custom, and self-esteem were considered to be harmless when weighed against a full purse. Those things did irreparable damage to my people. The world will never be able to measure, neither in dollars nor in anything else, just how much my people paid for America's full purse. I expect some white folks to belittle and gainsay that statement. But let no Black lips ever dispute my words when it comes to that! THE WORLD WILL NEVER BE ABLE TO MEASURE, NEITHER IN DOLLARS NOR IN ANYTHING ELSE, JUST HOW MUCH MY PEOPLE PAID FOR AMERICA'S FULL PURSE! NEVER! What we lost can never be recovered in its full measure. Despite the truth of that statement, this nation to this very day refuses to offer any type of real atonement for what it has done to the Africans within its borders.

The transatlantic slave trade was one hundred percent successful in cutting off the captive Africans from their physical homes in Africa; but it couldn't take the Africa completely out of their minds and physical bodies. Despite the terrible realities that the transatlantic slave trade—middle passage and plantation life included— heaped upon the backs of the enslaved Africans, it was not able to completely break their spirits or destroy the African culture within their bonded souls. We, the descendants of those proud Africans, have to this very day maintained a culture that in many ways is a direct descendant from our African roots.

The African culture that remained in the African slave in America was strong enough to make Paul Robeson insist on the assertion that "in every black man flows the rhythm of Africa." Paul Robeson, an African-American Renaissance man born in 1898, was an actor, singer, civil rights leader, and political activist. Dr. Henry Louis Gates Jr., who I consider to be a modern day African-American Renaissance man, also attested to the strength of the African culture that endured in the lives of the newly enslaved Africans. Dr. Gates said:

> [T]he African slave—despite the horrors of the Middle Passage—did not sail to the New World alone. These African slaves brought with them their metaphysical systems, their languages, their term for order, [and] their expressive cultural practices which even the horrendous Middle Passage and the brutality of everyday life on the plantation could not effectively obliterate. (Henry Louis Gates, Jr., in Gross and Barnes, eds., *Talk That Talk*, 1989)

I am proud of those Africans who were strong enough to keep the "rhythm of Africa" flowing through their veins under the most adverse set of circumstances to ever befall a group of people. Although they were brought to the New World in chains, those Africans laid the foundation for what we (as their descendants) were always to be throughout the Diaspora—survivors! The African will to survive against all odds has been passed down from generation to generation and lives today in our generation. I write these things because it is important for our people today to know that there is no survivor story known to mankind that is greater than the survival story of our people.

The Europeans have not been able to break our bond with the place where they kidnapped us from over four hundred years ago. I seriously doubt if anything other than the direct hand of the Almighty will ever be able to sever our ties with Africa.

After four hundred years, we are still African in ways that we will never be able to articulate into words. Africa is as naturally a part of us as the melanin in our skins. Africa not only comes alive in the so many things that we do, but it is alive in us. Dr. Maya Angelou told this truth when she wrote:

We had sung it in our blues, shouted it in our break-down. As we carried it to Philadelphia, Boston, and Birmingham we had changed its color, modified its rhythm, yet it was Africa which rode in the bulges of our high calves, shook in our protruding behinds and crackled in our wide open laughter. (Maya Angelou, *All God's Children Need Traveling Shoes*, 1986)

Remember sister Maya's words and revel in brother Robeson's assertion, I encourage all of you to dance Neslon Mandela style to the "rhythm of Africa" that flows within you. (In May of 1994, Mr. Mandela—an unbowed and unbroken septuagenarian—danced victoriously and triumphantly after South Africa's first democratic elections made him the country's first Black president.)

I know that we are African and I am proud of that fact, but I also know that the four hundred years of slavery in the Western Hemisphere has altered us in ways that were never a part of our original African genotype. The physical and mental environment created by our oppressors was so thorough in our collective castration that it was nearly impossible for our brains to process information that would allow our minds to maintain a positive image of our Blackness, of our African heritage, and of ourselves. In short, white people have gained control of what we think when it comes to how we look at ourselves and our history. They have made us ashamed of our Blackness, our African heritage, and ourselves. They have dared to do such a thing, when it is they who should be ashamed of themselves and their European heritage.

I can't think of any period in history that the white man has interacted with any of the dark nations with any type of noble intentions. You can ask all over the non-white world and everybody will say the same thing about the white man—maybe not to his face, but within their own, they will tell the truth. Throughout history, he has been an admirer of self and a respecter of none.

Why do we feel ashamed of who we are when it is they who should feel ashamed of what they have done? The answer is simple: the white man has brainwashed us. Our brainwashing at the hands of the white man, which has taught us to hate ourselves, has been the single most detrimental handicap that the white man has ever cast amongst our people; it is his greatest weapon against us. On a mass scale, their brainwashing of our race has been unquestionable. As a result, a new African phenotype was born through the use of the terms: nigger, darky, colored, and Negro—a phenotype that could not fully express the dominant pride of its African genotype.

The brainwashing and the brutal terror they imposed upon our people caused our African genotype to lay dormant for centuries, but neither brainwashing nor terror could remove it from our souls completely. And slowly but surely, we would re-awake to the drums and dance to the "rhythm of Africa" that flows through our veins and causes us to love our African heritage and ourselves.

Marcus Garvey planted the seeds of African pride within an entire generation of Black people. One of Garvey's seeds germinated in Malcolm X, and through Malcolm, subsequent generations were taught to love themselves, their color, and their heritage. Brother Malcolm continued to plant the seeds of Black pride and self-love that served as a catalyst to the Black power movement of the late 1960's. It was Malcolm who opened my eyes to the negative way in which we (Black folks) look at ourselves against this backdrop called America.

Unfortunately, despite the great efforts of brother Marcus and brother Malcolm, we still have a large percentage of our people not realizing their contemporary role in the historical struggle that has always existed between America and the Black folks within her borders.

The first thing that Black folks must realize is that the United States embraces a very Eurocentric value system that never intended for Black people to obtain any citizenship rights in America. The United States was created by white people and for white people. There was never any real intention on the part of the political power structure of the United States for the imported African slaves or their descendents to obtain the rights and privileges of citizenship. There was no graduated plan for the eradication of the enslavement of the African in America; slavery was intended to be a life sentence handed down from generation to generation.

Do you think that my statement is erroneous? If so, then ask yourself why were Black people still fighting and dying for our right to vote and our full citizenship as late as the 1960's in a country that won its independence in 1776. Seriously, stop reading for a moment and really ask yourself that question. What answer can you come up with to justify the amount of years between 1776 independence and the Voting Rights Act of 1965?

Forget what you heard, here's the answer: the founding fathers were not referring to those of African descent when they wrote the Declaration of Independence and the Constitution. Those documents and the words contained in them were written by white men and for white men. Black people were considered inferior and unworthy to be classified in the same category as white men. That's the white naked truth.

In the famous Dred Scott case of 1857, Roger B. Taney—former chief justice of the Supreme Court of America from 1836 to 1864—reinforced the American reality of Africans as inferior beings and their classification as property and merchandise. The chief justice of the highest court in the land reinforced the American reality de facto and de jure. Here are a few excerpts from his opinion rendered for the court in the Dred Scott decision on March 6, 1857.

> They had for more than a century before been regarded as beings of an inferior order and altogether unfit to associate with the white race, either in social or political relations; and so far inferior, **that they had no rights which the white man was bound to respect**; and that the Negro might justly and lawfully be reduced to slavery for his benefit. He was bought and sold, and treated as an ordinary article of merchandise and traffic, **whenever a profit could be made by it.**

> And in no nation was this opinion more firmly fixed or more uniformly acted upon than by the English government and English people. They not only seized them on the coast of Africa, and sold them or held them in slavery for their own use, but they took them as ordinary articles of merchandise to every country where they could make a profit on them, and were far more extensively engaged in this commerce than any other nation in the world.

> The opinion thus entertained and acted upon in England was naturally impressed upon the colonies they founded on this side of the Atlantic. And, accordingly, a Negro of the African race was regarded by them as an article

of property, and held, and bought and sold as such, in every one of the thirteen Colonies which united in the Declaration of Independence, and afterwards formed the Constitution of the United States.

No one of that race had ever migrated to the United States voluntarily; all of them had been brought here as articles of merchandise. The number that had been emancipated at that time were but few in comparison with those held in slavery; and they were identified in the public mind with the race to which they belonged, and regarded as a part of the slave population rather than the free. **It is obvious that they were not even in the minds of the framers of the Constitution when they were conferring special rights and privileges upon the citizens of a State in every other part of the Union.**

From the word go, the American way of life asserted the inferiority of Africans in language, in custom, and in law. It was against such a backdrop that the mental psyche of the enslaved African developed. The boulder of pride that once lived in the mind of the African was worn away to a mere pebble against the constant current of brainwashing that flowed throughout all segments of daily life in the United States.

White folks cut us off psychologically from our African roots. We were instilled with the notion that everything associated with being Black was bad, dirty, or inferior. We were taught that our S.K.I.N was our S.I.N. By some white folks account, we were enslaved by divine ordinance; our torment was justified as a result of the mark that was set upon Cain for killing Abel and the curse placed on Ham's youngest son, Canaan. (Genesis chapter 9 verses 24 and 25: Noah awoke from his wine, and knew what his younger son had done unto him. And he said, Cursed be Canaan; a servant of servants he shall be unto his breathen.) Based on biblical verse, white folks told us to accept our bond status and obey our masters.

Conversely, we were conditioned to believe that everything associated with being white was good, pure, or superior; white people's S.K.I.N. was their W.I.N. Free, white, and twenty-one, that was something that a Black person could never be and Caucasians knew that.

The white man's brainwashing efforts were so pervasive that it touched all parts of our thought. We thought —and some still think it today—that the lighter our skin the better off we were because we were closer to white. Can you even imagine such hogwash! It's almost impossible for me to believe, but I know that it is true because remnants of that type of thinking are still around even in this day and age.

I was teased as a child by many "light-skinned" children because my skin was of the darker complexion. It was just an accepted part of the culture that being dark-skinned automatically made you ugly or an object of ridicule. Our dark-skinned women feel inferior to this very day because of their skin tone. I suppose that's why we sold skin lightening cremes in some of our leading Black publications. The dark Black child was supposed to be ashamed of his or her skin color. Oh heaven forbid that you were dark-skinned with kinky (a.k.a. "nappy") hair.

All the Black children that I grew up with were taught that the straighter their hair was the better it was. I assume that all the Black children that I knew had been taught such a thing by their parents, who had been taught by their parents, and so on and so forth. You can trace the origin of that ridiculous assertion all the way back to the slaves who wanted to be as much like their white captors as possible. As a result of that kind of mental poisoning, many Black people have endured all sorts of chemical tortures in an effort to take the kinks out of their hair in order to alter its normal traits. I wish that I could write that I had never done such a thing, but I would be lying if I did.

Like many little boys my age, I wore a gheri-curl from the ages of eleven through thirteen. I can remember being so happy that the kinks had given way to a straighter texture of hair. I was happy that I could swing the straighter stringy hair from side to side. I was happy because I thought that I had "good hair" at that point. I hate that I even have to tell you something like that, but I know that my story isn't the only one of its kind. I hate it even more since my mother was the person who not only allowed me to do such a thing, but she actually put the gheri-curl perm in my hair. She had never grasped the point that Malcolm was trying to get across in his autobiography. In 1965 Malcolm said:

> This was my first really big step toward self-degrada-
> tion: when I endured all that pain, literally burning my

flesh to have it look like a white man's hair. I had joined
that multitude of Negro men and women in America
who are brainwashed into believing that the black people are "inferior"—and white people are "superior"—
that they will mutilate their God-created bodies to try
to look "pretty" by white standards. (Malcolm X, The
Autobiography of Malcolm X, 1965)

Most of us (African-Americans) have been guilty of renounc-
ing our God given features in one way or another in an effort to
embrace a more European model of beauty, culture, and success.
As soon as we get a few coins in our possession, we start talking
like the white man—talking all proper and justifying it with everything but the truth. The truth is that we're still trying to be more
like the "master" than ourselves. (How can such an imperfect man
think so much of himself as to make a whole group of people refer
to him as "master"?)

That type of psychological profile didn't appear out of thin air.
It has been cultivated for nearly four hundred years out of the soil
of slavery, segregation, discrimination, and prejudice. The job of
eradicating this thought process remains one of our biggest barriers to overcoming the problems that impact us in America. The
only way to overcome this particular obstacle is to reconnect with
our past and the values that we once held dear in our hearts.
Chinua Achebe was right about what the white man has done to
us. In his 1959 book, *Things Fall Apart*, the great Nigerian writer
wrote: "He has put a knife on the things that held us together and
we have fallen apart."

In a speech given to the Organization of Afro-American Unity
on June 28, 1964, Malcolm said:

We must recapture our heritage and our ideals if we are
to liberate ourselves from the bonds of white supremacy.
We must launch a cultural revolution to unbrainwash an
entire people.

The first battle in the revolution must take place in the mind. The
revolution of the mind is what Imamu Amiri Baraka was referring
to when he said: "There is no violent revolution except as a result of
the Black mind expanding, trying to take control of its own space."
Our greatest challenge in the 21st century will be to "unbrainwash"
ourselves, and our greatest revolution will be the "violent revolu-

tion" of the Black mind trying to expand to control its own space. That "revolution will not be televised".

BEAT THEIR
STRINGY HEADS

I took my first step in taking control of my mind when I read my mom's literature and I watched *Roots*, but by no means did I complete my journey. I reasoned to myself that the things discussed in the literature and in the scenes shown from *Roots* on the television screen were responsible for the big differences in the lives of the Black people that I knew versus the lives of the white people that I knew.

I had never heard anything about slavery at that point. I can't even imagine how that was even possible for a Black child my age. I was eleven years old and I had never heard anybody talk about slavery in the places where I had lived. I had never heard anybody talk about it in the schools that I had attended. Since I had never heard anything about slavery and the horrors associated with that "peculiar institution", I drew my own conclusion from my mom's literature and the images that I saw on television while watching *Roots*.

My conclusion was that I hated America and I hated white people; I hated them both for what they had done to me and to my people. But I hated them most for their continued betrayal through their silence. They weren't even sorry for what they did!

I didn't say anything about my newfound opinions to anyone living in my grandmother's house, but there was a definite change in my attitude and behavior. I began to hate the Pledge of Allegiance. I stopped saying it and I definitely stopped believing it! I didn't put my hand over my heart. I just looked at the flag with my hands behind my back and thought of it as a lie. I thought about its boasted claims of "liberty and justice for all" and what that had meant for slaves. I silently thought to myself where was the "liberty" for the slaves that I saw on *Roots* and where was the "justice for all" now when my life and the lives of my friends were so markedly different from the white children that we went to school with everyday. My hatred for the flag and America was matched by my hatred for white people. After all, they were the perpetrators of the crimes against humanity that my people suffered under the cruel whip of slavery.

Around the same time that I formed those opinions, I was enrolled in a band class where I played the drums at King Middle School. I was the only Black child in our small group of five to six white drummers. All the drummers in the band were required to purchase a drum pad to use while practicing. I can remember there were three sizes available at three different prices—the bigger the drum pad the more expensive the price. My grandmother could only afford the smallest drum pad and that was only after some creative budgeting on her part. A white boy who had the biggest drum pad available quickly brought it to my attention that I was the only one in the group with the small drum pad. He thought it was funny and tried to get the other kids to laugh at me too.

In the past, before *Roots* and my mom's literature, comments like that would have made me sad and I probably would've felt bad about my family situation. I would have been ashamed of my drum pad the way that I was ashamed of my lunch ticket at Stewart. That was the old me. After finding out how unfair Black people had been treated at the hands of whites during slavery, his comment only made me boil over with rage. I was a little black tea kettle that was ready to blow! But I held my peace … that day.

That night I thought about his comments and I grew even angrier than I was at school that day. I pulled out my mom's literature and began to read it again. I thought about the people who went around the town passing out the literature. The people around the neighborhood always referred to them as Yahweh people. I had never heard the word Yahweh before reading that literature; but after reading it a few times, I was convinced that Yahweh was the God for Black people.

Under the influence of the literature, I decided to write the word Yahweh on my drum pad with a permanent marker. I went to school the next day and I decided that I wouldn't look for trouble, but I wasn't going to run from it if it came. I had the mentality that Stokley Carmichael talked about in 1963 when he said: "Our godfathers and fathers had to run, run, run. My generation is out of breath. We ain't running no more." I was my generation, and I wasn't "running no more".

The trouble that I refused to run from that day came during my band class in the form of the same little white boy who had made the comment about the size of my drum pad a day earlier. He was starring at me with blazing contempt through the entire practice session and I met his stare with equal contempt. We exchanged a lot of dirty looks and a few insults, and then he dropped the word that took us past the point of no return. He silently called me a nigger by moving his lips and tongue in an exaggerated manner that made him seem like he had a mouth full of N's, G's, and R's. That was the straw that broke the camel's back! I signaled for him to meet me in the bathroom. He didn't hesitate in granting my request. Once we were in the bathroom, the fight jumped off immediately.

He was much bigger than I was (so was everybody else my age), but I was much stronger than my size suggested and my hand speed was far more superior. I also had the rage in me that made me want to avenge the fact that they made Kunte Kinte call himself Toby. It was truly a case of the old adage of: "it's not the size of the dog in the fight, but the size of the fight in the dog." I was fueled by a rage that had been inspired by the images in *Roots* of white people treating Black people worse than animals. That white boy had lost our fight before it actually started. I felt rage throughout my entire body, and it burned me through and through. It was that day that taught me that both rage and fury were the children of fire.

That day also taught me that I fought better when I was angry; I had never been that angry before in any of the little fights that I had in the neighborhood and I had never beat anybody up that bad. In the neighborhood, I had probably taken as much as I had given ... but that bathroom wasn't the neighborhood and there was nothing equal about that exchange.

Rage and fury caused me to pop that white boy in his face three or four times before he knew what hit him. He became incensed and began to mix his tears with his own fury, but it was all for naught because the flames of my fury burned seven times hotter than his fury. He couldn't hit me, but I was bull's eye accurate with every punch that I threw. My fists were made of brimstone, and I kept dotting his eye with jabs as I thought about how he called me a nigger. I was out to show him what kind of nigger I was. I wanted to knock every N, G, and R out of his mouth so bad that I could taste it.

Someone finally heard the commotion and came in to stop the fight. It was stopped much in the same manner and for the same reason that a referee would stop a one-sided prizefight—a mediator rushing in to save a battered victim from a more severe beating. I was out to whip his hide the same way they had whipped Kunte's back!

We were both marched down to the principal's office and given three or four swats each by the dean. The licks didn't really hurt all that much, but they hurt enough to make me not want anymore than the ones that I received. I had gone from giving the blows to one white male to receiving blows from another white male in a matter of a half-hour. By that time, the other kid's eye looked pretty bad. His swollen purplish-red eye combined with my non-remorseful attitude was probably the reason that the dean kept me in the office a little longer.

He kept trying to explain to me that the situation of someone calling me a name was not a good reason to hit anybody. I wanted to tell him that Kunte not wanting to be called any name other than his African name was no reason for the overseer to beat him into oblivion. I wanted to tell him that so bad that my bottom lip quivered, but I didn't say anything. I just sat quietly with the rage simmering just under my skin. He had already swatted my backside; I wasn't about to give him the satisfaction of thinking that he had actually made me sorry for what I had done.

If he hadn't already hit me, then there would have been a chance that I would have acted like I was listening to what he was saying. But it was too late for all that now, the damage was done; I didn't even pretend that I agreed with what he said. I sat there unbowed and unbroken with a defiant look on my face. I had gotten a real satisfaction out of beating the white kid up in such a convincing fashion. Besides the worst of the consequences were over for me, I knew that no one at home would find out about the incident. There was no way for the school to contact anybody at my house because we didn't have a telephone.

The dean tried to send a letter home with me, but that was like pouring water in a bucket that had a hole in the bottom—it just wasn't going to work. I was home free from home intervention and I knew it. Two weeks of not getting any word from my house and the dean knew it too. Perhaps if I didn't get bused in all the way from Palmetto and I lived right around the corner like the majority of the white kids, the dean would have actually paid my grandmother a visit. But I didn't, so he didn't. That's why the only way that my grandmother will ever know about that white boy and his black eye will be if this book gets published.

After the fight and my subsequent disciplining from the dean, things went on for me like the fight never happened. The only reason that I knew that it had happened was that I didn't have to worry about that little white boy anymore. He never said another word to me as long as I knew him, and I never said another word to him; but then again, he and I didn't need words to understand each other. He understood that I was ready, willing, and able to kick his butt anytime he felt like calling me a nigger. Other than our new understanding, the whole thing just went away.

My homeroom teacher taught the class to play chess (a few of the white children already knew how to play and assisted as instructors in teaching) and held a chess tournament. I took as much delight in beating all the white children in chess as I had in beating up my band class adversary. Although I had never played chess before, I went on to win the whole tournament for my class; I even beat the white children who had assisted as instructors. I enjoyed showing everybody that I could beat the white kids in my class with my brains.

The battleground for me to prove myself was everywhere, there was no sheltered rear. Any contest or any game was an opportunity for me to stake my claim to excellence and I did so with a ferocious intensity that came from deep inside of me.

It was ironic for me to recall that I felt like that years ago as a youngster and then to read the words that Dr. Du Bois wrote so long ago in *The Souls of Black Folk (1903)*. In referring to the delight he took in beating his white classmates, he wrote:

> Then it dawned upon me with a certain suddenness that I was different from the others; or like, mayhap, in heart and life and longing, but shut out from their world by a vast veil. I had thereafter no desire to tear down that veil, to creep through; I held all beyond it in common contempt, and lived above it in a region of blue sky and great wandering shadows. That sky was bluest when I could beat my mates at examination time, or beat them at a foot-race, or even beat their stringy heads.

FRIENDS & FAMILY

Shortly after my fight incident and the chess tournament, an all-school assembly was held in the gymnasium. The program's itinerary included a recognition portion for the top performing students of the previous school year. Students were called to come up in front of the entire gymnasium and given a certificate for achieving straight A's either for one quarter, for two quarters, for three quarters, or for the whole year.

My class wasn't eligible for the recognition that assembly because we had all been elementary school students the previous school year, but I made up my mind right then and there that I would be among those students recognized at next year's assembly. There was only one thing that I failed to take into account while making my plans to be recognized. I forgot to ask myself would I be at King the following school year. Considering my track record in transferring to different schools, that was always a very legitimate question.

The answer to that question soon began to manifest itself when trouble began brewing on the home front. At that time, my grandmother's house consisted of me, my grandmother, my mom and her boyfriend.

The trouble began with the relationship between my mother and her boyfriend. My mother's boyfriend had gotten himself involved in the drug game as a small time seller and as a user. I had already witnessed my mom smoke reefer as a small child, so I knew that the new drug was not my mom's first drug exposure. The reefer was now about to be classified as my mom's gateway drug because she was about to enter a whole new realm of altering her state of consciousness.

My mom was entering the dangerous world of crack cocaine. I didn't know much about crack cocaine at that time; but in the couple of years ahead, I would know more than I ever wanted to know and it would become an epidemic in Black neighborhoods all across America. My mom and her boyfriend just happened to get in on the ground floor of the IPO of crack cocaine in our town. It was 1984, and the little white rocks of crack cocaine would remain a part of my mother's life into the next millennium.

During an argument between my mom and her boyfriend, I heard her ask him two very sarcastic questions that bothered me a great deal. She asked him in rapid fire succession and repetitively, "is that why you keep me on that stuff?" and "is that why you hit me in my mouth?" She asked him those two questions after he said something to her that I was not privy to because he wasn't speaking as loudly as she was at that point in the argument. I didn't know at the time what "stuff" she was talking about, but I was furious to learn that he had been physically abusing my mother. I was also furious that my mother kept placing herself in positions to be abused and mixing me up in the crossfire. Later in life, I would find out that at least a portion of that "stuff" that she referred to was crack cocaine.

I was eleven years old and my mother had turned me on to two things that would be with me for life. The first thing was the music of Prince. She was a huge fan and I followed her right down the purple brick road of his Royal Badness to become a huge fan myself. Prince's music provided one of the few deep connections that I had with my mother.

She and I spent an unusual intimate afternoon listening to Prince's *Dirty Mind* album. We listened to it three or four times. I don't recall a lot of talking between us; but that wasn't unusual. My mom and I had never really talked to each other about anything. Nonetheless, that afternoon was intimate because we both enjoyed the music that was playing. Perhaps we were related after all. It was a shared experience between us. Despite the so-called controversial lyrics on the album, it was one of the very few times that I ever had a pure and innocent good time with the woman that birthed me. And I cherished it.

The second thing that my mom turned me onto was that Black literature. From the day that I picked up those pamphlets that she left lying around the house until this very moment I have always had an insatiable passion for Black literature. I define Black literature as any sentence, paragraph, article, or book that deals with the Black experience from a Black perspective. Black people are the only people who can produce true Black literature.

However, even those two heartfelt connections that I had with my mother could not endure through a crack addiction. One could say that any chances of any enduring connections that we might have shared were vaporized into smoke through a crack pipe ... just like the cocaine that she was using.

The situation of having crack cocaine being used in her house was a new experience for my grandmother. I knew that she was part afraid and part angry. Probably, the only thing that you could compare crack to in terms of the deteriorating effects that it had on folks and their families was that original narcotic destroyer of the Black community—heroin. I know from my readings and from listening to the speeches of Malcolm X that heroin really did a number on places like Harlem in the mid-1950's and early 1960's.

Around 1955 ... nobody wanted to kick the habit much. They were strung out, and they were really going down. They were ragged and beat-up ... They were people who had too much pride to put a dirty handkerchief in their pockets at one time. Now they just seemed completely unaware of how they looked. They would just be walking around dirty, greasy, looking for things to steal. The slang was always changing for heroin. They called it duji or shit or stuff or poison. (Claude Brown, *Manchild in the PROMISED LAND*, 1965)

[M]any of our people here in Harlem, and especially right here in this neighborhood have turned to that dreadful needle heroin ... Poison! Nothing but poison! But you turn to it seeking an escape from the misery that the brutality and the defeat of the white man has trapped us in here in Harlem. (Malcolm X)

145

My grandmother was from the South, so I don't know if she knew about the ghettos of the North and their past bouts with heroin. But I do know that she had never had the experience of having her child in the clutches of such a dangerous predator like crack cocaine. She was angry and afraid of the unknown.

I know that a portion of my grandmother's angry side was due to the lack of financial support that she received in the maintenance of the household in respect to things like bills and food. Crack is the most important thing in the world of a crack addict; everything else takes a back seat. Six days out of the week, she was on her knees scrubbing white people's floors for what she called "chicken change" and there she was carrying the economic burden of supporting the entire house.

I had heard her warn my mom a few times that she wasn't going to take care of grown people. My mom knew that that message was meant for her and her boyfriend; she should have also known that my grandmother was not the type of person who issued out too many warnings without following up with action. If she didn't know, then she could have asked me. I would've told her from the impromptu back slaps my lips had taken for "not staying in a child's place". My grandmother was an "I can show you better than I can tell you" kind of person.

Grandma Dot stopped cooking and stopped buying food for the house. She made sure that I had breakfast; she made sure that I ate lunch at school, and then she gave me money to go buy something to eat in the evening time for dinner. In the first week and a half, I thought that my grandmother's plan was a great idea. I was able to go to any fast food place within walking distance of my grandmother's house. There were a few to choose from, but when you were a kid growing up in my era you only had one true choice … McDonald's.

I visited the golden arches for dinner every night for two weeks. By the end of the two weeks, I had grown tired of McDonald's and the last night that I ate there was the worst. I think it was a combination between a physical and a psychological reaction. Physically, I had eaten there for two weeks in a row and my digestive system wanted to let me know about it. Psychologically, I was traumatized from dealing with the situation that was playing itself out inside my grandmother's house. I thought it was going to drive me crazy. Shakespeare posed the question: "to be or not to be" in Hamlet. My question to myself was to crack-up or not to crack-up. My mom had already made her choice.

On the last evening that I ate at McDonald's, I became so physically ill that it felt to me that I was regurgitating everything that I had eaten there for the last two weeks. What didn't come out through my mouth came out through the other end. I don't think if someone had offered me a million dollars that I would have been able to eat another bite of any of Ronald's burgers. The impression of that night was so strong for me that I didn't voluntarily go to McDonalds for years after that for anything. It is only within the last five years that I have voluntarily gone there for a soft serve cone or hot cakes and sausage. I still can't eat any of their burgers.

After I got sick, my grandmother realized that I couldn't go on under the present set of circumstances and she knew that she had very little power to change them at that particular moment in time. So she called her only son and arranged for me to stay with him and his white wife (he had married his girlfriend) and their baby boy.

My uncle and his new family lived in Bradenton and I was happy that he and his wife had agreed to take me into their home. I had had sporadic exposure to my uncle throughout my life and he was someone that I wanted to emulate. Although he and my mom were brother and sister, they were complete opposites. My uncle did not smoke or drink and I never heard him use profanity until I was well into my late teens. It always appeared to me that my uncle had nicer things than the rest of my family. His house had better furniture. His refrigerator had more things to eat and drink than any other place that I had lived with the exception of my uncle's café in Plant City.

My uncle would always wake up in the middle of the night to get something to drink. Whenever I heard him doing that, I would say to myself that I was going to have enough in my refrigerator to drink what I wanted to when I wanted to anytime I wanted to just like him. I thought the ability to get up in the middle of the night to get anything that your heart desired out of the refrigerator was the ultimate. However, what I liked most about my uncle was his black cars.

He was a mechanic by trade and he always had one of the baddest rides in town. He had to have a nice stereo to accompany his nice car to blast his favorite songs. When I moved in with him in the winter of 1984, he had a slick 1984 black on black Oldsmobile Delta

88. In contrast to his interracial marriage, his color of choice in cars was always black. I looked up to my uncle so much that my choice of colors in cars became black too.

I can still remember riding in his slick Oldsmobile Delta 88, with its black ragtop, blasting Klymaxx's jamming hit, *"Meeting In The Ladies Room"*. We rode around town looking at the world through illegal window tint. The Delta, as we called it, was a classic. I loved for people to see me getting out of it when he drove me to Bradenton Middle School (BMS) each morning. That was the school that I transferred to from King Middle School (KMS).

When the Delta pulled up to BMS, I always took longer than necessary to get out of the car. I lifted the latch to pull the back seat up at an extra slow pace, and I delayed an extra second before I lifted my book bag from the back seat. Every move that I made was prolonged and drawn out. I wanted as many people as possible to see me getting out of that car.

Getting out of the Delta at BMS made me feel a lot better than getting off the "poor Black kids" bus at KMS, but how I got to school wasn't the only difference between Bradenton Middle and King Middle. BMS was also different than KMS in respect to the racial composition. There were far more Blacks at Bradenton Middle than there were at King Middle. I'm sure that there were some white kids whose parents had money at Bradenton Middle because some of the kids who had played on my little league baseball team one year earlier went to Bradenton Middle, but it wasn't nearly as many as King Middle. All in all, you just didn't have such a polarized picture of race at Bradenton Middle as you did at King Middle.

It was much like the difference that I saw when I transferred from Stewart Elementary to Wakeland Elementary. At Bradenton Middle, I didn't see a white "I have everything group" versus a Black "I have nothing group".

I was much more comfortable in that environment than I was at King, but my individual comfort level was not indicative of the mood of the campus. The campus was hot, and before my sixth grade school year was done the racial tensions simmered into a race riot.

The riot pitted the sons of former slaves against the sons of former masters. It was a showdown between the sons of those who bore the yoke against the sons of those who prospered from the yoke. It was

Black against white. I can't say for sure if the riot was a small thing or something that was viewed as a serious incident. Everything in my world either revolved around home or school, so any event at either place ran the risk of me blowing it out of proportion. What I mean to say is that the riot could have been a tiny incident that received little or no attention from anybody outside of the school or it could have been an event that received considerable attention. Whatever the reality, I viewed the situation as a big event.

I remember that it started out with some of the Black boys who had reputations for being tough guys beating up some white boys. After that incident, a small buzz began to circulate among the student body that there was going to be a fight after school and it was going to be the Blacks against the whites. As the day went on, the buzz got stronger and stronger as each class period passed. The rumors that small fights had already broken out during a couple of periods were swirling around the campus. By the end of the day, the principal came on the intercom giving special instructions as to what he expected regarding our departure from school after the last class of the day. He made sure that he clearly spelled out the consequences for those who went outside those expectations.

I didn't get to see much of what took place after school because I rode the bus to my Grandma Mary's house in the afternoons and the bus riders were the first people dismissed from school, but I did see that there was a police presence on campus. The next day several of the kids reported that there were snipers on the roof with machine guns. I didn't see that personally, but I can't say either way; the buses were put on a tighter schedule than usual just to get as many kids off campus as quickly as possible.

Mentally, I didn't dwell on our brush with a race riot at Bradenton Middle because I did not really feel the urge to participate. I suppose that was ironic considering the recent fight that I had with the young white boy at King Middle School. I think the difference for me between the fight that I had at King and the fights that were taking place at Bradenton Middle was that I did not have an individual to target in the fights erupting around the campus of Bradenton Middle. My anger was only aroused to the point of wanting to fight during personal confrontations with whites.

My anger toward white people as a whole had also been somewhat tempered by the fact that I now lived with my uncle and his white wife. It was hard to think that all white people were bad when

149

you lived with one that made your dinner every night. She was a good cook too. I'm sure that my living with my white aunt had a lot to do with my lack of eagerness to run around randomly punching white boys in the face. A few months earlier, I probably would have relished that opportunity at King Middle School.

Besides the race riot, my sixth grade year at Bradenton Middle was otherwise uneventful … with the exception of meeting Floyd Watkins. The first time that I ever saw Floyd was after he came in late one day into our sixth grade science class. He was complaining that he had lost his lunch ticket. I had no idea at the time that he would become my best friend from the time we were in seventh grade all the way up until my twenty-sixth year of life.

It is not that we stopped being friends after I turned twenty-six years old; he just stopped being my best friend. By the time that I turned twenty-six years old, I had outgrown the boundaries of even the deepest of friendships that can exist between two heterosexual guys. Personally, I was moving toward the deeper kind of relationship that exists between a woman and a man. Spiritually, I was also moving in a different direction. By the time I turned twenty-seven years old (my age when I typed this sentence); I realized that Jesus Christ was my best friend. I had heard that He was my best friend at various points throughout my life, but I had never really tried to be worthy of that friendship in my daily thought and daily action. So, Floyd and I were still really good friends, but my perspective on life had changed and our friendship had changed accordingly.

Still, I counted Floyd Watkins as a person who had truly been a Godsend to my life, and I was eternally grateful for all the value that he had added to my life through his friendship. The friendship that Floyd Watkins offered to me validated the words of French born writer Anais Nin. In her diary, she wrote:

> Each friend represents a world in us, a world possibly
> not born until they arrive, and it is only by this meeting
> that a new world is born.

That's what Floyd Watkins was to me; he was the beginning of "a world possibly not born". Floyd … I love you man. You will always be my brother.

Floyd and I instantly became friends the moment that the 1985-1986 school year began. We were in seventh grade and no longer the new fish at Bradenton Middle. We had four out of six classes together and we both discovered that we loved to play basketball. Those two things, academics and basketball, would keep our paths crossed for many years to come. As a matter of fact, I don't know how much further I would have made it down my path without the support and inspiration that I received from watching Floyd on his path. He was the first peer that I looked to for direction and insight.

At the start of my seventh grade school year, I was still living with my uncle and his wife, but we had moved at least three times from the first time that I moved in with them from Palmetto. Lucky for me, each move that we made kept me in Bradenton Middle's school district.

We moved from an apartment to my aunt's mother's house. The house was in the part of east Bradenton where my baseball coach from fifth grade lived. We lived in that house with my aunt's stepbrother and his girlfriend. At that point, my uncle and I were living with three white people. That was different for me. I learned that white people had to wash their hair every day. I learned that they needed a blow dryer. For our part, my uncle and I introduced them to the gooey world of curl activator. They tried to keep their stringy heads dry and we tried to keep our wooly heads oily.

We didn't live in that situation too long before my uncle and his wife bought their first house. I was given my own room and slept on a waterbed. My uncle built me a basketball goal in the front yard. He put red, white, and blue chain nets on the rim and painted my name at the top of the backboard. I was starting to feel like I was a part of a real family. It actually seemed like I mattered. I felt really good about it. I can even remember inviting my friend, Michael Jermaine Williams, who I had met as a fifth grader at Wakeland Elementary over for Thanksgiving Dinner.

There was some irony in the fact that I was starting to feel like I was truly part of a family at my uncle's house because my beloved Grandma Dot was in Palmetto going through some very trying times with my mom and her new boyfriend. The drugs didn't stop after I left and the situation didn't get any better. I overheard my uncle as he talked to his wife about an incident that had taken place at my grandmother's house—strategic eavesdropping was how I usually got all of my information. No one really talked to me directly about things. I always had to pretend that I was totally absorbed in one thing or another while my ears strained to hear what grown-ups were saying.

My uncle told his wife that my mom's boyfriend had broken out all the windows of the house in a fit of rage. I was waiting for an explanation for his fit of rage because surely there must have been something to make one behave in such a way. I waited a couple of weeks, but the explanation never came. The waiting on the explanation and not receiving it reminded me of how I waited to find out why Peewee had attacked Frog in the parking lot of my uncle's café in Plant City during the summer of 1980.

I never got an explanation of the cause of the violent outburst, but I did find out that both my grandmother and mother were okay. That was my biggest concern. Still, I didn't know if they would be so lucky if there was a next time, and that scared me. It also made me glad that I had been sent to live with my uncle. We had moved three times, but at least I was eating home cooked meals and I felt safe. I wished that my grandmother felt safe, but I reasoned to myself that the odds of a person in her situation feeling safe were minuscule..

She was a single poor Black woman living in a house with a Black male who, in a fit of rage, broke out all of the front windows during the winter months. I guess he thought that the heat of his anger would keep the house warm. That was crazy logic, but I knew that he wasn't crazy. I don't know what he thought. I just know that when the drugs came through the door, any peace and love that existed in my grandmother's house went out through those broken windows.

Years after the window-breaking incident, I would hear a brother on television say that rage was the Black man's only alternative to insanity. Maybe rage was the only alternative my mom's boyfriend had to going crazy when he broke out those windows.

I wrote earlier that after attending an all-school assembly for the top performing students at King Middle, I told myself that I would be recognized the following year. At the time that I said that, I didn't realize that I would not be attending King the next year. To be quite honest, after transferring to Bradenton Middle, I had forgotten about King. I had forgotten that I had set a goal for myself to be recognized at the next assembly to show the white people that I could make straight A's too. I never received any report card from King because when I moved from my grandmother's house I just didn't have any connection with the school. I wasn't worried about the grades, so I forgot about them in the same way that I forgot about the goal.

That's why I was really surprised when King sent over my certificate in the beginning of the seventh grade school year to Bradenton Middle for achieving straight A's in the only complete quarter that I had spent there.

I felt some satisfaction in the fact that I had accomplished what I set out to do, but a lot of the satisfaction that I had expected to feel had been lost in the fact that I could not see the faces of the white people at the school. They are the ones who had inspired the anger that provoked me to set such a goal. But I'm glad that I couldn't see their faces; because that type of anger inspired achievement and anger inspired satisfaction was not healthy for me as an individual and probably would have led to more bad than good in the long run.

I was always angry when I attended King Middle because I couldn't see anything other than the blatant differences between the lives of the Black students and the lives of the white students. Those polarized lifestyles between the two races always bothered me in one way or another. Bradenton Middle didn't have such a polarized student body as far as race and socioeconomic class. On the whole, I adjusted much better to living with my uncle and attending Bradenton Middle than I did to living with Grandma Dot and attending King Middle.

I had a nice little surrogate family situation developing while living with my uncle, his wife, and their son, who was nine years my junior. I had two friendships with Mike and Floyd that would eventually prove to be lifelong friendships, I was starting to become really good in basketball, and I was developing less of a complex about whites. The key phrase in that sentence was "developing less of a complex about whites" because I did have an incident at the end of seventh grade.

I punched a white girl in the mouth as we waited in the school cafeteria for our bus to arrive. She called me a nigger. It was really a bad situation because her tooth went through her bottom lip. Unlike the situation when I fought the white boy in the bathroom at King, I didn't feel good about hurting the girl and it wasn't my intention to hit her at all. But when I heard the word nigger, it was just like my fist had a mind of its own. Before I even thought about it, my right fist flew right toward the place where the letters had escaped to form the word. I was called down to the office the next morning to get what was coming to me. As I walked toward the office, I felt like the dean was going to throw the book at me.

Unlike the situation at King, I did feel remorse for my actions. The fact that I expressed remorse must have had an impact on the dean. Instead of being suspended with three days home, I was given three days in time-out. Time-out was a sort of in-school suspension. That punishment was cool with me because the school still had no way of getting in contact with anybody at the place where I lived to inform them of the incident. That was the advantage in moving around so much and living in so many different places with different folks. No one really knew what was really going on with me in situations that I desired to keep a secret.

Toward the end of seventh grade, my uncle made two moves—a residential move and a professional move. The first move was a move from the house where I had my own room and a waterbed to a three-bedroom apartment. I thought to myself, wow I'm even being considered in apartment selections, which felt good. I felt good because they could have easily rented a two-bedroom apartment and asked me to share with my little cousin. I didn't particularly mind moving anywhere as long as I could still attend Bradenton Middle. There was no way that I ever wanted to go back to King Middle.

The second move was actually made in the summer after seventh grade. My uncle opened up his own automotive shop with his father ... my biological grandfather. My biological grandfather had never really been a part of my life up until that point. I knew who he was and I knew that my mom didn't have the greatest childhood when living with him and his second wife, but that was about the extent of my knowledge as far as he was concerned. However, that began to change when he and my uncle became business partners.

I started to see him quite frequently and we developed a descent relationship considering the fact that I had no previous relationship with him. I knew that our relationship could never turn into anything too deep because I was already thirteen years old; I had spent the first ten years of my life answering to Grandaddy Cee's country calls of: "Granboy!" Even though it was my biological grandfather's blood running through my veins, it was my memories of Granddaddy Cee that ran through my heart.

That 1986 summer Floyd and I became each other's ace, we had even began calling each other on the telephone. The thing that both surprised me and impressed me the most about Floyd was his incredible confidence. It surprised me because I did not see his confidence as being a reality-based kind of confidence. I was eight months older than Floyd was, but that didn't mean that he respected me as his elder.

It didn't matter what time of day it was, what day of the week it was, or what month of the year it was; Floyd would announce to me and anybody else who would listen that he was the best twelve-year-old basketball player in the world. Not in the school, not in Bradenton, not in Florida, not in America ... in the world.

Still, it wasn't the declaration itself that surprised me. I was surprised that Floyd actually believed his own words. He was sincere in his claim; he believed it with his total mind, body, and soul that he was actually the best twelve-year-old basketball player in the world. I didn't think that he was the best twelve-year-old basketball player in the world, but he didn't care what I thought or what anybody else thought. He was the best to the only person that mattered ... himself.

I was impressed by Floyd's total conviction in the statement and his all-around supreme confidence in himself as a person. I label his confidence as an all-around and supreme confidence because it was not just limited to basketball; it was the kind of confidence that knew no boundaries. It was almost a Muhammad Ali like confidence. Ali declared himself as the prettiest, the fastest, until he just summed it up as being The Greatest. Floyd, like The Greatest, could rattle off a verbal assault that would leave you dazed and confused.

The verbal assault part of Floyd's confidence had a three-part effect on me. The first effect was that it was often used to relegate me to a background position in the designated topic of discussion. There was no way that Floyd Watkins was going to say that anybody could read better than him, play basketball better than him, or was smarter than him. I oftentimes found myself taking his claims of superiority as a personal affront even when he wasn't talking directly to me.

For example, whenever we were playing 21 on the basketball court, Floyd would announce to everybody in the game that we were all playing to see who would get second place because he was going to win the game. That wasn't the part that really got me, it was the fact that he actually won the game enough times after such bravado that it made me play harder just to keep from hearing his mouth.

The second effect that his confidence had on me was that I began to do my absolute best in any area that I knew Floyd could draw a comparison between us because I knew that anything less would eventually lead to a verbal assault that I could not defend myself against.

The third and final effect that it had on me was one of inspiration. Whenever I wasn't fighting to prevent myself from being verbally assigned to a relegated position or concentrating on optimum performance in order to be able to put up a legitimate defense on my own behalf, I was studying and admiring the infrastructure of his confidence. I wanted to know how one person could be so truly confident.

It was hard for me to determine the origin of Floyd's confidence because I had not known him in his earlier years of life, but that was irrelevant by the time that I met him because the finished product was authentic and impressive. It wasn't a shallow confidence based on a greater fool theory where you had to ask yourself who was the greater fool the person doing all the talking or the person silly enough to listen. I had seen situations like that numerous times before I met Floyd. That's how I knew that his talking, no matter how crazy it sounded, had something behind it.

Floyd's talk was backed up by an unwavering confidence in his own abilities. He believed that he could walk it like he talked it. That made his ego impervious to all assaults. He wasn't going to let anybody define who he was and what he was capable of doing. He was too confident to let anybody else's opinion about him matter more than his own opinion about himself.

At twelve years old, Floyd had already discovered one of the keys to life. That key was expressed in a speech given by psychologist, Janice Hale Benson, at the African-American Child Conference in Detroit, Michigan in January of 1989. Ms. Benson said: "Know your place, but let no one tell you what your place is."

I spent so much time around Floyd that I was forced to adopt the age-old adage of: "if you can't beat 'em, then join 'em." Without his consent, and probably without his knowledge, I became a Floyd disciple. The beginning of the eighth grade school year found me responding to things the way Floyd responded to things. My responses were particularly funny when they produced an argument between the two of us regarding who was better in a particular area. I refused to sit idly by and let him claim that he was the best in any category that I fit into. Whenever he made his claim, I countered with my own claim that I was the best in that category.

I was pretty good at copying his style. I discovered that in order to be really good at copying his style I had to really believe what I was saying. I wouldn't say that the student was better than the teacher was at that point, but I became real good. I know that because of an incident that happened later on in that eighth grade school year.

I had gotten into another fight earlier in the eighth grade school year with a white boy. All of my fights with white people were about the same thing—the word nigger. The white boy called me a nigger as we were walking home from the bus stop. I still had not learned to control that intense anger that came over me when a white person said that to me.

My uncontrollable rage at the sound of a white person's voice calling me that word still existed even though the apartment complex that my uncle lived in was predominately white and I had more white friends at the time than ever before in my life. Actually, many of them cheered me on during that fight on the way from the bus stop. It was a very confusing thing to walk home with some of my white friends after just fighting a white boy for calling me a nigger, but I managed, although I felt awkward in doing so.

The funny thing about that situation was that I was pretty much in the exact same identical situation at the end of the eighth grade school year and I responded totally different. I know that it was as a result of me beginning to mimic the style and confidence that I learned from being around and watching Floyd.

Once again, the incident occurred when riding home on the bus from school. The same white boy who had called me a nigger during the beginning of the school year called me a nigger again; I guess he thought he would do better in a rematch than he did during our first fight. This time my response was totally different, I basically just laughed to myself. You see the word no longer had any impact on me because I had become bigger than that word and its previous effect on me. I wasn't only bigger than the word; psychologically, I had grown bigger than the boy was too. I actually thought it was funny that he thought that I should even care about what he called me—how pretentious of him.

When he realized that he couldn't make me angry enough to fight, he started repeating the word with more emphasis. The harder he said the word the harder I laughed. The more I laughed, the madder he became. At that moment, I stopped imitating Floyd's confidence. I actually possessed Floyd's confidence when it came to being proud of being Black. I knew that whatever I was had to be the best thing for me to be—God had made me that way. I have never wavered again. I have not cared to this day if some white person called me a nigger and I haven't thought for one second that another race was superior to my own. Or another person was better than I was.

I realize now that the word nigger itself had no power over me as an individual and that I was not fighting so much the people who had called me that name, but instead I was fighting the image of inferiority that I had allowed to exist within myself. Don't get me wrong, my early interactions with white people played a huge part in planting that seed of inferiority within me, but my lack of pride and self-love was actually the main ingredients that nourished my seed of inferiority.

My contact with Floyd gave me the self-confidence, self-pride, and self-love that was necessary to overcome my own feelings of inferiority. Floyd never really talked much about race, but he loved everything about himself so much—including being Black—that his self-love was not only obvious, but contagious too. It helped me to love myself too.

In overcoming my own feelings of inferiority, I overcame the pain and anger that had previously victimized me whenever a white person called me a nigger. I read a quote by Dr. W.E. B. Du Bois that appeared in the article, "Letter to Roland A. Barton"; it was featured in the March 1928 edition of the *Crisis*. A quote from that article explains perfectly what happened to me in the process of going from one who fought when called a nigger to one who laughed when called a nigger. Dr. Du Bois wrote:

Suppose we arose tomorrow morning and lo! Instead of being "Negroes," all the world called us "Cheiropoldi"- do you really think this would make a vast and momentous difference to you and to me? Would you be any less ashamed of being descended from a black man, or would your schoolmates feel any less superior to you? The feelings of inferiority is in you, not in a name. The name merely evokes what is already there. Exorcise the hateful complex and no name can ever make you hang your head.

In the process of adopting Floyd's thought process, I had effectively reduced, if not eliminated, my own feelings of inferiority. When I achieved that, I achieved a major victory in my life.

That victory wasn't the only victory that I celebrated during that 1986-1987 school year. All in all, things were going pretty well for me, considering all the things that I had gone through in the past. I was attending a school that I enjoyed attending. I had a best friend that was second to none (at least in his own mind). I was living in a stable household that was really the closest thing that I had ever had to a traditional family. In fact, most people actually thought that my uncle was my dad; on many occasions, I didn't bother to tell them any different because I wished that he was my dad. It was a situation that definitely beat trying to explain where my parents were and why I didn't live with them. That seemed to be a topic that I had been either explaining or avoiding since I started grade school. I hated it!

The stability of my home life actually showed up in my school attendance. I received the only perfect attendance certificate that I have ever received in my entire life during my eighth grade school year. I was very proud of that accomplishment because I never thought that I would be able to have a whole school year go by without me going through some home situation that caused me to miss at least a day or two of school. Life was improving and the world wasn't such a cold place anymore.

It was hard to believe that it could get better, but it did. Even with the private victory over my inferiority complex and the perfect attendance achievement, eighth grade offered more in the way of personal recognition for me. My private victories within myself yielded public victories for the entire school to witness.

The end of the school year included an awards ceremony to recognize the significant achievements of members of the student body. It was very much like the awards ceremony that I had witnessed at King Middle School. The awards were given to recognize the sixth, seventh, and eighth graders, so the entire school was assembled in the gymnasium. There were five awards given to the top student in each subject for each grade. The five subjects were language arts, social studies, math, science, and physical education. I received four out of the five awards for the eighth grade class of 1987 at Bradenton Middle School.

I was absolutely euphoric about winning eighty percent of the top awards. It felt like they called my name a million times before it was all said and done. I felt like Michael Jackson when he won all those Grammy awards for *Thriller* back in 1983.

On top of winning the awards, my uncle's wife and Grandma Dot came to the assembly. With all the stability that I had in my life, the school was finally able to call my place of residence. One of the deans of students realized that she went to church with my biological grandfather. By him being in business with my uncle, they had pinpointed the kid after eight years. I was glad that I was going to high school the next year. I didn't want to get used to having telephone calls home.

The school called my aunt to let her know that I would be receiving the awards and she called my grandmother. I was a real happy camper that day. I felt like the world was with me instead of against me. It was a very different feeling than what I anticipated when I had planned on being recognized at King Middle School in order to show white people that I was just as smart as they were.

First of all, I wasn't planning on winning any awards at Bradenton Middle. I was simply doing the best that I could in all the subjects that I had that year and the awards just happened as a result. I was selected as the top student for our eighth grade class in language arts, social studies, science, and physical education. Math was the only subject that prevented a clean sweep—which I really didn't mind because I was really starting not to like math.

I was particularly proud of the physical education award because it showed that although that I had advanced classes on the academic side that I had some athletic talent as well. I was pretty good at most sports, but I was starting to develop a small reputation for being a real good basketball player.

In our eighth grade students versus teachers basketball game we beat the teachers and that was a big deal at that time. Floyd and I both were selected as starters for that game and we both played pretty well. That game was where the majority of my small reputation for being a good player was derived.

I was enjoying life more than I had in a long time, but I had a feeling that it wouldn't last. Happiness for me as a child was like a rainbow in the sky after a rainstorm; it never stayed around long, so I tried to enjoy it while it lasted.

EVICTION, DEATH,
AND THE MVP

My bubble of happiness and newfound stability was turned upside down during the beginning of the 1987 summer. We were still living in the three-bedroom apartment that my uncle had moved us to after we moved from the house that had my basketball goal in the front yard. The only thing that had changed was the fact that my uncle's wife's younger brother came to live with us.

He was about five years or so older than I was. I am not quite sure what the circumstances were that contributed to him coming to live with us. Maybe he was like me when I moved in with my uncle two years earlier; perhaps he didn't have anywhere else to go either.

My uncle must've lost his shop by that point because he was working for a Nissan dealership and my aunt was working for a Kash-N-Karry supermarket. I remember that they were both working very hard. They were also working opposite schedules. The hard work, crowded house, and opposite schedules made for a tense environment. I could tell that the situation was having an impact on their relationship. Some say that a bad marriage kills the soul. I don't know if I am going to go that far, but I will concede that it wounds the heart.

I think that all those things added up one day to contribute to me being kicked out of the house. The reason given for me being kicked out centered around the fact that I was alleged to have eaten some food that I shouldn't have eaten. The food was prepared early because my aunt worked at night, and it was supposed to be dinner for that night. I didn't know that; the only thing that I knew was that I was hungry with no money, there was no one around, and the refrigerator was bare of any combination that might produce a meal—unless mayonnaise and water appealed to your taste buds.

I guess money had gotten tight after my uncle lost his shop because food started to act like a relative that owed you money. It just didn't come around as much as it used to. Since it wasn't visiting our apartment, I thought of all the places where I had seen it hanging out. There was a convenience store across the field from the apartment complex where we lived and my hunger made me seriously contemplate stealing something to eat from its shelves, but I was too afraid of being caught. I was so hungry that I couldn't think about anything else. There was only one option ... I ate some of the food on the stove.

My crime was that I had eaten a significant portion of the food and that there was not enough left for everybody. Those were the accusations that came toward me from my aunt. Her proposed punishment was to banish me from the house. The demand that I be evicted and made to go live somewhere else came in the form of an emotional and dramatic assault on my character and behavior. In the midst of her tirade, I found out that in my aunt's mind I was a pretty bad person and had been guilty of some pretty bad behaviors.

In my mind, I had eaten only the food that I would have eaten for dinner a little early. I don't know; maybe I ate more than I thought I did, I can't remember. True hunger has an impact on your ability to judge how much you eat. However, I do remember thinking that whatever crime I might have committed definitely did not measure up to the punishment that was being handed down.

My uncle made a case for me to his wife, mainly on the basis that anything that I had done her brother had been guilty of as well. But his argument was to no avail and her will to kick me out of the house was carried out in short order. I can remember feeling all mixed up inside. I was confused. I didn't know what I had done that was so bad. I don't know where she was getting all of the other stuff that she was coming up with and when my uncle went out for something I told her so.

I told her that she was just looking for a reason to kick me out so that she could have her own family. I knew that I was right because she had had a response for everything that I said up until that point. When I said that, she didn't say a word. Her silence was her betrayal to her lies.

I was hurt because I felt that I was unloved and unwanted by the world. I was angry that my uncle's white wife had enough power over my life to put me in a situation where I didn't know where I was going to live. Single-handedly, she had almost made me have a relapse into hating all white people again.

I felt betrayed because my uncle allowed me to be kicked out of the house so easily. But most of all I was scared, I was scared because I didn't know what I was going to do at that point. I turned to the only place that I could turn to at the time and that was back to Grandma Mary's house.

She took me in when I thought that my life was about to fall apart. It was ironic to me that Grandma Mary showed so much love toward me. I didn't have any relationship at all with the man that was her son; the man that was supposed to be my dad. Regardless of that fact, I was grateful that she let me come live with her because I truly didn't know where else that I could have gone. Grandma Dot was busy just trying to make it for herself. She had left my mom, her boyfriend, and their drugs behind in Palmetto. After that she had gone from living with a guy that she met to living in Sarasota with Grandma Cleo to living with my Aunt Gene. It was obvious to me that she had problems of her own.

I don't remember where my mom was during that time period, but I had a feeling that wherever she was living wasn't a good place for me to be. Plant City had long ago ceased to be an option. I shuttered to think what crack cocaine had done to Laura St.

My dad was never in as an option from day one. Besides he was living with some lady who had two little girls (one of which was his child, another little half sister that I would never know). So, in my mind, Grandma Mary's house was the only place that I could have gone.

Things were different at Grandma Mary's house; my grandfather had passed away in August of 1986 while I was living with my uncle and his wife. I think he had a heart attack. At least that was the speculation at the time around his death, but I never really found out for sure. Death is so final and irreversible that why and how are never as important as when.

I remember going to his funeral and trying to remember everything that took place. I did that so that I would never forget the man.

I had never received a harsh word from my paternal grandfather. Oftentimes, he had been a powerful ally to my cousins and me in helping us get what we wanted when we were small children.

He had a reputation for being a great singer, so naturally I paid attention to the songs that were being sang at his funeral. The one that I remember now is "Ship of Salvation". I remember that because I made a promise to myself that I would never forget my grandfather or that song sang at his funeral. As it was being sung, I wondered if my life would have been different if I would have been his son instead of his son's son. I felt emotions for my grandfather, but my soul was paralyzed when it came to my biological father.

The link between my grandfather and I was lost, but I knew that we were still a part of the same chain. That chain never felt stronger than it did at his funeral. At the funeral I thought about my grandfather's parents, each of whom I only had a small recollection of from my early childhood memories. When I read his funeral program and it talked about his parents, my grandmother, their children, and their children's children; I remember feeling like I was a part of who he was and that he would always live in me as a result.

It was a strange connection that I felt with him at the time of his death because I had spent so little time with him while he lived. I never really knew very much about him and his life. The few things that I did know were that he seemed to have only two kinds of clothes—blue-collar work clothes and church clothes, he always brought my grandmother his paychecks on Fridays, and he usually came home real late. No matter how late I stayed up or how early I woke up, he always went to bed after I did and was up the next morning before I was. I don't know when he slept.

He and I had never had any one-on-one conversations. My interactions with him were always interactions that I shared with my cousins. But that was irrelevant at his funeral; I simply thought of him as "my" grandfather. I felt that there was an easy peace between us at his funeral because the only thing that had ever existed between us when he was alive was love.

I say that even though I don't ever remember either one of us actually saying the words to each other. The love that I felt for him was my appreciation of the fact that the broad-shouldered man that worked so hard always took a moment to acknowledge my cousins and I with a smile or a playful gesture. My memories of him were a collection of those gestures and they seemed like one big long smile that never faded. His death was a very spiritual experience for me and I was grateful that the man had touched my life.

The fact that my grandfather had passed away wasn't the only difference at my grandmother's house. Another difference was the actual house itself. After my grandfather passed, my grandmother had two additional rooms added onto the house. One room was actually an extension of the front porch that became a living room and the other room was added to the back of the house and became an additional bedroom.

So my grandmother's house was now a four-bedroom house instead of a three-bedroom house. That may not seem like a big difference, but rooms were always important in my grandmother's house because there was always the potential of one or more of her wayward children coming back to live in the house.

The people that lived with my grandmother when I moved back were my Aunt Linda, her two daughters—Rhonda and Lynn, and my Uncle Willie. Willie was my grandmother's youngest son. I shared a room with him, but more important than that he had been my childhood sports hero.

My grandmother's house was full, but for the time being there were enough beds for all. Still, we all knew that at any point we could have more occupants than beds and the couch or the floor in the living room could possibly become an additional place for someone to lay there head at night.

As the summer went on, I adjusted to living in a house that never quite seemed to be the same without its alpha male coming in through the side door late at night to scrape the pots and pans to get all that had been left for him.

I attended my first basketball camp that summer. The camp was called the Manatee Christian Basketball Camp and it was being held at Southeast High School. Some Christian white folks from Minnesota and the coaches from Southeast High were leading the camp. I was happy that the coaches from Southeast were a part of the camp because I expected to start school there in the fall.

Everybody that I ever knew on a basketball level who was serious about basketball was at the camp. The camp was structured in such a way that we spent some time in the classroom learning about God with the remainder of the time being spent playing basketball games and receiving basketball instruction from various members of the staff. The camp was divided up by age. Floyd and I were in the pre-high school group.

The camp featured Kent Benson; he was the 1977 first round draft pick of the Milwaukee Bucks and the overall number one pick in the draft that year. He was twice an All-American at Indiana University. "Kent", as the campers called him, came in to talk with us about God and basketball in an effort to get us to understand the relationship between the two. Kent also talked about the trophies that would be presented at the end of the week. All the kids listened intently as he talked about the criteria associated with each trophy.

There was a Mr. Defense trophy for the best defensive player of the camp. There was a Most Improved trophy for the camper that showed the most improvement during the week of play. There was a MVP trophy for the best all-around player who was the most valuable to his team. Last, but not least, there was a trophy that was called Total Release. The Total Release trophy was explained as a trophy that would go to the camper who displayed the most athletic prowess on the court while performing equally as well in the classroom. The MVP and The Total Release trophies were the two biggest trophies; they both stood much taller than the other two trophies.

All the kids that I knew set their sights on the MVP trophy. Floyd and I were no different. The MVP competition would be no secret because there was a chart that was set up to keep score of the top performers in the categories that were being considered in the MVP selection. Needless to say, that chart was a top attraction each day as the camp progressed. It didn't take long to see that Floyd and I would both be in the running for the trophy. One of the scored categories was how well you did in one-on-one competition.

The one-on-one competition was tournament style and the winner would be called the best one-on-one player in the camp for their respective age group; there was the high school group and the pre-high school group. Floyd and I both defeated all comers in our group to make it to the finals to face one another. So there I was face to face against the guy who had taught me all that I knew about absolute confidence.

I was face to face with the guy that believed he was the best thirteen-year-old basketball player in the world; he felt that if the title was never taken from him at his previous age, then he automatically retained it going into his next chronological year.

It was the classic student versus teacher match-up where I was the student and he was the teacher. He ended up beating me quite easily in front of the whole gym. It looked like the teacher had showed the student ninety-nine out of the one hundred secrets in preparation for that very game.

I know that many of those who looked on that afternoon had suspected that Floyd would win based on his height advantage alone (Floyd has always been and continues to be almost a foot taller than I am). Although that may have given Floyd an advantage at that time, it was not the reason that he beat me so easily.

The reason that he beat me was the fact that he believed that he could; and more importantly, deep down inside, I believed that he could. That deep down in your soul belief in self when it is you against the entire world was the final and most important secret that the teacher had over the student, but it was also a lesson that I would eventually learn.

No one can teach you to believe in yourself when the world is against you and your chance of success appears to be against all odds; ultimately, it has to be something that each individual finds a way to do for him or herself.

For those of you who might need to be pointed in the right direction in finding a reason to believe in yourselves in the face of overwhelming odds, I encourage you to repeat the words of Philippians chapter 4 verse 13 that say: "I can do all things through Christ which strengtheneth me." You can claim victory over the entire world through confidence and faith in that statement. I don't know if that's where Floyd got his confidence, but later in life, that's where I would learn to get mine.

Floyd may have won the battle, but he would not win the war. The one-on-one tournament was only a portion of the MVP selection criteria and all the other criteria did not place me in direct competition against the confidence master. And against all other comers the ninety-nine secrets that the master had taught the student were sufficient to leave me alone atop the MVP chart at the end of the week.

I was really happy that I won the trophy because it took a little bit of the hurt away from the feeling of being kicked out of my uncle's apartment just one month earlier. It also gave me a little recognition going into high school that fall. I had proven myself to be the best by the camp's basketball scorecard; I was the MVP and I had the tallest trophy in camp to prove it. I put it next to my Uncle Willie's trophies on the shelf. It wasn't orange and blue, but it was just as tall.

BIG MAN ON CAMPUS

In the fall of 1987, I fulfilled a boyhood dream of attending Southeast High School. The orange and blue trophies that belonged to my Uncle Willie which lined at least two shelves at my paternal grandma's house had inspired my dream when I was a fifth grader attending Wakeland Elementary. That dream had remained with me all the way up until the first day of school when I finally stepped off the school bus onto the campus.

In my mind, I had taken my first step in placing my own orange and blue trophies on my grandmother's shelves. I had dreams of becoming the big man on campus before I finished my journey at that school.

The only problem at the beginning of the journey was that I was one of the smallest kids in the whole entire school. I had always been small for my age, but now I was in a school with eighteen-year-olds, some of whom had already physically matured into men. I had to be one of the smallest freshmen that ever seriously thought that he was going to be a high school basketball star. Nevertheless, I was undaunted.

Floyd and I both received invitations to try out for the junior varsity basketball squad. The invitation alone was somewhat of an honor considering that we were both freshmen and the junior varsity was usually reserved for sophomores. In his usual fashion, Floyd announced that he knew that he would make the team and even planned on being a starter.

I wasn't quite as ambitious as Floyd was because I knew that at my size I was really going to have to play the best basketball of my life if I was going to make the junior varsity basketball team as a freshman. I did have one thing going for me. The coach of the junior varsity team was a former teacher at Bradenton Middle School. He had played on the faculty squad that we beat in the 1986-87 eighth grade students versus faculty game. The day after that game, he came up to me personally to tell me that he thought that I played an excellent game. However, even with that working in my favor, I was still fighting an uphill battle. The guards were all bigger and stronger than I was and I was sent to play on the freshmen squad. Floyd, on the other hand, made the junior varsity team ... just like he said he would.

The freshmen squad proved not to be such a bad thing for me. I was the team's starting point guard and the captain of the squad. My friend Mike, who I had known since my fifth grade year at Wakeland was also on the team. Our schedule consisted of playing the other county school three times for a total of nine games. I don't remember what our record was, but we did beat every team in the county at least once. I knew that we would have been much better than we were if Floyd had been playing with us instead of with the junior varsity.

During our respective seasons, he and I talked on the phone every night to keep one another informed about what was going on with each other. But after my freshman season ended, that was a conversation that no longer needed to take place because I was moved up to the junior varsity squad.

It was the custom that one or two of the best freshmen players from the freshmen team be moved up to the junior varsity squad at the end of the freshmen season. Our freshmen coach recommended two players from our team to be moved up, and I was thrilled to be one of those players.

The junior varsity team still had about fourteen games remaining on their schedule. Floyd acted as if my being moved up was no surprise to him. He told me that I should have been there all the time. Floyd always had my back like that and we were happy that we were back on the same court again—at least until game time.

I spent the majority of those fourteen games on the bench while Floyd actually played. The idea of moving freshmen up to the junior varsity team was for the freshmen standouts to gain experience through practice time, not game time.

I just pretended that the practices were the games without fans. To me basketball was basketball, and I played the game for the feeling that it gave me. I really didn't mind the role at all because the junior varsity team traveled everywhere the varsity team traveled and that travel kept my body and my mind away from my empty home life.

I still hadn't fully recovered from being kicked out of my uncle's apartment, but basketball was definitely helping with the healing process. I was getting my first taste of what being an athlete at Southeast High School was all about. When I was with the team I didn't need anything.

Most of our clothes were provided for us. We were all given a travel shirt to wear on the way to games and we wore our uniforms during the game. We were even given shoes and socks. We were given money for our pre-game meals. I was so happy that I didn't even mind going to McDonald's when that's where the team was taken. I just ate what I could and threw the rest away before it made me sick. My life as an athlete was getting off to a pretty good start, especially considering the alternative of my makeshift home life. I was a kid with no parental support and inconsistent support from other family members.

I mean don't get me wrong, Grandma Dot was doing all she could when she could and Grandma Mary was making sure that I had a roof over my head and food in my mouth. But even with the support that they were giving me, there were many times that I would have been in some real bad shape without basketball.

Basketball actually became a surrogate parent in a certain sense. It was feeding me on some days; it was broadening my horizons with the travel and different exposure to different people; it was boosting my self-esteem; and it was fun. But what basketball gave me more than anything else during that first year was an escape; it gave me an escape from the pain that had become my life.

I was happiest when playing basketball, but there were still some days that I had to find my way through. I was living the life of a child, who at times, felt like he wasn't wanted or loved by anyone in the world. That nobody's child feeling that I used to get when I was a small boy in Plant City came back knocking on the door of my soul. On some days, it took all that I had not to give in to it. On the outside, I appeared to be doing as well as the next person; but on the inside, I was hurting. My pain was a lonely pain that I couldn't express to anybody. My private trials and my inner feelings were my secrets; painful experiences had written them into my essence.

I kept up the mechanics of school and basketball and I went through the motions of day-to-day life really well, but it was all a hoax. On those days where I felt like nobody's child, I was bleeding from the outside in. My wounds were only visible to my soul. I don't remember any specific events that triggered those episodes where that feeling would invade my being, but I do remember that I used the same medicine each time to chase it away. I used hope.

I didn't realize it at the time, but I was only doing what my people had done for centuries when I used the medicine of hope to get me through to a better day. Hope was the only cure for what ailed me on those tough days. Faith, the substance of things hoped for was all I had. I hoped that life would one day offer me more than what I had been offered up until that point.

It was ironic because it was during the times where I felt like nobody's child that I felt the most secure in the fact that I was God's child and that He would make a way out of what seemed like no way. During those days that I felt so terribly all alone, it was definitely one set of footprints along life's beach; they belonged to the Lord because those were days that He truly carried me. I was still a sinner, but all the religion of my early childhood had driven the heathen out of me. I didn't have wisdom or understanding, but I did believe.

Basketball season and my freshman year finally came to an end. From what I have told you up to this point, you would think that my high school experience was simply made up of the joys of basketball and the doom and gloom of my personal family situation. While those two extremes did in fact combine together to contribute significantly to my freshman year experience, my remaining three years of high school would include much more.

CRACKING UP

My sophomore year at Southeast found me living with my uncle and his wife again. I had spent half of my ninth grade summer living with Grandma Mary and working as a custodial aide at Wakeland Elementary. It was weird going back to work there as a fifteen-year-old. When I was ten, the hallways seemed a lot bigger. It reminded me of the feeling that I got when I went back to Laura St. for the last time; the strip didn't seem as big as it appeared to be when I was a little snotty nose kid standing on a crate to shoot pool. I realized that it was always small—a couple of juke joints, a bar, and a café. It just seemed bigger than it was because my whole world was no bigger than what I could see in front of me.

The custodial job at Wakeland was sponsored through a county program for kids who came from low socioeconomic backgrounds. I was definitely qualified. I was grateful for that job because I knew going into the summer that I would have to buy my own school clothes for my tenth grade school year. The previous summer of 1987 included a basketball camp and playing basketball at the park, but the summer of 1988 offered little room for basketball. I was dealing with life issues that I knew were not going to be handled unless I took care of them myself. I had a roof over my head and food in my mouth; but outside of that, I was truly on my own.

I was moody because I knew that I wouldn't be able to attend any summer basketball camps. I had to work for the things that I needed. I had come to terms with that, but the conditions at Grandma Mary's house were making everything more difficult. The house was starting to get crowded and my grandmother wasn't able to regulate things with a couple of her wayward sons the way that she once did.

After my grandfather passed away, the house was missing that muscle mass that it needed to defend itself against adult males who refused to cross over into manhood. That's why I jumped at the opportunity when my uncle's wife said that I could come back to live with her and my uncle in the middle of the summer.

In truth, I still had not gotten over being kicked out of the house during the 1987 summer. I also missed the benefits that my uncle's apartments always included. One of those benefits was central air and heat. Grandma Mary's house didn't have central air or heat and there was always intense competition for the one fan in the house. In the summertime in Florida, central air makes a real difference concerning how comfortable you can be. No cool air to combat the muggy heat made it impossible to chill out.

It was unbearably hot at times. A heavy layer of thick hot air stayed in the house all day long and sometimes all night too. Besides, my uncle's house was the lesser of two evils in terms of being able to offer more of a traditional type of family environment. Dinner was a good example. At my uncle's house, everybody ate dinner at the same time around the kitchen table. At Grandma Mary's house, it was more of a free for all. If you waited too late to fix your plate, you ran the risk of missing out on dinner altogether. On the nights where I was the last one to rattle the pots, I learned to eat sleep for dinner.

By the end of the summer, I had enough money to buy all of the clothes that I needed for the new school year with enough left over to buy me a basketball hoop and a bicycle. I was going to use the basketball hoop to work on my shooting and I was going to use the bicycle to take me where I wanted to go. I thought that I had everything that I needed when school started again. I had worked hard all summer and it had paid off. I was excited to get back in the groove of high school.

All things considered, I had emerged from my freshman year in a relatively good position. Academically, I earned a 3.42 GPA for the first semester and a 2.85 GPA for the second semester. My cumulative GPA was 3.14. I wasn't satisfied with the second semester, but I was cool with the cumulative average. Athletically, I had done very well as the starting point guard on the freshmen squad and I hadn't done anything to hurt myself when I was moved up to the junior varsity squad at the end of the freshmen season.

With all of the life changes that I had gone through from the summer of 1987 until the fall of 1988, I was still on track with my grades and with basketball. I had a B average in an honors based curriculum and I was slated to be the starting point guard on the junior varsity squad for the upcoming basketball season. With one year down and three years to go, my plan to be a big man on campus was shaping up nicely.

Prior to the start of the basketball season, everything was going well. The actual start of the season was the turning point. My decision to work over the summer as opposed to concentrate on basketball began to show up during game time. Game speed was always just a little faster than practice speed. In the games, I wasn't able to handle the increased pressure that came at me on the junior varsity level.

My fatal game—the game where I lost my starting position— came during the fourth game of the season. It was an eight turnover performance against Sarasota Riverview. Anybody who knows anything about basketball knows that eight turnovers in one game from the point guard position is usually enough by itself to cause a team to lose a ball game. The coach had seen enough after that game and he inserted a new kid that no one had ever seen before because he was from another city.

The new kid being moved into the starting line-up proved to be just as catastrophic for me as the eight turnovers because he could really play. He always seemed to do better in games than he did in practices. That was kind of frustrating for me because I was doing better in practice. I would have a strong practice on Monday, and he would go out in have a strong game on Tuesday. I knew that a strong game on Tuesday beat a strong practice on Monday any day of the week.

I was a real good on the ball defender and I held him in check pretty well in practice; but then we would play some team with point guards who he blew right past, shot over the top of, or just plain outsmarted. During some games, I wished that I were on the opposite team just to see if he could do that to me in a game situation.

I didn't really want to be on a different team, I was just licking my wounds. I just couldn't help thinking that if the new kid hadn't done so well in the games, then maybe I would have gotten another chance to prove that I could do the job. After a few dazzling game performances by the new kid in town, I became a forgotten man. I went from premium minutes to some embarrassing minimal appearances to a few DNPs (a basketball stat that means 'did not play'). I was crushed.

My confidence really went down the tubes and I don't know what I would have done without Floyd; it seemed like he was the only friend that I had left in the entire basketball world. He would always tell me that I could do it and not to give up. I know that sounds like a simple message that wouldn't do much good, but those words from him were like a breath of air to a drowning man. My basketball life depended on them.

Floyd believed in me when I wasn't strong enough to believe in myself. Most of the guys tried to stay out of the whole thing by not talking to me at all. But not Floyd, he started calling me more just to try to keep me in it. He never tried not to talk about my situation; it was always at the top of his agenda to tell me to keep fighting. He acted as if my giving up would have hurt him more than it would have hurt me.

I didn't want to let my best friend down. I had a choice to make in my mind. I was either going to choose to fight to get my starting job back or I was going to quit because the role that I had been reduced to was simply unacceptable to me.

I chose to fight and I know that I wouldn't have made that choice without Floyd in my corner. He saved my basketball life.

I decided that I would hang in there. I told myself that the new kid wasn't really better than the best me that I could be; he was only playing better than me because I had not prepared myself properly over the summer. I had taken basketball for granted.

I had to keep telling myself that if I had done what I needed to do over the summer that I would have easily been able to keep my position. It didn't matter whether that was the truth or not, what did matter was the fact that I could use that to motivate myself to work harder. I reasoned to myself that hard work was the shortest distance between where I was and where I wanted to be. So instead of sulking, I went to work on my game.

I eventually overcame my battle on the basketball court by regaining my starting job back with about five games remaining in the season. I was excited to be a starter again, but it was a half-hearted victory. It was true that I had worked hard and improved my play significantly, but the new kid helped my cause tremendously with his behavior off the court. It wasn't like I just came storming back to reclaim my starting position with outstanding performances on the court.

I was a competitor and a true competitor wants to win out on superior skills or merit on the court; no true competitor wants to win out on some off the court issues. If you are a boxer, then you want to win or lose in the ring. If you are a basketball player, then you want to win or lose on the court. You always want to take that last inch; you don't want it given to you. When there is trouble in your way, you don't ask the Lord to move your mountain; you ask him for the strength to climb!

Nevertheless, I did receive some satisfaction from knowing that I had persevered through a very tough time period where I wasn't sure if I could actually make it. I had won an important internal victory. Looking back on that time in my life, I know that my being able to handle and overcome that particular adversity involving my junior varsity basketball season did a lot to shape my future character. It was a major influence on the way that I dealt with adversity from that point forward.

In the end, I had lost my starting position for the majority of my junior varsity basketball season, but I had added strength to my character that I still draw from today. It wasn't such a bad trade-off. I lost a little, but I gained a lot.

The adversity on the basketball court wasn't the only adversity that I would have to overcome during my tenth grade year. After the season, with about three months left in the school year, I came home one day to find that all my clothes had been packed up and set out in the living room. No one was home when I first got to the apartment, so I didn't really know what to think about the situation.

I searched the other parts of the apartment to see if anybody else's clothes had been packed up. I wondered if my aunt and uncle had decided to move to a different place without telling me. I searched the other rooms, but I didn't see any other belongings out of place that would indicate that the whole family was moving. I went back into the living room to examine things to see if it was all of my stuff or just some of my stuff because if it was just some of my stuff, then maybe there was a logical explanation behind the mystery. After careful examination, I concluded, that it was all of my stuff.

I thought for a few minutes through all of the possible reasons why my belongings would be packed up in the middle of the living room. My mind kept trying to avoid the logical conclusion that I was being kicked out of the house for the second time in two years. Seconds seemed like hours and minutes seemed like days.

As my mind settled in on the fact that I was actually being kicked out of the apartment, the apartment began to shrink and the walls began to close in on me. I can remember feeling like I had to get out of there before they all closed in around me. I don't know what an anxiety attack feels like, but I know that that was the closest that I ever came to having one. Luckily for me, I wasn't afflicted with agoraphobia.

I left the house and jumped on my bicycle to escape the situation. I didn't know where I was going and I didn't care. I just peddled. I can't remember one single car on the road. I rode the streets around our apartment everyday and there were always cars to avoid; but on this day, if they were there, then I was completely unaware of them. I was in a daze in my own little private purgatory.

As I peddled down the road on my bicycle, the tears just ran down my face as I thought about my future. The immediate future was staring me right in the face and asking me: "where are you going to sleep tonight?" The future that lies beyond the immediate future was standing right behind the immediate future looking over its shoulder and asking me: "what's going to happen to your life and does anybody care?" The worst part about it was that there was no future standing after the second one. It seemed as if I had been born to fulfill a destiny of having no long term future.

I didn't have any answers to the self-posed questions about my future. I felt totally alone in the world. I felt so alone that I felt like my own soul had left my body. If you have ever felt like that, then you know that it is a very empty feeling. I didn't know what I was going to do. I just wanted to disappear off the face of the earth leaving no evidence that I had ever existed at all. I thought about various ways to do that, but the impulses to go through with them were blocked by the last ounce of hope that I had left in my body. It was out of that last ounce of hope that I found the strength to pray to God.

Through the emptiness that I felt and the tears that I cried, I began to pray to God and ask Him for His help. I thought about all the lessons that I learned from the church services that I had attended as a small boy when I lived with Grandma Mary. I thought about the concept of faith that had been involved in so many of those lessons and how the folks who attended the prayer meetings with my grandmother seemed to have an immeasurable amount of faith in the Lord. As I continued to peddle, I felt my own faith that I had in the Lord began to reclaim the soul that felt like it had left my body.

After I prayed long, hard, and earnestly I still couldn't answer the question of where I was going to sleep tonight, but I did have faith that the Lord would take care of me. Faith was the only thing that I had.

In looking back, it's funny that the only thing that I had in the situation turned out to be the only thing that I needed ... sort of like David and his stone. Sometimes the only thing that you have is really the only thing you need when you get God involved. That thought makes me want to ask the question that the preacher asks on Sundays: "Ain't God good?"

Everybody was home by the time that I finally returned to my uncle's apartment. I tried to compose myself as I entered into what seemed like a Venus flytrap. My uncle and his wife were already arguing about the situation. If I had any hope that I wasn't going to be kicked out of the house, then it vanished as I listened to their argument.

I remember my uncle asking my aunt questions about my future and how this would impact my grades at school. In response to his question about my grades, his wife said something that I will never forget. She said: "Ah! He will do fine! He has always done fine!" I didn't disagree with her, but I did feel very angry about the comment.

I was angry because it seemed that people always assumed that I would be fine no matter how terrible the situation was that I was facing. I knew deep down inside that I could achieve in school against almost any odds if I really put my mind to it, but I was still extremely bothered by the position of the statement. It just didn't make sense to me how she could make such an arrogant and cold assumption. I wondered if she knew that just a few hours earlier that I wanted to disappear off the face of the earth ... I wanted to know if she considered that feeling as doing fine. I wondered if she didn't know where she was going to sleep that night would she be doing fine.

I don't think that she or anybody else realized just how hard it was to be me and keep it all together at the same time. I was myself, my mother, and my father all rolled into one. I had major problems, but all she could say was: "Ah! He will do fine! He has always done fine!" In a brief moment of rage, I wanted to punch her in the face as hard as I could and then tell her that she would be just fine.

After I listened to them argue for the next hour or so, it became apparent that my uncle was going to lose that argument the same way that he had lost the argument that they had in 1987 over whether I would stay or leave. He must have realized the same thing because he began to load my stuff in the car as he shouted back and forth with her about the situation. I began to help him load the car, not because I wanted to leave, but because the walls were closing in on me again.

We finished loading the car and began to drive away from the apartment. I wondered where he was driving me to because I didn't have a clue. I decided to sit back and wait rather than ask. At first it didn't seem like we were going anywhere in particular, it just seemed like he wanted to drive and talk for awhile.

He tried to explain how sorry he was about not only this situation, but also the situation with my parents as well. He starting telling me how unfair life was and how hard things were. The way he was talking I thought that he was about to drop me off to some kind of shelter or something.

I couldn't figure out where he was going to take me so I just listened to what he said. Part of the reason that I listened was because I had never heard my uncle sound the way that he sounded that evening. The other reason that I listened was because I had not had any Black man seriously talk to me about anything real since Grandaddy Cee left five years earlier.

I could tell that my uncle was sincerely sorry about the situation. He tried to explain that his hands were tied. He tried to explain how much he loved me. He tried to explain that I was almost old enough to take care of myself and that I could make it if I could just hang on a little while longer. He told me that he couldn't make me any promises about the future except one. He promised me that if I worked hard and finished high school that he would buy me a car for graduation. That made me feel good, but I just couldn't help thinking about what I was going to do until graduation. I had over two years of high school left.

When my uncle finished saying all the things that he wanted to say to me, he began to drive down the familiar roads toward my Grandma Mary's house. He told me that his wife had already called and spoke with my grandmother about the situation earlier in the day.

I was relieved in a sense because at least I knew where I was gonna sleep that night. At the same time, I was embarrassed. I didn't know what the conversation had been between my grandmother and my uncle's wife. My uncle's wife always accused me of things that I didn't think that I was guilty of doing. There was no doubt in my mind that she had told my grandmother some things that I didn't do.

I was ashamed that I had chosen to accept her apology for kicking me out the first time. It was my belief in that apology that caused me to leave my grandmother's house in the first place. Nonetheless, my uncle dropped me off and we unloaded my stuff. He told me good-bye and that was that.

I was pretty familiar with my grandmother's house, so it wasn't like any big shock to my system or anything. It was lucky for me that my aunt decided to kick me out during a time when my grandmother's house wasn't very crowded. I easily scored me a bed to rest my head for the night, but I didn't sleep much. I just kept thinking about the events of the day. In the midst of my thoughts, I felt hunger pains piercing my side. In between leaving my uncle's house and arriving at my grandmother's house, I had missed dinner at both places. I was hungry from a physical standpoint, but I was filled from a spiritual standpoint.

As I lay there, I remembered my prayer to God and I felt that He had really come through for me. That bed and that pillow underneath my head felt like the most comfortable bed and pillow in the entire world. I really appreciated having a warm bed to sleep in because earlier that day I didn't know if I would be sleeping in a bed that night or not.

I went to school the next morning and I told Floyd the story. He said that he had called my uncle's house the night before and my uncle told him that I wasn't going to be living there anymore and that I was at my grandmother's house. He asked me some questions about the situation, but he could tell that I didn't really feel like talking about it that much. I just felt bad the whole day.

I must have looked like a zombie in class because of the way that I felt. My grades were already down during the first semester from the confidence crisis that I went through with the junior varsity basketball season. I pulled down a 2.85 GPA during the first semester and it knocked my cumulative GPA down lower than I wanted it to go. I knew that the last three months were going to be tough, but I was totally unprepared for what actually took place.

My course schedule was an honors course schedule and it was brutal considering my psychological state. Even when life wasn't kicking me around, homework and studying had never been my strong suit; but it went from bad to worse in a New York minute. I stopped even taking books home with me. If I couldn't understand the material from when I halfway paid attention in class, then it just wasn't going to happen.

The only time that I opened any book was when I was in the actual class trying to look like I was paying attention. I only opened my geometry book in geometry class and I only opened my chemistry book when I was in chemistry class. You get the picture.

For my lack of efforts, I received an F in both geometry and chemistry; those were two classes where you had to pay attention or else. Even though I knew that I probably wasn't going to do to well that semester I had the nerve to be surprised when I got my report card and saw a 2.00 GPA looking right back at me. I was glad that the summer saved me because I probably would have ended up with a worse GPA than that if the semester didn't end when it did.

My academic confidence was shook right along with every other form of confidence that I possessed. I was supposed to be an honor student and I received two F's while barely falling into the C average range for my semester GPA. What was I doing? I was letting everything just go down the drain. My cumulative GPA had fallen from a solid 3.14 at the end of my freshman year to a 2.79 just one year later.

My academic performance during my sophomore year was unprecedented for me, but there was a brief period of enlightenment that I experienced in one class. The class was English Honors II and the assignment that triggered that wonderful experience was the reading of Richard Wright's 1945 autobiography, *Black Boy.* I had read many books about Black people when I was a boy attending elementary school. They had all been books about my sports heroes. When I thought I was going to be a professional football player I read books about Jim Brown, Walter Payton, Tony Dorsett, Gayle Sayers, and any other book about a Black football player that I could find in the school library. But those were short stories mostly about their athletic careers and they were written on an elementary school level. Richard Wright's book was an in-depth novel that was talking about his everyday life experiences growing up poor and Black. Those were two things that I could definitely relate to.

When the teacher first assigned the book, I had no special plans to read it. I figured I would skim through it just enough to be able to talk about it or write a little something about it if she asked us to do so. That's what I did with all of the other books that I had been assigned to read. That's probably why she was so surprised when I took such an interest in the discussions regarding that book. To be honest, I even surprised myself.

At first, I picked up the book to just glance through it. But after a couple of pages, I couldn't put it down. I had never read a book so fast in my life. I read it the way that I ate Grandma Dot's fried chicken; I devoured it.

I had never read a book before that addressed the issues that Mr. Wright's autobiography addressed. The issues in the book were dealing with both being Black and being poor. I saw my own struggle in the struggles outlined on its pages. I gobbled up the material and became an active participant in the class discussions. When she asked us to do a writing assignment to articulate what we had gotten from the book, I turned in a paper that earned rave reviews from her. Although I never took any real interest in any other book she assigned, she went on and on about my paper until the end of the semester. It's unfortunate that that type of academic engagement was an isolated incident because it felt really good to read, to talk about, and to write about something that I could relate to my own experience.

Speaking of my own experience, the summer after my tenth grade year was challenging. It was 1989 and I knew that the summer of 1989 could not find me spending more time working for money than it saw me getting ready for basketball. I knew that the fall would prove to be a very tough challenge for me on the basketball court. After my junior varsity experience, I would have to prove that I could make the varsity team. The varsity basketball team at Southeast was not like the varsity team at the other county schools.

The talent at Southeast was plentiful and nothing was guaranteed. For example, during my freshman season, the varsity team consisted of at least fifteen people. That's a situation on a basketball team where not everybody is going to get to play. During that particular season, two starters from the previous year ended up quitting the team due to lack of playing time.

The two guys would have kept their starting positions at other high schools in the area, but not at Southeast. That's how deep the talent ran and how shallow the guarantees were at Seminole Alley. My sophomore season saw the same kind of depth on the varsity team and some of the same would-be-stars on other teams riding the pine. Needless to say, I was nervous about my upcoming junior year and the varsity situation.

I wanted a spot on the team and I wanted to play. I was ready to put my bad experience from the past season behind me and get back on track. I put a weight bench and some weights that I got from a friend in my room. I had my own room at my grandmother's house by that time.

I lifted those weights all summer while working on my ball handling. I attended the Manatee Christian Basketball Camp, the same camp that I attended in the summer of 1987 where I out dueled Floyd for the MVP trophy in the little kid division. This time I was older and I was in the big kids division. Unlike the first time I attended the camp, I really paid attention in the classroom portion of the camp where bible study and the importance of Christianity was the topic of discussion.

I paid attention more and participated more during that camp session because I still had not forgotten what the Lord had done for me after I got kicked out of my uncle's house. Although my life was still a struggle, I felt blessed. I knew that it could have been a lot worse without my faith in the Lord.

At the end of the camp, I was presented with the Total Release trophy, which was awarded to the camper who best embodied the principles learned in the classroom while performing equally as well on the court.

By the end of the summer, I was feeling a lot better about basketball and life. I promised myself right then and there that I wasn't going to leave the security offered by Grandma Mary's house ever again until it was time for me to go out into the world on my own. I didn't want to be kicked out of anywhere else again and I knew that while my grandmother's house may have had its drawbacks that I wouldn't be kicked out.

I also made up my mind that I was going to give it my best with the basketball thing and if it didn't work out it wasn't going to be because I didn't try or I wasn't at my best. That was a much different attitude than the one that I had the previous summer going into my sophomore season where I expected to be the man on the junior varsity squad.

The other thing that was different about the start of the 1989 school year than the start of the previous school year was my financial situation. At the start of my sophomore year, I felt pretty good about my financial situation because I had worked the entire summer. I had enough money to buy a decent amount of clothes to start the school year, but that wasn't the case going into my eleventh grade year. I had to rely on Grandma Dot. She was living with my Aunt Gene during that time. Relying on my grandmother wasn't so bad because she came through for me like she always did, but what happened shortly before school started was something that I will never forget.

About a week before my junior year; I spent three days riding my bicycle to different stores to get the best deals for the money that my grandmother had given me to buy clothes. There was no logical person for me to ask to take me to the stores, so I didn't ask. I could see people with a car looking at me like I was crazy if I had asked them to take me around school shopping. That was something that parents were supposed to do.

My grandmothers usually saved me in situations where I had nowhere else to turn, but neither of them had a car or knew how to drive. I decided that it would just be easier to ride my bike to the stores. I carried load after load from the stores to my grandmother's house until I had finally bought everything that I needed for the year. That's when the tragedy unfolded.

I had separated all of my new clothes from all of my old clothes in the closet in my room. I can remember looking at them and feeling good that I had done a good job. I bought a lot of stuff and I had the latest fashions; I had a closet combination of value and style that would keep me dressed slick for the first two weeks of school. But it wasn't just the clothes; I was feeling good all around. I had improved a great deal on the basketball court, I had gotten a lot stronger from lifting weights all summer, and I felt more secure in my home life because I knew that as long as Grandma Mary was breathing that I could stay in her house.

I was in good spirits until I came home one afternoon to discover that someone had broken the back window of my grandmother's house and stolen my brand new school clothes. They took everything with the exception of a couple of shirts. They had also stolen some of my youngest cousin's new clothes. I was devastated and enraged all at the same time. I didn't know what to do. I just cried.

It wasn't the kind of crying that a child does. It was the kind of crying that comes from anger and hurt mixed together because you can't rise above a situation. If any of you have ever seen director John Singleton's 1991 debut film, *Boyz N the Hood*, then you might be able to understand. There was a scene where the Academy Award-winning actor Cuba Gooding Jr. was crying to his girlfriend (Nia Long) after an incident where he had been harassed by the L.A.P.D. The police officer put a gun to his head and accused him of thinking that he was tough. The officer thought that he was a suspect in a possible 187 because he was driving a blue Volkswagen. It turned out to be a case of mistaken identity, but the damage had already been done.

If you saw the type of crying that Cuba Gooding Jr. did after that incident in the film, then you can get a picture of what kind of crying I was doing after I discovered that my clothes had been stolen. It was the kind of crying that's produced when you mix the emotions of anger and fury with the emotions of helplessness and hopelessness. It makes you look like you are cracking up. It's a strange mix, that crack-up cocktail; but every Black man seems to be destined to drink one at least once in his life.

I walked around the house in a hateful mood. I hated the fact that I was even in a situation where that kind of thing could happen. I hated the fact that I knew that I was in a situation where I didn't have any more money to replace the clothes. I hated the fact that I was too poor to just go out to the stores to replace the clothes. I hated the thought of wearing my old clothes on the first day of school. I hated always getting the short end of the stick.

My grandmother called the police and they came out and took some fingerprints around the area where the glass was broken in my grandmother's bedroom window. They asked the neighbors some questions and looked around for clues. I hated the neighbors for claiming to not have seen anything. I wanted to scream at them: "how can you live right next door and not have seen anything!"

The search for fingerprints, the questioning of the neighbors, and the search for clues all yielded the same result of no information. There were no fingerprints, no answers from the neighbors, and no clues around my grandmother's bedroom window. The police told my grandmother that the majority of break-ins were committed by someone that you knew because they knew what your patterns were and when you weren't going to be home. None of us doubted that fact because we knew some shady characters.

We didn't tell the police that because we suspected that the guilty person was someone that we knew extremely well. We suspected the person to be a member of the family. I am not going to reveal any names or what relationship he had to the family because the goal of writing this book is to tell my life story; not indict anybody on charges that were never substantiated.

Well, some might ask why I brought it up if I wasn't going to call any names. I consider that to be a fair question so I'll answer it. I brought it up because it will shed some light on what it's like to have a member of your family on crack cocaine.

The particular family member that we suspected was a family member that we all knew smoked crack cocaine. It was impossible not to know. The person would quickly go through a whole week's pay before the weekend was over when he was smoking or basing (that's what we called it) crack.

The evidence of the addiction was more than circumstantial because the individual would sometimes come into the house with a wide-eyed stare look in his eyes. When you saw him that way you just knew that he was on something. And when you were on something in 1989 that made you look like that, more than likely it was crack cocaine. My grandmother had even found a saucer that had the crack residue on it; it was hidden way behind some stuff under the bathroom sink.

Our family wasn't the only family that had to endure the pain and the problems associated with having a crack addict in the house. It seemed that everybody that I knew had a relative who was involved with crack, either at that time or at some point in the past. Those who were lucky enough to have a relative who had beat it were always thanking the Lord and praising Jesus; while keeping their fingers crossed that their son, daughter, father, mother, aunt, or uncle wouldn't have a relapse.

There were certain rules that you learned when you had a person that was addicted to crack in your house or in your family. You learned that items with any kind of value had the potential to just disappear. If the addict was supposed to be a contributing member toward household finances, then you learned that it was going to be times when they would not have the money that they were supposed to have to cover their agreed upon contribution. The biggest rule that you learned was that there was no limit that a crack addict would not go beyond in search of that next high. A base head would go all out to feel that intense high that they got from that killer crack cocaine.

We had all learned that rule, as well as a few others, and that's why we all thought that that relative was guilty of staging the break-in and exchanging our school clothes for crack cocaine. My grandmother wasn't willing to tell the police of our suspicion, but she did confront the relative.

Of course the relative denied the charges, but none of us expected a person addicted to crack to tell the truth—lying was as essential as having a crack pipe. My grandmother insisted that she had lived in her house for all those years and never had a problem. She asked the relative if he expected her to believe that all of a sudden someone breaks into the house and only steals school clothes. The discussion went on for a few minutes without anybody giving ground. My grandmother didn't give any ground in her charge and the relative didn't give any ground in his defense. I just sat there, feeling like the relative was guilty and hating him for ruining what seemed to be my life at the time.

We never found out for sure if the relative took the clothes or not, but we knew it was a strong possibility considering his penchant for sticking glass crack pipes in his mouth.

For those of you who have or have ever had a crack addict in your family, you know the difficulties that the situation brings and how it negatively impacts the lives of everybody involved. Several members of my family have used crack cocaine, so I think that I can attest to the devastating effects of the drug.

The negative impact of the drug is definitely not limited to the user; it is a drug that can cripple entire families. If you never had anybody in your family who has suffered from a crack cocaine addiction, then you may not be able to understand how bad it can be. You may have a hard time grasping my story about the break-in and why we suspected the relative. You all will have to trust me when I tell you to consider yourself fortunate not to have had personal experiences with a crack addict in your family. I am going to leave you with a quote by Dorothy Riley that you better believe if one of your family members ever becomes addicted to crack cocaine. Ms. Riley said: "Blood may be thicker than water, but it is not thicker than crack cocaine." And that's real.

Regardless of who stole my clothes, they were gone and I didn't have any more clothes or any more money to buy new clothes. I called the only person I could to help get me out of the situation of having no clothes to start school. I called Grandma Dot. I had a lot of faith in my grandmother's ability to get me out of tough jams, but I wasn't expecting her to be able to really help me because she had just given me the money to buy the clothes that were stolen.

Grandma Dot loved me more than she loved herself, but I knew that money didn't grow on trees. Still, I explained what had happened and miraculously somehow she brought me some money within the next couple of days. I don't know how she got it, where she got it, or who she got it from; but I do know that she got it.

I don't know why I was surprised because Grandma Dot had no pride when it came to me. She would beg or borrow from anybody if it came down to me needing something and she didn't have it or couldn't get it herself. When she was able to get it herself, it involved her getting on her knees scrubbing the floors and cleaning the houses of the white folks that she worked for as a housekeeper. If she couldn't beg, borrow, or get on her knees to scrub floors for white folks; then she would get on her knees to the Lord. The point is that somehow, when she knew that I needed something, she got it.

When she brought me that money, I remembered something that I had overheard my Aunt Desoline from Plant City say years earlier. I didn't know what it meant at the time because I was a small child, but it hit me that day. I had heard my aunt say the following words to another lady about my grandmother: "you know Quincy is her heartstring". As I said before, I didn't know what those words meant at the time, but it made me feel good because it sounded so nice.

I had never heard the word "heartstring" before and I haven't heard it too many times since that time I heard my aunt say it, but I know what it means. I know what it means because the love that my grandmother has shown me over the years has taught me what it means. Grandma, if you ever read this book, I want to say thank-you and I want you to know that I love you. You are my heartstring.

I bought me some clothes right before school started. I didn't like them as much as the clothes that were stolen because I had actually shopped for the clothes that were stolen. The replacement clothes were hurried purchases that were made to fill a need at the very last minute. Nevertheless, I was grateful that I had anything at all to put on my back considering the circumstances. My grandmother had been there for me again, like she had been so many times before. Crack cocaine may be thicker than blood, but it's powerless against a strong Black grandmother who always runs to God when she has a problem. And that too … is real. Hallelujah!

HINDSIGHT;
MY TWO, ME TOO

Hindsight: Understanding after the fact; the ability or opportunity to understand and judge an event or experience after it has occurred.

After the Egyptian and Indian, the Greek and Roman, the Teuton and Mongolian, the Negro is a sort of seventh son, born with a veil, and gifted with second-sight in this American world,—a world which yields him no true self-consciousness, but only lets him see himself through the revelation of the other world. It is a peculiar sensation, this double-consciousness, this sense of always looking at one's self through the eyes of others, of measuring one's soul by the tape of a world that looks on in amused contempt and pity. **(Dr. W.E.B Du Bois,** *The Souls of Black Folk,* **1903)**

Before I can go on with my story, I feel that it's important that I lay the foundation of what happened to me from a psychological standpoint. With the benefit of hindsight and a better of understanding of life, I can explain it to you in a way that will help you gain a better understanding of some of the things that will be written about in the following chapters of this book. I think that it's significant to do this at this point in the book because my junior year in high school was the genesis of some serious things that would turn out to have a meaningful impact on my life. Of course I couldn't know that then, but in hindsight it is as clear as a glass ceiling.

Dr. W.E.B. Du Bois introduced me to a concept that he referred to as "two-ness" in his 1903 book, *The Souls of Black Folk*. Some have called that book the most important book ever written by an African-American. I first read the book and came across the concept as a twenty-six-year-old and I was absolutely euphoric. I had never come across anything in print that described so accurately what I had felt so deeply for so many years.

By the time I was twenty-six years old, I had felt for years that I lived in two different worlds that required different thoughts and actions. I lived in a Black world and a white world, two worlds that were segregated by thoughts and actions.

The rules of the Black world that I had always known did not translate very well into the white world that I began to discover as a teenager at Southeast High School. The rules that I discovered in the white world did not translate well into the Black world that I had been submerged in throughout my entire life experience. So I learned the rules to both worlds and applied them appropriately as I moved from one world to the other.

I had two modes of operation, which were often completely opposite in nature. Imagine that. Two opposite forces within one mind and one body. Dr. Du Bois referred to this position of the Negro as "two-ness". He wrote the following in *The Souls of Black Folk* in respect to the Negro and his opposite natures:

> One ever feels his two-ness,- an American, a Negro; two souls, two thoughts, two unreconciled strivings; two warring ideals in one dark body, whose dogged strength alone keeps it from being torn asunder.

When I read that sentence I was like, yeah! That's exactly what I feel like Doc! It was such a beautiful and accurate diagnosis of the ailment that I had never quite been able to explain or articulate with my own words. His words, written nearly one hundred years ago, made me feel for the first time that somebody knew what I was going through trying to be Black in America. I felt a validation and exhilaration that made me sweep through the pages of the book.

I had grown up Black and my experiences rooted me firmly in the Black world as a child; but as I grew older, I began to notice a different world. I began to notice a white world dominated by white people. Once I noticed the white world, it would not go away. It was everywhere. I realized that the white world was the mainstream world and my Black world was an island in the midst of a sea of whiteness.

I also noticed that the white or mainstream world would not allow me entrance into its world unless I adopted its accepted thoughts and actions, which were different than the thoughts and actions of the Black world. Many things that were accepted without question in my Black world were either questioned or frowned upon in the white world. My talk, my walk, my hair, my dress, my attitude in general, were all things that had to be modified in order to escape scrutiny and disapproval in the white world.

On the other hand, as I learned the rules that allowed me more entrance into the white or mainstream world, I noticed that some elements of the Black world would not always accept me back upon my return from the white world. The possible exile from the Black world made me realize that the decision to go into the white world was a serious dilemma. It was a dilemma because more often than not, acceptable entrance into the white world was the way to material prosperity, a better education, a better job, or a better life in general.

I know that this dilemma is not my burden alone; I think that most Black people deal with it on some level or another. Subconsciously, we all know that our pot to piss in and our window to throw out of is correlated to our ability to convince some white person of our merit or usefulness. We all have our different methods, but the madness is the same for us all. We are all shaped by the larger whiteness that surrounds us.

Once I was able to recognize and rationalize my own struggle with "two-ness", it became easier for me to see the same struggle in other Black folks. In my opinion, there are three approaches that I believe are the most commonly used methods to coping with the Catch-22 nature that being at odds with oneself causes.

Most people have seen the stereotype that portrays the angry Black militant who believes that there is a conspiracy in everything that white people say and do. That stereotype represents the type of person who deplores white or mainstream culture and deals with the two worlds by loving the Black world unconditionally and almost to a fault, while despising the white world. That extreme approach is the favorite extreme of many whites because it inappropriately blames white people for all of our problems.

I know that that seems like an odd statement on the surface, but it really makes a lot of sense. Considering all of the problems that plague the Black community at large, it is quite easy for anybody to dismiss a claim that blames whites for all of our problems; and it is in that ease in dismissing the charge that many whites find favor with the charge. It would be like a guilty criminal of one particular crime finding favor with being charged for many different crimes that he or she can't possibly be convicted of by a just court of law. He will beat the bogus charges and falsely claim innocence on the legitimate charge.

At the other extreme, most of us have also been exposed to the stereotype of the Black person who has totally abandoned their Black world in an order to blindly embrace a "white is right" type of mentality. The Black community usually labels people who adopt that attitude as a sell-out. That's a charge that carries some serious weight for any African-American who has any love for his or her race. Both of the extreme approaches have serious drawbacks.

The first extreme leads you down a road that will ultimately lead you to the same destination of racial hatred that inspired you to adopt your position of angry Black militant in the first place. Racial hatred on the part of whites is usually what inspires racial hatred on the part of Black militants. That is a formula where race hatred produces race hatred and that's a lose-lose proposition where neither the white perpetrator nor the Black perpetrator of the racial hatred can claim a moral position.

Don't get me wrong, *I am not saying* that I don't understand the militant approach, because I do. Sometimes people just get tired of being victimized; and when they get tired, they will do anything within their power to bring about an end to that victimization. *What I am saying is* ... that a righteous cause cannot be maintained on any front that supports blind racial hatred or intolerance of any individual or group—regardless of the reason for that hatred. There is no virtue or justification for hatred. God is love; and hate is an antipode of love.

The second extreme of "white is right" will never allow a Black person to embrace the beauty that is to be found in who we were as a people, who we are as a people, and who we will be as a people. In effect you will be severed from your past, present, and future only to find that there is no sustenance in the end you seek by chasing a Euro-centric model that does not value what you bring to the table. The reason that a Euro-centric model will not value what you bring to the table is simple—it all has to do with love and respect. If you do not love or respect yourself enough to be who the Lord made you to be, then how can you reasonably expect anyone else to love or respect you? I hope you consider that question to be rhetorical.

I believe that one would get further by embracing a philosophy that says it is better to love and respect yourself for who and what you are, because then and only then, will others be able to love and respect you for who and what you are. Is it feasible for me to look in the mirror and hate myself, and then turn right around and ask or expect someone else to love me?

That's my analysis of the two extreme approaches to the dilemma of being faced with the two unequal and uncompromising Black and white worlds. They are both negative analyses because they are extreme and fixed in their positions. There is a third approach that is somewhat more moderate and flexible, but it too has its drawbacks. One who chooses the third approach faces potential peril from both worlds along with the danger of losing one's real identity.

The third approach to the perplexity proposed by the two worlds allows the individual to go back and forth between the two worlds. The journey offered by this approach was the path that I started on in high school. At first, it was like a game for me, but I realized quickly that the game could leave me emotionally injured.

I have "played the game" for eleven years and it is from that experience that I am writing about this approach. The skill in the game of successfully going back and forth between the Black world and the white world is contained in the highest form of knowledge. You have to know the difference between the two worlds. More importantly, you have to know when to apply that knowledge in the appropriate situations. To know is not enough; one must know and act accordingly. The correct application of the knowledge is the highest form of use.

I have found out that the inability to apply that knowledge in either world could lead to isolation, ridicule, scorn, denied opportunity, or some combination of the four. Too many mistakes in going back and forth between the two worlds could have a devastating impact on one's sanity, one's career, or one's entire life.

I realized early on that there was also a danger in losing your real identity in going back and forth. When you go back and forth you are constantly aware and constantly monitoring your situation for feedback of either acceptance or disapproval. You are forced to become what is known in social psychology as a high self-monitor. In a sense, you are adapting to your different situation so much that you might forget who you really are. Playing the game of going back and forth is almost like being in a constant state of incognito.

I don't know too much about the originator of the next quote, Ms. Cheryl McCourtie, but the quote itself is a very accurate description of what I'm trying to describe about the identity danger of the third approach.

In an article titled, "Where I Enter", that appeared in *Essence* in April of 1989, Ms. McCourtie said: "One of the most difficult aspects of being a Black American is that in addition to my ever pervasive otherness, I have also become identityless." Notice that her quote from 1989 dealt with the same two elements that Dr. Du Bois talked about eighty-six years earlier in 1903—Black and American—only he referred to Black as Negro as was the custom for his day.

The problem of trying to be both Black and American is still having an impact on the psychological welfare of Black Americans today. I suspect that some Black people will either be so in denial about the dissonance associated with being Black in America or so ignorant of their ignorance that some might be asking themselves right about now, "what is he talking about?" Well, in an attempt not to lose anybody, let me give those people some real life suggestions to do that will show them what I'm talking about.

> Invite your closest white friend or associate over to your house to watch and discuss any video episode of *Roots* together.

> Invite your closest white friend over to your house to listen to and discuss one of Malcolm X's speeches together.

> The next time you find yourself in mixed company having a political conversation, raise the subject of reparations for African-Americans for the centuries of enslavement of the African in America.

Ask yourself how would you feel right now, if the United States were to openly declare war on an African nation. Would you fight? If so, try to imagine how you would feel.

I have come close to the edge of my sanity on several different occasions while dealing with my "twoness"—being Black and American. Yet, I don't think that I have actually ever lost my identity in my eleven years of playing the game. But by the same accord, I have never been so severely tested as I have been tested over the last two years of my life (referring to the time period between the ages of twenty-five and twenty-seven). So in the words of Melle Mel: "Don't push me cause I'm close to the edge, I'm trying not to lose my head".

I don't know ... maybe I will lose my identity if I am unable to reconcile my worlds into one world in which I can just concentrate on being a human being. Even if that single focus of thought and energy of just being a human being only lasts for one day, it will be a welcomed moment of respite from the grueling and unremitting battle of being a Black male in America.

It will be one day that I didn't have to be reminded every single day that I'm a Black male in a country that has many different perceptions of me regardless of whether those perceptions are based on characteristics that I actually possess as an individual or not. It will be one day that I didn't live in a country that belittles (at its best) my plight as a Black man, unless it is to introduce me to the criminal justice system when I fall victim to a society and a system that doesn't care about my diminished life chances. It will be one day that I didn't live in a country that uses the improbable success of a few African-Americans as token examples for the majority of African-Americans for whom it is nearly impossible to overcome the racism and discrimination that they are confronted with in their daily lives.

It will be one day that I didn't have to hear electric door locks snap to a locked position because of my approach. It will be one day where I did not have to go out of my way to make someone else feel at ease in my presence—as if to offer some sort of sign that I intend to do them no harm. It will be one day where I didn't have to be followed around a store—as if my only purpose for being in a retail establishment was to steal what others were expected to buy.

It doesn't matter how much money I've had; I've been followed with the same amount of zeal when I had thousands of dollar at my disposal as when I had two dollars in my pocket. They register my skin tone instead of my buying potential.

It will be one day where I didn't have to bear the burden of being a member of a "poor race in a land full of dollars". It will be one day where I could be a human being first and foremost, a brother to all and a pariah to none. It will be! Someday! Maybe not in America, but somewhere!

The cry for respite from the battle and the need to be simply regarded as a human being does not belong only to the average or less fortunate Black citizen of America. It can even be heard from the mouths of those Black Americans who have ascended to unprecedented heights within American society. Michael Jordan, who is an icon in American society and one of the most highly regarded human beings in the whole world, lends credibility to my testimony in an article tilted, "Michael Jordan in His Own Orbit", which appeared in *GQ* in March of 1989. Jordan said: "I'm happy to be pioneer. When I say, 'Don't think of me as black or white,' all I'm saying is, view me as a person. I know my race."

In looking at the socioeconomic status of someone like Michael Jordan and the socioeconomic status of someone like me, one can see that the need to be regarded as a human being and an individual first is a need that knows no socioeconomic boundary. It seems that in this country that both the white world and the Black world are very focused on making sure that you are considered and defined as either a Black man or Black woman first and foremost on every subject matter.

I don't think that many Black men or Black women have a problem with being a Black man or a Black woman; in fact, many are very proud to be Black men and Black women. I know that I am proud to be Black. I say it loud the way James used to say it, "I'm Black and I'm proud!" But the fact that we are Black men and Black women should not precede our humanity or individuality every single minute of every single day.

That is true for any race and given any circumstance; but the prejudice and discrimination that Black people have always been confronted with in this country on a daily basis makes it especially true when you talk about Blacks and America. The prejudice and discrimination that Blacks face is so ingrained and pervasive in American society that both the white world and the Black world are constantly aware of race.

Race is the subject that is always lurking right beneath every issue. It is the issue that nobody wants to discuss openly and honestly in a multi-racial forum—especially when it means really talking about a redistribution of any type of resources or opportunities. Shhh! Hush your mouth!

Being quiet becomes the order of the day when it's time to talk about and implement real change, because "when you start dealing with real change, you are talking about interfering with those who are in possession of something" (Kwame Nkrumah, *Promise of Power*, 1973). Those in possession can't have those that are not in possession interfering with their possessions. No sir! The haves cooperate in any and all areas where mutual benefits can be obtained; the have-nots don't cooperate in any areas, they merely compete against one another for the crumbs that drop from the table. If you are one of those people who think that the system ain't what it is, then you are merely setting yourself up for a slap in the face with reality.

Another thing that I have found out in my eleven years of playing the game of going back and forth between the two worlds is that both worlds are consistent in their general disapproval of interracial dating. The disapproval is passed out through the glares, stares, and comments of the un-silent majority of both worlds. I analyzed my own situation and the situations of all of those around me. Based on that analysis, I believe that the disapproval of interracial dating seemed to be unavoidable for even the most skilled of those who chose to go back and forth between the two worlds. In my own experiences regarding interracial dating, I found that the two worlds would try to harass me to the point where I would have to choose between the two worlds.

There has been many an issue where I've had to fight simultaneously in both worlds against those members of the two races who disapproved of my choice to date a white woman. Black eyes and white eyes, through disdainful glances and hard stares, sent messages my way letting me know that I should stay with my own kind. Other times, those who were less timid or more vocal would actually have the audacity to voice their unsolicited opinion about the person that I was dating. Depending on my mood, I either ignored them or struck back in a manner that let the person know that neither would I tolerate their interference into *my life* nor would I apologize for loving a white woman.

I knew that my reactions could lead to considerable backlash from both worlds. I realized that I might be an enemy and outcast in both worlds, but I was willing to risk it. Even if that risk meant that I would have to live in a world made up of only two people who wanted to be human beings and individuals instead of races and groups.

When I realized that I could possibly create a destiny of being an outcast in both worlds if I chose to continue to date a white woman, I resisted the thought. I didn't resist it out of fear; I resisted it because I had come to find value in each of the two worlds and I did not want to be locked out of either world. I had discovered that what I found to be rare in one world might be found in abundance in the other world or sometimes I just simply enjoyed the diversity that existed within the two worlds.

I enjoyed the freedom of being able to go back in forth as my mood suited me. I did not want to reject the things that I loved about being Black in order to be accepted in the white world and I did not want to sacrifice the experiences that I found in the white world to be accepted in the Black world. I didn't want to be confined. I wanted to choose on my own what I would maintain and dismiss from my Black experience and what I would absorb and reject from my participation in the white world. I wanted to make those choices so that I could become the best possible person that I could be as determined by my own cognition.

Once again, the intellect of Dr. Du Bois was able to give voice to my feelings nearly one hundred years before I had them. He commented on my "strife" in *The Souls of Black Folk*. He wrote:

> The history of the American Negro is this strife- this longing to attain self-conscious manhood, to merge his double self into a better and truer self. In this merging he wishes neither of the older selves to be lost. He would not Africanize America, for America has too much to

teach the world and Africa. He would not bleach his Negro Soul in a flood of White Americanism, for he knows that Negro blood has a message for the world. He simply wishes to make it possible for a man to be both a Negro and an American, without being cursed and spit upon by his fellows, without having the doors of Opportunity closed roughly in his face.

Both worlds at different points in my life have tried to constrain me to the boundaries that they had set for me as a Black male. In the process, they made it very difficult for me to exist as a human being first. Each world has declared, at times, that I must always be a Black male first and foremost in the face of every question presented to me. Even questions on simple subjects, such as love, were expected to be dealt with on a racial level first.

I thought that the true answers to questions that pertain to the person that one falls in love with were to be found in humanity and being a human being first. I say that because when you began to exalt race over humanity, you will confound the rules of logic every time. You will find that to be true as long as the fact that all races are human continues to be a universal law. Race has to be discussed within the confines of humanity, not outside or above humanity. Humanity must encircle race, not the other way around.

I know that many people in both worlds will always find fault with interracial dating and marriage. Still, I find it comforting to know that one of my mentors, Malcolm X, in his last days on this earth saw the subject of interracial dating and marriage the same way as I see it now. I don't see it the way that I see it due to personal reasons. As I type these words on August 12, 2000, I am neither in an interracial marriage nor am I dating someone outside of my race. I'm in love with a beautiful Black woman that I will give my very next breath of air for if she needed it … even if it meant that I would never breathe again.

I see it the way Malcolm described it in his last television interview before his death because I believe that it is the way that God intended for it to be. However, at the same time, let me make one point clear. Although I don't agree with the racism often associated with interracial dating, I do understand the racism from the African-American perspective. Allow me to explain what I mean.

You see what we are dealing with are two opposing views. You have a spiritual view versus a worldview. The message within the spiritual view is one that instructs individuals to be in the world, but not of the world. This simply means that an individual should base his or her thoughts, beliefs, and actions on rules that stem from religious or spiritual teachings and not the rules of a sinful world. When you do that, it becomes very difficult to justify any racist attitudes or behavior against another human being.

In my religion of Christianity, I can't justify it because the bible instructs me that we are all one in the body of Christ with Jesus being the head of that body. So I can't agree with having a racist attitude or taking racist action against another individual. Therefore I can't be against an interracial marriage. In Christianity, marriage is viewed as a positive thing between a man and a woman who love one another; it doesn't make an exception to that based on race.

On the other hand, when you look at the situation from a worldly perspective, I can see why some Black people get upset about the situation. The message of the world tells individuals that in order to make it in the world they need to rely on their experiences in the world. Well, based on the ways of the world, Blacks should be hesitant to form intimate relationships with white people. First of all, there are enough historical facts concerning the ill treatment of Blacks in America by whites to make Black people distrustful of the intentions of white people for another thousand years. And yes, I know that some whites will argue that there are historical facts that exist that will show ill treatment of whites in America by Black people. But the rebuttal to that argument is simply this; any and all ill treatment of whites in America by Black people is a reaction to the hostile conditions that whites have created for Blacks within this society.

I don't have time to prove this to be true on every specific example of ill treatment of white people by Blacks that a white person might come up with in defending their argument. But I don't have to prove this on every example that a white person may produce because I don't have to go any further than the phrase of "Blacks within this society". Our very presence in this country and how that presence came to be is enough all by itself to prove that Blacks started off reacting to ill treatment by whites. Mr. Charles (the British version of "Mr. Charlie") started all of this idiocy in America. He and his other European friends did the same thing in Africa with colonialism.

The fact that we were brought to the shores of this country in the hulls of slave ships under some of the most wretched conditions that one could ever imagine ... on a journey that spanned all the way across the Atlantic Ocean is proof enough. The fact that we endured such a voyage just so that we could be worked for the duration of what ever natural life that we had within us from "can't see in morning to can't see at night" for no pay is also proof enough. When you throw in the fact that upon arrival we would be lynched, our women raped, and our families ripped apart, disenfranchised, and discriminated against for the next four hundred years; then it becomes an open and shut case.

There is nothing else to prove because we have never had an opportunity to stop reacting to the horrible conditions under which we have been forced to live with from the arrival of the first African slave until this very day. So I understand why some Blacks have a problem with interracial dating or marriage. In fact, I overstand it! Therefore, I can't be completely upset with those Blacks who don't like or accept interracial dating or marriage because they are justified from a worldly perspective. It is only from a spiritual point of view where they are not justified. However, white people—in their disdain of interracial relationships—are justified in neither a spiritual view nor a worldview.

My personal opinion on the subject is a case where my spiritual view is overpowering, but not eliminating, my worldly interpretation. That's the point Malcolm reached before he died. His spiritual view overpowered his worldview, but it did not eliminate it.

Malcolm's last television interview took place with Pierre Berton in Toronto on January 19, 1965 prior to his February 21, 1965 assassination. Berton asked Malcolm did his 1964 trip to Mecca and his contact with the original world of Islam change his views on integration and intermarriage. Malcolm replied:

> I believe in recognizing every human being as a human being, neither white, black, brown, nor red. When you are dealing with humanity as one family, there's no question of integration or intermarriage. It's is just one human being marrying another human being, or one human being living around and with another human being. I must say, though, that I don't think the burden to defend any such position should ever be put on the black man. Because it is the white man collectively who has shown that he is hostile towards integration and intermarriage and towards these other strides of oneness. So, as a black

man, and especially as a black American, I don't think that I would have to defend any stand that I formerly took. Because it's still a reaction to the society and it's a reaction that was produced by white society. And I think that it is the society that produced this that should be attacked, not the reaction that develops among the people who are victims of that negative society.

I suspect that for a person who only knows the popular and fiery image of Malcolm X, his last words on interracial marriage might be a little surprising. I think it's critical that I explain that Malcolm had changed many of his views towards the end of his life. Shortly before his death, Malcolm was undergoing a profound change in his philosophy and how he viewed the world. Those individuals or groups who simply want to dismiss Malcolm as a demagogue or a racist often slight Malcolm's change, but in truth Malcolm was a very complex man who, by the time of his death, had evolved into the type of leader that transcended race. That is not to say that Malcolm was not a race man at the time of his death, but it is to say that he was not a racist at the time of his death.

There is a big difference between a race man and a racist. A racist harbors hate or intolerance for other racial groups while a race man simply demonstrates a great love for his people. Throughout his leadership, Malcolm had always demonstrated a great love for his people, but it was his last days that saw him embrace the idea of all of humanity as one family. The fact that Malcolm did not have more time on this earth to distinguish his new philosophy from some of his old philosophy is one of the things that made his death an even bigger tragedy.

I consider his death, along with the death of Dr. Martin Luther King Jr., to be one of the greatest tragedies in not only African-American History or U.S. History, but in World History. I write those words because we will never be able to measure the full impact that those two Black men might have made. Only God knows what might have been if they would have been allowed to live longer lives. Malcolm's death in 1965 and Martin's death in 1968 embody the prophetic words, written by Dr. Du Bois, in *The Souls of Black Folk*. He wrote: "Throughout history, the powers of single black men flash here and there like falling stars, and die sometimes before the world has rightly gauged their brightness."

Wow! I really went off on a tangent during the last few pages, but it was all for the good of setting a solid foundation that will promote a better understanding of the things to come in this book. My next two years at Southeast High School was where my foundation began in respect to my most significant passing between the two worlds of Black and white.

I had been aware of the existence and differences between what I viewed as a Black world and a white world; but high school was the place that I really began to venture into the white world with the feeling of being an equal. I felt like I had nothing to prove on any level to any white person; I had also ridded myself of the racial chip that I had on my shoulder. As I talk more about the next two years at Southeast High, I think you will understand what I mean by entrance into the white world and why I felt it was important to bring the concepts of "two-ness" to light as it was introduced to me by Dr. Du Bois. You will also be able to see why I discussed interracial dating.

BLACK SOUNDS
& WHITE GIRLS

The first day of school of my junior year was upon me; I was a junior at Southeast High School! I was officially a part of the junior/senior group known as the upper classmen. I was excited and nervous all at the same time. I was excited because of the new opportunity that a new school year brings. I was nervous because I didn't know if that was going to be a good thing or a bad thing for me.

It started off well because everybody could tell that I had lifted weights the whole summer. That was funny to me because I had spent the previous week worrying about my clothes being stolen, but people were noticing my body instead of the clothes that I had on my body. I mean don't get me wrong, it wasn't like I was rippling with muscles or anything, even as a junior, I was still one of the smallest cats in the school. But it was the change from being short and skinny to being short and well defined and somewhat muscular. Everybody was noticing; my friends, the varsity coaches, and the girls. Well, a couple of girls.

The comments that I cherished the most were the comments of the varsity coaches. They had preached the importance of weight training before the start of the summer and they could actually tell that I had taken their advice. My new body sent a message that said—*hey, I'm willing to work to be a part of this.* They seemed to respect my strong commitment because it led to visible improvement.

I carried the positive momentum that I had received from the acknowledgment of my hard work from the coaches all the way up until the varsity tryouts. But the momentum from their comments was stopped dead in its tracks on the first day of tryouts. The first day of tryouts gave me a visual of just how many people wanted to be a Southeast Seminole basketball player that year.

From the end of my freshman year to the point of walking into the gym that day, I had gone from having plans on being the man to just hoping to make the team. I had planned on the best and expected the best instead of planning for the worst and hoping for the best. My glass was always half-full; but when I walked in that gym, it seemed as if someone just walked by and deliberately kicked my glass over. My dreams were spilled all over the hardwood.

After the initial shock of seeing just how many people were interested in playing varsity basketball that year, I decided to give it my absolute best. I just went after it; I knew that my basketball career was hanging in the balance. It was a "do or die" shot.

The ball handling drills that I had concentrated on during the summer showed themselves during the tryouts. That was a major plus because I had to overcome the reputation of not being able to handle pressure that I created for myself during the first few games of last season as a member of the junior varsity squad. At the end of the tryout period, I felt that I had performed well, but I still didn't know which way it was going to go for me. Floyd was supportive and confident just like he had always been, but to be honest with you the only opinion that I wanted to hear at the time was the opinion of the head coach. That opinion came shortly after the tryouts.

He called me into his office, which I interpreted as a very bad sign. He told me that he held a team meeting with all of the seniors on the team and asked them what they thought about keeping fourteen guys on the team as opposed to the traditional twelve guys. (Keeping more than 12 guys had always been a part of the varsity program, but it had caused so many problems coach really didn't want to deal with it again) He explained to me that he informed those guys of who the extra two guys would be and let them decide on the issue. He said some more things after that, but I don't really remember what they were until the words "you're on the team" came out of his mouth.

He added that he was pleased that the seniors decided to keep me on the team because he felt that I had worked hard over the summer and it showed. He went on to say that I probably would not see a lot of playing time. He told me that I couldn't get upset about not playing and that I couldn't become a disruption for the team. I didn't have a problem with the things that he said; I wouldn't have had a problem with very much that he said that day because I had accomplished my initial goal of making the team. I was on the team! Far from being the man, but on the team!

Our team was something that year. I mean don't get me wrong, the varsity teams that we had my freshman and sophomore years were both twenty game winners which is laudable, but 1989-90 team had the makings of something really special. One of the reasons was due to the fact that we had a 6-10 All-American who had already signed a full scholarship during the early signing period to play for North Carolina. Dean Smith himself came to Bradenton, Florida to recruit our All-American center. The team also had six other seniors who had nice skills in their own right. That team accomplished a great deal that year.

We were ranked number one in the state for most of the entire second half of the season and we were cocky about it. We would walk out, not run, with a number one signal on our right hand. We would enter the gym during home games and our fans would make a special sound ... it was a very Black sound and I don't think that there is a correct grammatical spelling, but I will do my best to write it. It was a chant of: "Whuuuuuup! Whuuuuuup! Whuuuuuup!" Most Blacks have heard that sound at one time or another. It was a sound that was made when you thought somebody was about to jump bad about something. Every jump ball of the season, our fans knew that we were about to jump bad on the opposing team. We were bad and we went for bad.

With our number one fingers in the air and the sound of the long drawn out "Whuuuuuups!", the atmosphere was one that said that this is the baddest team in the state and they are all about kickin' tail and taking names. Since I was the shortest man on the team, I was the first to pop through the door to initiate the "Whuuuuuup!" chants. I was thrilled to be the first "Whuuuuuup!" through the door!

A lot of nights that warm-up process was the only time my feet touched the court during the entire game, but that was fine with me. We were winning and I was happy to be a part of what was truly a unique experience.

Because of our resident All-American, we went to a couple of the more prestigious tournaments that included top ranked teams from all over the nation. It was truly first class, at least in my opinion. We stayed in fancy hotels and ate a Red Lobster every night ... for free. Those were things that I had never done at that point in my life. I would learn later in life that some well-to-do white people looked down on restaurants like Red Lobster; but for a kid in the ghetto who liked seafood, Red Lobster was even better than red Kool-Aid.

We had giants in the college basketball world at our school like Dean Smith, Phil Ford, and Dick Vitale. I was having a wonderful time and to top it off there was even a stretch of about six consecutive games where I not only played, but I scored points. We never needed any points that I scored, but they always made me feel good about myself.

I knew that scoring points made me feel better about myself, but I didn't know that other people noticed. The 6-10 All-American, who was quick to cut jokes, announced to the whole basketball study group that I had walked around the school the whole day with my chest stuck out because I had made a lucky shot on a cat from Booker High School. The whole study group thought that was funny. I thought it was funny too, but I had to let him know that it wasn't luck. I hit a double pump scoop shot off the glass in traffic that made the crowd say ooohhhhhh! It was sweet, but it wasn't luck.

Not to be out done, the 6-10 All-American said that he had seen my eyes close when I took the shot. I told him even if that was true, which it wasn't, he wished that he were good enough to make a shot like that with his eyes closed.

We finished that regular season undefeated in the state of Florida with our only losses coming at the hands of three out-of- state teams that we ran into at the prestigious Christmas tournaments. I think that two of them were out of New York City ... maybe Brooklyn Lincoln or Bronx Tolentine or something like that. I think the other was a Kentucky team with a white shooting guard that blazed us. I don't know; there were so many teams there that it's a little fuzzy in my mind.

Still, it was an honor and a privilege to be on that 1989-90 Southeast High basketball team. I remember being treated like the cock of the walk for much of that season. It was a first class experience. However, the end of the season was somewhat disappointing because we lost in our district championship game to a team that included three players who would be All-Americans the very following year. Despite that unexpected and abrupt end, I felt good about our experience and the things that we accomplished.

My junior year brought me something else besides basketball to feel good about. I mentioned earlier that I had received some comments from girls about the new body that I had come back with as a result of working out the whole summer. That was a new experience for me because I had been considered cute before from a couple of girls, but it was never enough to get me anywhere with any of them. Cute meant that you weren't ugly, but you still weren't going to get any real play or serious rap.

Well after receiving a few comments, I felt that I had a chance to improve upon my past track record with the ladies. Besides, I was an upper classmen now. As a freshman and sophomore, I watched all the girls flock toward the upper classmen. For two years, I watched that happen. When I say all the girls flocked toward the upper classman, I do mean all the girls. The freshmen and sophomore girls were dating juniors and seniors too. Now that I was an upper classman, I felt like it was my turn.

There was this one Black girl who I thought had to be the finest girl in the world. She was a bad mama jama with a brick house body! She was built; she was stacked with everything that a woman needed to get a man. She would have made Carl Carlton and the Commodores proud. I was having a pretty good day one day, so I decided to ask her for her phone number and she gave it to me. I acted cool on the outside, but I was in utter shock that she actually granted my request.

I asked myself a thousand questions on why she had given me the phone number. Was it the new muscles (she had commented on them)? Was it because I was a junior and she was a sophomore? Was it because she thought I was more than cute? Was it because she thought I was nice? Was it because I was on the number one ranked basketball team in the state? She knew that I didn't play a lot, but I was on the team—I knew that sometimes that was enough.

I never came up with a satisfactory answer, but whatever the reason was didn't matter all that much. What mattered was she actually gave me the number. She gave me the number! In high school you got player points for having the courage to ask for a number in the wide open in front of your boys. You got extra player points if it actually worked. You got an extra player card if the girl was super fine. I got the whole deck that day.

The whole key was to act cool no matter what the outcome was. If you didn't get it, then act like it didn't matter anyway. Act like you did her a favor by asking for her number. If it did work, then act like you never had a doubt that she was going to give to you; but still act like you did her a favor by asking for her number. Like I said, act cool, no matter what the outcome was.

I called her over the next few weeks and we had good conversations. She even called me a few times. But she would never give me the opportunity that I needed to show her that I was real deal serious about being her boyfriend. I think that one of the reasons was that she was a bona fide brick house and she had a lot of guys who wanted to be her real deal serious boyfriend. I knew some of them and most of them went to Southeast. I say most because a bona fide brick house was never confined to the guys at one high school. A bona fide brick house usually had guys from at least two or three counties trying to push up on her with talk game.

The guy that she ended up choosing was a 6-5 superstar small forward from Sarasota High School. After she did that, I wondered if I ever had a real chance in the first place. I was closer to 5-5 and I was nowhere near being a superstar. I didn't even have a car. I was just a nice guy, and most nice guys really did finish last in high school. To this day, I think that if it weren't for practicality, that most chicks will tell you that nice is boring.

I didn't actually get the outcome that I had desperately wished for on that day when I decided to ask her for her phone number, but we became what most nice guys and brick houses become—good friends. However, all was not lost, because as that situation was not materializing another one was developing.

The developing situation was one that I had never encountered before in my entire life—not on a personal level. There was this white girl that I had seen around and I might have said a few words to her in passing in the halls, but I don't remember ever having any intentions of trying to initiate any kind of relationship with her. As a matter of fact, I don't even remember how I started interacting with her on that kind of level. One day the thought just hit me. I realized that if I did have any intentions on initiating some kind relationship with her that she wouldn't be opposed to the idea. It wasn't until after I came to that realization that I started to think about it.

Interracial dating was something that was common enough in our school that the students were not going to stone you to death if you decided to be involved in that sort of thing. My uncle was married to a white woman, but to be honest, I had always thought of it as taboo. I say that because I had heard all the things that Black people said about interracial couples when interracial couples were not around.

I thought about it as taboo when I was alone, but when I was with her the only thing that I thought about was how much I liked her and how pretty she was. I was seriously thinking about pursuing the situation, especially since my bona fide brick house was wearing Sarasota Sailor t-shirts to school. Still, I was hesitant about pursuing an interracial relationship. Her color was the thing that I thought about the most, but her age was also something that I thought about. She had a birthday that fell late in the year and my birthday fell early in the year; that made it seem that I was so much older than she was. She was born in 1975 and I was born in 1973, but with the birthdays as they were, it seemed like I was three years older than she was instead of two. Nonetheless, even with the issue of race and her age on my mind, I decided to test my theory and see if she was interested in a relationship with me.

The truth of the matter was if I had not asked her, she would have asked me. Before I could get the question out of my mouth good, she was already saying yes. It was really that simple. That's how we became a couple.

I had to learn about being a couple in high school because I had never had a girlfriend that you were supposed to hold hands with, supposed to walk to and from class with, and where kissing was the rule instead of the exception. After a few kisses, I found out that I liked being a couple. I liked her even more than I thought I would. I began to like her so much that I thought I would tell her so, but when the words came out they transformed themselves into I love you. Oops—too late! I said it. I was a sucker for love at such a tender age.

I couldn't take it back; the longer I thought about it, the more I decided that I didn't want to take it back. Not long after I said it to her, the reciprocal in kind was returned unto me from her lips and that's when our special relationship really began. We were each other's first loves. And while we were happy with our relationship, I did start to notice others who were not so happy about the new zebras walking down the hall holding hands.

There were a few Black girls who let me know that they were not at all happy with my decision to date a white girl. I also noticed some different reactions from some of the white folks. I expected the reactions from the white folks, but the disapproving comments from the Black girls were totally unexpected. They were unexpected because the Black girls that made the comments seemed liked they could have cared less about my love life before I started dating a white girl. They had never given me the time of day before they saw me with a white girl. I thought they were being totally unfair. I didn't know how or why a girl who had never taken one second of her time to acknowledge that I ever existed cared about who I was dating.

It didn't matter, I had my mind made up that no matter what criticism I received and who I received it from that I was going to do what made me happy. She apparently must have reached the same conclusion because she received criticism as well. I don't know if she received criticism from people at school right off the bat, but I was quite aware of the fact that she did receive criticism at home from her family.

Her father seemed to be the one who was most opposed to the situation, but that's not to diminish the disapproval of the other family members. They were all against the idea, but he was the most powerful figure in her household and he had the most to say about it. Once he found out that I was Black, he tried to prevent her from talking to me and tried to keep a strict record of where she was and who she was with. My Black skin was all that he could see; nothing else mattered to him. My skin was my sin when it came to his creamy complexioned daughter. He didn't want his milk mixing with my coffee.

He couldn't see that I was in honor classes and well liked by most of the faculty at the school. He couldn't see that I was a nice guy that only wanted the best for his daughter. He couldn't see any of that, but he could see that his daughter was in love with a Black guy. I could also see that his daughter was in love with a Black guy because my girl never let the pressure of her family, or anybody else for that matter, sway her opinions or feelings about our relationship. She seemed to be ready to defy the world for our relationship.

Her love was penetrating, pure, and innocent. I reciprocated her affection with love from the deepest part of my soul. The love that she sent flowing toward me had to be a strong love in order for me to feel it the way that I did because I wasn't an individual who was accustomed to receiving a lot of love. My childhood experiences had placed a hard shell around my vulnerable emotions, but she cut right through that shell like a hot knife through butter.

Another thing that I wasn't accustomed to was mixing in so deep with the mainstream white student population. My new relationship, my membership on the varsity basketball team, and the fact that my honors classes were predominately white all came together to place me in the mainstream of white folks like I had never been before. But I found out that I didn't mind it all that much. After awhile, I thought it was kind of fun, so I went with it like it was nothing. It was definitely a lot easier than carrying around a big chip on my shoulder and a mind full of hatred toward white people like I had done in both elementary and middle school. So I mingled among the mainstream and had a good time with my new world, but I soon began to realize that as I moved further into my new world that my old world was watching me.

The world of Black folk and Black culture was watching me to see how far I planned to go into the white world. The Black student body kept letting me know that it was one thing to date a white girl, but it was quite another to become what was termed a sell-out by occupants of the Black world. The former wasn't necessarily kosher, but the latter was unforgivable. They wanted to see if I changed my talk, if I changed my walk, or if I changed my attitude. I tell you that if any of those elements about me would have changed in the course of my journey into the mainstream, then I would have been regarded as a total sell-out.

A total sell-out defined in the Black world was anybody who gave up or severely compromised established Black patterns of behavior or thought in an effort to gain acceptance by the white or mainstream world. I was hip to the game, so I went out of my way to let the Black folks know that I would always be the same. By doing that I kept my credibility and acceptance into the most intimate circles of most of the Black folk at the school, but I must admit that I did lose the endorsement of a few who refused to forgive me for what they saw as going beyond the point of no return.

Conversely, the white or mainstream world was watching me too. It was watching to see if I would change my talk, if I would change my walk, or if I would change my attitude. It was watching because those things determined just how far they would let me in considering the fact that I was all ready breaking the rules by dating a white girl. It was sizing me up in order to see if I was different, the fundamental question was: "is he like the rest of his kind or is he different". I was aware of their stealth attempts to gather this information before reaching their verdict, so I gave them what they wanted. I learned their rules on the fly and I played by them when in their presence. By doing this I gained acceptance from a great many of the white folks at our school.

I had watched both worlds watch me. I watched them from a third eye that belonged to my third conscious. My third conscious was neither Black nor white; it was just human. As if it were a card game, I let each world play its hand before I played my card. My play was always a reaction to their play.

I had Black cards that I played in the Black world and white cards that I played in the white world. I was becoming a master of both decks so to speak. I never dealt the cards; I just played them. I played the cards in a manner that would allow me to fit into both worlds. I was playing a dangerous game. I was playing two hands from two decks too often; my "twoness" had begun. I was ready to either prove or disprove the words of F. Scott Fitzgerald:

> The test of a first-rate intelligence is the ability to hold two opposed ideas in the mind at the same time, and still retain the ability to function. (F. Scott Fitzgerald, *The Crack-Up*, 1945)

If I had played the game of academics as well as I had played the dual social worlds; then I would have had a much more successful junior year. I received an F in each of my two junior year semesters, but the comparisons of the two semesters end there. The F during the first semester was the only blight on what was an otherwise respectable grading period. The second semester was just bad all the way around.

My GPA for the first semester of my junior year was 2.86. That wasn't so bad, but my report card was stained with an F in Algebra II. The F in Algebra II wasn't legitimate; I'll explain what happened with that class real soon. If you take that F away, then I would have done fairly well considering the problems that I had at the end of my sophomore year.

The reason that I did better the first semester of my junior year than I did the second semester of my sophomore year had to be attributed to a more stable home life. I was able to concentrate more when I was in class and my grades improved. I say that because I still wasn't doing any homework—at least not at home. Everything that I did was in school. As a matter of fact, I still wasn't taking any books home with me. I had stopped trying to fool myself; I knew that it just wasn't in me to do schoolwork outside of school. I had to deal with life outside of school, and I couldn't get any life lessons out of the books that they gave me.

Despite my unconventional approach to my studies, I felt like I was much closer to being back on track academically. Not counting my Algebra II performance, I pulled down a 3.33 GPA for the first semester. However, any attempts at an academic recovery were quickly derailed by my second semester performance.

The second semester was atrocious. I received another F, this time it was in Accounting and it was legitimate. It surprised the teacher because I got an A during the first semester. But the F wasn't a surprise to me. Anybody who has ever taken accounting knows that it is a cumulative course where everything that you learn builds on the things that you have learned earlier. The simple concepts that I learned in the first semester were being replaced with complex concepts that required you to study outside of class. Anything outside of class was out for me, so when it came time to take the test I couldn't use my head to figure out the answers like I did during the first semester.

The tests of the second semester required much more than just my natural sense, which had served me so well during the first semester. I knew that I was going to get an F. I did care, but not enough to start taking books home to study and to do homework. Besides, I knew that I would be the only one at my house who even knew about the grade.

There was no one at Grandma Mary's house that had ever asked to see my report card. That practice wasn't just limited to my paternal grandmother's house; there was no one on either side of my family that ever asked to see my report card. My grades were only for me because there was no one else who asked about them. And that was cool with me; I had been signing my own report cards since I was a little kid. I had never had any parental or guardian supervision as far as my school performance was concerned. So when I got the F and the 1.85 GPA, the only person that I had to answer to was my basketball coach.

I didn't anticipate having to answer to him because I had never given an account or a reason why to anybody. He really surprised me when he told me that he needed to talk me to about my grades. At first, I couldn't understand why he would want to talk to me, but I figured that the only reason that I had to talk with him was that my grades were too close to placing me on the ineligible for athletic participation list.

In Manatee County, no athlete would be able to participate in athletic competition if they did not maintain a GPA of 1.5 or better. My 1.85 placed me closer than I had ever been. In addition to that reason, my coach knew that I was in honor courses. He knew that I had a good head on my shoulders and he didn't want to see me waste my potential.

He and I talked about the fact that I had barely succeeded in my make-up attempts of Chemistry I Honors and Geometry. I had failed those two courses during the second semester of my sophomore year. I made them up during my second semester of my junior year, but I barely escaped my second attempt at learning the difference between ionic and covalent bonds in Chemistry I Honors with a D grade. Geometry wasn't much better; I was thankful that Mr. Pythagoras let me out of there with a C grade.

We talked about the F in Accounting and in Algebra II. We agreed that I could just write accounting off, but he told me that I would need the Algebra II grade if I went to college. So we outlined a game plan where I would take Algebra II again during two summer school sessions in an effort to make up that grade. He said that if I didn't, then it might impact what courses I started off with in college.

His advice on college was the first time that anybody had ever talked to me about college from an academic perspective and it made me start to really think about college. Sure I had thoughts about college before, but they were always centered on athletics. I had completed three years of high school and I had watched many different athletes from Southeast High get athletic scholarships to this school or that school during those three years. I had taken for granted as a freshman, that Floyd and I would also sign a college hoops scholarship at the end of our four years at Southeast. However, with all the problems that I had at home, in the classroom, and on the court during my sophomore and junior years, the idea of college for me had just faded into the background.

I didn't replace the idea of a college future with any other ideas for the future. The future for me was dark, uncertain, and scary. I literally did not know what I was going to do with my life. I had no direction. I knew that if I didn't get an athletic scholarship that nobody in my family could afford to send me to college. I knew that if I didn't go to college that it would be very difficult to succeed in life.

When I really sat down and thought about the situation my feelings were ambiguous. There were some days that I didn't care about my lack of future plans. On those days I just went with the flow of enjoying being a relatively popular high school student who seemed to be doing just as well as, if not better than, the next fellow. Those were the good days, but there were bad days too. Sometimes it really bothered me that I didn't know what I was going to do with my life after high school. On those days my whole life came crashing down on me.

I lived a life with no parents. I lived a life with no stability. I lived a life that had been one struggle after the next since birth. I realized that my whole life was a life of diminishing chances and I had no one to talk to about it. I felt like I was headed nowhere fast.

The day that I failed Algebra II was a day when my life was crashing down on me. I entered the classroom and I sat down. I had no intention of paying attention, but I didn't have any plans on being a disruption either. I had no plans at all. It was one of those days where I was just there. I was neither a positive force, nor a negative force. I was just there. I wasn't participating in the Black world or white the world; I was a member of that universal world of despair that one sometimes feels when life treats them unkind. I was full of despair and devoid of faith. That's the kind of mood I was in, but before I go on, I need to give you some background on my relationship with my Algebra II teacher.

We didn't have a good relationship and I don't know which came first, me not liking her class or her not liking me. In reality, they probably contributed to one another. Although I didn't like her class, I had no real problem with her, but maybe she couldn't separate herself from her class.

It was pretty obvious that I didn't like the class because every day I did the same thing. I came in, sat down, shut-up, and tried not to get called on to answer any questions. I did that in all classes that I found no personal reason to pay attention. On most days, she seemed to realize that I was content with taking up space and she left me alone. Still, it didn't take long for me to notice that she didn't particularly care for my approach to her class. I accepted that and said to myself that if she could accept the fact that I wasn't going to be an active participant in the class; then I could accept her seeming dislike for me.

Well, on the particular day that I am about to describe, the fragile truce that I thought we had between the two of us went awry. I came in, sat down, and shut-up. But as I had mentioned earlier, my life was crashing down strong on my head on that particular day. I felt darker than blue.

In order to make a long story short; there was a bee in the front of the classroom. She was already in the process of standing in front of the class going over the homework when she saw the bee buzzing around. She really began to panic in a way that was sort of funny. After the bee was killed, she told the whole class that she was allergic to bees; but prior to finding out that she was allergic to bees, some of the members of the class thought that the spectacle that she had made of the situation was pretty funny. She was already a pale lady, but her fright from the bee seemed to make her turn three shades whiter and she was flailing her arms wildly in an attempt to keep the bee away from her body. She looked like a pale white lady who had caught the Holy Ghost.

I wasn't one of those people who thought that it was funny; on that day, I didn't think anything was funny. Still, after she calmed herself down, she lit into me with a verbal assault about how I thought it was so funny and how I thought that I was so cool and so smart. I thought that was interesting, since I was one of the few people who had not even cracked a smile. She went on and on and on. On any other day, I would have just accepted her attack on me as just treatment for the way that I treated her class. But not that day! Her last comment was something about how arrogant I was … but before she could finish her next accusation I just snapped. I had had it!

She had made antagonizing remarks about me before, but today was not a day that I was in the mood for those kinds of comments. Especially, since I was one of the few class members who had not reacted to the situation at all. I stood up from my seat and began to angrily refute her charges. I let her know that I had not laughed at her and that I didn't think that I was so smart or so cool. I told her that if she thought I was arrogant, then that was her opinion. She was stunned at first—my voice had always been soft, but it had a strange inflection when I was angry. Nevertheless, she recovered quickly. She yelled: "Get out of my classroom and go to the office!" She kept yelling that over and over.

I mean in hindsight, I guess that was not such an unreasonable request. But at that moment she might as well had said solve for X, Y, and Z squared in a quadratic equation because I was incapable of honoring that request. I wasn't going anywhere unless she felt like she could make me leave the class and take me to the office herself. With fire streaming from her nostrils, she said that she would call the dean. With flames flaring from my own nostrils, I snorted back: "No! *You* put me out of the class! *You* take me to the office!" I yelled that repeatedly as I began to take steps toward where she was standing. Her combativeness momentarily changed to fear, but before I could get any closer a classmate whom I had known since sixth grade bolted from his seat to grab me. I'm glad that he did because I was ready to "float like a butterfly" and "sting like a bee".

After he grabbed me and I allowed him to pull me toward the door, her fear changed back to combativeness as she shouted words that I was too angry to hear at that point. I told my middle school friend that I would be okay and that he could go back to class because I wasn't going to the office. I was totally unafraid of any consequences that might have resulted from my actions.

On that day, I figured that there was nothing worse than my own past and my diminished life chances. In my mind, there wasn't anything that anyone could have made me face that was darker than my future. I was a poor Black ghetto child with no parents, poor and uneducated family members, and no idea what I was going to do with my life. I wouldn't say that that attitude and perception of my life made me overly aggressive in a neutral environment, but it definitely gave me a lower tolerance level in a threatening or confrontational environment. I say that because as I walked toward that teacher, I literally did not care what happened to me … or to her.

I'm just relieved that my classmate prevented the situation from escalating to a higher level than it did. He was a Black guy who always acted way older than his age from the first day that I met him. He carried a briefcase instead of a backpack around when we were in sixth grade. I was never more appreciative of his maturity than I am right now, because who knows what could have resulted from that situation. It definitely could have turned out a lot worse than it actually did. My mature classmate became senior class president of the class of 1991 during our senior year. I definitely made sure that I voted for him.

As it turned out, the front office had received complaints regarding my Algebra II teacher's attitude from other students. That was a big plus for me. When the dean combined the previous complaints from the other students with the fact that I had never gotten into any other kind of trouble before, he decided that leniency was the right method of punishment. It didn't hurt that I had an excellent reputation among most of the faculty and staff; I didn't receive any consequences other than a strong recommendation to withdraw from the class. It was lenient punishment because it could have been a lot worse. However, it still hurt me because I ended up with an F in Algebra II instead of the low C that I would have gotten if I stayed in the class. Because of my withdrawal, I had to attend summer school for the very first time in my life before the start of my senior year.

SAY IT IN MY FACE

At first I really hated the fact that I would have to attend summer school because it was something that I had never done before; but once I got there, it turned out to be fun. I'm sure that the fact that Floyd was in my class had a lot to do with the fun that I had. I don't remember why Floyd was taking the course, because he was an honor student and summer school wasn't a part of his summer protocol either. So we probably both appreciated each other during those two summer sessions.

We talked to each other about our senior year basketball plans more than we paid attention in class, but I still managed to get an A for the first session and a B for the second session. I remember wanting to make good grades for both sessions because I felt like I had to redeem myself as an honor student and plus I was thinking about college more than I had ever thought about it before.

Now that my back was up against that senior year wall, I knew that I would really have to step up my performance in the classroom and on the court in a big way if I wanted to get a college education. I had one year to make it all work. I knew that performance was the only thing that would take me where I was trying to go. I also knew that I had the ability in both the classroom and on the court; I simply needed to apply myself to achieve success.

The concept of applying one's ability in a situation for improved chances of success seems like such a simple concept, but I tell you that far too many of our children do not have a fundamental understanding of that concept. And it is not their fault. Too many of them start out in life without the proper support from the adults in their life and they never even recognize that they have any ability. But for those who do recognize it, the lack of proper adult guidance or support may lead them down a path that doesn't value the application of their ability.

If we expect our children to have even a fighting chance, then it is of the utmost importance that we create environments where they understand that they have to apply themselves in order to succeed. It is a simple message that not only tells our children that they have ability, but to apply that ability. This message is nothing new; I'm only passing on the words and wisdom of Dr. Benjamin Mays. Dr. Mays was an educator, a Baptist minister, and the mentor of Dr. Martin Luther King Jr. In his 1971 book titled *Born to Rebel*, Dr. Mays exhorted: "You have the ability, now apply yourself." We must exhort our kids today the same way that Dr. Mays exhorted yesterday.

I applied myself in a lot of areas during the summer of 1990. I got a job working for a leading area newspaper selling subscriptions door to door. The reason that I took that job was the fact that they advertised no transportation needed. That was important because I didn't have a way to get to and from anywhere let alone a job that would depend on me to be there when I said I would be there. It proved to be a wise decision for me because I was good at the job. One of the things that helped me the most was my ability to connect with the different people that I encountered.

The experience of bounding back and forth between the Black world and the white world during my junior year proved to be invaluable. I sold subscriptions in rich white neighborhoods as well as I did in poor Black neighborhoods. And since our pay was based on commission, that was to my advantage. I applied my ability to appeal to both groups to achieve success. Soon I was the top producer on our crew and received the top-level pay that was reserved only for those who sold a designated number of subscriptions.

I worked about twenty-five hours a week and brought home, after taxes, over $200 a week. Considering the fact that I spent at least twenty percent of the twenty-five hours riding in the van, I was making somewhere around $10/hr for actually selling subscriptions. In 1990, $10/hr was excellent money for a high school kid.

My determination was not limited to the classroom or the job that summer, I also concentrated my efforts on becoming the best basketball player that I could be. I knew that if I could do that, while hitting the books, then I would improve my chances of going to college. The success that I had on my new job allowed me to be flexible with my schedule when I needed to be away pursuing basketball opportunities. Those opportunities included a weeklong basketball camp at the University of South Florida and an AAU team that included many of the county's top players.

The camp at USF was a team camp that included the people who were expected to play on the varsity team during the 1990-91 season. I had been the only junior point guard on the team last year, now I was the only senior point guard on the team. But there were two very good junior point guards right behind me. The fact that they were juniors and I was a senior didn't mean much because they were both thought of highly by the coaching staff. That put me in a position where I had to prove myself in order to be the starting point guard. I knew that the camp at USF was my first serious test.

Coach awarded me the starting point guard at the camp because I had believed in his system and worked hard. I sat on the bench without complaining during the 1989-90 season and practiced hard everyday. Those were attributes that he endorsed and now he was giving me my opportunity to show him that I could get the job done. I respected him for that because it was a fair situation. However, he also let me know in no uncertain terms that I had two point guards behind me that he felt were very capable of being starters. I don't know if he was expecting the added pressure to make me fold or what, but I wasn't thinking about who was behind me; I was just focused on being able to blow by any defender standing in front of me.

I performed well at camp against some of the best guards in the Tampa Bay area and we had a good camp overall as a team. I think that both areas were a pleasant surprise for coach. I think I was a surprise because I had never been seriously tested on the varsity level and my sophomore season on the junior varsity level was disappointing. I think that the team's performance was a pleasant surprise because we had lost our 6-10 All-American to the University of North Carolina along with six other seniors.

The only player on our new team who had started any games during the 1989-90 season was Floyd. We also had one 6-7 rising junior who had seen some significant playing time. The rest of us were inexperienced as far as varsity game time was concerned. For the most part, when it came to varsity game time, we were a group of guys who were more accustomed to sitting on the bench than lining up for the opening tip-off. So like I said, I think that the coaching staff was a little surprised at my personal performance and the team's performance. But they also knew that one basketball camp did not make a season; the jury was still out on me and the jury was still out on our team.

I think it was appropriate that that was the camp that I learned the acronym for fear. The acronym, as it was explained in the camp literature, read: **F**alse **E**vidence **A**ppearing **R**eal. I say it was appropriate because it gave me a chance to prove that the evidence against me was false. Circumstances had only made it appear to be real. I showed that I could get the job done as a starting point guard of a winning team. The U.S.F. Basketball Camp was the first place where I crossed my critics over and left them and their opinions without merit. I knew from that point on that they didn't have any power over me. I knew that I had the power to triumph over fear.

My next basketball opportunity came to me in the form of an AAU (Amateur Athletic Union) basketball team. I had played AAU the previous summer and we won the state competition for our age group, but most of the credit for that success was due to the 6-10 All-American on our team. That team was made up of some top players from the surrounding area and my high school coach coached it. I didn't figure very prominently on that team, so I decided that I wanted to get a different experience playing under someone other than my high school coach during the 1990 summer.

It wasn't that I disagreed with the role that I played on his team last summer; I just wanted to get a different experience under someone who would judge me by what I was doing today without being influenced so heavily by what role I had played in the past. The fact that Floyd was trying out for the new team was also a huge factor in my decision to try out for what turned out to be somewhat of a Manatee County all-star team. Floyd and I tried to play together as often as we could.

I say it turned out to be a county all-star team because all the top players from the other county schools were at the try-outs. That was a little intimidating for me at first because my hoop resume couldn't touch most of the other guards who were at the try-outs. A couple of them were three-year starters for their teams and leading scorers for their teams. If a stranger had looked at the basketball credentials of the other guards versus my basketball credentials prior to the start of the try-outs, then I would have been laughed out of the gym. And I knew that, but I made up my mind that I was going to compete at my highest level in order to make that team.

I took every play seriously and I didn't back down from the other guard's superior reputations. After I made the team the coach told me that he admired my toughness. That comment meant a lot to me and gave me the confidence to continue to compete at a high level. Once the group was dwindled down to just the guys who would be on the team, the jockeying for starting positions began and I was determined to stake my claim. I must admit that I was a little skeptical, because there were two point guards who had both been starters and top scorers on their respective high school teams.

The skepticism that I felt only came through when I was off the court, because when I was on the court I used all the energy that I had in my body to do the best that I could to stake my right to the starting position. After a couple weeks, the coach pulled me aside and told me that I was his starting point guard because he liked the way that I played the game. He said that he couldn't put his finger on what it was that I brought to the table, but he knew that good things happened when I was out there on the court. His words were the best compliment that I ever received regarding basketball, because that's how I felt about myself. I did what it took to help the team win, not to make myself look good. The tougher the situation, the better I played. The more others choked up, the bolder I became. I was all about winning.

His decision to start me over two more well-known point guards in the area was a huge confidence builder for me because someone other than Floyd was saying: hey that kid can play basketball! It also helped me in terms of my quest to remain the starting point guard for the upcoming 1990-91 season at Southeast.

We had to beat the team that my high school coach from Southeast was coaching in order to advance to state competition. His team was made of all the up and coming Southeast players with the exception of Floyd, a rising junior point guard (he was one of the guards who was rumored as a possible starter if I couldn't handle the job), and myself. Considering what I already told you about how our up and coming 1990-91 team was a young team, you might say that the county all-star team should have easily defeated the Southeast team. But there was only one thing that I left out. The 6-10 All-American who was on his way to North Carolina was still young enough to compete in AAU competition. So between his McDonald's All-American game and the Dapper Dan Roundball Classic, he played with the Southeast AAU team.

We knew that we would have to beat the Southeast team in order to advance to the state competition. We knew that because the general opinion in the high school basketball circles was any team that had the 6-10 All-American became an automatic favorite. The guy had only averaged 35 point per game, been selected as Mr. Basketball for the state of Florida during his senior year, and personally recruited by Dean Smith to play basketball for the University of North Carolina in the fall of 1990. By 1994, he would be the 16th pick overall in the NBA draft. The dude was phenomenal on the basketball court.

We had all the best rising senior players in the county, but people were not seriously expecting us to be able to beat the Southeast based team led by the All-American. They expected us to get to the title game, but they didn't expect us to beat them.

The inevitable match-up between their team, which was really my teammates for the up and coming season, and my temporary county all-star team came to pass just as everybody had expected. I knew that that game had double implications for me. My performance either positive or negative was going to impact my standing with both teams. If I played poorly, then it would make both coaches doubt whether I could handle being their starting point guard; my temporary coach would doubt it for the rest of the summer and my high school coach would doubt it for the up and coming basketball season. However, if I played well, then in their minds I would live to dribble another day as a starting point guard. So, I had a lot to lose if I played bad that day; but I chose to look at it as an opportunity.

Before the game I told myself that I deserved to be a starter and then I went out onto the court and showed that I deserved to be a starter. I knew that I couldn't confuse efforts with results; I had to produce. My maternal grandmother had taught me that you could always show'em better than you can tell'em. Success in life is based on show and prove, because everybody is either a critic or from Missouri. I was cool with that, so I did what I had to do.

Both my high school coach and my AAU coach told me that I played a great game after we defeated the 6-10 All-American led Southeast team. My team had won that game, but I think that I won an even bigger personal battle. I played like the best point guard in the building that day, just as one would expect from the starting point guard for the winning team, and I felt good about it.

I felt good because on my AAU team I had started the game ahead of people who were "supposed to be" better than me and I had played well enough for our team to win. I was a big reason that our team did win. I felt good because I outplayed a talented Southeast guard who, from the Southeast coaching staff's perspective, was breathing down my neck for my starting point guard position for the up and coming varsity season. I felt good because I knew that I could get the job done.

That game was the highlight of our AAU summer season because we had good and bad times as a team after that win over the Southeast squad, but I think that for me it was even more than the highlight of the summer AAU season. It was a moment when I knew that I could play basketball against some of the best guys that our area had to offer. It was a moment when I proved to myself that I could reach deep down inside of myself when all the chips were down and come up with an effort that I could be proud of no matter what the outcome. It was a moment that I knew that I could beat the odds. And that was the feeling that I took with me into my senior year at Southeast High School. I was ready to rise up against the challenge of all rivals—just like Rocky running up those stairs.

I was going to beat the odds. I wasn't going to have a repeat of what happened to me on the basketball court during my junior varsity season and I was not going to be an underachiever in the classroom like I had been during my sophomore and junior years. Despair wasn't going to get the best of me. I decided that I was going to give it my very best shot and let the chips fall where they may. If they didn't fall my way, then it wasn't going to be because I didn't give it my all.

When I was a small kid growing up in Palmetto, I had gotten into a couple of fights and seen many more. All of them started off with some sort of trash talk; that was just a part of it. However, that talk didn't necessarily mean that there was going to be a fight that day unless one of the participants had enough audacity to say something directly in the face of the person to whom he was talking. If the target of the taunt wanted to save his reputation, then he would usually warn the aggressor to get out of his face or else. If the aggressor ignored the warning, then the person was left with no other alternative than to go for what he knew in the knuckle game. To do anything less meant a daily dose of getting punked.

There was more credibility in fighting and losing than there was in being afraid. The quickest way to be proved a coward was to let a person put you down directly in your face and not do anything about it. Fighting words from a distance rarely led to fights, but fighting words said in your face had to lead to a mandatory standing eight count for somebody.

Going into my senior year, big bad life was standing two inches away from my face telling me what it was going to do to me. Popping its gums about how it was going to deny me opportunity and smear my face in my own failures. It was saying those things right in my face! I had no choice but to knuckle up and go for what I knew! Win, lose, or draw; it was going to be a fight. Me and life were going to go toe-to-toe; backing down wasn't in my protocol.

HOW YA LIKE ME NOW

I hit the campus the first day of school full of confidence. My senior year was do or die and my last chance to dance, but I was ready. I told myself that I could erase the previous two years of academic underachievement with one last strong effort in the classroom during my last two semesters. I knew that was going to be a task easier said than done since I still had to take courses like Trigonometry, English IV Honors, Economics, and Psychology. I had even signed up for a prep course to help me when I took the SAT.

I hadn't thought enough ahead to take the test sooner in order to give myself a chance to improve if I needed a better score, so I signed up for the prep class to give myself a better chance of getting a good score on the first go round. That decision would later prove to be an invaluable move, not because of the SAT preparation, but because of the teacher that I met while taking the class. Her name was Mrs. Debra Valcarcel. I will talk about her a little later, so remember that name.

As the semester progressed, the time for basketball season moved closer and closer. Floyd and I were excited and I knew that the rest of our teammates were excited, but the local media was billing our upcoming season as a failure before we ever played our first game. They were saying that we would have to go through a rebuilding year because we lost our All-American and a host of other seniors.

The reporters shamelessly asked the question of who were the no-name players that would replace the talented seniors who led Southeast to hold the number one ranking in the state. Our coach told us to disregard the talk in the newspapers and any other talk that suggested that we were not going to have a successful season. He told us that we didn't rebuild at Southeast High School. He told us that we reloaded!

Oh, it was a great line and the whole team fell for it hook, line, and sinker. I would go so far as to say that everybody at the school who was interested in basketball believed in the reload statement. I really don't remember anybody, outside of the press, telling me that they didn't think that we had enough talent to win over twenty basketball games (twenty games was a benchmark for a successful high school basketball season at Southeast).

The reloading concept did a lot to boost the confidence of the team, the faculty, and the students, but it did little to shield me from the doubts that some of the Black students had about my ability to keep my starting position throughout the entire season. A lotta cats were looking for a repeat of what happened to me during my junior varsity year.

The rumors started during the summer at the local park in the neighborhood where we all gathered to play basketball and they continued into the start of the school year. As a matter of fact, they didn't stop until the second game of the season. Sometimes things were said directly to me, sometimes things would get back to me like they got back to Glady's and Marvin; "I Heard It Through the Grapevine". No matter how it got back to me, whether direct of indirect, it seemed like it was a lot of talk concerning the situation.

The word on the street and at Southeast High School was that Quincy Smith wouldn't be the starting point guard for long. I understood that most of the Blacks that were talking about the subject were basing their opinions and predictions on my sophomore basketball season. I can't say that I blamed them for feeling the way that they did; I had not really proved that I could handle a starting point guard position at Southeast High.

I had had a really great basketball summer among some of the best players in the county coming into my senior year, but I had never done it at Southeast. In addition to my lack of proof that I could get it done at Southeast, the two junior point guards behind me were talented and would have been starters on many other teams around the area. So, for the most part, I could really understand why people were skeptical. Still, there was something additional in some of the comments that were coming from a smaller segment of the Black student population. I didn't like the extra content because I thought that it was based on personal reasons more than past performance issues.

That smaller segment of the Black student population supported their opinions and predictions with the same facts that the other Black students used to validate their opinions and predictions, but the extra had to do with how they saw me as a person. I know that that small group of Blacks saw me as somewhat of a sell-out. I don't think that the majority of the Black student body saw me that way, but I am quite sure that the group that I'm talking about did see me as a little soft. I think the reason that they saw me that way had a lot to do with my venturing into the white world.

The group of Black students that I'm referring to were mostly males; by that time, most of the Black girls, even the ones who didn't like the fact that I was dating a white girl, either thought I was a nice guy or cute. Some of the girls thought I was both, but to the small group of Black males that I'm talking about I was a sell-out.

The guys that I am talking about were the first guys in the neighborhood to play N.W.A.'s 1989 debut album Straight Outta Compton (I didn't really start listening to N.W.A. until my first year of college). They were guys that wouldn't hesitate to spit the word cracker out of their mouth any more than they would hesitate to spit a sunflower seed on the ground.

I couldn't say the word cracker, because I was dating a white girl. I couldn't say the word cracker because I was highly respected by faculty members who were mostly white. I was too involved in the white world to say the word cracker. Even if I did say the word, my deep involvement in the white world prevented me from saying it as openly and defiantly as they said the word. I had too much skin in the white game to be a straight-up NIGGA.

That view that those individuals took of me was new to me. I had never been perceived as too close to the white world to not be down for the cause in the Black world. Still, I understood why the group of guys that I'm talking about viewed me that way. I just didn't agree.

I had a very different image of myself. I knew that I had been down for the cause in the most militant of ways since I was a child. I was militant way before I knew what the word meant. Just eight years prior to my senior year, as a fourth grader at Stewart Elementary, I had written my first speech against racism. Six years prior to my senior year, as a sixth grader at King Middle, I had been disciplined for beating up a white boy for calling me a nigger. That same year that I dotted the white boy's eyes, I had made straight A's in defiance just to prove to white people that I was just as smart as the smartest of my white counterparts. Five years prior to my senior year, as a seventh grader at Bradenton Middle, I had punched a white girl in the mouth for calling me a nigger. Four years prior to my senior year, as an eighth grader at Bradenton Middle, I had gotten into another fight with a white boy for calling me a nigger. So I didn't see myself as soft or a sell-out, but I did see change.

I saw myself change from a person who had punched a white girl in the mouth to a person who was kissing a white girl in the mouth. And while it was true enough that I had changed my thinking and feelings about white people, I still felt that I identified as a Black male. I was just tired from all the fighting that I had done during all the years of elementary and middle school. I was tired of hating white people. I was tired of hating period.

The years of hating had worn my soul down. I knew in my heart that my soul was not meant for such a misguided purpose of hating other people based on the color of their skin. I was tired of all the Black and white issues. I realized that I had become the hate that hate produced and I didn't want to be that anymore. I just wanted to engage in the fullness of my own humanity. So I did. But I didn't see myself as a sell-out; I was merely trying to take my soul out of the deadly game of hating people.

That was the first time that I had an element of the Black world label me as a sell-out or as not down for the cause, but it wouldn't be the last. I felt that it was important to touch on it now because it was the first time. It also provides the first illustration of how an element of the Black world tried to constrain me to the boundaries of their viewpoints by imposing limits on my ability to just be me without being Black first. It wasn't a particularly strong attempt by that particular element of the Black world and I didn't have too much difficulty in dismissing it; but nonetheless, it was an attempt.

I disregarded all the naysayers' opinions of me. I blocked them and their reasons on why I wouldn't last as the starting point guard on our team out of my mind. I didn't listen to their statements of how I didn't keep my starting position as a sophomore. I didn't listen to their statements about how the two junior point guards were better than I was. I didn't care if they thought I was soft or a sell-out. I just didn't listen and I just didn't care. I knew what I had to do! The time for talk was over and the time for action was beginning. As the season drew closer and closer, I began to focus on the task of being the starting point guard for Southeast High School for the entire season. Beyond that, I also wanted to perform well enough during the season that I would get a college scholarship after the season. I had serious business to attend to; I didn't have any time to pay attention to what others were thinking about me. I had my business and their opinions of me were not included in that business.

The season finally began and I was the starter, but I knew that if I didn't perform well or if the team didn't perform well under my leadership that I would be benched in favor of one of the other point guards. I was definitely in a compromising position because not only did the coach name me the starter, but he also made me a co-captain. He was gambling that I could get the job done. I know that my play over the summer was the reason he was willing to take that gamble.

He chose me and Floyd to be the co-captains for the entire season. His decision to name me as a co-captain was really a shot in the arm for me and I took great pride in that honor. He was doubling down on me and I didn't want to let him down; even though his bet was big, my bet on myself was even bigger. I had my whole life riding on the season. In my mind, I had to either make it this way or make it this way. There was no that way; there was only this way.

I had come a long way from that disastrous junior varsity season. If the story ended with me being made a co-captain, it would have been a happily ever after kind of story. But Lakeland Kathleen, the team that we opened the season against, wasn't in the mood for my personal storybook ending or beginning.

The Kathleen team was the state runner-up in the state basketball tournament during the 1989-90 season and they returned a squad of veterans. Here we were this team full of first time starters, with the exception of Floyd, going against one the state's best in our very first game. We played tough; we led after the first period, we were down by four at the half, and we were down only six points going into the final period. That wasn't bad against last year's state runner-ups that hadn't lost any people. Some would have said that it was pretty good. Then it all went downhill like a boxer who had been hit by a Joe Frazier left hook that he never saw coming.

The final eight minutes saw the game turn into a rout. We ended up losing the game 76-51. The coaches were upset, our very first game and we lost ... blew out in the fourth! We were 0 and 1, and that's not the way that Southeast teams were supposed to start the season or end ball games. The whole team from player one through twelve was questioned on what kind of season we were going to have if we played every game like we played that final eight minutes. That first game was a defeat for the whole team, from the coaches on down to every player, because the whole concept of reloading had been thoroughly defeated in the final eight minutes of game number one. The season was too long to start it out that way.

You could feel the doubt in the atmosphere of the locker room that an opening loss, especially a blowout loss, brings into existence. The "team question" of whether or not this team would have to go through a rebuilding year after the loss of so many seniors and an All-American was looming large. The loss also brought into question each individual that we had on our team; I could feel the question of did we have the right people in the right places to get the job done circulating around the locker room. It was posted on the brow of all the coaches.

Normally, that type of questioning would have fallen squarely on my shoulders, but it couldn't on that night. Because even though we lost the game, I had shown what would prove to hold true the entire season. I showed that we would not be able to be pressured into turning the ball over as a result of any type of full-court pressure. No team would even be able to think about pressing us without me instantly killing their notion.

I didn't have any turnovers during the Kathleen game and turnovers were one of the question marks that the coaching staff had about me. In fact they were one of the questions that I had about myself. I had lost my starting job my sophomore year as a result of not being able to handle full-court pressure. And while it was true that I had played all summer on the AAU team without any problems, my actual performance as a starting point guard for Southeast High School was an unknown at that time. Nobody knew how I would respond to the pressure, not even me. However, what I did know was that since the day that I lost my starting position as a sophomore I had worked on dribbling the basketball more than any other aspect of my game. On many a night, Grandma Mary or the neighbors that lived around her house had to tell me to "stop dribbling that ball" because it was time for people to go to sleep.

My persistence in practicing my ball handling had paid off in a huge way. Not only could I handle intense full-court pressure, but I also didn't need to pass the ball to any of my teammates in order to do it. I just dribbled through every point in the traps and through all the pressure until it was gone. My thoughts and actions were one concept. My body instantaneously executed any dribble move that I thought that I needed to trick a defender. I only needed tricks for two or more people; if it was just one man, I just blew past him like he was standing still. I could move just as fast dribbling a ball as I could move without a ball. I was probably faster with the ball. The ball was like a part of my hand. Later on in the year, when teams were forced to try to press to get back in the game, my coach wouldn't even ask for a press-break offense. He would yell: "give the ball to Quincy and get out of the way!"

The second game was even more revealing as far as my personal improvement was concerned. We were on the road again, this time we were up against a team called Sarasota Cardinal Mooney; it was one of those private schools where it seemed like rich and white were part of the prerequisites for admission. They were a totally different team than Lakeland Kathleen, but they were solid enough where we had to play well in order to win. They were a whole bunch of white boys who tried to fundamental you to death.

I knew that if we started this season off with a 0-2 start that our reloading concept would be down the drain and the doubts of the starting line-up would creep ever closer to the forefront of the coaching staff's mind. Those thoughts were turning themselves over and over in my mind before the start of the game, so I sat in an empty corner of the bleachers in order to try to make my peace with them. Just as I really started to ponder the possibilities of being pulled out of the line-up as a starter due to a poor start to the season, another person sat down beside me on the bleacher bench.

I looked over and saw that it was my girlfriend's father, the man who tried to prevent me from having any relationship with his little girl because I was Black and she was white. It was a move that took me by surprise, but I was cool and my surprise didn't show through my mask of cool pose. For a minute, I forgot about the game for which I was mentally preparing.

His intrusion into the space by my side broke my whole vibe. My mind roamed across all the possibilities that would make him sit right beside me in a remote area of a gym that had plenty of other seats available. I fortified my outer appearance of cool with an internal fire that was ready to combat any reason that he could give for him not wanting me to date his daughter. I knew that I would morally win out on any reason that was founded along racial lines, but I also knew that it took more than morals to beat a racist.

I was ready to go to battle if that's what he had come for; I rarely backed away from serious confrontations. The racial tension between us had made my posture strong and manly. That bolstered my otherwise adolescent physique to a level that it had never known. I stood my ground and sat up erect like a man who was prepared to meet the challenge of another man. It was a good feeling because I knew that a countless number of other Black men before me had stood in the face of prejudice with the same courage that I felt flowing through my body. I was ready for whatever he brought, but I decided that given the unknown of the situation that discretion was the better part of valor.

I decided that the best thing to do was to wait and see what he wanted. Under that approach, we sat and we sat some more. All in all, it must have been about ten minutes of this uneasy silence between us, as I sat closer than I had ever anticipated to the man who thought that Black was Black and that Black was wrong for his white daughter.

He never broke his silence and I never knew what he wanted to say to me. After the ten minutes of uncomfortable silence, I got up to go get dressed in the locker room. I was ready to deal with whatever he brought to the table, but I didn't have all night to wait for him to do whatever he came over to do. His delayed methods were starting to interfere with custom; I always went into the locker room before the second half start of the junior varsity game.

I did that just so I could be alone before everybody poured into the locker room with the high-five jive that was never my style before a game. I believed that playful high fives should be reserved for after you won the game. I wasn't opposed to giving high fives because I knew that some of the other guys needed that kind of thing, but I also knew that I had to be alone to get really focused.

Alone in the locker room, my mind resumed its thoughts about the potential consequences of a 0-2 start. I knew that point guards were the first to be blamed when a team didn't do well. That's just the way it was; all point guards knew that. The thoughts stayed with me all the way up until the tip off of the game.

As if the first half of the game was scripted to bring all my pre-game worries into fruition, we got off to a terrible start. After the first quarter we were down by a score of 22-8. At the end of the second quarter the score was 37-24. We played the first two quarters the same way that we had played the fourth quarter of the previous game.

The halftime speech was fierce; considering how awful we played the first half, I really didn't know if Coach would make changes right there on the spot or not. As the coaching staff ranted and raved about this and that, I blocked out all the words that dripped from their lips and focused deep within myself. I told myself that I had worked long and hard to be a starter again and that I wasn't about to let it be taken away from me without giving it my very best shot. I knew that basketball was a team sport, but the things that I was saying to myself were very individual. I told myself that if I was going to go down, then I was going to go down fighting. Life was in my face telling me that it told me so; telling me that I might as well get used to being a failure right now. It was looking me dead in my face asking me what was I going to do about it. It was a moment of truth where I had to answer with authority or acquiesce to defeat.

I zoned back into the halftime tirade just in time to hear our head coach say that the same five that started the game would start the second half. To be honest, I didn't know if he would say those words after the first half that the starters had just played, but he did and that's all I needed to hear.

I was determined to show that I should be the starting point guard and that our team could win with me in that position. The third quarter was a completely different story. We outscored them 24-6 in the third and took a 48-43 lead into the fourth quarter. We went on to hold on in the fourth quarter to produce a 64-61 win, but the third quarter was the big difference. In my mind, we had won that game as soon as we stepped back on the floor after half-time. I had won a personal victory with my own individual effort. Even though I had been named the starter during the first game of the season, the second half of the second game was where I truly became the starting point guard.

I was very satisfied with the fact that we won the game and that I had prevailed in the battle of self versus self, but I was even more satisfied after I woke up the next morning to find out that I was the star of the game. Both the Sarasota newspaper and the Bradenton newspaper opened their coverage of our game with my performance. Although they reported different final scores, they both confirmed that I had played well. The headline for the Sarasota newspaper read:

Southeast Comeback Dooms Mooney 64-61

The headline for the Bradenton newspaper read:

Seminoles slip past Cougars

Both of the opening paragraphs for each article talked about my game performance and the role that I played in helping us to win the ball game. The Sarasota newspaper staff reporter wrote:

Southeast's Quincy Smith scored 10 of his team-high 18 points in the third quarter to key a 24-6 run that led the Seminoles to a 64-61 come-from-behind win over pesky Cardinal Mooney Friday Night in a high school basketball game.

The Bradenton newspaper even included a quote from our head coach about the way I played, the staff reporter wrote:

Quincy Smith had 18 points and four steals Friday night to lead Southeast to a 64-60 high school basketball victory at scrappy Sarasota Cardinal Mooney. "Smith played a great game," according to Seminole Coach Bob Carroll.

Before I could enjoy my personal satisfaction of my performance or the celebration of the team victory, we were on to another game the very next day. This time we were playing a St. Petersburg High school team that we just ran away from to post a 71-51 victory. I scored nine points, before coach decided to empty our bench to allow everyone a chance to play. During my junior season, I would have loved that type of game. That kind of blowout game was the only time that I would have gotten to play. But that was then. Three games into the season I had solidified my role as the starter and the co-captain of the team, so the blowout game found me on the bench during half of the third and all of the fourth quarter enjoying it all. It was fun.

We played three games in the opening week and the reloading concept was still alive; we had made a huge recovery from the opening game loss that we suffered at the hands of Lakeland Kathleen. The back-to-back victories earned me some much needed respect from the coaching staff and some breathing room to have a turnover or two before somebody decided that the world was ending.

I also gained some recognition from some of the student body. Apparently they had read the newspaper over the weekend and saw the fact that my name had been mentioned in both articles covering the two wins. At Southeast High School, getting your name in the newspaper for football or basketball was something that carried some rank. Southeast High School was a school that was proud of the success of its athletic teams and the athletes that made those teams successful.

As it began to appear that our team might have a chance at success and that I would be one of those athletes that would be responsible for that success, my status in the school began to change. People that usually walked right past me began to stop for brief conversations. The conversations weren't about national security or anything; they were just trivial exchanges about any small topic. I started to understand what being a starter on a successful team at Southeast High School was all about. It made people want to talk to you; they didn't want to talk about anything big; they just wanted to talk period.

Our fourth road game and fourth game overall only validated my understanding of being a hoop star. We defeated Arcadia Desoto by the score of 85-78 in a game where I scored 16 points and another newspaper reference. Life was getting sweet.

A lot of people, students and teachers alike, read the newspaper at our school, but many of them had not had an opportunity to see me play since my struggles as a sophomore point guard. I've already written about the lack of playing time that I received as a junior, so I won't revisit that again. Combine that lack of playing time as a junior with the fact that our first four games were on the road and it was easy to conclude that a lot of people had not seen me play basketball in a long time. With the exception of Floyd, that was pretty much true for our entire team; we were all relatively new to playing major minutes on the varsity level. So our fifth game, which was our first home game, was a big game for me personally and the majority of our team.

Yes it was true that we were on a three-game win streak. Yes there were written and verbal reports that suggested that we might have a good team. But to most people, "seeing is believing". We had a big crowd who wanted to see if we were for real or if it was all mere hype. We were playing a visiting Sarasota Booker team that had always played us tough in the past, but that game would prove that the past was exactly that ... the past. By the time the dust had settled, we had seriously defeated the Booker team by a most embarrassing score of 108-57. We didn't just beat them; we routed them!

The Booker boys caught a drubbing, a shellacking, and a beat down all in the same game! I scored 10 points in the win, but it was really Floyd's scoring show. He scored 23 points in what would turn out to be his first of several big scoring games that he put in for our team. It was a really impressive total considering the fact that the starters only played half of the game. Due to the serious hurting that we put on Booker, the bench played the other half the game. The game was almost over before it started.

The crowd that came to see if we were for real got its money worth that night. They saw a team that used the full depth of its bench to literally destroy another team. They saw a lot of new faces on the court, but it looked like we were definitely prepared to continue the same old tradition of Southeast excellence that had been established by multiple seasons of twenty wins or more. The twenty-win season streak began five years prior to my senior year. The 1989-90 team had punctuated that streak with a number one state ranking. We were trying to keep it all going.

If anybody wanted to see if I was for real or not, then they also got their monies worth. Although I only scored 10 points, which wasn't bad given the fact that the reserves played more than usual, I had shown something that you just couldn't always count on to show in the box score. I had shown that I was a leader, not only competent, but also far better than anyone could have predicted. I showed that I was smart and that I was tough. I also showed that I knew how to win a basketball game without scoring one single point. I took charges, I played great defense, I knew how to get the ball to the people where they could do something with it, and I didn't turn the ball over.

I was super quick and I could handle the ball like it was an extension of my hand. I had a huge desire to win and I played with the heart of a champion. That kind of play not only helps to win games, but it also inspires the human soul. Ultimately, by season's end, it would be those traits that set me apart from many of the top area players who scored more points.

The fact that I was the shortest man on the court ninety-nine percent of the time had a lot to do with the inspiring part of my basketball skills. I can remember one teacher coming up to me and saying that he overheard another student of a short stature just gushing over the fact that I could play so well against players who were oftentimes so much bigger than me. The comment totally took me by surprise because I had never even considered my height as an obstacle in any endeavor. I knew that it was a concern for other people from time to time—mostly coaches, but it had never been a concern for me. Still, I took the comments from the teacher as a positive and I felt good that I was having a positive impact on a person who did view height as a big factor.

For some reason, after the teacher told me that story, I thought about a stupid song that one of my uncles teased me about when I was younger. It was a popular song that claimed that short people had no reason to live. It talked about their little hands and their tiny feet. My uncle didn't know it then, but when he teased me with the words of that song, I only grew from it. I grew in heart and I grew in character. I am glad that he teased me because I would learn later in life that a big heart would carry a person much further in life than big hands, big feet, or a tall stature. I also learned that a short person could stand on the content of his or her character and become a giant. So short people do have a reason to live; they should live to stand on their character and become giants.

The positive impact that I was having on people was even carrying over to the media. As we won more and more games, I was appearing in the newspaper quite regularly. After the Booker game, we went on a run that boosted our record from 4 wins and 1 loss to a very impressive 15 wins and 2 losses. In the process of our team raising our record to such a respectable level, my individual role received considerable attention. By the time we reached 15 wins, I had become somewhat of a media favorite.

I had been quoted in the paper commenting on our "surprising" success after losing an All-American and a number of senior starters. My defensive ability had been highlighted (I was particular proud of my defensive ability; by the end of a thirty-two game season I had over one hundred steals while the next closet person on my team had forty-eight). My name had appeared in the headlines in a few articles. My dribbling ability had been highlighted. My ability to save games down the stretch with clutch free throws had been highlighted. The head coach had been quoted on how pleased he was with my individual play. In summation: I had gone from a guy struggling to make the varsity team as a junior to a guy who was receiving a great deal of press coverage as the starting point guard of a team with a record of 15 wins and two losses.

I had planned on being a basketball star at Southeast High School from the very moment that I first stepped onto the campus as a freshman, but for a long time it appeared that my plans would never be reality. I had gone through so much in my home life, in the classroom, and on the court that my freshman year plans just sort of got lost. At the start of the season, I was just fighting to survive; but by the time we had played our seventeenth game, I was so much more than just a survivor. I was a winner. And the next newspaper article that I appeared in just might have made me a local star.

All of the previous articles that I had appeared in were articles that reported on actual game results, but the next one was an exclusive article that was all about me and my personal triumph over adversity. The media saw me as this guy who just came out of nowhere and they loved to play that "out of nowhere" aspect to the maximum. In one article, a reporter for the Bradenton newspaper had actually written:

> Before this year, Quincy Smith had never been a starter
> on any basketball team, anywhere. Now, Smith a senior
> point guard at Southeast High School, is not only start-
> ing the games, but winning them.

Of course that wasn't true, but since they had never heard of me before; the only sensible thing that they could conclude was that I had never been a starter on "any basketball team, anywhere". That didn't appear in my personal story article. It appeared in an article where our head coach said: "Quincy has won several ballgames for us. We didn't know (how he'd respond to pressure situations). He was one of the question marks. He'd never been tested."

My personal story article was just like me in a sense because it just came "out of nowhere" too. Our head coach came up to me one day and told me that a reporter from the Bradenton newspaper wanted to schedule an interview with me and that he had already arranged for it to happen. I had seen personal articles on many of the local athletes during my years at Southeast, but I never thought that I would have my own article. I say that because the articles were primarily reserved for either the athlete who had out-of-this-world statistical performance or the athlete who exhibited consistent and long-term excellence in their respective sport or sports. I had done neither, but I guess my personal triumph and the intangibles that I played the game with were inspirational to a lot of people. Apparently, it was newsworthy.

I went to meet the reporter during my Research class that was taught by my head coach. The man who called the shots for our basketball team didn't want any of his players to miss any other teacher's class, so he scheduled the interview during the class where he was my teacher. I was nervous and excited, I really didn't know what to expect, but after a couple of minutes the interview turned out to be more like a casual conversation than a structured question and answer session.

I wasn't the type of person to try to take a lot of individual credit for group success, especially when our strength as a team was really rooted in our depth. I also shunned a lot of personal credit for my individual success. The reporter gave me plenty of opportunities to blow my own horn and I tried to blow it, but my words could only be true to what I was thinking and feeling.

The more questions he asked me, the more I thought about how much Floyd had helped me make it through. He was the only one that believed in me when I was down and out. He was that lone voice that kept telling me that I was a good basketball player when everyone else was ready to write me off. I don't think that the reporter expected the interview to go the way that it did, but I talked about Floyd so much that he decided to focus on our friendship along with basketball.

The article appeared in the paper about a week later and most of it highlighted the strong friendship that Floyd and I shared. I didn't know it at the time, but he called Floyd for a telephone interview later that day after he spoke with me. I was really happy with the article because I had never told Floyd how much I appreciated all that he had done for me as a friend and as a basketball player. The article gave me a chance to do that. It also talked about my ability to make clutch free throws and included some comments on my play from our coach.

The article came out in the Friday, January 18th, 1991 edition of the newspaper and was featured on the front page of the weekend sports section with a full color photo of me posing as if I were about to shoot a free throw. The layout of the article and the photo, which was right in the middle of the page, was among all the national sports news and events of that day. My story was center stage amongst stories talking about the impact of the Persian Gulf War and its impact on the upcoming Super Bowl and other sporting events. My headline read: "Quincy Smith: tough in the clutch" and the caption above the article read: "Mental Rehearsal pays off".

The following is an exact replication of the text of the actual article as it appeared in the above-mentioned edition of the Bradenton Herald. Mark Moring, a reporter for the Bradenton Herald, wrote:

> When Bob Carroll gave the assignment, Quincy Smith jumped.
>
> Carroll, who teaches a scientific research class at Southeast High School, told his students they were to undertake a project in which subjects would practice the art of mental rehearsal.
>
> Students were to conduct experiments in real-life situations, if possible, recording data and documenting results.
>
> The moment he heard the assignment, Smith knew exactly where he was headed.
>
> To the gymnasium.
>
> The topic: Mental rehearsal
>
> The situation: The waning moments of a close basketball game.
>
> The task: making free throws in the clutch.

The subject: Himself

Smith, the starting point guard for the 15-2 Southeast boys basketball team, which Carroll also coaches, wanted to test his response in such a situation.

So he rounded up a handful of fellow hoopsters and headed for the hardwood.

The gym was empty for the experiments, so the participants had to do their best to simulate game situations.

'We had low-stress situations and high-stress situations,' said Smith, a senior.

They shot free throws in a quiet, empty gym. Then they shot them in a noisy gym, with players waiving their arms behind the baseline, trying to simulate a pressure situation.

And, finally, they didn't shoot them at all, taking a session to simply *visualize* successful free-throw attempts. They just sat at the foul line and thought about making baskets—mental rehearsal in action.

Did it work?

The numbers seem to say so.

Smith has won at least two games for Southeast at the foul line this year. He went 5 for 6 at the stripe in the fourth quarter in a 71-70 victory at Sarasota last week, and went 9 for 10 in the fourth quarter in a win over Boca Ciega last month.

He shoots a laudable 72 percent from the line but he guesses that figure is much higher in the fourth quarter, when it matters most.

'I just want to be the guy shooting the ball or getting fouled at the end of the game,' Smith said. 'I don't really get nervous in those situations, I just go up there to make the free throw, that's all. I block out the distractions. If you think too much, then you get nervous.'

Smith says the research project made a difference.

'It helped me a lot,' he said. 'It made me believe it a little more. It reinforced what was already there.'

'Quincy has a lot of confidence in himself,' Carroll added. 'He's learned to think positively in those situations.'

Smith wasn't always so confident.

Two years ago, he underwent a mild confidence crisis.

As a sophomore on the junior varsity, Smith was scrawny and barely five-and-a-half feet tall. He wasn't seeing much playing time, and he was down.

'I don't know how confident you can be coming off the bench,' Smith said. 'I had lost confidence in my ability.'

Enter teammate Floyd Watkins, Smith's best friend since sixth grade. Watkins, who was the star of the JV team, gave his buddy plenty of pep talks.

'Without Floyd,' said Smith, 'I don't think that I would have made it through that stretch … A combination of hard work and a dose of Floyd Watkins will cure anybody.'

Watkins, downplaying his role, says he helped Smith 'inadvertently.'

'We would go to the park and play one-on-one,' Watkins said. 'He knew he was a good ballplayer. He just didn't think he was appreciated. So I appreciated him. I knew his talents more than anybody. He just had trouble showcasing them when his confidence level was down. (But) he knew what his abilities were.'

Smith regained his confidence and worked to become a better ballplayer. Today, he's one of the steadier point guards in the area.

He's not flashy, and he's not much of scorer; he averages just 8.1 points per game. But he's a fine ballhandler who averages almost five assists and less than two turnovers a game.

Smith likes to take control of a game.

'I try to think a little bit more than the other guy, and do what the coaches ask of me,' said Smith, who carries a 3.1 grade point average. 'Basketball's at least 50 percent mental, and I pride myself on being a smart basketball player.'

Carroll says he wouldn't want anyone else bringing the ball up the court or running his club.

'There hasn't been a team this year that's hurt us on the press,' Carroll said. 'That's how well (Smith) can handle the ball.'

And Watkins, who leads the Seminoles with 15.4 points per game, says he wouldn't want anyone else to have the ball when the game is on the line.

'He is our team leader,' Watkins said. 'Everybody wants Quincy Smith to have the ball late in the game, because you know he's always going to do something good.'

Smith, who only played about two minutes a game last year, has come a long way.

'He has worked hard and has believed in our program,' Carroll said. 'We've told our kids, "You'll be rewarded if you stick with it."

'Quincy has shown me he was a leader and can do the job. And that he was a winner. He's done what we've expected of him, and he's exceeded that.'

Smith attributes much of his success to Watkins, who has not only helped his confidence, but helped him as a player, too.

The two play one-on-one whenever they can, which at first glance looks like a terrible mismatch: The 6-foot-6 Watkins is nine inches taller than Smith.

But the rivalry is dead even, says Smith, who keeps a log of their series. Seventy times they've played. Smith has won 35, Watkins 35.

Yes, David can still slay Goliath.

Amazing what a little confidence—and some mental rehearsal—can do.

By the way, Smith did quite well on that research assignment.

He made an A.

STAY IN YOUR PLACE

After the article appeared in the newspaper, I went back to school that following Monday and found myself to be one popular guy. Some of the teachers had posted the article on their boards in their classrooms and many of the students made positive comments to me as they passed me in the hallways. I was more popular than I had ever been. It was a popularity that extended to include most of the students, most of the teachers, and most of the faculty; but I can't say that I was everybody's favorite person.

I already mentioned the fact that a small element of the Black student population had problems with me. I have speculated as to why I felt that those problems existed; but after the article, I started to experience problems from another group. I began to notice that there were some white adults at the school who seemed to be very against the fact that I was dating a white girl.

I began to feel the weight of their stares as I walked down the hallways, sometimes arm-in-arm, with my girl. I don't know, maybe they just couldn't stand to see her white skin so close to my Black skin when we held hands. Maybe they were afraid that my new and sudden popularity would cause copycat couples. I don't know, whatever their reason, their hostility was definitely growing.

My girl had actually told me of a few verbal warnings that she had received from a few "well-intentioned" teachers that warned her against the potential pitfalls of interracial dating. Her stories always brought the spirit of rebellion and anger in me right to the very surface of my personality. It was a spirit that I had just successfully put away before entering high school. Each time she told me about one of the stories, I tried to conceal my rebellious anger because I knew that she wouldn't understand.

I knew that she couldn't fully comprehend the feelings that permeated every fiber of my being. She would not understand my anger as a reactionary energy that was brought into existence only as a result of continuous injuries to the deepest part of my human psyche. She would not understand the sheer force of the hurricane strength winds of emotion that battered rage back and forth against the constraints of my soul. I knew that I would have blown her away if I ever unleashed what I was feeling when she told me what the "well-intentioned" white teachers said to her.

The thing that bothered me the most was that some of the white teachers at school that told her those things were also some of the same white teachers that smiled at me or acted cordial toward me in some other way. I realized that their smiles were nothing more than grand deceptions meant to fool me. I couldn't decide if I was more upset with them for their deceit or more upset with myself for being foolish enough to be deceived. I waffled back and forth between those two, but my anger never wavered.

Like the blade from a guillotine on the morning of an execution, my anger was sharp and decisive. If I had my choice, some heads would have definitely rolled. I was tired of being bothered for no reason other than my Black skin. From my very first day of significant exposure to white people right up through that moment in my life, some portion of the white world had harassed me. I wondered if my entire life was going to be that way. Their harassment always made me feel that they were trying to make me get it through my head that there was a certain place that I was supposed to occupy as a Black male.

One day after she told me about one of the comments, I didn't go to my next class. I went to the boys' locker room and just thought about it all. I suppose that they reasoned that if they could get me to accept such a notion as knowing my place, then it would be easier for them to effectively use my color against me to make me feel that I was inferior to white people in all areas of importance. Once they accomplished that task, then I assumed that their next step would have been to try to make me feel that I was somehow less than a whole and complete human being. The harassment itself didn't always manifest itself in the same way every time, but it always seemed to be centered on making me understand my place.

As I began to try to develop a more positive attitude toward race relations between Black and white, the accumulation of slights that I collected from white folks began to hurt more and more. The more I hurt, the angrier I got. I was tired of being looked upon as inferior by white folks who did not feel that my race was important enough or human enough to be included in its goals of "life, liberty, and the pursuit of happiness". If they didn't want us here, then they should have never stole us from the coasts of Africa!

I had vigorously and violently fought the bigotry of the white world in elementary and middle school without success. I had tried to compromise with the moderates of the white world throughout my high school career; but judging from some of the reactions that my girlfriend was getting from home and from some white folks at school, I had not succeeded with that approach either. Nonetheless, I was still somewhat encouraged by my perception that the number of whites who were *openly* opposed to me dating a white girl was a smaller number than the ones who were minding their own business. However, that small encouragement was pummeled into melancholy by a conversation that I had with my head coach.

One day, shortly after my article appeared in the newspaper, he called me into his office in the basketball locker room. I had no idea why he was calling me into his office because there was no reason for such an occasion. I was playing well and we were doing great as a basketball team. As a matter of fact, our team had just recently been ranked in the top ten in the state.

I knew that I wasn't in any academic trouble because my performance in the classroom was better than it had ever been as a freshman, sophomore, or junior; so it couldn't have been about academics. I knew that he couldn't have wanted to talk to me about behavior or conduct issues. Outside of those things, I couldn't figure out any other reason that he would need to talk to me during that point in the basketball season.

I went into his office with no idea of what to expect. As I sat in his office for a couple of minutes and he began to talk, I quickly figured out what the meeting was all about. He had called me into his office to talk to me about my relationship with my white girlfriend. After listening to him for a while, it became clear that my coach—the white man, had been involved in a conversation with my girlfriend's father—another white man. It seemed that the father had expressed his displeasure to my coach about the fact that one of his Black players was dating his white daughter. I knew that my girlfriend's father wasn't pleased with the fact that I was dating his daughter, so that part of the conversation was not a surprise for me. But the fact that my coach was sitting across from me trying to convince me that my relationship was not worth all the problems that it was causing was a big shock for me. I thought that he was on my side. He wasn't talking to me in a blatantly racist way, but something about the whole tone of the conversation made me feel the twinge in my body that I felt whenever I thought something was race motivated.

I couldn't figure out why any of that situation was his business, I was angry that he had intruded into an area of my life where he had not been invited and where he had no legitimate authority to be. As he continued to talk about all the people who were opposed to the relationship and the reasons why it was more trouble than it was worth, my anger turned into sadness. I was sitting across from a man that I had believed in for over two years as he preached the benefits of being loyal to his system and the Southeast High School basketball program. I had heard him say that there were three things that should be top priority in our lives as a Southeast High basketball player. According to him, those three things were God, family, and school; school included academics and the team. I wondered which priority had I violated with my relationship with a white girl.

I knew that God had no preoccupation with color; I wasn't doing anything that my family didn't approve of because I already had a white aunt; and I wasn't hurting my grades or my team by dating a white girl. I had been loyal to him and his program; he had been quoted saying that I had won "several ballgames" for the team. I wanted to know where was his loyalty to me. I wasn't doing anything in my relationship that could have been a cause for concern. It was a very innocent high school relationship involving two people who loved each other. My girlfriend was so under lock and key that we had never had a chance to do anything.

Our relationship was based upon the purest of things that most relationships aspire to develop. It was that way if for no other reason than the fact that we were never allowed to see each other outside of school. We talked on the phone, walked each other to and from class, and literally stole kisses during the rarest of moments when the opportunities presented themselves. More than anything else we laughed together and expressed our deep personal commitment to one another. In a sense, we were more tragic than Romeo and Juliet. But it was a sweet tragedy.

As my coach continued to talk, I began to seriously ask myself what was his reason for having this conversation with me. My eyes peered at and through him, while my mind searched for the crime that I had committed in order to receive that unfair judgement from him. He had a daughter that was in the same grade as my girlfriend; I wanted to ask him if he would still be having that conversation with me if I were dating his daughter. I wanted to ask him if he would've, as a father, gone to a coach of a Black athlete if his daughter had decided to date a Black athlete. If I had thought that his answer would have been worth me asking the question, I would have made sure that he knew that I was talking about an amateur Black athlete. That way it would have been all about the Black penis, not the green dollars.

Regardless of what his answers would've been to those unasked questions, I would have still felt the same way about the situation. At that moment, I didn't feel like my coach was a straight-out racist like my girlfriend's father; but I felt like he would've had a problem with me dating his own daughter much the same way that my girlfriend's father had a problem. I felt like I was good enough to dribble basketballs for them, shoot hoops for them, but I wasn't good enough to date their daughters. I felt that that was the bottom line. It didn't matter how innocent the relationship was or how nice I was. When it came to dating their daughters, the only thing that they could see was my Black skin. My skin was my sin … yet once again. They could only hope that my girl and I had not already done the nasty.

In their minds, when it all came down to it, I was still a nigger. And niggers and basketballs was one thing, but niggers and white girls was quite a different thing. I guess my place was to learn the difference between the two.

I listened to everything that my coach had to say in total silence. I left his office without a word because I didn't know what to say. My soul felt an unutterable pain caused by betrayal from a man that I had come to respect and admire a great deal over the years; but from that point on, my great respect and admiration for him was severely diminished. He had effectively managed to undue three and a half years of respect and admiration in a span of fifteen minutes. If he had presented the situation in a way that were only passing on information from a racist parent, while maintaining my rights as a human being; then that would have been one thing, but his conversation was heavily laced with his own personal opinions on the matter. To put it in simple language, the fact of the matter was that nobody would have had any problems with anything that I was doing if I were a white male. But that was something that I was clearly not capable of being ... ever. It was also something that I would have never chosen to be ... ever.

NO COMPROMISE

I was Black on the outside and I was Black on the inside. I went back and forth between both worlds very well, but I was Black through and through. All of my life experiences, no matter at what level, were funneled through my identity as a Black male. On top of that, I liked being Black. I liked the things that most Black dudes my aged liked. My hair was cut into the latest Black style; I had a split-level hi-top fade that was "cooler than a polar bear's toenails".

I liked the style that set us apart from the mainstream white world—the style that set us apart, but at the same time forced the mainstream white world to drop by just to see what we were doing. I liked the cool vernacular we used when we spoke to each other. For example, we would say "what's up baby" to another guy and not feel the least bit like we were being soft. I didn't know it at the time, but we were just continuing in the tradition of Black male expression. Claude Brown talked about that expression in his 1965 book. He wrote:

> The first time I heard the expression 'baby' used by one cat to another was up at Warwick in 1951...The term had a hip ring to it, a real colored ring. The first time I heard it, I knew right away I had to start using it. It was like saying, 'Man, look at me. I've got masculinity to spare.' It was saying at the same time to the world, 'I'm one of the hippest cats, one of the most uninhibited cats on the scene. I can say "baby" to another cat, and he can say "baby" to me, and we can say it with strength in our

voices.' If you could say it, this meant that you really had to be sure of yourself, of your masculinity...The real hip thing about the 'baby' term was that it was something that only colored cats could say the way that it was supposed to be said. (Claude Brown, *Manchild in the Promise Land*, 1965)

For me, being Black meant a lot of things. One of the things that it definitely meant was being cool. To be Black was to be cool. During my senior year, my homeboys and I were so cool when we played the wall before school that it seemed that everybody in the school had to pass through at least once a morning just to check out our scene. They couldn't stay on our corner too long without catching a cold. We blew cool so hard that we had to drink anti-freeze for breakfast instead of orange juice to keep the wall from freezing. That's saying something when the headquarters for Tropicana was less than five miles from every one of our houses.

Cats outside of our click couldn't lean on the wall; it was too cold, too froze. To lean up against it was to invite chattering teeth and blue toes. We were that cool. Still, we were merely imitators; the progenitors of the cool that we knew were the Africans that we had always known, but never met—at least not in the physical form. Those cool African progenitors lived inside of us.

The progenitors of African cool made the voyage to America via the Middle Passage. It was their cool that kept us from cracking up inside the belly of the beast and burning a hole through the hulls of the slave ships. We were just cool people. They tried to beat and lynch the cool out of us during slavery, but they couldn't do it. Cool rhythms just flowed through our bodies.

When our bodies couldn't contain the cool, we let the cool escape through our voices and musical instruments. We were so cool that we invented ragtime, jazz, rock and roll, and rap; each became a world craze, but they started out just as another reason for us to relieve tensions and give each other dap. We were hip and we hopped and we didn't stop, we rocked it to the bang bang and made the boogies jump up to the rhythm of the beats. We were the most digable people on the planet. We were cool like that! We were Black like that!

The music that we invented was so cool that it turned full circle to re-enter our bodies to create some of the best dancers that this world has ever known. "Body African", not "Body English", controlled their physical movements and their cool set the world ablaze with icy-hot rhythm.

Most of time, people of European descent just tried to steal our moves without ever thanking us for what we had given to them. But that was cool too, because you can't copy what you can't do; Black expression through dance ain't as easy as whitey see whitey do. You cool with that, "baby"?

It's the entire Black experience that makes us move like that; and experience can't be bought, taught, or stolen. It must be lived. And there ain't a white person on this planet who wants to dance bad enough to live the entire Black experience. Our experiences have caused our souls to grow deep like rivers, and the art of dance flowed from their depths.

I am very proud of our contributions to the world in the area of music and dance. We should all be very proud. Yet, we should also understand the words that Dr. Maya Angelou wrote concerning music and dance. Her words were true before she wrote them, they were true when she wrote them, and they are still true today. It will forever be in our best interest to always remember them. In her 1981 book, *The Heart of a Woman*, Dr. Angelou wrote: "I knew no race could sing and dance its way to freedom."

Dance to the music, but don't just dance, listen to what it has to say. Listening to what the music had to say had always been a big part of the cool rhythms that Black people used to get through life. It was a big part of "we" as a collective, and it was a big part of me as an individual.

I had been hooked on Black music since my first night on Laura Street. I guess that I was really no different than any other Black male in America who had been pulled in at an early age to the sounds of his day. Those sounds have changed over the years. The spirituals and slave songs started it all off; they were soon to be followed by ragtime, the blues, swing, bebop, Jazz, R&B, Rock and Roll, Reggae, Funk, Disco, and Rap.

The funny thing about Black music is that the constant has been that the white man has used it to get his hands on some green. I have heard numerous rap artists complain (conversely, rap artists are also breaking new ground in the business of music and achieving unprescedented financial success) about what they got in the end when it came to their music. I ran across some history about ragtime and couldn't believe how much it reminded me of the same concepts that I hear the rappers dis today. With Ragtime, the Black man had the talent and creativity, but the white man got the money ... the epitome of the Black talent/white management model.

> This was ragtime music, then a novelty in New York, and just growing to be a rage, which has not yet subsided. It was originated in the questionable resorts about Memphis and St. Louis by Negro piano-players who knew no more of the theory of music than they did of the theory of the universe, but were guided by natural musical instinct and talent. It made its way to Chicago, where it was popular some time before it reached New York. These players often improvised crude and, at times, vulgar words to fit the melodies. This was the beginning of the ragtime songs. Several of these improvisations were taken down by white men, the words slightly altered, and published under the names of the arrangers. They sprang into immediate popularity and earned small fortunes, of which the Negro originators got only a few dollars. (James Weldon Johnson, *The Autobiography of an Ex-Colored Man*, 1927)

I grew up through my very early years with R&B, but I was born into a generation when a Black male was most likely to choose Rap music. The Sugar Hill Gang burst on the world scene with the first commercial rap song and the scene hasn't been the same since. Kool Herc, Afrika Bambaattaa, Grandmaster Flash and the Furious Five—the originators of rap—continued to *rock the planet* with their *messages* and the rest is Hip-Hop history *"baby bubbah"*.

By the time I reached high school, rap had re-invented itself a few times over. I had gone along for the ride each time. The latest form to take shape during my high school days was "gangsta rap". I was a little slow to catch on to the pioneering "gangsta raps" of N.W.A because I was still more captivated by the educational, political, and socially conscious rhymes of Kool Moe Dee, KRS-One, and Public Enemy. I was attracted to the knowledge that came across in their music. I was hooked on how they addressed situations that I could relate to. I was emboldened by the vibe of revolution that laced their lyrics. They were talking about more viable forms of revolution than what I had known before hearing their music.

Earlier in my life, I had tried to punch or fight white people whenever I felt like the direct victim of their racism. The big problem with that approach was that I always felt like a direct victim of their racism, so I was always fighting in one way or another. I had fought to master their curriculums just to prove that I was just as smart as they were. I fought with my fist. I fought with words. I fought all the time. My type of fighting was always directed at an external enemy. I had really never been exposed to the type of revolution that begins with the knowledge of self and is directed at the internal enemy (ignorance) that lives within us.

Kool Moe Dee, KRS-One, and Public Enemy didn't exclusively talk about knowledge of self in their lyrics. However, they did talk about it enough to introduce me to the concept as a way to revolt against a world that did not want to include me on the level that I should have been included. I had learned very early on that you couldn't punch or kick your way through racism; the effort to do so only left you exhausted and unable to continue in the struggle. The three artists above were telling me that there were also other ways to strike. It was really ironic because at the very same time that some of my more militant Black male classmates were considering me a sell-out; I was actually becoming more sophisticated in my revolutionary thinking. The sophistication was shaping anger into knowledge.

Kool Moe Dee, KRS-One, and Public Enemy were saying things that I personally wanted to hear. They were saying things that I needed to hear as a Black male adolescent. I was growing up in a world that didn't really care about the diminished life chances that I had faced in my past in order to get to where I was at that time. I was living in a society that didn't care about the diminished life chances that I faced every single day in order to have a future. Their lyrics gave me a viable option to express my anger, my pain, and my rebellion toward a white or mainstream world that seemed to be engaged in a constant battle to belittle my humanity and marginalize my existence. I needed to express my anger, my pain, and my rebellion. I had come to the conclusion that I would never acquiesce to a world that did not accept the fullness of my humanity or my right to exist in my entirety.

I had made up mind that I would never make peace with any elements or individuals of the white world that I perceived to be opposed to granting me my full rights as a citizen or a human being. It was a very either/or proposition for me. In my mind, it was either accept me on equal terms or prepare for a battle that would last until I drew my very last breath on this earth.

That proposition was no different than the 1775 cry of Patrick Henry at the revolutionary convention of Virginia when he said: "I know not what course others may take, but as for me, give me liberty or give me death!" That proposition was no different than what Malcolm said in his 1965 "Ballet or the Bullet" speech: "It's the ballet or the bullet; it's liberty or death; it's freedom for everybody or freedom for nobody".

Like those two, I made up my mind that my proposition was of the non-negotiable type where there was no room for a middle ground. W.E.B. Du Bois, being the prophet that he was in terms of the social conditions of Blacks in America, wrote about the non-negotiable mentality of the American Black man in his 1935 book, *Black Reconstruction*. He wrote:

> This the American Black man knows: his fight is a fight to the finish. Either he dies or he wins. He will enter modern civilization in America as a Black man on terms of perfect and unlimited equality with any white man, or he will enter not at all. Either extermination root and branch or absolute equality. There can be no compromise.

I made my decision, I was going to die or win. No other alternative was acceptable. At the time, I didn't know the full measure of consequences that went along with a decision like that. I had endured many hardships early in life that made me somewhat precocious, but I couldn't possibly know then the things that I know now. I know now that such a decision will always keep one in a constant battle. I know now that an American Black man who makes that decision is in a fight that will last his entire life. I know now that his victory may never be achieved until he dies.

In the spiritual sense that's how it was for Jesus. In the human realm, both Malcolm and Martin were resigned to such a fate. Thus, the precedent has been set for all that tend to accept no compromise when going against extreme power. The result will be complete and total exoneration or physical death. Through physical death, a righteous man prevails either way, but that victory of the spirit results in death of the flesh.

When I think of all the Black men that have had to die in the flesh in order to overcome a white man's world that has dreaded them so, I ask myself why. Then I ask why ask "why"; when, "is", is all that there is?

I don't have an answer for that one. I can only recall the words of Zora Neale Hurston from, *Their Eyes Were Watching God*, her 1937 book. Hurston wrote: "A man is up against a hard game when he must die to beat it."

IRONY

Sometimes life seems to be nothing more than a great attempt at irony. I suppose that's why I have heard the phrase: "irony is humanity's sense of propriety". At the very same time that my Black conscious mind was expanding and cementing in my psyche a permanent militancy against some elements of the white world, I was also developing very close relationships with two white individuals. Those two relationships were very important because they allowed me to keep my ability and my human desire to connect with all of humanity. Perhaps if it weren't for those two individuals, I would have had a Coke and a smile while consigning all white folks to hell.

The relationships that I shared with those two individuals were on terms where the fullness of my own humanity wasn't challenged. The first individual was my girlfriend; we shared a love that really transcended skin color. The love that we shared was a deep and innocent love where one first discovers the strong emotions associated with their first true love. It seems somehow that we both knew that. If we were the only two people in the world, then that would have been enough. But we weren't the only two people in the world.

Some elements of the white world and some elements of the Black world tried to impose their own ideas of what love should look like upon our relationship. Their attempts were irritating and frustrating, but I didn't see them as real obstacles that couldn't be overcome.

My girlfriend's love was enough to insulate me against falling prey to seeing the world from the narrow way of thinking that some individuals were trying to impose upon me. The feelings that

I felt for her were so right that I knew that it was wrong to segment humanity or any of its components—in this case the component of love—by something as superficial as skin color. I say that because love is love, no matter the color of the skin. Love's ability to conquer all other emotions is an absolute and universal law that will emerge triumphant in the end no matter who the opponent is or what the obstacles might be. Love is invincible because God is love and God is invincible.

If you don't believe that last sentence to be fact, then ponder this for food for thought. A man's body may live for as many years as he is able to draw breath into his lungs, but the very day that he ceases to have the ability to draw love into his heart is the day that marks his spiritual and most permanent death. Love alone is omnipotent because God alone is omnipotent. The arms of color/race prejudice are too short to box with love simply because they are too short to box with God. So I say it again, God is love and God is invincible. That's a timeless universal truth.

The second individual who affirmed my personal belief in all of humanity as one family was a white lady who taught an advanced reading course that was designed to prepare individuals for the SAT. Her name was Mrs. Debra Valcarcel. My enrollment in her Advanced Reading class was a part of my plan to maximize my chances of being able to go to college after I graduated from high school. I thought that a good score on the SAT would boost my chances of receiving either an athletic or academic scholarship. I had no idea at the time, but the teacher herself would prove to be far more instrumental in me going to college than any techniques that she would teach me in preparation for the SAT.

The May 17, 1954 decision rendered by the Supreme Court of the United States in the case of *Brown v. the Board of Education of Topeka* effectively declared that racial segregation had no place in public education. However, I still found myself in a segregated classroom in my Advanced Reading course. The course wasn't so much racially segregated as it was mentally segregated; but there was a high correlation between the different mentalities and race.

There were predominantly two groups of students with two trains of thought among the students in my class. There were a number of athletes (the majority of them were Black) who all stood a pretty good chance of receiving college scholarships based on their athletic talent if they could achieve a passing score of 700 or above on the standardized test. There was also a number of students (the majority of them were white) that were pursuing a score in the 1100 -1300 range in order to receive a college scholarship based on their academic aptitude. These two groups did not represent the total composition of the class, but they made up the majority of the class and they voluntarily sat on opposite sides of the classroom.

I didn't really fit neatly into either group, so I didn't sit with either group. I sat by myself in the divide that was left by their rift. I was an athlete, but I didn't have the athletic resume of most of the athletes who were in the class. God gave me a heap of sense, but my transcript couldn't go toe-to-toe with any of the brainy side of the room without losing by a TKO. I had suffered too many academic setbacks that hurt my GPA during my sophomore and junior year.

As a senior, I was playing well on the court and I was performing well in the classroom. I was an athlete that had a chance at an athletic scholarship, and I was an honor student that had a chance at an academic scholarship. In both cases, I knew that a good SAT score would enhance my chances of going to college a great deal. My chips were doubled down on the two bets; I was either going to beat the dealer or go broke all in one hand. That's how life was when you were Black and coming from my kind of situation ... most of the time you couldn't do jack about it, but play the cards that you were dealt and go for broke. We called it do or die. What the mainstream called a gamble, we called our only shot.

I don't think that my double reasons for needing a good score was the only factor that made me stand apart from the rest of the class, but I know that it contributed to the interest that Mrs. Valcarcel took in me. After the first few classes, she told me that I was not like the others and that I was different. I asked her what she meant and she told me that I was gifted. She said that some people just had it and that I was one of them. She told me that I was incredibly smart and that I could do whatever I wanted to do if I put my mind to it.

Deep down inside, I had always felt that I was "different", "gifted", and "incredibly smart"; but I had never had anybody else to tell me that I was those things in such a matter of fact way. She told me those things as if they were laws of the universe that were beyond refutation. She asked me a lot of questions that no one had ever asked me before. Many times I wasn't prepared to answer. She asked questions like: "what do you want to be or do?" and "where do you want to go to school?" When I couldn't find any answers to those questions, she rattled off her own suggestions and recommendations in rapid succession. She suggested what seemed to be anything and everything under the sun. She always finished up her speech with: "it doesn't matter, your potential is endless and you can do anything that you want."

The first semester of my senior year came to an end with me receiving an A in Mrs. Valcarcel's class and a 3.57 GPA for the semester; my GPA would have been much higher if it were not for a C in Trigonometry. After the course ended, I still visited her class when I got a free moment. I suppose we had grown fond of each other. For her part, Mrs. Valcarcel's made it a point to attend some of my basketball games. She didn't stop there. She also talked to me about her family and she talked to her family about me; in fact, she talked so much that I felt that I knew her family and that her family knew me.

Mrs. Valcarcel eventually became a part of my life and I guess I became a part of her life as well. She had seen me and my girlfriend walking together in the hallways and she began talking to me about interracial dating and love. She asked me if I loved my girlfriend and I told her that I did, at which point she told me that that was all that mattered and not to pay any attention to people who had no clue about life. She talked as if she was a world traveler who happened to get stuck in a small and unrefined town. She actually appeared to be upset at the people who opposed the relationship that I had with my girlfriend based on race. She said that made no sense at all. After a while, she even began to develop a personal relationship with my girlfriend.

In the span of about six months, Mrs. Valcarcel was involved in my scholastic life, athletic life, and love life. She was more involved in those parts of my life than any parent or guardian had ever been. I knew that we were heading toward a point that I had never shared openly with anybody in my whole life. I knew that she would eventually get around to asking me about my family situation and my parents.

I decided that I would tell her if she asked me. That was a very different decision from any of the previous decisions that I had made in the past. Usually when I sensed that someone was going to ask me that question, I would subtly change the course of the relationship in an effort to prevent it from being a topic of conversation. But it was different with Mrs. Valcarcel. I just felt that I could trust her with the pain that I had locked away in the depths of my soul. I hadn't opened that place of pain since I was a small child.

The inevitable subject came up in an odd sort of way. It was during the second semester and she asked me what schools had I applied to at that point. I told her that I hadn't applied to any schools yet. When I told her that, it was just like I hit her in the head with a brick. She was dumbfounded. She asked me what was I waiting for and why was I waiting. I told her that I didn't know what I had to do and that I wasn't aware that there was any special timeframe that I had to get things done. She went on and on, in her staccato style, about all the things that I should have already done and all the things that I needed to start doing right away. Somewhere in the middle of her rapid succession delivery of all the things that I needed to do, she named one or two things that my parents would have to do. It was those things that she said that my parents would have to do that ignited our conversation.

I told her that anything that I needed from my parents was going to have to come from somewhere else because I wasn't in contact with either of them and had not been for a long time. The first brick must have been a boomerang because it looped back and hit her again; for the second time, she was dumbfounded. I told her that my dad and I had never been close and that my mom was going through some problems with drugs. I told her more about the situation than I thought I would, but I didn't tell her as much as I wanted to tell her.

I didn't tell her that I basically had no emotions attached to the man who everybody else referred to as my dad. I say everybody else, because I didn't refer to him at all. He would occasionally come back to live at Grandma Mary's house during my high school years that I spent living there, but that didn't mean anything to me. The love for his mother and the twenty-three chromosomes he dropped off with his semen were the only things that he and I ever shared. When I did see him at my grandmother's house, we walked by each other in the narrow hallways like two strangers in a dark alley in a large city—guarded.

By the time that I began high school, I had not known him as a person; so there was no way that I could have known him as my dad. I was distanced from him emotionally the way that Pluto was distanced from the sun. Our relationship was nothing more than ice and rock—it was cold and hard. The fact that I really didn't inherit any of his physical features made it easy for me to distance myself from him physically too. He didn't act like my dad and he didn't look like my dad, so I acted like he wasn't my dad and I didn't look at him like he was my dad. I didn't look at him at all.

The only thing that I felt for my dad at all was a burning anger in the pit of my stomach. He was a man that never talked to me, and the few times when he did say something to me, it was in words that I never understood the first time because he mumbled. I usually had to ask him to repeat whatever grunt or groan he hurled my way.

Normally he didn't have an impact on me one way or the other, but sometimes I would feel intense anger in his presence. I thought that I would have been better off if I had been the son of Cronus. I guess my anger was fueled more so by curiosity than anything else. I wondered why he acted as if he had nothing to do with the fact that I was a living and breathing creature in this world. I wondered why he had never apologized for any of his lack of involvement in my life. I wondered why he had never offered any sympathy for what I was going through growing up in a world all by myself.

After thinking such thoughts, I always came to the conclusion that I would go out of my way to help another Black child avoid the same feelings of isolation and pain that had been such an integral part of my own life. It didn't seem to be anything that I could do about my situation, but maybe I would have the opportunity to help someone else in the future.

My feelings of isolation and pain couldn't be attributed only to my dad; my mom also played a tremendous role in creating those feelings. My relationship with my mom was more complex because I actually loved my mother. I had spent some time around her in my early youth, so I knew more about her as a person. But that knowledge of her as a person was where my problems began.

It seemed to me that she would rather be doing almost anything else instead of being my mother. As a small child, I watched her choose to indulge in the streets of Plant City like the streets held all that was good about life. As she ran the streets, she neglected her duties as a mother like somehow our mother-infant bond had never been fully developed. Perhaps it was a premature mother-infant bond because I was born three months early.

Our relationship never recovered from our time together in Plant City and we only grew further and further apart as the years went by … but I never stopped loving her. By the time that I became a high school senior, I had no idea of what my mom's life was like; and she had no idea of what my life was like. I had no idea what she was doing on a day-to-day basis, but I knew that it wasn't good and I worried about her from time to time. Yet, the pain and anger would always be just a few thoughts behind the worries that I had for her.

I just didn't understand why my life was the way that it was and I wondered if the two people who were responsible for me being in the world had ever even talked about my future. I wondered how they thought that I was supposed to make it in the world without parents. I wondered if my mom had even seen the newspaper article of her son on the front page of the sports section.

I wanted to tell Mrs. Valcarcel all those things, but the only thing that came out was that anything that I needed from my parents was going to have to come from somewhere else. I told her that my substitute parent list was short. I told her that my mom's brother was probably the best direction to look in for any involvement from my family. Both of my grandmothers were great at the food, clothing, shelter thing; but neither of them knew much about higher education and the process of applying to a university or college. I told her that my uncle probably didn't know much about applying to colleges either, but he would be better than any other option.

Mrs. Valcarcel took the new information about my family situation and took her involvement in my life to a new level. I guess she concluded that if the things that needed to get done were going to get done, then she would have to be the one that made sure that they got done. She began to use the fax machines, copiers, and computers in the main office of Southeast High School like they were the exclusive assets of Get Quincy Smith to College Inc. She had me filling out paperwork for financial aid; she had me applying to the University of Florida, Florida St. University, and the University of Central Florida.

It seemed to me like we were sending information everywhere in an effort to get me anywhere that was a good school and that would provide some financial assistance. She thought the "good school" part was essential, she said I was too smart not to go to a "good school". She stayed with the state schools because she thought that I had the best chance of getting the most money.

All of Mrs. Valcarcel's efforts to get me to one of Florida's universities would yield some dividends, but my path of choice would lead me to Eckerd College. Our basketball season ended with a loss to St. Petersburg Gibbs in the district championship game, but not before we had silenced all critics and doubters by posting a final record of 26 wins against 5 losses.

I had also played well enough to silence my own critics and doubters. The last part of the season wasn't as strong for me as the first part of the season; my new view towards my coach after our little talk about my white girlfriend didn't help. Nevertheless, I suppose I played well enough to get a look from Eckerd College. Eckerd had been interested in Floyd all along, but I had played very well at the Eckerd College Christmas tournament during our Christmas break. So when they found out that Floyd and I had a strong friendship they showed an interest in me as well.

In a phone conversation, it was arranged for Floyd and me to meet the Eckerd coach at a junior college tournament game that was being held at the Manatee Civic Center; we all just watched the game and talked a lot about basketball. After the game, the coach began discussing the possibilities of the two of us attending Eckerd. I remember being very excited about that because Floyd and I had always planned to go to the same college, but for a long time it just looked like it wasn't going to work out that way. The words from the coach gave us new hope that our plans were going to work out after all. The next day, I told Mrs. Valcarcel the news and she immediately began to do research on Eckerd College.

After researching the institution, she told me that it was a very well regarded academic institution and that she thought it would be a great opportunity if I had a chance to attend the college. She did mention that the college was very expensive at over $16,000 dollars a year. She asked me if I had discussed finances with the coach and I told her no, but I did mention that the coach had said that he would call me in a couple of days. She said that the only thing to do was to wait for his call and to address the finances at that time.

When the coach called back, he said that he could put together a package that would cover a little over $13,000 dollars a year (including federal money). I promptly reported the offer to Mrs. Valcarcel. She said that I could easily get the rest of the money in loans to attend Eckerd, but that I might be able to get a full ride from one of the state universities based on academic performance and federal money. I told her that the Eckerd package was good enough because I considered the opportunity to play college ball with Floyd to be priceless. I told her that Floyd and I had always talked about playing college hoops together since we were both eighth graders at Bradenton Middle School. She wanted to hold out for the full ride state option, but when she heard how excited I was, we both agreed that that was the deal for us. She was satisfied that I was going to a fine academic institution and I was satisfied that I was going to play hoops with Floyd. So just like that, my future included a college education.

The newspaper came out to take a picture and do a write-up when Floyd and I signed our letter of intent to play for Eckerd on April 10, 1991. I actually signed my letter of intent twice; I signed my own name on the line provided for the student and then I signed my mom's name on the line provided for the parent or legal guardian. The signatures looked completely different because I had learned over the years to sign my mom's name differently than I signed my own. It bothered me a little that I didn't have at least one blood family member with whom I could really celebrate the joy that I felt about actually getting a chance to go to college and play basketball, but I shrugged it off like I always did. I felt too good to allow melancholy to blow my high.

I felt good because good things were happening for me; and it seemed that whatever happened to me also happened to Floyd. We were both one of sixteen seniors out of a class of two hundred ninety-three seniors to be chosen as Senior Notables for our contributions in the area of basketball, academics, leadership, and racial harmony. Picture that, who woulda thunk it; me chosen for racial harmony.

We were also invited to an invitation only try-out for a summer AAU team that would be made up of the top players from the Suncoast area of Florida. From my best assessment of the situation, the Suncoast area included players from Pinellas, Manatee, and Sarasota counties. The Pinellas area was strong; the St. Petersburg Gibbs team could boast three All-Americans by itself.

I was very excited to be invited to the try-outs because it meant that I had gained considerable credibility on the basketball court.

The invitation did a lot for my mental psyche because I had never been considered an elite player amongst my peers. The invitation was my chance to show that I did belong to that group and I set out to prove it.

The try-outs were designed to have the final twelve players after three cut periods. After the second of the three cuts, I was the only player left from my county and I knew that if I made the last cut that I would have done something that nobody expected me to be able to accomplish. However, on the day of the last cut, the coach pulled me over and told me that he wasn't going to be able to keep me. He said that he would have liked to, but he needed combination guards who could play both the point and the shooting guard positions—guys who were six feet and above. He said that I should have been proud of the way that I played at the try-outs because I sure made it a very difficult decision. So, I was released, along with one other player. I never counted for sure, but it appeared to be about thirty or so players invited to the try-outs, and I made it to the top fourteen. Shucks, I was just two short of the final twelve.

I wasn't too disappointed by not making team Suncoast, because I walked away from the try-outs with a confidence that I had played extremely well among some of the state's best players. I also walked away from the court with the respect of the people that I had competed against over the course of the try-outs. That might not mean something to some people, but to anybody who has ever played the game and really cared about it; they know that respect is everything. On the basketball court it was, is, and shall be a must that you make people respect you (basketball imitates life).

I felt like I should have made the team. I know I played well enough to make it; but what did that mean? It was just an early lesson about something that I would come to know later in life. It was written in Ecclesiastes 9:11:

> I returned, and saw that under the sun, that the race is not to the swift, nor the battle to the strong, neither yet bread to the wise, nor yet riches to men of understanding, nor yet favor to men of skill; but time and chance happeneth to them all.

I knew that most basketball coaches measured the game in feet and inches; I just came up short with that particular coach. I knew that I had the heart of a giant, but there aren't too many folks who take time enough to measure the heart. That's ironic because heart wins just as many games as feet and inches.

Undaunted and unfazed, I felt good about where I had taken my basketball abilities. Other people were also recognizing the fact that I could play the game. I had always had dreams of playing professional basketball since the eighth grade, but those dreams had been buried under the difficulties of my sophomore and junior seasons. However those dreams were starting to resurface. During the try-outs, I had proven to myself that I could play with some of the best that our state had to offer; and with four years of college to improve my game, I felt that I had as good a chance as anybody else. Besides, I was on top of the world. I thought that I could accomplish anything that I set out to accomplish. Confidence was my middle name—Quincy Confidence Smith.

The last month of school was a breeze. Everything was going just great. My SAT scores came back and I had eclipsed the 1000 mark with a score of 1040. During the last week of school, I realized that I was going to achieve my first 4.00 GPA of my high school career. I thought about all that I had gone through as a sophomore and as a junior, and decided that it was all worth it in order to feel the feeling of euphoria that I was now experiencing as a senior. I felt like I came; I saw; I suffered; and then I conquered!

That conquering feeling was enhanced during the summer when I received letters from the University of Florida, Florida State University, and the University of Central Florida. They all wrote me to inform me that I had been selected to receive an academic scholarship to attend their institutions. Those letters and the scholarship to Eckerd gave me a sense of power; I felt that if I wanted to get it done, then I had the skills and work ethic to get it done. I felt that way because the start of my senior year was full of uncertainty, but I overcame that uncertainty through hard work and the use my God given talent. Still, I wasn't ready to rest on my laurels; I wanted to achieve even more on the collegiate level.

I couldn't wait to go away to school. I was so ready to leave the atmosphere at Grandma Mary's house I could taste it. I loved my grandmother and the family that sheltered me when I could find no other shelter, but it was an atmosphere that I couldn't wait to escape.

My mom's brother aided me in my escape when he fixed up a Volkswagen Rabbit as my going away present. He had promised me that he would buy me a car if I graduated from high school. He made me that promise after his wife kicked me out of the house as a tenth grader. At the time when he made that promise, I didn't know if I was going to make it to my high school graduation or not; but when I look back, I see that I did much more than make it to graduation. I say that "I" did much more than make it to graduation, but in my heart I know that it was the Lord who made it all possible.

On that fateful night that my uncle made that promise to me, I prayed a long prayer to God because I had no place else to turn. I just want to take this moment to say: thank-you Jesus for delivering me from a day filled with fear and doubt. I choose to write that "thank-you" in print because whoever might stumble across the words on this page might be able to look back and remember the long way that the Lord has brought them along their journey in life. Perhaps in looking back and remembering, that person might offer praises to the One who sits on the Right Hand of God with all power in His hand; because He, and He alone is worthy to be praised! Amen.

I want you to go to school, because I believe that an education is the key you need to open up a new world and a new life for yourself ... It is the only key that can do that, and only those who seek it earnestly and perseveringly will get anywhere in this white man's world. Education will open doors where none seem to exist. It'll make people talk to you, listen to you and help you; people who otherwise wouldn't bother. It will make you soar, like a bird lifting up into the endless blue sky, and leave poverty, hunger and suffering behind ... Above all, it'll make you a somebody in this world.

Mark Mathabane,
Kaffir Boy
1986

Education consists not only in the sum of what a man knows, or the skill with which he can put this to his own advantage. A man's education must also be measured in terms of the soundness of his judgment of people and things, and in his power to understand and appreciate the needs of his fellow man and to be of service to them. The educated man should be so sensitive to the conditions around him that he makes it his chief endeavor to improve those conditions for the good of all.

Kwame Nkrumah,
speech given at the institute of African Studies
25 October 1963

BET IT UP

College

"College provides a glimpse of the higher life, the broader possibilities of humanity, which is granted to the man who, amid the rush and roar of living pauses four short years to learn what living means"

W.E.B. Du Bois, **Speech given at Fisk University commencement,** *(1898)*

I can still remember the day that I left for school. I loaded up the car that my uncle fixed up for me and I hit Eckerd College like I had a new lease on life. I had dreamed about that day for a long time. Not so much from the standpoint of going to college, but more so from the standpoint of finally escaping my environment. Living with so many relatives other than my parents had caused me to carry around a feeling of being an unnatural fit in most of the households in which I lived. I carried that feeling with me throughout my entire childhood.

In the normal paradigm of society, a child is supposed to live with his or her parents. However, rising divorce rates and the increasing number of single parent households forced the "normal" paradigm to be adjusted in order to accommodate single parents. Therefore, if you grew up with at least one of your parents, then you could include yourself in the "normal" category.

I had grown up not living with my parents, so no matter where I laid my head at night during my childhood I always felt like I was not really supposed to be there because my parents weren't there to complete that model that society considers "normal". And if they were there, they definitely were not there in a primary support position for me or for the household. In the majority of the instances where I did live in the same household as one of my parents, he or she was being taken care of in the same marginal way that I was being taken care of. The fact that we were both being taken care of by other adults significantly impaired the "normal" parent-child relationship. Yet, because of the legitimate biological relationship between us, we couldn't be brother, sister, or cousin; so it was almost like we weren't related at all. The natural order of things wouldn't allow for us to be anything but what we should have been. They were supposed to be my parents and I was supposed to be their child, but they never acted like my parents. Truth be told, they didn't act like anything; we weren't even friends. I was their kid ... genetically; but nothing in our environment corroborated the biological evidence. Because of the situation, the only thing that we were was abnormal.

When I left for college, I knew that it was going to be an experience that would greatly reduce that maladjusted feeling that I always carried inside of me of never feeling like a natural fit. By going to college, I was entering into the same situation that a countless number of "normal" kids were entering into. No matter how untraditional my home may have been, I was leaving home just like "normal" kids were leaving home. I was expected to live without parental supervision ... just like "normal" kids were expected to live without parental supervision. I was expected to live with someone new that I had never lived with before ... just like "normal" kids were expected to live with someone new with whom they had never lived. So the experience of starting college for me, in one respect, was an ending of years of what I had felt to be an abnormal childhood experience where I was different from everybody else. It was the beginning of a very "normal" late adolescent experience that I would share with countless others.

I relished in the opportunity to feel what it felt like to be "normal". The opportunity to be able to participate in a conversation of present experiences with the knowledge that I would find common ground with another human soul was something that I looked forward to doing.

Throughout my life, I had avoided or learned how to skillfully divert conversations where other people were talking about their parents or their family life experiences. I did that for at least two reasons. The first reason was because it hurt too much for me to voluntarily talk about my parents. There was a lot of pain for me in the fact that I had such an abnormal relationship with my parents. The second reason was that when one is a child it seems that one has a strong need to belong or fit in and I knew that my story was a story that did not belong or fit in with most other children.

I expected college to provide me with a more common experience where my additions to the conversations would belong or fit into the mainstream spectrum of normalcy. That was my only initial expectation of college save one exception. I planned on becoming a basketball star. Other than those two expectations, I arrived at Eckerd College with no idea of what to expect. But I took comfort in that; I suspected that ninety-nine percent of the college freshmen across the nation had arrived at their respective institutions not knowing what to expect. I was "normal".

The first month of the semester began in August for freshmen at Eckerd. It was a period called Autumn Term and it was only for freshmen. In order to offset that month, non-freshmen students participated in a similar term called Winter Term during the month of January. The freshmen students were excused from any course of study during the month of January. By the end of the year the freshmen and non-freshmen ended up with the same amount of course study.

The freshmen that participated in Autumn Term were responsible for only one course of study over an intense three-week period in August. That was comparable to the one course of study that non-freshmen were responsible for during the month of January.

Autumn Term was designed to acclimatize freshmen to the college life and a new environment over a three-week course of study before they undertook a full course load. The non-freshmen students did not return until September, so during the month of August the campus was more or less the exclusive domain and territory of the freshmen. I suppose it was all a clever system of trying to provide the freshmen students with the maximum chance of success at the start of their college careers by reducing the initial shock of rigorous study and leaving home.

Floyd and I had registered for the same autumn term course called African-American Women in Literature. It was a course centered on the works of prominent female African-American writers like Zora Neale Hurston and Toni Morrison. In hindsight, I sincerely wish that I had taken the course more serious than I did because I think that I could have gotten a lot more out of it than I did.

Our entire class with the exception of two white girls was filled with Black students. That was cool with me, because it provided a freemasonry that made the class more interesting.

Despite the material, Floyd and I did not let class take up too much of our time; our main goal was to have fun. We thought that we were on the first real leg of a journey that we knew would lead us to the good life of professional athletics on the basketball court; and more importantly, we were doing it together just like we had planned since the eighth grade. As far as the class went, we did what we had always done in high school.

We read just enough of the assigned readings to sniff out the theme of the book; if that proved to be too difficult, we simply found two or three important passages that were deep enough to allow us to write a short paper or participate in class discussions. We thought that we were being smart ... our goal was to make the best grade while doing the least amount of work. In hindsight, we know that we missed out on some really great books; but you couldn't tell us that then, the amount of free time that could be gained by doing it our way was too good to pass up. We seized our ill-gotten gains and spent the extra time making ourselves known to whoever was around.

We had plans on taking over the school and we both decided that we weren't going to wait around until our senior year like we did at Southeast High. We figured that a successful takeover on our part would require a strong promotion and marketing campaign. I mean Floyd had never been shy or at a loss for words since I had known him and by that time in my life one would have never known that I was his understudy because I had learned to match Floyd's verbal assaults word for word with excellent marksmanship.

During the first few days of autumn term, our marketing campaign efforts were very limited, but it wasn't too long thereafter that we were given a forum to step them up. Our opportunity presented itself in the form of a nighttime weekend party sponsored by the college for all the freshmen on campus. The event was pretty dull, so we decided that we would take it upon ourselves to add some excitement.

As we looked around the room for something that would help us accomplish our goal; our eyes simultaneously settled upon two microphones on the stage at the front of the auditorium.

We both thought that the rap that Floyd had done at the senior show at Southeast was the bomb. Since Floyd had spent years making it up, I had heard it enough times to know enough of it by heart to help him out in performing the lyrics. We both agreed that that party needed something to keep everybody awake, so we engineered an agreement with whoever was over the school-sponsored event to let us get on the stage to rap.

We got on the stage and did our thing. The performance did not go over as well as it did when Floyd did it by himself at the senior show at Southeast. I don't know if it was fair to expect people who had only known us a few days to respond the same way as people who had known Floyd for years. I would much prefer to look at it that way as opposed to citing myself as the possible culprit who hindered the performance of a proven successful solo artist.

Despite the diminished success, there were still enough people in the audience who gave us enough positive feedback where we weren't embarrassed by our performance. As far as Floyd and I were concerned, we had accomplished our goal; the performance had kept us awake at what had to rank near the top of the list as one of the most boring college parties ever. We laughed about it for most of the night.

After that night of laughter, the positive memories that I associate with that rap performance end like the period at the end of this sentence. I don't write that because of anything else that happened that particular night at the party, but more so because of the context in which I was next reminded of the rap performance.

The Director of Multicultural Affairs at Eckerd, who happened to be an African-American, called me into her office and informed me that there had been some bikes stolen from campus on the night of the party where Floyd and I did our Run-D.M.C. impression. She said that there was one witness who described the perpetrators of the crime with one statement: "they looked like the guys who were rappin' on stage at the party".

I was stunned. First of all, I had never even come close to even thinking about stealing a bicycle in all of my life. The second reason was because it didn't even make any sense for me to steal a bike when I had a car. The third and final reason that I was stunned was that out of any of the expectations that I had of college the out and out racism that inspired that trumped up bogus charge was not one of them.

I had never seen any two guys together that looked like Floyd and I in all the years that I had known him, but some white female at the party managed to see two guys that looked like we did in a matter of hours. He was 6-6; I was 5-8. He was light-skinned; I was dark-skinned. We were complete opposites in appearance as individuals; as a pair, we were rarer than rare.

I wasn't going for it; I knew that it was more about the color of our skin than a legitimate case of mistaken identity. The only crime that Floyd and I had committed was trying to liven up a dead party and being Black. I don't know if she had actually seen two Black guys or if the whole thing was a lie. Either way, I was willing to bet that whoever she did or didn't see did not look like me and Floyd. But I knew that some white people thought that all Black people looked alike anyway. (Later on in my college career, I found out that there was actually a thing called Cross-Race Identification Bias: The tendency for people to be better at identifying members of their own race than members of other races).

I learned from that experience that racism had the ability to rear its ugly head at anytime and any place. I learned that it could smack you in the back of the head like a brick when you least expected it ... leaving your soul battered and bloody if you let your guard down. All of my old environments had taught me that lesson, but I guess I thought that a college campus would be different ... more enlightened I suppose. Unfortunately, I was wrong ... and the brick-hard accusation against my skull let me know it (It was definitely an oops upside yo head!).

A couple of other school officials asked me a few questions, but ultimately nothing in the form of action was ever taken. I suspect that the reason was that there wasn't any real evidence to support such a preposterous claim. For example, what had we done with the bicycles? That was a question that no one could answer. Despite the lack of aggressive prosecution, the indictment had made its mark on me, I was keenly aware of my race at Eckerd College from that day forward. You would never catch me on stage again trying to give a dead white party some Black soul. Nope ... never!

My awareness of race was heightened even more as Autumn Term came to an end and the non-freshmen students arrived for the start of the 1991 fall semester. I saw the campus fill up with white people. I kept looking for the Black element of the school, but I found none. I thought to myself, surely there must be more of us at this school than what meets the eye. Although I didn't like stereotypes, I found myself desperately hoping that the old stereotype of CPT (colored people's time) was the reason for our late arrival. However, as the days went on, I realized that only a very small number of Black people attended Eckerd College.

It hit me that the greater majority of the African-American males at Eckerd College were on the basketball team or had been on the basketball team. Eckerd did not have a football team and the baseball team was all white with the exception of one Black outfielder. I accepted the fact that the chances were very good that when I saw another Black male student that I was looking at one of my future teammates or an ex-member of the basketball team.

In my heart, I wished for more of a Black presence on campus; but in my mind, I was determined not to let race be a huge factor in my college experience. I was trying to continue on the journey of becoming a whole human being. I was attempting to view all people in the broader context of humanity instead of through the narrow lens of race. I had not yet been exposed to the words of James Weldon Johnson. As a matter of fact, it would be years before I even knew who Mr. Johnson was, let alone know his words. In the 1927 edition of his book entitled, *The Autobiography of an Ex-Colored Man*, Johnson wrote:

> And this is the dwarfing, warping, distorting influence which operates upon each and every coloured man in the United States. He is forced to take his outlook on all things, not from the view-point of a citizen, or a man, or even a human being, but from the view-point of a *coloured* man.

The practical experience of living my life would ultimately convince me of the veracity in Johnson's words, but at the tender age of eighteen, I was too immature in life experience to accept the narrow neck of the race funnel as the passageway for my thoughts and actions. I was optimistic enough to believe that the wide neck of the humanity funnel could still be the way of the world. I had begun to actively seek the humanity funnel in high school. I felt that it was the right position to take in the eyes of God and it made me feel better about the world. I used those two reasons as motivators to help me overcome some of the racism that I encountered in high school. I was hoping that I could use them again to help me overcome any racial issues that I encountered in college as well.

After I shrugged off the charge of stealing a bicycle, I decided to give the old forgive and forget philosophy another try. I attributed the false allegation to a case of mistaken identity instead of the color of my skin. I had worked hard to get to college and I planned on having as much fun as I could during my four years; I didn't want to get caught up in the whole race thing again. I had played that game before, so I knew that there wasn't any fun in it.

Determined to have a good time, my first year—with the exception of an incident with the Sarasota Police Department and an injury at the end of basketball season—was a year filled with fun.

The try-outs for the basketball team were where the fun began. I had practiced hard all summer long and I was playing the best basketball of my life. I was quick, confident, smart, and competitive. I was intense and all about business on the court. Plus, I could see that I had gotten the coaches attention. By the same token, they had gotten my attention as well. I soon understood that college basketball was much more demanding than high school basketball and that it would take everything that I had to do well. At the end of the tryouts, I was one of the twelve men on the Eckerd College Men's Basketball team. That was more of a feat than I realized at the time.

As our season began, I realized that we traveled in style when we went on the road. We traveled on chartered buses with televisions and VCR's on board. I had more fun on the trips than I did during the games. I wasn't getting into many games, but that was alright because I knew that I was becoming a better basketball player by the minute and that I would eventually get a chance to show what I could do in a game. If my experience at Southeast High School had taught me anything, it had taught me how to be patient. I knew what I could do because I was doing it in practice everyday. But anybody who has ever played sports knows that there is a big difference between practice time and game time, so I waited patiently for my game time.

That time came halfway into the season during a game where our starters had moved comfortably ahead of the team that we were playing and the coach decided to play the bench during the last part of second half. It was a period where the other team was desperately trying to catch up by applying a full-court press. Coach put me in the game along with four other reserves. It was a reserve group that had worked on breaking full-court presses extensively in practice, but usually I just defeated the need for following the play because I could dribble through the press all by myself. In that millisecond that lasts an eternity in basketball time, I decided that the full-court pressure from the game was the same as the full-court pressure from practice. I reasoned that I could dribble through our opponent's press the same way that I did in practice. So that's what I did.

I dribbled the ball behind my back and through my legs all the way through their pressure. I did that every time they tried to pressure us the length of the court. My fancy darting and weaving usually led to me dishing the ball to a teammate for an easy basket or to me shooting foul shots as a result of them fouling me. By the end of the game, I had scored four points, dished out five assists, and had no turnovers in the span of about 8 minutes of game time. But more than that, I had become a crowd favorite.

Every time that I dribbled the ball through their defense the crowd went crazy like we had just slam dunked the ball, hit a home run, or scored a touchdown. Without being able to pressure the ball, the opposition's effort to catch up was futile. After the game, the coach gave me a ride back to my dorm. He said: "You think you played a pretty good game tonight don't you?" I said: "Yeah, I did alright." He said: "Well, remember one thing. I'm the show at McArthur Center." I never knew exactly what he meant by that comment and at the time I didn't care because I knew that I had been the show at the McArthur Center that night, so I didn't give him or his words too much thought.

Life was going great for me. I was playing college ball, Floyd and I were teammates and roommates, and in my mind I was well on my way to a very promising college career. I was really becoming quite popular on campus. Although I didn't play much in the majority of the games, people knew that I was a really good player. And if they didn't know, my self-promotion routine was usually pretty convincing. Between basketball and my pursuit of social activities, it seemed liked my studies were something that I paid attention to from time to time. I was in school to party and play ball, if I had time to do class assignments after that, then that was cool too.

I approached my semester coursework the same way that I approached my Autumn Term coursework. I did enough to keep up and to get by, but I never let it get in the way of basketball or any social activities. Nevertheless, I still did pretty well during my first full semester of college. The first semester, including my Autumn Term course, ended with me earning a 3.00 GPA. My grade summary report for the 1991- 92 Fall Semester read:

African-American Women in Literature: A

Western Heritage I: A

Math Analysis for Management (Quant. Methods): C

Analytic/Persuasive Writing: B

Elementary Spanish: C

Shortly after I received my grades for the first semester, I was sitting around talking with a group of my friends. The group included Floyd along with three other freshmen basketball players. I didn't know it at the time, but over the next three years, we would all become as inseparable as five fingers on one hand. At our very best, we closed ranks to become as tight as a fist. It was a Florida group composed of Floyd, two other Black guys, one white dude and myself. One of the Black guys was from Ft. Lauderdale, the other was from St. Petersburg, and the white dude was from Melbourne. During the particular conversation to which I'm referring, we were all sitting around talking about our grades for the semester when an argument broke out.

The white dude, who seemed to be in a perpetual worry mode about one class after the other, was expressing his dissatisfaction about one of his grades when I made a mistake in the timing of one of my own comments. I would soon come to realize that the arguments between him and I were going to be an essential part of our friendship. They didn't turn out to be a negative because we both learned from one another. Actually, I think that our arguments caused us to develop a healthy love and respect for one another. However, in this case, an impartial observer would have been hard pressed to find any of the love or the respect that would develop later in our friendship.

As he was finishing up with his statements of discontent about his grades, I made a comment that was ill timed at best and insensitive at worst. I said that I had earned a 3.00 GPA without even trying. I went on to say that I thought that I could easily get a 4.00 GPA for the spring semester if I really tried. My comments trailed off at the last part of his comments about his disappointment with his grades and they met in the air the same way that hot water meets an ice-cold glass. You could hear the cracking sound in the air.

I hadn't meant to start any argument or offend anybody with my comments, but my assertion of what I felt to be factual information infuriated my white brother. He told me that I could do no such thing and that "I was just shooting off my mouth like I was always doing". I thought, well! Tell me how you really feel!

It was on from that point on! In response to his charges, I began to shoot my mouth off even more. We went back and forth about whether I could pull off a 4.00 GPA for the spring semester. The argument was long and intense. Mentally, it took me back to the time period in my life during my sixth grade experience at King Middle School when I made good grades just to show white people that I was just as smart as they were.

We were both unequivocally fixed in our opposite points of view regarding whether I could actually get a 4.00 GPA for the semester. Finally, we both got tired of arguing about the issue and decided that we would let the results from the spring semester settle the debate. He acted as if he had found the perfect way for him to prove his point. Undaunted by his confidence in my imminent failure, I told him to "bet it up".

I was fuming, and although the spring semester was a month away, I had to get started immediately. I started with a promise to myself that very day that I was going to go for broke in my efforts to get a 4.00 GPA. I wasn't going to let anybody, let alone a white dude, tell me what I could and could not do. By him telling me that I couldn't do it, he had made me all the more sure that I could do it. (A white man telling a Black man that he can't do it should be the first real indicator to that Black man that he can do it. We had a nation full of white men tell us that we weren't fit to be anything other than slaves, and look at some of us now. Colin Powell, the descendant of an ex-slave, is the Secretary of State).

The fact that he was white definitely had a lot to do with how I responded to him. I wasn't sure why he thought that I was so incapable of getting a 4.00 GPA. I didn't know if it had to do with my color or some other trait that he had observed in me that made him so sure of my cognitive abilities. I was hesitant to convict him as a racist, but I didn't dismiss racism as the basis for his charge. For me, the raw energy of the argument had dragged race into the matter and I couldn't let it go. I was going to show him that the days of the white male imposing limitations on the cognitive ability of the Black male were long gone—at least for this Black male. Who did he think he was to tell me what I couldn't do; better yet, who did he think I was to think that I would let him tell me what I couldn't do?

Oh yeah, it was definitely a bet that I knew that I wouldn't lose. On the strength, it was on. The defiant African spirits that flowed through me told me to bet the house on it!

WHAT'S THE CHARGE

In order to win the 4.00 GPA bet, which was strictly a wager of "you can't" versus "I can", I knew that I would have to pay more attention in class and try harder to stay on top of things like homework. Those two adjustments would have to prove sufficient to get the job done because I was having too much fun in my social life to cut back any hours from that department. A party popped up every weekend, and Floyd and I seemed to be in sync with that phenomenon because we popped up at every party. We were what we called "on the scene!" It seemed that my life outside of the classroom was one big road trip with the basketball team or one big party on campus. I loved every minute of it!

When I did get a free moment, I went back to Bradenton to catch a basketball game at Southeast or to visit my high school friends. On one of those trips back to visit my friends in Bradenton, I ran into a problem with the police; but before I get to that, I think it's best that I give you a little background information.

By the time Floyd and I graduated from Southeast, we had many friends of all different races, but there were three Black cats that we hung around with as seniors at Southeast who we would remain close to over the years. On this particular trip back to Bradenton, I decided to go out to a teen club in Sarasota with my three friends and a couple of guys that I had known for a long time as acquaintances. So all in all, it was six of us rolling in two cars—my home-boy's Chevy Chevette and my VW Rabbit that my uncle fixed up for me. In order for you to get a full understanding of how my homeboy and I felt about our cars, I must tell you that we saw those cars as much more than a Chevy Chevette and VW Rabbit.

Neither of us had known the freedom or joy of having access to a car for any extended period of time in high school, so now that the two of us had cars it was like bliss. The cars were on their last legs when we got them, but we treated them like they were a Benz and a Beamer. As a matter of fact, the day that my uncle gave me the Rabbit with its fresh $99 paint job, my friend and I detailed it up with a coat of the most expensive turtle wax that money could buy.

In addition to the new paint job, my uncle put some 6 X 9 speakers that had red sequence lights that flashed on and off through my hatchback window. If that wasn't enough, I had saved up some money over the summer to buy me some wide low profile tires to go over some GTI rims that I got from Floyd's girlfriend's brother. You couldn't tell us that we weren't rolling ghetto fabulous that first day that we pulled up to the courts in my freshly waxed ride.

Shortly after I got my VW Rabbit, my homeboy got his Chevy Chevette complete with a speaker box of four non-matching 6 X 9 speakers. So on the night that the six of us rolled to the club in Sarasota, the way we stuck our chests out, one would have thought that we had rolled to the club in a Benz and a Beamer instead of a Chevette and a Rabbit.

Everything was fine on the way to the club and inside the club, but we ran into a problem after the club. We had spent a good portion of our time at the club on the dance floor, so by the time the doors closed we had all worked up a late night appetite. There was a Subway sandwich shop on the main strip that we took to get back to Bradenton. We decided that we would stop there to get a sandwich and drink before we called it a night.

It was around 1:00 am or 2:00 am, I can't remember; but it was past the time where you could eat inside of the Subway. The drive-through was the only part of the business that was open. We ordered our food through the drive through and parked in the Subway parking lot to eat our food outside of the cars. The last thing that we wanted our cars to smell like was onions, pickles, oil & vinegar, and hot peppers. Long story short, we were all standing outside of the cars in the parking lot of the Subway eating the sandwiches that we had just purchased.

We were almost done with the sandwiches when the police pulled into the parking lot. I had already started to walk toward a dumpster to throw my garbage away when they got out of their car, but I could still hear them as they began to question my friends. They asked them what they were doing in the parking lot and where were they coming from at that hour. My friends said that we were eating our food that we just bought from the Subway and that we were just coming from the teen club up the street. I had just started back form the dumpster when I heard them tell my friends that we were going to have to leave immediately.

My friends curiously responded to their request by asking them what kind of problem were we causing by sitting in a parking lot of a restaurant where we had just purchased food. The cops said don't worry about all that, just get into your cars and leave. My friends said, well we would like to know what law we are breaking and why you are asking us to leave when we haven't finished our food that we bought from "this restaurant". The two policemen seemed to become irritated with the questions and grabbed two of my friends while informing them that since they didn't want to leave that they were going downtown.

Both of my friends attempted to pull their arms away from the cops. That's when all hell broke loose! The police slammed my two friends against the car with great force and then onto the ground with even more force. One officer wasn't convinced that that was enough, so he sprayed one of my homeboys in the face with some pepper spray. They slapped handcuffs around their wrists, threw one of them into the patrol car, and left the other one lying on the ground. Right at that moment, two more cops arrived on the scene to offer their support to the other two by shouting at the four of us that we needed to get into our cars and leave or we would be next.

I felt rage as I watched my friend in the back of the squad car with his eyes searing from the aerosol that was sprayed into his eyes. My feeling of rage quickly shifted to a feeling of helplessness as I looked at the high powered firearms on the hip of each cop. At that point, I told my friends to get in the car, but yelled to the cops that we were going to follow them to the station to make sure that's where they were being taken. One of the reasons that I said that was because we were all streetwise enough to know that cops did some shady things in situations like that one. But I think the main reason that I said it was to fill the void between the rage and the helplessness that I felt in the pit of my stomach. I wanted to say and do more, but I knew that all that I could do was yell a pseudo aggressive statement that had no power.

The policemen got into their cars and we got into our cars and followed them to the police station. I knew that it was impossible for the pepper spray to evaporate from my homeboy's eyes as quickly as our fun had evaporated into the night air, but still the pained look that I saw on his face made me wish for it to be so.

On the way to the station, we were now two deep in my car instead of three deep. Normally two would have been sufficient for conversation, but the only sounds you could hear were my low profile tires rolling over the pavement. I was quiet because I just couldn't understand how my two friends ended up in handcuffs in the back of police cars when we had broken no laws. We had gone out on the town to have a good time and stopped to get something to eat before going home, that's all. I just couldn't help thinking that if we weren't Black males and the officers weren't white (three white males and a white female) that the whole thing would have played out very differently.

For some idiotic reason, I thought that I could go into the police station and explain the situation to some person with some sense and our friends would get to go home with us. Boy was I dumb! I might as well had walked into the station and started talking to a brick wall because nobody was going for it. They said that nobody was going anywhere unless my friends could post a bail of $250 (ten percent of $2,500).

In describing the Gestapo tactics of the police, the brothers in the hood changed the official police motto from "to serve and to protect" to "to serve, protect, and break a nigga's neck". But now the cops were showing me that they would also serve, protect, and take a brotha's paycheck. We didn't have $250 dollars, so we had to leave while our two friends stayed behind in jail.

We left the police station in a daze wondering how we went from dancing at the teen club and eating sandwiches in a parking lot to two of our friends being locked up behind bars. The four of us who escaped incarceration decided that we would split up the task of going to tell our homeboys' folks the news of what had gone down in the last two hours after leaving the club.

I did most of the talking at my friend's grandmother house. I told her about the situation and how it all went down. At the time,

I was still angry about the whole thing, so my voice was filled with emotion. I can remember how calm and relieved my homeboy's grandmother seemed to be after she learned that her grandson was not seriously hurt. It was almost like she was thankful that nothing more happened than what I was describing to her.

The more outraged that I became over what actually did happen; the calmer she appeared to become about what didn't happen. My best guest is that she probably knew then, what I know now ... and that's the fact that many young Black males don't live to walk away from confrontations with the police; it doesn't matter whether the confrontations are warranted or not. Five-O, the po po, one-time, the fuzz, the pigs, whatever you called the police in your town or in your era, it doesn't matter because the story been told one million times—the boys in blue have gotten away with all sorts of crimes.

From the days of slavery and the overseer (the overseer served as the police officer on southern plantations) until these very days of the 21st century, Black males have always been in grave danger when it comes to confrontations with officers of the law. Any incident between a cop and a Black male is a most serious matter that could turn into a matter of life and death in a heartbeat. We need to imprint that fact in the brain of every Black male child in this country. We have always been in and continue to be in serious peril when involved in any type of situation with so-called law enforcers of this nation.

For those who think that my words on this issue are extreme, I am going to use the words of others who have explained real scenarios from yesterday and today where innocent Black men have lost their lives when dealing with law enforcement officials. The overseer of yesterday and the officer of today, even the two words are similar. KRS-One pointed that out on his 1993 song, *"Sound of Da Police"*. He said: "Overseer, overseer, overseer, overseer, overseer ..., officer; yeah officer from overseer. You need a little clarity, check the similarity".

In his 1855 autobiography, *My Bondage and My Freedom,* one of the greatest and most courageous champions of justice, Mr. Fredrick

Douglass, described the character and behavior of an overseer on a plantation where he was enslaved. In describing the character of the overseer, Mr. Douglass wrote:

> Mr. Gore was one of those overseers, who could torture the slightest word or look into impudence; he had the nerve, not only to resent, but to punish, promptly and severely. He never allowed himself to be answered back, by a slave. In this, he was as lordly and as imperious as Col. Edward Lloyd, himself; acting always up to the maxim, practically maintained by slaveholders, that it is better that a dozen slaves suffer under the lash, without fault, than that the master or the overseer should *seem* to have been wrong in the presence of the slave.

In describing the behavior of the overseer, Mr. Douglass wrote:

> All the coolness, savage barbarity and freedom from moral restraint, which are necessary in the character of a pirate-chief, centered, I think, in this man Gore. Among many other deeds of shocking cruelty which he perpetrated, while I was at Mr. Lloyd's, was the murder of a young colored man, named Denby. He was sometimes called Bill Denby, or Demby; (I write from sound, and the sounds on Lloyd's plantation are not very certain.) I knew him well. He was a powerful young man, full of animal spirits, and, so far as I know, he was among the most valuable of Col. Lloyd's slaves. In something—I know not what—he offended this Mr. Austin Gore, and, in accordance with the custom of the latter, he undertook to flog him. He gave Denby but few stripes; the latter broke away from him and plunged into the creek, and, standing there to the depth of his neck in water, he refused to come out at the order of the overseer; whereupon, for this refusal, *Gore shot him dead!* It is said that Gore gave Denby three calls, telling him that if he did not obey the last call, he would shoot him. When the third call was given, Denby stood his ground firmly; and this raised the question, in the minds of the by-standing slaves—"will he dare to shoot?" Mr. Gore, without further parley, and without making any further effort to induce Denby to come out of the water, raised his gun

deliberately to his face, took deadly aim at his standing victim, and, in an instant, poor Denby was numbered with the dead. His mangled body sank out of sight, and only his warm, red blood marked the place where he had stood.

The prevailing attitude and actions of the overseer that Mr. Douglass describes from his experience in the 1800's have not wholly disappeared from today's American society (today referring to the age of the 21st century). Today's police officers patrol poor Black communities throughout the country in much the same manner that overseer's patrolled the plantations throughout the South. One can very well argue that the February 4, 1999 fatal shooting of Amadou Diallo was a modern day reenactment of the type of judge, jury, and executioner police tactics that was employed on plantations throughout the South during slavery.

Mr. Diallo, a Black man, was gunned down by an assail of forty-one bullets fired from the weapons of four white New York policemen. Nineteen out of the forty-one shots fired hit the unarmed and defenseless Black body of Amadou Diallo, pinning him against the door of his home until his lifeless body slumped to the ground and his head lay against a wall. The officers, who suspected Mr. Diallo of being a rapist, fired upon his body because they suspected that he was reaching for a gun. However, when they approached the body of the innocent dead man, they found that the object in the twenty-two-year-old's hand was only a black wallet. It was only a wallet, not a gun!

My proposal that a person could easily argue the similarity between the murder scene described by Mr. Douglass in his 1855 autobiography and the murder scene surrounding the death of Amadou Diallo in 1999 will undoubtedly be dismissed as erroneous by some. Others will simply dismiss it as plain foolishness. But for those who know something about the history of this country and something about the infrastructure and practices of the police departments in inner-city neighborhoods around the country, the connections between the two scenes are crystal clear.

In comparing the two situations, let's move beyond the simple comparison of unarmed Black men being shot and killed by white men. In the case of Mr. Diallo, let's move past the argument of whether the white officers shot and killed him because he was Black or because they thought that his wallet was a gun. I say that because the only people who truly know why Amadou Diallo was shot and killed are the officers that pulled the triggers forty-one times. But I also say it in order to move past the speculative arguments. In order to see the real similarities of the two situations you have to examine the role of the broader environments where the shootings of the Black men took place. It is the broader environment where the unequivocal similarity really exists.

I want to be clear on this point, so I repeat, let's move past the simple comparisons of unarmed Black men being shot and killed by white men (overseer and officers). Let's also move past the speculation on whether the police officers shot Mr. Diallo because he was Black or because they believed his wallet was a gun. Let's move past both those points; cast them out of your mind for the sake of this comparison.

If you examine the situation where Mr. Gore, the overseer on Col. Lloyd's plantation, shot the slave known as Denby in a county in Maryland some time between 1824 and 1826; then you would know that Maryland was a slaveholding state recognized by the U.S. government during that time period. That information is important because it establishes the framework of the environment where the slave known as Denby was shot and killed by Mr. Gore.

The environment of a slaveholding state was an environment where a Black man had no rights as a citizen. That non-citizenship status meant that Black men had no rights to equal protection or fair treatment under the law. If you wanted to go deeper, then I could go on to factually write that Black people that lived during the historical time period of slavery were regarded as property and had no rights at all. The lack of rights for Black people was an indisputable fact recognized on every slave plantation. In fact, the U.S. Government legally supported the lack of rights among Blacks on Southern slave plantations in America on the local, state, and federal levels.

I don't see the necessity of indulging too much to establish what has already been proven and generally accepted as historical fact, so I will hasten to establish my point. Mr. Gore was guilty of actually pulling the trigger in the shooting and killing of the slave known as Denby, but it was much bigger than that. Mr. Gore was a part of a corrupt system where the broader environment created by the local, the state, and the federal government allowed a white man to shoot and kill an unarmed and defenseless Black man ... and get away with it.

The examining of the broader environment where Mr. Amadou Diallo was shot and killed by four white N.Y.P.D. police officers will require a little more analysis than the environment where the slave known as Denby was shot and killed. A lot of the framework of the environment where Mr. Diallo was killed isn't as widely known or accepted among today's American public. That's only because racism is much more complicated today than it was during the time period in which Denby lived.

The neighborhood where Mr. Diallo was shot and killed was in the Soundview section of the Bronx. It is a neighborhood densely populated by a large number of African-Americans and Hispanics. On the night when Mr. Diallo was shot and killed, New York City's Street Crime Unit (SCU) was policing the streets of Soundview.

At the time of the Diallo incident, the SCU consisted of nearly four hundred officers who were given only three days of intensive training before being assigned to the special elite unit. Three days of training, no matter how intensive the training, is a very questionable duration of time to prepare an individual for such a difficult task. I say that if you are going to send an officer into a high crime area with extremely powerful weapons and the license to use them, then that officer should be thoroughly trained to handle a variety of situations because people's lives are at stake.

In addition to the lack of adequate training that the officers received, the N.Y.P.D. recognition and reward system for performance was heavily bent toward arrests and convictions. There is nothing wrong with a system that rewards and recognizes arrests and convictions of a police officer if that system also includes someone to police the police. In a system like that you need someone to makes sure that the arrests and convictions are arrests and convictions that obey both the actual and the intent of the law. Without that, there is little more than "scout's honor" to prevent an ambitious cop from being overly aggressive in his/her lawful duties.

In the case of the SCU, there appeared to be an absence of effective supervision of the police who were being paid by taxpayers' dollars (including the residents of Soundview) to protect all citizens. The fact that the special elite unit had the freedom to search, frisk, and arrest suspects freely throughout the city's poorest neighborhoods while having no official responsibility to any precinct lends support to the idea that the unit was poorly supervised.

Adequate internal supervision of a city's police officers is the responsibility of police chiefs, mayors, governors, and presidents. In other words, adequate and effective internal policing of the police is a local, state, and ultimately a federal accountability. The lack of adequate and effective internal supervision that undermined the success of the SCU is evident in the racial profiling that the members of the SCU used to make arrests between 1997 and 1998.

The racial profiling can be seen in the statistics reported in an article written by Howard Chua-Eoan. "Black and Blue", appeared in the March 6, 2000 issue of *Time Magazine*. It stated that the SCU, in order to make nine thousand arrests, stopped and searched forty-five thousand men. The overwhelming majority of the forty-five thousand men were African-American and Hispanic.

Considering the five to one ratio of stops to arrests, along with the fact that the majority of the men were either African-American or Hispanic, one has no choice but to conclude that a great number of innocent African-American and Hispanic males were being stopped and searched by the SCU. If you want to be exact about it, you could say that over thirty thousand innocent African-American and Hispanic men were stopped by the SCU between 1997 and 1998. I guess their skin tone was enough probable cause for the dutiful lawmen to stop and search them. In eighty percent of the forty-five thousand cases, there wasn't even enough evidence for an arrest, let alone a conviction. That should be appalling by any standard.

Let's go over the points of the broader environment where Mr. Diallo was killed.

1. There was a lack of adequate or effective training for the officers in the SCU.

2. There was a flawed system of recognition and rewards based on arrests and convictions without adequate or effective internal supervision of the officers in the SCU. A Brooklyn sergeant was actually quoted in the "Black and Blue" article in *Time Magazine* as saying: "If there is anyone who should have been on trial, it is the department. Those guys went out for numbers— they didn't go out to kill anyone—but the department wants guns and numbers."

3. The allowance of racial profiling—permission and approval to stop and search citizens and taxpayers for

no other reason than the color of their skins or where they live—that took place within the ranks of the SCU was allowed to exist by the local, the state, and the federal government.

From those three points, I draw my conclusion. Either through action or lack of action, the local government of New York City, the state government of New York, and the federal government of the United States conspired to create a racist environment. Yeah it was racist; it doesn't go down that way in white neighborhoods. In the poor neighborhoods of New York City, the method of policing used to reduce the crime rate adhered to an "ends justifies the means" strategy.

That type of policing strategy reduced the crime rate in the Soundview neighborhood where Amadou Diallo lived, but it came at a great social cost to the residents of that neighborhood. There were many costs, but the ultimate cost in this particular case was the shooting and the death of an unarmed and innocent Black man. The words: shooting, death, unarmed, and innocent rings in the ears of our people with "piercing familiarity".

I understand that the local government, state government, and the federal government all want a reduced crime rate. I think that all law-abiding citizens of all races want a reduced crime rate and safer streets in this country. However, I feel that it is imperative that government officials on all levels realize that there is a better way to do it than the way that it was done in the Soundview section of the Bronx where Amadou Diallo was shot and killed. Those officials would do well to recognize that there is a strong connection between the conditions in which people live and their disposition toward criminality. That is to say that local, state, federal officials, and the collective whole of America would do well to heed the wise council of Dr. Cornel West. I quote his words from his 1993 book *Race Matters*. In the book, Dr. West instructs:

> First, we must acknowledge that structures and behaviors are inseparable, that institutions and values go hand in hand. How people act and live are shaped—though in no way dictated or determined—by the larger circumstances in which they find themselves. These circumstances can be changed, their limits attenuated, by positive actions to elevate living conditions.

Local governments, state governments, and the federal government should focus more time and energy on improving the living conditions in higher crime areas. Let them aggressively seek to eliminate poverty, unemployment, homelessness, poor schools, and hopelessness in the poor neighborhoods the way that they aggressively seek to reduce the crime rate. At the same time, they should work diligently to eliminate the type of environments that I have described in reference to the SCU and the N.Y.P.D.

Until those officials do that, then they are just as responsible as the four white officers who pulled the triggers in the death of Mr. Amadou Diallo. The four white officers guilty of pulling the triggers in the shooting and killing of Amadou Diallo were a part of a corrupt system where the broader environment created by the local, the state, and the federal government allowed white men to shoot and kill an unarmed and defenseless Black man.

In a logical construction of what I knew to be true about the SCU and the shooting death of Amadou Diallo on February 4, 1999; I was able to write the same exact words that I wrote about the shooting death of a slave named Denby between 1824 and 1826. The only difference is I had to change white man to white men. In both situations, the perpetrators of both crimes were a part of a corrupt system where the broader environment created by the local, the state, and the federal government allowed white men to shoot and kill an unarmed and defenseless Black man ... and get away with it.

That's a real shame that in almost two hundred years we have traveled so little as a nation. The bigger shame is that both murders went unpunished by the justice system of the United States.

The four officers who shot and killed Amadou Diallo were cleared on all criminal charges in an Albany, NY courtroom on March 3, 2000. Twenty-four "not guilty" verdicts rang out in the decision to clear the officers. That's a small number considering the forty-one shots that rang out in the shooting and killing of Amadou Diallo.

The whole sickening verdict reminds me of a sentence that I read in Claude Brown's 1965 book. In *Manchild in the PROMISED LAND*, Brown wrote: "Yeah, they ain't gon do anything to a white cop for shootin' a nigger, even if it is New York." It makes me think that *we (you and me)* should start doing something about it—something more than we've ever done before.

Compare the Diallo verdict with what Fredrick Douglass wrote concerning the outcome of the shooting and killing of the slave known as Denby by the overseer on Col. Lloyd's plantation. In his 1855 auto-biography, *My Bondage and My Freedom*, Mr. Douglass wrote:

> All that Mr. Gore had to do, was to make his peace with Col. Lloyd. This done, and the guilty perpetrator of one of the most foul murders goes unwhipped of justice, and uncensured by the community in which he lives. Mr. Gore lived in St. Michael's, Talbot county, when I left Maryland; if he is still alive he probably yet resides there; and I have no reason to doubt that he is now as highly esteemed, and as greatly respected, as though his guilty soul had never been stained with innocent blood. I am well aware that what I have now written will by some be branded as false and malicious. It will be denied, not only that such a thing ever did transpire, as I have now narrated, but that such a thing could happen in *Maryland*. I can only say—believe it or not—that I have said nothing but the literal truth, gainsay it who may.
>
> I speak advisedly when I say this,—that killing a slave, or any colored person, in Talbot county, Maryland, is not treated as a crime, either by the courts or the community.

I too, like Mr. Douglass, know that what I have written here about the shooting and killing of Amadou Diallo, the SCU, the local government of New York City, the state government of New York, and the federal government of the United States will be dismissed and gainsaid by some. Those that will dismiss it do not think that such a system could exist in an American city in the 21st century. For those people that think this country to be above such a situation in the 21st century, I will ask that you do a little research. You can take the same issue of Time Magazine (March 6, 2000) that covered the Amadou Diallo verdict and read an article written by Adam Cohen entitled "Gangsta Cops". Read that article and it should be plain to see that all cops ain't heroes, all Black men ain't always guilty, and the system ain't always innocent. Black people already know that; we know that "every shut eye ain't sleep, and every goodbye ain't gone".

I almost forgot that I was writing an autobiography. I got off on a tangent where I became a trial lawyer indicting America for its crimes against the Black community. Well, the prosecution rests

...at least for now. In picking up with my personal story, I reiterate to the reader—in the form of my best guess—that I know why my homeboy's grandmother seemed so calm and relieved when she found out that her grandson was not more seriously hurt than what I reported to her on that night of our confrontation with the Sarasota Police Department. She probably knew then, what I know now—and that's the fact that many young Black males don't live to walk away from confrontations with the police.

I rode back to the St. Petersburg campus of Eckerd College the next day feeling very uneasy about the ordeal that my friends and I had gone through the night before. I played my N.W.A. tape on the ride home because I needed to validate the angry feelings that I was experiencing. I needed an outlet that dealt aggressively with the forces that had dealt aggressively with me and my friends for no justifiable reason at all.

Like so many Black men before me, I turned to music to deal with the hostile world around me, a world that seemingly went out of its way to give me a hard time. The tradition of the African expressing his sorrows, his joys, his pains, and his frustrations through music came over with the first slaves that were brought over from the motherland.

The fields of the South were the birthplace of the songs of the slaves that eventually led to the Negro Spirituals. All other subsequent forms of African-American music—ragtime, the blues, swing, bebop, Jazz, R&B, Rock and Roll, Reggae, Funk, Disco, and Rap —sprang from that tradition of expression that was first heard on American soil through the deep soulful holler of the field hands on the southern plantations. Phyl Garland, the jazz musician, does a great job of explaining the relationship that has always existed between the Black man in America and his music. She said:

> The relationship of the Black listener to the music that he regards as 'his' always has been a very deep and personal one, quite often reflecting a great deal about his subordinate position in the society. In contrast to all the things the Black man has not had in this country, he has always had his music. (Phyl Garland, c. 1988)

Rap music was the music that I most regarded as mine. It was the chosen form of music by many young Black males of my generation; it was the youth music that carried on in that tradition of deep soulful expression started in the fields of the South. It was the music that most honestly dealt with the issues of the Black community, while offering no apologies to an oppressive mainstream white world. On too many occasions it was the only honest outlet that I had to express a lot of the feelings that I felt.

Mainstream America blames rap music for a lot of things, and some of that blame may be justified. But what mainstream America doesn't realize is that the music keeps a lot of Black men from going off the deep end by allowing both some of the listeners and some of the artists to release pent-up anger and frustration. The alternative to releasing the frustration and anger is insanity. When it comes to a lot of Black men in America, there is a lot of truth in Melle Mel's warning of: "Don't push me, cause I'm close to the edge. I'm trying not to lose my head".

As I crossed the Skyway Bridge to the anti-police lyrics of N.W.A., I still couldn't figure out what crime my friends had committed or what law they had broken. My friends were charged with disturbing the peace and resisting arrest. The disturbing of the peace must have happened when my friends asked what law had they broken by eating sandwiches in a parking lot where we had just purchased the food. And the resisting arrest must have occurred when they had a problem with being handled with undue force for no legal reason. The true charge that night was that we were six Black males. Six white boys and no one would have been arrested or charged with anything. The more I thought about it, the harder I bobbed my head to the beat and the louder I chanted: "———Tha Police"!

CAN YOU PLAY

I hit the entrance of Eckerd College and it was like I was driving into a completely different world than I had just left the night before. The sun was shining, the landscape was manicured, and the water was glistening. The college's motto at the time was "The Right Climate for Learning". As I drove to my dorm, I can remember thinking how glad I was that it was a different climate than what I had been accustomed to all of my life. I didn't care if it was the right climate for learning, just so long as it was a change in climate.

The campus environment was definitely unlike the one filled with police cars, overzealous cops, and big guns that I had visited the previous night. In less than twenty-four hours, I had driven less than fifty miles, but I might as well had driven halfway around the world because the two surroundings were as alike as oil and water. Later that day, I sat by the sea wall and thought about life. I wanted to take my mind off the police encounter and settle back into my college routine.

My college routine was made up of basketball, a fun filled social life, and academics. The bet that I had made with my white friend forced me to take the books portion a little more serious than I probably would have if we had never gotten into such an intense argument about whether I could get a 4.00 or not.

Despite my new focus on books, basketball was still my favorite part of the college routine. We were winning and I was a better basketball player than I had ever been. I worked hard on the court to improve my game and I worked hard in the weight room to improve my strength.

At the rate that I was going, I knew that I would be in a position to be the starting point guard much quicker than I was at Southeast High School. It was just a matter of time before I would have to be given an opportunity to get some real time in a game. In my mind that opportunity was all that I needed because I knew that I had the skills. I wasn't the favorite of the coaching staff because I probably had a little bit more personality than they wanted to see, but even they knew that I was all about winning and I had the skills. I knew that ultimately they would not be able to deny me the chance to show what I could do in some serious game action. I knew that they weren't going to give me anything, but I was very confident that I could forcefully take what they wouldn't freely give. Right about the time that I came to that conclusion, the unthinkable happened. The thing that all athletes dread; I was injured. I hurt my ankle worse than I had ever hurt anything in my life.

The regular season was winding down and we were just a few games away from getting ready to enter the conference tournament. The injury happened after a relatively light practice. A few of the guys decided to stay around to play some three-on-three, so I decided to stay and play. I would spend years regretting that decision because I feel that it drastically altered my collegiate basketball experience. It's amazing how you spend years reliving one single moment. I jumped into the air and came down in such a way that my ankle twisted in every direction but the right direction. I heard a strange cracking sound as the pain shot through the area. I knew that I had done something very serious.

I knew that I was in trouble as my friends carried me into the training room. The trainer said that my ankle wasn't broken, but it was a very bad sprain. As he poked and prodded, my ankle already looked like a balloon with a helium addiction. I had sprained my ankle many times before, but I had never experienced any pain like I did at that time. The pain was so intense I felt dizzy.

The trainer gave me some crutches because I couldn't put any pressure on the injured ankle. That was the first time in my life that I could remember where I was unable to walk. He told me to ice the ankle as often as I could and gave me some ibuprofen for the pain and swelling; while advising that I keep it elevated. He also scheduled me for treatments during practice time. As he finished explaining our treatment plan of action, I kept thinking that I needed more medical care than he was giving me. I needed an X-Ray or something. The pain in my ankle was screaming that something was seriously wrong, but those screams would never be heard.

My family situation prevented me from going to see a doctor under any health insurance plan. I was on the default SOL plan that served as the default selection for the poorest inhabitants of this country. I thought that I was finally going to be able to escape the consequences of not having parents when I got to college … wrong thought. I can truly say that the fact of not having the traditional support normally provided by either one parent or both parents hurt me big time in the case of my ankle injury. Where most kids would have called up their parents and gone to the doctor under their parents' healthcare coverage, I was stuck like chuck and didn't nobody give a … care.

My scholarship/financial aid package only provided for my room & board and tuition; the school did offer a separate healthcare plan that could have been purchased, but that was something that had never come up in my discussions with my family members. It was my old case of being sort of half-raised by people who were not directly responsible for me being in the world.

The ankle injury brought back the many painful memories of childhood where I felt like I was nobody's child. It brought back the memory when no one was there for me to give me a ride home after my baseball games as a ten-year-old child. The realization that I was still in the same boat of needing at least one of my parents as an eighteen-year-old hurt almost as much as my ankle injury.

I resolved to accept my fate that I was done as far as the remaining 1991-92 basketball season was concerned. I turned my competitive focus to making sure that I won the bet of whether or not I could achieve a 4.00 GPA. I was still in a good position to achieve the goal when I hurt my ankle, but I knew that my performance on my final exams would determine if I kept my A's. I informed my white friend of my progress as my finals moved closer and closer. He stood firm in his position, relying heavily on my scores from my final exams to save him from the verbal assault that he knew that he would get from me if I earned a 4.00 GPA. My ankle was hurt, but my mouth worked fine.

The semester finally came to an end and I was one grade away from my coveted 4.00 GPA. My score on my Accounting final was the only thing that stood in between my goal and me. I took the Accounting final on a Friday; my professor said that she would post the grades on the door of the classroom by Saturday. Floyd and I went to Bradenton for the weekend; so I had to wait until we got back in order to find out my grade. My patience depreciated over the course of the weekend and I was anxious to get back to campus to reconcile my course account.

We arrived back on campus Sunday night and I immediately asked Floyd to walk with me to see what grade I had gotten on the exam. I remember the walk to the classroom like it was yesterday. I had on some flip-flop shoes that exposed my feet to the wet grass with each step that I took. My toes became so slippery from the wet grass that I could barely hold on to the flip-flops, but I pressed hard with a brisk pace. My injured ankle was throbbing like it usually did whenever I walked with any kind of determined purpose. I reached the door of the classroom and looked up and down the list looking for my student ID number until I found it. My eyes quickly read from left to right until I saw the A in the column designated for course grades. I exulted in personal triumph as I screamed self-approvals in Floyd's direction. And like the true friend that he had always been, Floyd exalted with me. We took great delight in the fact that my report card for the Spring Semester of 1991-92 would read:

Elementary Spanish: A

Western Heritage II: A

Business Law: A

Principles of Accounting I: A

As Floyd and I walked back toward the dorms, I was so busy feeling good about my achievement that I almost forgot what had motivated me to focus my eyes so diligently on the prize. My memory was jarred to the bet that I had made with my white friend when I began to extol my ability to do anything that I set my mind to doing. I remembered how my white friend had said that there was no way that I could do it and the joy of achievement intensified. I had defeated his attempt to define my ability and impose a limit on what I could achieve. I was going to be able to stop him from shooting off his mouth about what I could and couldn't do.

My white friend really didn't know with whom he was dealing when he so arrogantly asserted his feelings in regards to my ability.

I was blessed with a strong will to survive from the moment I drew my very first breath of life as a premature baby. On top of that, I had graduated from the Floyd Watkins School of Confidence (it existed in the only place that mattered, my own mind). Floyd's philosophy could best be summed up in the words of Ms. Janice Hale Benson. Ms. Benson said: "Know your place, but let no one tell you what your place is."

Before I met Floyd, I knew what confidence was and I knew what achievement was. My achievements usually preceded my confidence. That's how it works for most people. Floyd taught me how to take being confident to the next level. He inspired me to have the kind of confidence that preceded achievement. You know you can do it before you even do it. You are already there before you even get there. You can walk it like you talk it, because the only thing that you really need to achieve it is to really believe it. No one save Jesus can stop you once you reach that stage.

Floyd showed me how to know confidence, how to rationalize confidence, and how to use confidence in life. When it came to me believing in myself, Floyd had taken me through the three forms of knowledge that Amiri Baraka spoke about in a 1998 rap session with a group of aspiring writers in New Orleans. Baraka asked:

> Can you understand the levels of what knowledge is? The first level of knowledge is perception. Perception is nothing but a sponge. Everything you are around, you pick it up. You might not even know it, but your mind is just picking up stuff like a blotter. The second level is rationalization, you actually name it. Oh, that was this. But the highest form of knowledge is use. For example, I can say I know about the piano. I know all kind of stuff about the piano, about music, but then they say: can you play? I say, oh, no I can't play. (Amiri Baraka, in "Advice to Young Writers: Amiri Baraka," *The Black Collegian Online*, February, 1998)

That's the thing in life; you have to know how to use knowledge in order to really make it work for you. The words on this page are providing you with knowledge if you read them. But to be in possession of some knowledge about how to be confident is not enough, if you truly want to be confident you have to read between these lines to take that knowledge to its highest form. You have to be able to play confidence in the key of life: set goals, apply yourself, believe that you can achieve it, persevere in the face of adversity ... and you will get there.

My ankle stopped me from playing basketball that year, but it didn't stop me from playing the game of life. At some point, we all have to answer the "can you play" questions in life in order to get from where we are to where we are trying to go. When it came to making straight A's, I knew that I could do it; the actual achievement of straight A's was simply being confident enough to play that knowledge in a virtuoso performance.

CHASING PAWNS

My high from hitting my 4.0 GPA for the spring semester rolled right into the summer. I was feeling good about my academic accomplishments of my freshman year; I had a 3.44 GPA and a head full of ideas. I had already declared Business Management as my major and I had a plush bank job in Bradenton lined up for the summer. I got the job through a program called Step Up!.

Step Up! was a Manasota Industrial Council program that was designed to provide employment opportunities for young Blacks and Hispanics. The council partnered with several businesses of Manatee and Sarasota counties to create internships. One of the main goals of the program was to show "young, bright, and motivated" Blacks and Hispanics that they did not have to move out of the area in order to find good employment opportunities.

On the flip side, the program wanted to demonstrate to the local business community that minorities were good prospects for management-level, decisions-making positions. Last, but not least, the program set out to demonstrate to the community that opportunities in the local business world were based on ability and motivation, not on race.

The program had some lofty and admirable goals now that I look back on what it was trying to achieve, but at the time I really didn't care much about the objectives that the program was trying to accomplish or why such a program was needed. The only thing that I really cared about was the fact that I was going to have the opportunity to earn $5.50 an hour working in a bank; $5.50 an hour was a whole $1.25 higher than the $4.25 minimum wage for 1992. Besides the money, I figured that if I went to work everyday and applied myself that I could pick up some knowledge that I could really use.

The only problem that I saw with the summer was that I didn't have any wheels. During one of my last trips to Bradenton before school adjourned for the summer, I ran the VW Rabbit hot and blew the heads. Floyd and I broke down right before we reached the Skyway Bridge. The Skyway not only connected Pinellas County and Manatee County, but more importantly it provided safe passage over Tampa Bay. It had crashed once and a lot of folks died, but no one wanted to think about that ever happening again.

We popped the hood of the car and even our amateur eyes could see that the car had overheated. I am almost embarrassed to write that the two bright young men who were enrolled in and doing well in college courses actually pondered the thought of putting water from the bay (Tampa Bay is a large body of salt water) in the radiator. We were so ignorant and desperate that we couldn't figure out if it was the most ridiculous idea we had ever come up with or if it was the greatest idea that we had ever come up with. Perhaps there is some saving grace in the fact that we decided to label it as the most ridiculous idea. Yet it was so tempting … a boiling engine and all that water just twenty yards away.

After my uncle accessed the damage done to the car, I reasoned that I would not have lost anything more if I had put salt water in the radiator. He said that it would cost more to fix the car than it was actually worth, so he was hesitant to fix it. That meant that I wouldn't have any way to my new job unless I stayed somewhere where someone could give me a ride to work every morning and pick me up every afternoon. My uncle and his wife's house was the only logical choice when I considered the need to be able to depend on someone to get to and from work. Besides, they were really the only family that I had real contact with throughout my freshman year. They came to several of my games to see me sit on the bench before I hurt my ankle.

I think that they looked forward to the games because it was a nice get away for them. I suppose their life had become so routine that the games gave them a chance to take a shower, put on some clothes, and go somewhere. So all things considered, it was almost like my uncle's wife and I had never had any problems with one another. For me, their family was the closest thing that I had to a whole and complete family, so I let the past roll off my back.

My ace in the hole, Grandma Dot, came through for me when it was time for me to buy the appropriate clothing for my new job. My grandmother always came though for me like that when I really needed something that was vital in order for me to do something important for my future. I had no idea what I should wear, so my uncle picked out most of the clothes that my grandmother bought. So that first day that I got dressed to go to work, I couldn't tell you much about my clothes or the way that I looked on the outside, but I can remember feeling like a million dollars on the inside.

I met the man who would be my mentor for the summer. He was a big shot and he looked the part. His official title was VP of Residential Lending. His office wasn't really that big, but it had expensive looking things adorning the desk. In addition to the expensive looking decor, there were a few awards recognizing him for his various accomplishments during his career.

My first impression was that he was a cool middle age white dude that I might be able to learn something from if I paid attention. Later, I would find out that my first impression was right on and then some. I was supposed to meet with him periodically during my eight-week employment with the company to talk about how I liked the organization and to ask him any questions that I might have regarding different aspects of the banking industry.

My main job duty during the program was to assist mortgage reps in arranging files for customers that were interested in re-financing their mortgages at lower interest rates. That was mainly making sure that the files contained all the proper paperwork in order to be passed onto the rep. In hindsight, I realize that I was a secretary. But at the time, I didn't think about my title or my role, I just did what I was asked to do. I quickly mastered the task of arranging files and I was soon able to do it without too much mental effort. After a few weeks, the repetitiveness of the job became boring, so I jumped at the chance when my mentor offered to let me accompany him to an offsite meeting. The chance to get away from the never-ending refinance vault was more attractive to me than the lower interest rates were to the homeowners that kept my little cubicle so filled with big stacks of files.

On the way to the meeting, my mentor had a headset that allowed him to talk on the phone while he was driving. I had never seen anybody actually talking on a car phone for real live business purposes with equipment that seemed to be made with that exact purpose in mind. That wasn't the only thing that I discovered on that trip.

On the way back from the meeting, through general conversation, I learned that the company was providing my mentor with the leased sports utility vehicle that we were riding in to get to and from the meeting. He told me that the truck was his to drive back and forth to work until the lease expired. After that lease expired, he said that the company would lease him another vehicle. I asked him who paid for the gas for the vehicle. He said that he had an expense account that he used to make fuel purchases. I thought to myself: "wow—I could really style and profile through the neighborhood in a company leased vehicle all day long if I didn't have to pay for gas". I was still a small-time thinker.

I caught myself having small-time hood fantasies sitting in the passenger seat of Mr. Big Shot's leased SUV. I thought: "wow—if I played the role with his headset phone, I would really be a ghetto superstar. I could pull up to a red light or cruise real slow through the spots to make sure that everybody saw me in my ride looking like I was engaged in some big-time business deal".

I was too ignorant to respect the difference between looking like I was engaged in some big business deal and actually being engaged in some big business deal—at the time, pretending and have people believe it was enough for me. I was like the emperor and his new clothes; naked when it came to the understanding that the real was always more important than the fake—no matter how many people went along with the fake.

When I snapped back to reality, I found myself wanting to test the sound system to see if it had the proper bass output that was required to really cruise the neighborhood in style. Apparently, my mentor didn't care for the deep bass sound; he had the channel tuned to some real low-key radio station with the volume barely audible. I didn't let that stop me from my hood fantasies.

I had hood fantasies before, but they were usually based on me basking in my imagined limelight after I achieved fame and fortune as a star basketball player. I had never had any fantasies based on becoming a big shot executive. One of the reasons was that I didn't really know anyone who was a big shot executive. Realizing that I didn't know or have access to anyone that was a big-time executive, I wasn't about to let my opportunity pass me by to learn as much as

I could about being an executive from my mentor. That white man had some keys to the game and I was going to pick his brain the way thieves picked pockets. I was going for as many keys as I could to unlock my unknowns.

After the trip, I paid attention to how my mentor dressed, talked, and his general overall demeanor. I noticed that he was extremely well dressed, not in flashy way, but in an impeccably sharp and conservative manner. Everything was in place, and neatness must have been one of his top priorities.

I was lucky to be assigned to my mentor, because I quickly realized that he was well respected by his peers. He spoke amongst them as one who had a strong command and an extreme knowledge of every area of his business. After a little exposure to how he carried himself and after witnessing the respect that he commanded from his colleagues; my mentor went from being a cool middle age white dude, in my mind, to a kind of player that I never knew. I started to admire him for his style much the same way that I had admired some of the players from my childhood days on Laura Street in Plant City.

Although the players and hustlers from Laura Street and my mentor were operating in two different worlds, I found myself admiring them for the same reasons. I saw more similarities than differences.

I watched my mentor work a meeting room with a finesse and competence level that was sure to win the day ninety-nine percent of the time. For me, it was no different than watching an extremely competent hustler from Laura Street running the poolroom in games of 9-ball. They both took on all would be challengers to their dominance and they never let anybody test their cool. However, the thing that really made my mentor and some of the Laura Street players seem so similar to me was the overall confidence that they had. It wasn't a false confidence based on arrogance; it was a confidence based on the ability to deliver time after time.

For those who have never been around that type of confidence and need a modern day comparison, look no further than Michael Jordan; MJ knew that he was going to deliver time after time. He knew it and he made you know it. It didn't matter if you were a friend or a foe, you knew that he was going to hit that shot and flail his fist wildly in the air in exaltation. You just knew it. In that sense, the confidence of the players from Laura Street and my mentor was a Jordanesque confidence. That type of confidence translates into success from the poolroom to the boardroom; it is master of its domain, no matter where the domain happens to be.

I felt that I had that type of confidence and I felt that it was based on ability, but I knew that I had a long way to go to turn my confidence and ability into the success of my mentor. I knew that my $5.50 per hour was a long way from the cash that he was making. I knew that the clothes that I was wearing were a long way from the stylish conservative threads that he wore everyday. I knew that I had a lot to learn to be able to command the respect of my peers the way that he did. I knew that me getting dropped off and picked up in my aunt's Nissan Sentra was a long way from him driving to and from work in a company leased SUV that he didn't even have to pay for gas to drive. I wasn't too small time to know that.

Speaking of driving, my car breaking down was really cramping my style for the summer because I was confined to the house after I got off from work. One day my uncle came home and told me that he could get me a real nice car for about $1,000 dollars. I was like yeah right … and I got a bridge in Brooklyn that I want to sell you. He said that he was serious; he explained that one of his customers, a white lady, couldn't pay the bill for the repairs and that the car was going to go back to the bank if she didn't make her next payment that was due in one week. He told me that it was a Renault Alliance and that it looked real nice. I still had the Brooklyn Bridge skepticism going until he drove me up to his shop for me to take a look at the car.

The car was much nicer and newer than my VW Rabbit. It had a nice deep blue color with nice tan upholstered seats. It looked a lot like some of the cars that I had seen in the parking garage at the bank. Unlike the Rabbit, I wouldn't need a paint job or seat covers, the only problem I had was I didn't know where I was going to get a thousand dollars in one week. I had never seen a thousand dollars all at one time in my whole life and now he was asking me to come up with a grand in one week. I only knew of two ways to get that kind of money and both ways were illegal, so I dismissed the thoughts almost as quickly as they flashed through my mind. Besides, I didn't have the right mindset for either activity. I wasn't built to jack anybody and I didn't even know how to sell crack cocaine (rocks).

My uncle encouraged me not to give up on the idea; he convinced me that there had to be a way to get the money with all the people that I knew. He kept bringing up the fact that I worked at a bank and there had to be someone there who could help. At first, I didn't think that he was familiar enough with banking to know how difficult it was for a person in my financial position (broke) to borrow money from a bank. The words broke and loan didn't appear in any of the lending formulas that I had seen. It was a case of "them that's got, get"; banks blessed the child that had his own and told the rest to go to hell.

Banks only lent money to people who already had some form of wealth. Still, he talked long enough until he made me believe that I could actually pull it off. That night I went through angle after angle in an effort to try to figure out what was the best approach to take in order to get the funds for what would be the nicest car that I ever had. After tossing and turning half the night, I concluded that I needed more information. I decided that my mentor was the best source for that information.

The next morning, I dropped by my mentor's office when I thought that he would have the most time to talk. That was a challenge in itself because he seemed to be engaged in one perpetual task that went on and on and on. He only thought about yielding to a break after five o'clock.

I dropped in anyway, I assured him that I would only take up a few minutes of his time and then I laid down the facts of my grand predicament. He told me that I would have to go through consumer lending. He warned me that that department didn't typically make loans for that small amount of money. He suggested that I get the money from a relative. I wanted to tell him that an ice cube had a better chance in hell than I had of getting a grand from any of my relatives. That kind of money was too tight to even mention in my family. All of my relatives were livin' just enough for the city; wasn't nothing going on but the rent.

My eyes must have told the story that my mouth was too reluctant to speak because after he made his suggestion, he wrote down some notes on a piece of paper. He confirmed my hourly wage and the time period remaining in the intern program. He did a quick calculation and told me that he would get back to me in a couple of days. When he went back to his to-do list, I knew that I was done and it was time for me to leave him alone for the day. As a mentor, he taught me just as much by not spending time with me as he did when he did spend time with me. He made me realize that busy people placed a very high value on their time; and they didn't like their time wasted, frivolously spent, or disrespected.

After I left his office, I wasn't too optimistic about my chances, but at least I had more of a chance than I had before I went into his office. I tried very hard to kill all hope over the next forty-eight hours so I wouldn't be disappointed when he told me that it was a no go, but the thought of me having what I considered to be a dream car was pushing me to keep hope alive.

True to his word, my mentor called me into his office in a couple days with some follow-up information. He told me to go see one of the reps in the other department and that everything had been worked out, so I should be able to get the car with extremely low monthly payments. I never had a desire to kiss a white man before that time or since that time, but my mentor almost got a big fat one across the lips. Instead, I decided a heartfelt thank-you and a firm handshake was a better career move. Someone had told me that people in power respected firm handshakes. I also realized that there was a big ring of truth in the old adage of: "it's not what you know, it's who you know". My uncle couldn't give me the money, but he had enough sense to know that I could get the dollars if I used my brains enough to open my mouth to the right people.

My internship at the bank and the summer came to an abrupt end with little fanfare. It didn't bother me though because I was going back to Eckerd College in style in my fresh new ride. I can remember being very excited about having that car because in my mind it was a very nice car. In looking back, I can see that it was really just a regular car. But coming from the environment where I was coming from it was really easy to mistake a regular car for a really nice car.

One of my funniest memories about that car that I still laugh about today was the time when Floyd and I were driving down the road in it when we saw a police car. I looked at Floyd with all the conviction in the world, as I slowed the car down to a snail's pace and said to him: "I better not let the police see me driving this car".

I made that statement because I knew that the police stopped Black males that drove nice cars. But that wasn't the funny part; it was a well-known fact that the police had been targeting brothers in tight rides for those "routine traffic stops" for a longtime. The funny part occurred to me a few years later when Floyd and I recounted the story and I told him that I must have been crazy if I thought that that car was tight enough to even make a policeman look twice.

When I look back, I think that the police should have arrested me on the spot for thinking such a ridiculous thought. Floyd, who always seemed to be a half-a-step ahead of me when it came to culture, said that he thought I was kind of crazy when I said it at the time. He said that he didn't say anything because he thought that I knew something about Renault Alliances that he didn't, so he decided to just go along with it. We both laughed hard for a longtime, and to this day that statement that I made to him of not letting "the police see me" in that car has become a running joke between us whenever we reminisce about how small-time my thinking was during that time. Boy was I ignorant! But I'm not going to be too hard on myself though, because I just didn't know any better.

I had been raised in the ghetto and by the ghetto, so I had a ghetto mentality. It's hard to explain, but being raised in the ghetto gives a person a flawed sense of reference in comparison with the mainstream world. In the ghetto, Kool-Aid isn't just a cheap substitute for juice or soft drinks; it's an exquisite drink with a premium placed on its availability. An empty container would always evoke an angry question of: "who drunk all the Kool-Aid?" The way that it was said, one would have thought that someone had sold the last barrel of oil without taking thought to drill for more.

In the ghetto, sometimes small things were considered to be big things and sometimes things that were really second or third tier were considered to be quintessential. I can remember being so excited when Grandma Mary brought home second hand clothes from the white family for which she worked. My cousins and I would grab up the clothes with all of the glee of a person who had won a shopping spree at a fine department store. We wore the old clothes of the two white kids with pride because they were often name brand clothes that we couldn't afford.

I suppose that that part of my upbringing was a contributing reason to why I thought that my car was the quintessential of what a car was supposed to be. I would later realize that anybody outside of the ghetto mentality would have viewed the car as just a regular car, but you couldn't tell me that then. I was so ghetto that you probably had plenty of people within the ghetto mentality who thought that I was trippin' with the views that I had about that car. Because the car definitely wouldn't make any policeman ask the question of how did that Black man get that car as I had suggested it would.

Being raised in the ghetto also puts a person at-risk to possess a mentality that makes you think that things that are really of no real significance in the grand scheme of the game of life are big things. The ghetto mentality is pervasive across all planes of life, but it definitely rears its head in a few categories more than others. Cars, clothes, and jewelry usually top the most wanted list of a person with a true ghetto mentality. A person with a true ghetto mentality chooses cars, clothes, and jewelry over home ownership. They might pull up to their rented apartment in a brand new luxury vehicle, jump out of their rides sportin' the latest high priced fashions, with expensive jewelry adorning their bodies. Platinum and gold chains are viewed as more valuable than platinum and gold credit ratings.

Nathan McCall's best-selling 1994 autobiography entitled, *Makes Me Wanna Holler*, describes the mentality better than any other description that I have ever read. In his book, which is one of my all-time favorites, he broke the ghetto mentality down during a game of chess. McCall actually recounted the breakdown as it was broken down to him by a cat named Mo Battle that he served some prison time with while completing his sentence for armed robbery. McCall wrote:

> One day, I made a move to capture a pawn of his and gave Mo Battle an opening to take a valuable piece. He smiled and said, 'You can tell a lot about a person by the way that he plays chess. People who think small tend to devote a lot of energy to capturing pawns, the least valuable piece on the board. They think they're playing to win, but they're not. But people who think big tend to go straight for the king or queen, which wins you the game.' I never forgot that. Most guys I knew, myself included, spent their entire lives chasing pawns. The problem was, we thought we were going after kings

DÉJÀ VU

My sophomore year in college was the beginning of what was to be a serious assault on my ghetto mentality. Basketball proved to be the catalyst for that attack. The ankle injury that I suffered at the end of my freshman basketball season still wasn't completely healed at the start of my sophomore year, but even more importantly it had left me without my biggest asset for the entire summer. That asset was my drive to put in tremendous amounts of work in order to achieve my goals.

I was the kind of the person who always felt the most confident and most comfortable when I felt that I had worked hard enough to deserve whatever it was that I was working to achieve. I knew that I had not put in enough work over the summer to deserve what I wanted.

I wanted to work on my game more than I wanted to do anything else, but my injured ankle just would not allow me to do what I needed to do in order to prepare like I needed to prepare. Still, even with all that said; I wasn't expecting to face what I faced as a sophomore.

By the time tryouts rolled around, my ankle was just well enough for me to run halfway decent. My quickness was reduced considerably, but not nearly as much as my confidence. I just didn't feel right on the court anymore. Everybody moved too fast and jumped too high. I just couldn't perform the way that I had performed before the injury.

I remembered the words that my junior varsity basketball coach at Southeast spoke when he would encourage us to work harder in order to get better. He would always say: "men, you never stay the same, you either get better or worse."

I was definitely not the same and I wasn't any better, so I had to be worse. I knew that I was worse; I just couldn't do anything about it. My mind would tell me what to do in situations, but my ankle wouldn't let my body execute. A life full of good ideas and poor execution is a formula for failure. I saw my chance at being the starting point guard sliding through my hands because my feet wouldn't let me move. Inevitably, the end of try-outs came with me feeling dejected about the way that I had played, but I still wasn't expecting what happened at the end of the tryouts.

My coach asked me to take a ride with him at the end of the last day of try-outs. We went to McDonald's, a place that I hated since I was a sixth-grader, but I ordered to be polite. He asked me how I thought I did during the try-outs and I told him that I was disappointed with my performance. He said that he wasn't happy with my performance either and that as a result he wasn't going to be able to keep me on the team.

As the words poured from his lips, I could feel my heart began to expand in my chest and my stomach began to drop. The mind/body connection that took place with me as my mind absorbed the words that he was saying to me was scary. I wanted to interrupt him and say something that would not only make him stop saying what he was saying, but also make him take everything back that he had already said.

I wanted to get on my knees and beg that white man for a spot on his team. If given a chance, I would have got on my knees and done my best impression of James Brown: *"Please, Please, Please"*. I wanted to be on that team so bad. Oh boy, how bad I wanted…

I wanted to tell him that he was making a big mistake. I wanted to let him know how many obstacles that I had overcome in my life and that my ankle injury and poor try-out performance was no different than any of the other setbacks that I had overcome. I wanted to let him know that I had been counted out before, only to get up at the count of nine to comeback to score a last round knockout. I wanted to let him know that I was the comeback kid who refused to lose. I wanted to let him know that he was wrong to bet against me. I wanted to tell him that I was a winner and if he stuck with me that there was no way he could lose. My mind was screaming: "tell'em!, tell'em!, tell'em!" But my mouth was unable to speak; in fact, I think I lost all of my senses during that conversation.

It seemed that my soul slowly left my body until there was no feeling left in my physical body. The assault on my five senses continued with my ears. I saw his mouth moving but my ears were no longer able to distinguish the words that were dripping from his lips. I could only hear the tone of his voice. His speech was in a tone that suggested that our discussion was hurting him more than it was hurting me, but I knew that was impossible.

The incapacitating effects of the words coming from his mouth moved from my ears to my nose. The distinctive aroma of the McDonald's french fries that were right under my nose lost their ability to stimulate any olfactory activity. I picked up a fry or two in a weak attempt to appear grateful for the meal and put them in my mouth, but the normally salty fries had no taste. The inability to eat a sandwich from Mickey Dees came back to haunt me from the experience I had as an eleven-year-old and my stomach started to churn.

My eyes followed suit, joining the exodus of the rest of my senses. The longer I looked at the man that I had called coach a couple hours ago, the more my eyes began to water and lose their ability to focus on his face. I didn't want to cry in front of anybody, let alone a restaurant full of strangers, so I put my head down. In the end, I couldn't tell you if I actually cried or not; and if I did cry, I couldn't tell you who saw me. Because I couldn't feel the tears or see who was watching me.

After I lost my senses, I couldn't tell you how much longer my ex-coach spoke to me, because I was not even there. I was in a stupor like state. I didn't come back to life until I heard him talking about a doctor. I pieced his syllables together the way that you put together a jigsaw puzzle and figured out that he was trying to tell me that I should become a doctor.

My hearing returned in time for me to hear him tell me that I was really smart and that I could be anything in the world, including a doctor. (Ironically, I had only heard that kind of tribute from two white people. That should never be the case for a Black child or adolescent.)

In hindsight, I realize that I should have taken that as a compliment and actually listened to what he was trying to tell me. But where I was coming from, as far as my background, the only doctor that I knew and wanted to emulate was Julius Erving. Erving was known throughout the world as "Dr. J"; he was a perennial ABA/ NBA all-star whose popularity was only matched by his incredible jumping ability.

Instead of taking his advice as I compliment, I took it at as an insult. In the ghetto, hoop dreams were far more common than dreams of becoming a doctor ... and I was a child of the ghetto. Ebonically speaking, I didn't wannabe no doctor and I didn't want no advice 'bout being one. I wanted to play basketball. If he wasn't going to give me the opportunity, then I didn't want to hear anything he had to say. He didn't realize that I could go back home and get much more clout as his starting point guard than I could from saying that I was studying pre-med, pre-law, or engineering. When I look back, I realize that his advice was on the money; but back then, I was still suffering from the ghetto mentality that said that a basketball was much more important than a stethoscope.

Unfortunately, even as a sophomore in college, I still didn't understand that if I applied myself that I had a much better chance of becoming a doctor, lawyer, or engineer than I had at becoming a professional athlete. And even more importantly than that, I didn't understand that my people needed doctors, lawyers, and engineers just as much as they needed professional athletes. One of our challenges of this Black generation is to make sure that every Black child knows at an early age the full spectrum of possibilities that lies within their potential and that every Black child has the resources to pursue their potential to the fullest.

I was having such a hard time dealing with the reality of being cut from the basketball team that I just went into a cocoon. I wanted to block out the world. I had spent my entire freshman year telling the Eckerd College world that I was going to be the man on the court. Many of those people actually believed that I would be the man based on that one game that they had seen me steal the show in the final minutes of a blowout. The whole thing would have been really embarrassing if I still cared about what people thought, but I was too devastated to be embarrassed. I could care less what people thought.

I discovered that there was something between basketball and me that had nothing to do with anybody else. It was a relationship between the game and me, a relationship that I realized that I had grown to love. I didn't want to talk to anybody. I didn't want to eat with anybody. I didn't want to eat period. I didn't want to go to class with anybody. I didn't want to ever interact with another person again. It was like basketball had been a part of all of my interpersonal relationships, and when it was taken away from me, I lost a part of all of my relationships.

As basketball players, I think that my friends understood; but I had a new relationship with a girl that I had met during the spring semester of my freshman year and I closed myself off to her completely. She and I had really started hanging out a lot after I decided that my high school girlfriend's father's hate was too strong for me and his daughter to be involved in a relationship where we weren't enrolled in the same school.

My high school girlfriend's father would have rather locked his daughter away in a prison for the remaining two years of her high school career than allow us to see each other outside of school. I didn't want her to go through that and miss out on what was supposed to be one of the best time periods of her life, so I let her go on one of my trips home during my freshman year.

That's when I really started to hang out strong with the new girl that would become my girlfriend from my sophomore year of 1992 until 1998. Everything was going fine in the new relationship until basketball broke my heart. I was all prepared to break her heart and let her go, but she wouldn't let me. I let her stay because she was so determined not to be pushed away … and stay she did, for seven years.

In a matter of months, I had gone from dating one white girl to dating another white girl. I didn't really see a problem with dating a white girl, so I never gave her race a second thought. I saw love as an emotion that was colorblind, but not everybody on the campus looked at love the same way that I looked at love. I was about to set myself up to get hit in the face with a big piece of déjà vu.

Eckerd was a small college with an even smaller number of African-Americans. I would venture to say that throughout my whole four-year tenure that there were never more than ten African-

American women who lived on campus during a given academic year. Combine that with the fact that at least two or three of them were saving themselves for some dude that they left back home, and you had slim pickings.

Still, I knew that some of the African-American women who did live on campus were upset about the frequency in which the African-American males chose to date the white women who lived on campus. In some cases they were upset about the frequency in which the white women chose to date the African-American males who lived on campus. You see that's the old myth that claims that Black men can't resist chasing white women; a lot of times, that's at least equally true in the reverse: some white women can't resist chasing Black men. Either way, some of the sisters were upset about all the interracial dating going on at Eckerd College. Some referred to it as "the fever", an obvious take from Spike Lee's 1991 film, *Jungle Fever*.

One of the sisters, a particularly vocal sister, decided that she was going to let her feelings be known about the situation of interracial dating during an Afro-American Society (AAS) meeting. AAS was a school-sponsored club primarily put in place for the college's African-American students. It wasn't limited to one particular race, but it was always ninety-nine percent Black during my tenure at Eckerd.

The ninety-nine percent Black make-up of the club did not equate to one hundred percent participation by all of the Black students at the college. Some of the school's scant African-American student body attended the meetings and participated in the various activities of the club and some did not.

Well, the particular meeting that I am writing about happened to be my first AAS meeting. I really did not know what to expect, so it would be fair to say that I was highly impressionable about the club. The particularly vocal sister was also an officer in the club and she almost single handedly ruined my impression of the AAS when she started to speak.

She began to spout her personal views about interracial dating and the brothers who would "stoop so low" as to be involved with a white girl. She went on for a good little while, as the rest of the room just kind of fell silent. I didn't know if the women were silent because they agreed, because they disagreed, because they were shocked that she was saying those things outside of the confidence of their circle, or a combination of all of that. I didn't know if the fellas were silent because they were embarrassed, because they were angry, because they were intimidated by the power in which she was bringing her message, or a combination of all of that.

I was silent because I was past angry. I was "thirty-eight hot", that's the kind of hot that my maternal grandma got when someone really made her mad and she was thinking about going to get her mythical .38 caliber pistol and blowing their "dooty hole loose". If it were humanly possible, my nostrils would have expelled fire and brimstone. As I listened to her talking about the issue, I began to tell myself that I didn't come to the meeting to be spoken to, at, or about the way that she was speaking.

I went to the meeting because I was curious. I was curious to see what Black people who went to college talked about. I went to the meeting to find out if the club was into things that stimulated my Black consciousness on the predominately white campus that I was supposed to call home for the next few years. I went to the meeting searching for that feeling of fusion between Blackness, unity, pride, and power that I got from Public Enemy lyrics. Needless to say, that didn't happen.

I was in for a feeling all right, but it wasn't the kind of feeling that I was searching for when I sat down in the campus apartment that served as AAS headquarters. The more she spoke, the angrier I got and the more I felt that I had to say something. It seemed that the vocal sister took the silence in the room as acquiescence; the longer she spoke, the haughtier her tone became. I couldn't stand it any longer; I knew that my silence was my own betrayal. I also knew that I wasn't the only Black guy in the room that was dating a white girl. Still, I took her diatribe personally.

Before I could figure out what I was saying, my emotion filled voice rang out into the air to meet her emotion filled voice in a mid-air collision. In my opinion, there is something about the voice of a Black man when it is filled with sincere emotion that has the ability to trump the voices of all other groups. I suppose that Dr. Maya Angelou was right in her opinion when she wrote:

> The voice of an American black man has undeniable tex-
> ture. It has a quality of gloss, slithery as polished onyx,
> or it can be nubby and notched with harshness. The
> voice can be sonorous as bass solo or light and lyrical
> as a flute. When a Black man speaks with a flat tone, it
> is not only intentional but instructional to the listener.
> (Maya Angelou, *The Heart of a Woman*, 1981)

My voice was winning in the midair collision; I was ready to instruct her as to what was and what wasn't any of her business. I talked over her until she relinquished the stranglehold that she had over the room. I told her and anybody else that was in that room who agreed with her that I would date whoever I wanted, whenever I wanted, and that nobody—and I meant nobody—would define for me who was acceptable or unacceptable for me. There's a lot about life that's collective, but some things about life are individual.

My voice was ranging out and my message was strong, even those who would have never dated outside their race were forced to consider the substance of what I was saying. However, it seemed that the silent room was still a divided camp on the issue when I said that I didn't want to be a part of any organization that would frown upon who I chose to date on the basis of skin color alone. After I felt that I had firmly established my position on the issue, I left the meeting. The feeling of fusion between Blackness, unity, pride, and power that I searched for was replaced with a disturbing uneasiness and sadness. Still, deep down, I felt that the things that I had spoken were right.

I was privately bothered by the interaction at the meeting for a couple of days, but I did feel a little better when the Director of Multi-Cultural Affairs & AAS advisor called me into her office and apologized for the comments that were made by the particular vocal sister. She was the same lady who had called me into her office and informed me of the stolen bike situation during Autumn Term of my freshman year. She said that she was surprised that an officer of the AAS would say such things at a meeting that was open to all. She did most of the talking as I listened. As a school representative, she was giving me the political answer that was mandatory on any college that claimed to place any value whatsoever on diversity in the 20th century. But I knew that political answers would not solve the emotional divide caused by the interracial dating dilemma that existed among Black folks.

That issue has divided our people the way Moses parted the Red Sea ... at least since white men in America stopped hanging Black men with their genitals stuffed in their mouths for the so-called rapes of so-called "pure and chaste" white women.

I would love to hear what a contemporary group of African-Americans would have to say in an interracial dating forum about the fact that Fredrick Douglass was involved in an interracial relationship with a white woman during the latter part of his life. Would they say that the great champion of the African in America had "the fever" or would they say something else?

When I left the office of the AAS advisor, I still had an uneasy feeling because I knew that the topic of interracial dating was bigger than the personal differences of opinion between two individuals. I knew that the issue was something that was impeding the ability of African-Americans to work together on problems that were common to us all.

BARBERSHOP TALK

T he situation at the AAS meeting wasn't the only place where I found myself in a discussion on race matters in a predominantly Black setting. Unfortunately, it also wasn't the only time that I left the situation feeling uneasy about the ability of Black people to rally together to work on common problems while putting aside individual differences.

The next time that I found myself in that state of affairs was at the barbershop. Excluding the ten dollars that I was spending on each haircut, I loved going to the barbershop because of the atmosphere that it provided. It was a one hundred percent authentic Black environment. That environment was a direct contrast to the extreme whiteness of the campus life of Eckerd College. During the five-minute drive from campus to the barbershop, I literally drove from one world into another world.

I used the world of the barbershop to bask in the Blackness that was missing from my life at Eckerd. The walls of the barbershop were usually covered with different promotional material about various events that had taken place or that were going to take place. The promotional material included everything from fashion shows to invitations to different local grassroots political meetings. Sometimes between all of those promotional materials that boasted of the vibrant and diverse cultural life of the area was a flyer that asked for any information about the whereabouts of a person who had been missing for a prolonged period of time.

The combination of the diversity of promo information and the numerous materials posted for the various hairstyles of Black men and women transformed the wall into a cultural collage. I could have easily spent an entire visit to the barbershop just looking at the different things posted on the wall, but I usually split my time between doing that and rummaging through the different periodicals that were piled on the end table.

I would pick up *Jet* to look at the music charts in the back of the book and the "Beauty of the Week" that was usually found around page forty-three of every issue. I looked through the contents of *Ebony* to see if I could run across a topic that grabbed my interest. I scanned *Sports Illustrated* to see if I could read up on one of my favorite sports personalities. That end table full of magazines was just as diverse as the collage of information on the wall, but neither the wall nor the array of different magazines could compare to the different kind of people that walked through the doors of that shop.

Ninety-nine point nine percent of the people that I saw walk through the doors were Black people (I saw a white mailman come in once), but within that group were all different kinds of Black people. I thought that at least a part of the reason for the differences in the patrons of the shop was that there were three different barbers that cut hair there. Those three different barbers were so different in so many ways that the only visible similarity between the three was the fact that they were all Black men.

One barber was an old light-skinned Black man who looked to be in his sixties or seventies, but who still had an incredible zeal for life; he probably could best a man twenty years his junior. He was the owner of the shop and he had a shiny new Cadillac parked outside the front window just to prove it.

Another barber was a muscular dark-skinned brother who stood about 6 feet 2 inches who looked to be in his mid-thirties or early forties. He was the man that a brother from Eckerd recommended to me when I asked where he got his hair cut. That was the primary reason that I always went to his chair to get my trim.

The third barber was a brown-skinned man who looked to be in his early to mid-twenties. He was a cool brother who didn't talk much unless someone was talking directly to him. He was a direct contrast to the loquacious owner who seemed to be engaged in a perpetual conversation from the time a customer sat in his chair until he finished that haircut. Most of the older Black men usually went to the owner of the shop, while the younger cats my age and slightly older went to the cool quiet brother.

The dark-skinned muscular brother, who cut my hair, had a cross section of everybody. He cut heads of all kinds and was easily the top draw of the shop. His manner was just as all-inclusive as his clientele was. He went from having exclusive conversations with those in his chair to voicing his opinions about various topics back and forth across the shop.

Given his top draw status, the line for his chair was usually the longest. So at first, before I learned to call ahead for a good time frame, I would spend a lot of time at the shop just waiting in line to get into his chair. I spent that time just listening and watching the different people as I flipped through magazines. You had some street people, some professional people, and some people who I couldn't quite figure out what segment they fit into. You had some deeply religious people and you had some people who seemed to be at odds with religion. I listened and watched them all.

One day after I had been getting my haircut there for a while, some of those people had an opportunity to listen to and watch me. The dark-skinned muscular brother had already engaged me in enough of his "exclusive conversations with those in his chair" to know that I was from Bradenton and that I played ball for Southeast during my high school days. He also knew that I went to Eckerd College, and that I was a former Eckerd basketball player who wasn't on the team anymore. None of that information was what led to the situation that put my views on center stage for the whole barbershop to hear. The thing that did that was a discussion over the use of the term "African-American".

It seemed to me that the topic had already been lightly debated before I arrived at the shop, but that light debate was about to turn into passionate exchanges. My barber asked me what I thought about the term. It was something that I had never really thought about before, but after thinking about it for a few minutes I told him that I guess it was an O.K. term that paid homage to our past African heritage while properly noting our current American citizenship. I thought that it was a descent answer. I was about to expound when the cool quiet brother busted in with a response to what I said.

He began to talk about all of the injustices that Black people have faced in America; injustices that he said true citizens of a country would have never had to face, so my idea of attaching the word American to the word African based on U.S. citizenship was erroneous. He went on to add that we were African when whites stole us from Africa, and that that fact didn't change when they brought us to America.

He explained that the originating location or origin of a person or thing was the proper way to refer to that person or thing. He continued by declaring that all Black people could trace their origins to one place and one place only—Africa! He said that the problem with Black people was that they were always trying to run from their African roots and their Blackness to something American and its whiteness. The cool quiet brother, who had now become the fiery vocal brother, went on to say that anybody who would attempt to do such a thing was a fool and wasn't worthy to participate in the inevitable revolution that would go down between Black people and white people.

After his lecture and stern admonishment of my statement, I was shocked. Not so much because of what he said, but more so because I had never seen that side of him. I actually agreed with a lot of what he said and was proud that he had so much conviction in what he was saying. He spoke like a man with iron in his words who was prepared to die for that in which he believed. In my mind, there was something impressive about the way a person came across when he or she truly believed in what they were saying to the degree that they were willing to pay the ultimate price of death.

Dr. King identified the willingness to die for something that you believe in as a prerequisite to an individual's right to live. He said: "For if a man has not discovered something that he will die for he isn't fit to live." Historical records show that many Black men throughout history were willing to die for their beliefs and our freedom. Oftentimes their words and actions attested to that fact before their actual physical deaths.

Since that barbershop conversation, I have heard the willingness to die for beliefs in the voices of Malcolm X, Dr. Martin Luther King Jr., and Medgar Evers. Their words always inspired and impressed me. The same trait was just as inspiring and impressive when I heard it in the voice of the brother in the barbershop. Perhaps it was more impressive simply because he was an ordinary cat from around the way.

With all that said, I still didn't agree with everything that he said. I didn't think that by attaching the word American to the word African that a person was trying to run away from their African roots and their Blackness to something American and its whiteness. I thought that by attaching the word American to the word African that one was recognizing the fact that Black people in the United States were indeed African and would always be African. In my opinion, the American attachment was in recognition of the four hundred years worth of contributions that we have made in the United States.

I reasoned that our legacy in America was significant enough in its contribution to the building of this nation that it gave us just as much right as anybody else to be called American. When you call a spade a spade, the only other group that may have more right to this country than we do is the Native people of this land.

I knew that one thing was definitely for certain; our ancestors and elders didn't build this country for free, just to let others enjoy all the fruits of our labor. White people tried to make it that way, but too many of our ancestors and elders sacrificed to make a different day with a different way. I wanted to ask the fiery vocal brother how many times did he think that our ancestors and elders had to bite their tongues almost in half while they mumbled to themselves: "there gon be another day".

I agreed with the fiery vocal brother that a great number of white people wanted to withhold the citizenship that our blood, sweat, and tears had paid for many times over. But I didn't care what white people wanted to withhold. Our citizenship was paid for in the form of hundreds of years of forced and free labor. Our citizenship was paid for in the form of numerous significant contributions to all facets of American life. Our citizenship was paid for in the form of dedicated service in America's wars. Black people had anted up and kicked in to save this country too many times. Not only had our citizenship been paid for when we built this country for free, but America owed us some change back from our overpayment.

I thought that those whites who didn't want me to enjoy full citizenship in America as a Black man should have thought about that before they loaded our people in the hulls of their slave ships. I thought that they should have thought about that before they sent our people to fight in their wars. I thought that they should have thought about that before they eagerly accepted all that we gave to enrich American life. I thought that they should have thought about all that feces from the git-go!

I wasn't prepared to give up our due citizenship rights—that included every letter of the word American if I wanted it—in America because some whites did not want our people to posses them. By the same token, I wasn't willing to giving up anything because some Blacks thought that it was denouncing Africa and Blackness while pursuing America and whiteness. No, no—not I.

I couldn't equate America with whiteness, when I looked at our contribution to the land, I saw Blackness. In some of the cases it was stolen Blackness, but it was Blackness nonetheless. The Blackness that I saw in America was beautiful, so beautiful that if it were extracted, America would not exist at all.

America wouldn't be America without Black people. America ought to get on her red, white, and blue knees and thank us for what we have done for this country. Because of our suffering, this country was able to rise to prominence in world affairs at a much faster pace than it would have without the unfair competitive advantage that it gained as a result of slavery and Jim Crow. No one can deny that. If they try, then I suggest that we talk about the free labor and the money that was never paid ... not to mention the 40 acres and the mule. If they try, then I suggest that we talk about the commerce and all the money that was made from Black toil and suffering. Let that be the prelude to the gainsaying of those that dispute the charge.

I knew that a great part of America had fought hard to keep the U.S.A from being the country of the Black man, but its might was no match for the Black man. The Black man fought courageously and suffered hard and long to make the U.S.A. his country and the country of the little Black boys and girls that were to come behind him. The best men within our ranks did not do so because they despised Africa, but because their African souls believed that after what we'd been through that Black folks had just as much right to America as anybody else.

They stood boldly and defiantly in the face of all opposition and asked who would be a match for them in denying them the fruition of their full American citizenship. They looked into the face of that opposition and stared them in their eyes. Out of their mouths, they spoke words that had iron in them. David Walker, Malcolm X, W.E.B. Du Bois, Richard Allen, Fredrick Douglass, and Paul Robeson were all such men.

> Let no man of us budge one step, and let slave-holders come to beat us from our country. America is more our country, than it is the whites—we have enriched it with our *blood and tears*. The greatest riches in all America have arisen from our blood and tears. (David Walker, Appeal to the Coloured Citizens of the World, 1829)

This is our contribution—our blood. Not only did we give of our free labor, we gave our blood. Every time [we] had a call to arms, we were the first ones in uniform. We died on every battlefield the white man had. We have made a greater sacrifice than anybody who's standing up in America today. (Malcolm X, "The Ballot or the Bullet", 1965)

Your country? How came it yours? Before the Pilgrims landed we were here. Here we have brought our three gifts and mingled them with yours: a gift of story and song—soft, stirring melody in an ill-harmonized and unmelodious land; the gift of sweat and brawn to beat back the wilderness, conquer the soil, and lay the foundations of this vast economic empire two hundred years earlier than your weak hands could have done it; the third, a gift of the Spirit. Around us the history of the land has centered for thrice a hundred years; out of the nation's heart we have called all that was best to throttle and subdue all that was worst; fire and blood, prayer and sacrifice, have billowed over this people, and they have found peace only in the altars of the God of Right. Nor has our gift of the Spirit been merely passive. Actively we have woven ourselves with the very warp and woof of this nation,—we fought their battles, shared their sorrow, mingled our blood with theirs, and generation after generation have pleaded with a headstrong, careless people to despise not Justice, Mercy, and Truth, lest the nation be smitten with a curse. Our song, our toil, our cheer, and warning have been given to this nation in blood-brotherhood. Are not these gifts worth the giving? Is not this work and striving? Would America have been America without her Negro people? (W.E.B. Du Bois, *The Souls of Black Folk*, 1903)

We were stolen from our mother country and brought here. We have tilled the ground and made fortunes for thousands. This land which we have watered with our tears and our blood, so it is now our mother country. (Richard Allen, *The Life Experience and Gospel Labors of Richard Allen*, 1887)

We can be modified, changed, and assimilated, but never extinguished. We shall never die out, nor be driven out. We are here and this is our country. (Fredrick Douglass, "The Destiny of the Colored American", *North Star*, 16 November 1849)

So I won't be singing, except for the rights of my people for the next couple of years. No pretty songs gentlemen, no pretty songs. Time for some full citizenship. Understandable? (Paul Robeson, Here I Stand, 1958)

If I had known those words from those men at the time that I was having the discussion with the fiery vocal brother in the barbershop, then I would have used them. But even without the words of my ancestors, I could tell that my points made sense and hit just as hard as the fiery vocal brother's points hit when he made his comments. There were just as many people in the shop who agreed with me as the number of people who agreed with him during his speech.

I went on to further press the issue with those who agreed with me by declaring that if a successful Black revolution was going to take place, then it would need Blacks to be united across all fronts and not just Blacks who shared the same opinions and philosophies. I proclaimed that a fragmented Black revolution, based on partial participation, would not only fail; but it would not lead to the higher goal of humanity that regarded all men as brothers. So ultimately, after we both went back and forth, the two issues that we were the furthest apart on were who would participate in the Black struggle and what should be the ultimate goal of the revolution.

The cool quiet brother, who was still in his fiery and vocal mode, said that the revolution that he was referring to would only allow the Black people who were willing to disassociate themselves from whites to participate. He said that those would be the only Black people that could be trusted not to sell-out. I knew where he was coming from and I understood completely, but I knew that an effective and successful Black revolution couldn't exclude all the Blacks who would have been excluded under his rationale.

I believed that there were too many Blacks who did associate with whites, but who would have also been completely committed to a plan of action if it meant a possible change in the way things were done in this country. I was one of those Blacks, so in effect, I was arguing for my own participation and I let that fact be known.

I kept telling him that in order to succeed that he would have to let me participate. I punctuated a lot of his sentences with my own statement of: "Yeah, but you would have to let me participate!"

I commented on the fact that the revolution, if it was to truly replace bad with good, would have to *eventually* get away from the whole Black and white question all together and regard all people the same. Oh boy! Why did I bring that up? I really set myself up. He had a hundred examples of all the attempts at that philosophy and a hundred and one failures to go along with his examples—my failure to recognize reality being the latest. I didn't really have a whole lot to throw back in defense against the things that he was saying, so I went with the only ammunition that I had. I responded with the Christian concepts that I had learned from going to church with my paternal grandma as a small boy.

Although I had not been to church in a long time, I had actually retained a lot of basic Christian teachings from the prayer meetings and the long Sundays at church with my grandmother. I remembered the teachings that said that you were to love thy neighbor as thy self and that all men were brothers, so I focused on that aspect of Christianity.

His questions to my Christian messages were terse, but I couldn't give him any confident answers. One question that he asked me was how long did I expect Black people to keep turning the other cheek, while forgiving and trusting white men who had never shown any brotherhood toward our people. Another question that he asked me was if I thought that Black people should just suffer here on earth, continuing to love the white man and to forgive his evil ways until we all died and went to heaven.

I struggled to find answers, but they were weak attempts at best. I didn't recognize it then, but during later years of my life, I would realize that opposing Black views on Christianity was something that had been around for a long time. The most opposing views centered on the white man and his behaviors.

Under one view, we were expected to forgive the white man over and over under the guidelines of the New Testament and the doctrine of Jesus Christ. That willingness to forgive made some Black folks some of the most ardent followers of Christianity and the most faithful of servants to the Lord. People who support this view believe with all their heart that those who serve the Lord shall surely be saved from the wrath of God. Thus, they epitomized the phrase: "forgive and forget".

Under the polar opposite view, some Black folks vehemently denounced the white man and *his version* of Christianity. They did so based on the fact that the white man's version always seemed to place him and his people in a superior position to all other groups of people in the world. God is white, Jesus is white, angels are white; everything is white.

The blatant hypocrisy between the white man's deeds and his Christian doctrine was another thing that left a sour taste in the mouths of the Black folks who turned away from the white man's version of Christianity. Oftentimes, those people said the hell with the white man and his image of a white Jesus. Some became atheists and others sought other forms of religion to satisfy their spiritual needs ... religions that were not so insistent on having a white wash on all of the prophets. They wanted to believe in something where the followers were not so determined to make God a white man.

Compare and contrast the two polar views as presented by sister Maya Angelou in her 1981 book, *The Heart of a Woman,* and brother Malcolm X in, *The Autobiography of Malcolm X,* written by Alex Haley in 1965.

Maya Angelou

As for spirituality, we were Christians. We demonstrated the teachings of Christ. We turned other cheeks so often our heads seemed to revolve on the ends of our necks, like old stop-and-go signs. How many times should we forgive? Jesus said seven times seventy. We forgave as if forgiving was our talent. Our church music showed that we believed there was something greater than we, something beyond our physical selves, and that that something, that God, and His Son, Jesus were always present and could be called 'in the midnight hour' and talked to when the 'sun raised itself to walk across the morning sky.' We could sing the angels out of heaven and bring them to stand thousands thronged on the head of a pin. We could ask Jesus to be on hand 'to walk around' our deathbeds and gather us into 'the bosom of Abraham.' We told him all about our sorrows and relished the time when we would be counted among the numbers of those who would go marching in. We would walk the golden streets of heaven, eat of the milk and honey, wear the promised shoes and rest in the arms of Jesus, who would rock us and say, 'You have labored in my vineyard. You are tired. You are home now, child. Well done.' Oh, there was no doubt that we were spiritual.

Malcolm X

'Peaceful coexistence!' That's another one the white man has always been quick to cry. Fine! But what have been the deeds of the white man? During his entire advance through history, he has been waving the banner of Christianity ... and carrying in his other hand the sword and the flintlock.

You can go right back to the very beginning of Christianity. Catholicism, the genesis of Christianity as we know it to be presently constituted, with its hierarchy, was conceived in Africa—by those whom the Christian church calls 'The Desert Fathers.' The Christian church became infected with racism when it entered white Europe. The Christian church returned to Africa under the banner of the cross—conquering, killing, exploiting, pillaging, raping, bullying, beating—and teaching white supremacy. This is how the white man thrust himself into the position of leadership of the world—through the use of naked physical power...

The black man needs to reflect that he has been America's most fervent Christian—and where has it gotten him? In fact, in the white man's hands, in the white man's interpretation ... where has Christianity brought this *world*?

... Many black men, the victims—in fact most black men—would like to be able to forgive, to forget, the crimes.

But most American white people seem not to have it in them to make any serious atonement—to do justice to the black man.

Indeed, how *can* white society atone for enslaving, for raping, for unmanning, for otherwise brutalizing *millions* of human beings for centuries? What atonement would the God of Justice demand for robbery of the black people's labor, their lives, their true identities, their culture, their history—even their human dignity?

I wish I knew then, some of the things that I know now; I would have been able to answer the fiery vocal brother's barbershop questions better than I did. I would have hit him with the words of Mahatma Gandhi. The man that many referred to as "the great soul" said: "Where there is injustice, I always believed in fighting. The question is do you fight to change things or do you fight to punish? For myself, I've found that we're all such sinners we should leave punishment to God".

That was the essence of my question. My issue was not whether to fight or not fight injustice. It was how do you fight injustice, and what did you fight for to take its place? But I wasn't mentally strong enough at that point to articulate such a thought in clear and concise words, so I left the barbershop with a one last: "yeah, but you have to let me participate!" He couldn't realize it, and I couldn't make him see that we were two brothers standing on the opposite shores of the Nile; we needed each other to confirm that the other side did in fact exist.

I thought about that conversation for a long time after that day. My thoughts were always accompanied by mixed emotions. I was happy that I had met somebody who was relatively close to my age who had thought about the race issue as much as I had. The fiery vocal brother seemed to be very committed to his beliefs about the issue; I respected that. Still, I was uneasy because I knew that his views wouldn't let him put aside our differences and allow us to work together on the issues that we both felt very strong about.

My views and my associations with the white man and his daughter made the fiery vocal brother see me as an outsider who couldn't be trusted not to sell-out. I understood where he was coming from, but I didn't agree. I didn't know if he understood where I was coming from, but I did know that he didn't agree. The problem was that we could not get to a point where we could agree to disagree and still work together. That made me sad.

I couldn't feel good about the possibility of all of our people coming together, when I hadn't been successful in coming together with just one other Black man. We were both chained together in facing the obstacles of being Black males in America, yet we were separated by our viewpoints. Upon leaving the shop, I wish that I had left the fiery vocal brother with the words of LeRone Bennett, Jr.

"[T]he quest for black unity ... must begin in an attitude of active love for black people. Not an attitude of false agreement, nor an attitude of blindness to faults and political divergences, but an attitude of active love embracing the idea that many, perhaps most, Negroes are salvageable on the level of operational unity ... That's the key point. And I stress that point because a real quest for unity might require us to give up our organization, or it might require us to work with individuals of different viewpoints. Some men, of course, draw the line at that point. Paradoxically, some men are willing to give their lives for black liberation but are not willing to give up their claims to organizational or ideological supremacy within the black community." (Lerone Bennett, Jr. *The Challenge of Blackness*, 1972)

HEART OF HEARTS

I had some serious problems to deal with during my first school year without basketball since 1987. I was cast out of that brotherhood that existed between guys on a sports team. There was a lot to miss about the camaraderie that I had been able to take for granted. We ate together, we practiced together, we traveled together, we faced the agony of defeat together, and we rejoiced in the thrill of victory together. I was a part of that we, but that was no more; I was only left with me.

I was an outsider now and that hurt. It hurt all the more because Floyd was my roommate and a constant reminder that I was an outsider. My best friend in the whole world was powerless to protect me from feeling shunned and isolated. Basketball had a powerful mojo and it was using my best friend against me.

I watched Floyd go to practice and I watched Floyd come from practice. I wished for the days when our lockers were side by side and we both opened it up to find a clean practice or game uniform waiting for the both of us. All of that was gone now. I watched him pack for trips to away games and reminisced about the two of us listening to our headphones on the bus or just lounging and trippin' out with the rest of the team. It was funny how we always laughed with the guys, but always had our own jokes within their jokes.

Our jokes within their jokes were funny things that could only be understood after seven years of friendship. It seemed that every day made me realize how much of our friendship had been built around the dream of playing basketball together. I watched him go to pre-game shoot around and pre-game meal before home games, with a longing to do those things so that we could continue our dream of playing hoop together. I wanted to create new jokes and stories to add to our archives. But what I wanted and what was happening were two different things. The pain that I felt was so intense that I could not muster enough support for my longtime friend to attend one single game during that season.

I hurt so much that I would have chosen not to be around anyone if I could help it, but I was in a new relationship with a girl who I couldn't push away. Although the pain was great and the motivation was strong to let her go, I couldn't do it. She was so compassionate to my pain and so supportive about the whole situation that I couldn't find a reason to let her go. After awhile I was even glad that she was around.

We started doing things that I had never had time to do when I was playing basketball. We did things like going to nature parks and museums. Neither were things that I would have done on my own, but it was cool to do them with her. So somewhere in between her compassion for my basketball situation and doing things that I would not have normally done on my own, I fell in love with a white girl … for the second time in my life.

All the while that I was hurting over basketball and falling in love, my grades kept me company by hurting and falling right along with me. At the end of my freshman year, I had finished with a bang and I knew that I could repeat the straight A performance if I really tried. But with basketball out of my life, my drive to hit the books just wasn't as strong. I actually had to withdraw from one of my fall semester classes due to my lack of motivation.

The persistent pace of Microeconomics and its demanding course syllabus left retreat as my only sensible option. After a couple of weeks, I knew that I wouldn't be able to keep up. It was one of those courses that required you to read on your own before class in order to understand the next class lecture and to pay attention in class every minute in order to understand the next reading. As if that wasn't enough, it was all cumulative learning that didn't afford you the opportunity to miss one beat. With a wounded heart from basketball, I knew that I would miss plenty of beats.

One of the curious effects of the basketball mojo was to cause me to zone out for days at a time. During those times, I didn't feel anything and I was totally incapable of serious study. Aside from all that, the professor was on top of his game and wasn't accepting anything less than one hundred percent effort from his students. With him, a point received was a point well earned. So after I weighed all the factors, I decided to cut my losses at a W, for withdrew, instead of risking a D or an F.

It proved to be a wise decision, not only because I avoided a D or an F, but because having three classes gave me a better chance of focusing on my remaining three classes. Two of them, Human Sexuality and Computer Applications, were perfect fits for my preferred modus operandi. I followed along with the class discussions and crammed a couple of days before each test. That formula gave me huge amounts of free time for two or three weeks at a time, but it also put me under a great deal of pressure during the two or three days before the exams.

Given the fact that we only had three or four exams during the whole semester, I was willing to make the sacrifice of two or three hell days in exchange for weeks of free time. I hated the hell days and always vowed that I would never put myself in that position again, but my success at pulling it off and the lure of blocks of free time made me repeat the same cycle over and over again.

The third class was Introduction to Logic and it was tough. Not only did I have to pay close attention to class lectures, complete homework assignments, and do well on the exams; but I also had to deal with an 8:00 AM start time. In the life of real world adults or school age children, that time may not seem like any big deal. But to a college student that has neither the real world demands of some adults nor the parental supervision of some school age children, that 8:00 AM class can seem like the curse of all curses.

A lot of students at Eckerd, myself included, didn't even think about going to bed until 2 AM. On weekends that time was adjusted to 3:30 AM. That's not to say that you actually went to bed at that time, that's just when you started thinking about it.

I heard all about the dreadful 8:00 AM time slot from a few people, but the course title was something that interested me enough to disregard it all. Perhaps the time that I signed up for the class was just as important as my own intrigue. I held that schedule request form in my hand in the afternoon when I was fully awake, but not fully aware. Had I been fully aware of what it felt like to be up on a college campus at 7:30 AM, I am not sure if I would have made that same choice. It's all speculation at this point and I shall never know.

But one thing that I do know is that I was in the grasp of one of the most common desires known to man. I was gripped by the desire to know. I wanted to know about logic.

I associated logic with the ability to think. I had heard the phrase: "It defies logic", but I knew that phrase was used in the wrong context more often than not. Logic was a powerful tool that could be used to reduce many complicated situations or problems into simple situations. Even as a ghetto child, I had run across the names of Socrates, Aristotle, and Plato. I had gotten my hands on one of my uncle's school textbooks on philosophy during my pre-teen years and it introduced my mind to all three men.

I tried to read the book and I did read some of it, but at that age, I couldn't stay with it too long. It seemed dry to me and it was difficult for me to understand. Nevertheless, I read enough to know that all three men were regarded as great thinkers. The respect that the author gave those men in that text made me want to be a great thinker too. Thus the seed was planted. I put it in the back of my mind that I too would command respect for my intellect. I hadn't thought about becoming a great thinker in a long time, but when I saw the Intro to Logic class offered I figured that it was time for me to move toward my childhood goal.

The material in the Intro to Logic textbook was heavily laced with a lot of Latin terms that made me wish that I had been one of those chosen few elite intellectuals of my high school who were convinced of the virtues of studying Latin. Back in high school, I had always wondered why kids, who were supposed to be so smart, were stupid enough to take a dead language. But when I saw some of the phrases in Intro to Logic, I wished that I had been stupid enough to take that dead language as well.

The Latin terms proved Maya Angelou's brother Bailey right. In *I Know Why the Caged Bird Sings* (1969), Dr. Angelou wrote that her brother once told her that "all knowledge is spendable currency, depending on the market". I discovered that there were fallacies of logic known as Ad Hominem and Post Hoc; I was in a market where I had no currency to spend.

Later in the class, I learned that Ad Hominem was a Latin phrase traditionally translated in English as "against the man" or "against the person". The fallacy (a fallacy in logic can be thought of as an error in reasoning) occurs when a person attacks the character, circumstances, or actions of the individual making the argument and then claims to have defeated the argument of that individual. It is a fallacy because the attack is made on factors that may be totally irrelevant to the truth or falsity of the actual claim of the argument.

Post Hoc fallacy derived its name from the Latin phrase "Post hoc, ergo propter hoc." In English the traditional translation is "After this, therefore because of this." The Post Hoc fallacy occurred when a person claimed that A caused B just because A happened before B. While in some cases A may actually be the cause of B, the precedence of A before B alone is not enough to make a sound logical argument.

When we went over fallacies like Ad Hominem and Post Hoc in class, I realized that people, myself included, committed those fallacies all the time. Some of the examples were quite funny. The funniest fallacy to me was my favorite fallacy. It was also the one that I thought that people committed the most. It was called the straw man fallacy.

The straw man fallacy was committed when a person substituted the original argument of an individual with a similar, but usually weaker, argument. By substituting a similar weaker argument for the original argument the person had a better chance of defeating the weaker argument.

The only problem with that was once they defeated the weaker argument they would actually claim to have defeated the original argument. So basically, it's like constructing a straw replica of a real man, destroying that straw man, and then claiming that you have actually destroyed the real man. That's why it's called the straw man fallacy.

Once I learned what the straw man fallacy was, I identified it in many conversations. I would listen to the person who made the original argument spend wasted energy by erroneously defending the substituted weaker argument as if it were their original claim. It was a clever trick that was highly successful more times than one might think.

There were numerous times when I witnessed the perpetrator of the straw man fallacy carrying the day as if he or she had won the argument based on sound reasoning. Every time that happened, I marveled at how easily one could counter the straw man fallacy by simply restating their original claim. By restating the original argument, the substituted weaker argument was easily identified as an imposter and the argument could be determined unsound.

The fallacy was then exposed for all to see. As I said, I got a big kick out of the whole thing.

After the kick in the head that I received from my basketball coach, I needed all the good kicks that I could find. I found one of those kicks in my report card for my first semester without basketball. With the exception of the W that I received for withdrawing from the microeconomics course, I managed to pull down straight A's for the second consecutive semester. My report card for the Fall Semester of 1992-93 read:

Introduction to Logic: A

Human Sexuality: A

Principal of Microeconomics: W

Computer Applications: A

I had my second 4.0 GPA in as many semesters and my cumulative GPA was 3.58. My GPA figures took some of the sting off the hurt of not making the basketball team, but it couldn't take away all of the hurt. The campus was full of all the reminders that there was basketball being played and that I wasn't picked to be on the team, so I sought ways to get off campus.

One of the most productive means of escape from campus was to get a job; so during the Christmas holidays, I applied to a shoe store in the mall and got the job. It reminded me of the selling that I had done for a leading area newspaper in high school. It made me feel good that I was just as good at selling shoes as I was at selling door to door newspaper subscriptions. Shortly after I was hired, I was competing with the most experienced salespeople in the store.

My commission based paychecks made me feel that I had really made a good decision to get a job, but as fate would have it, I had to quit selling shoes a few months later because my car broke down. The infamous car that I couldn't "let the police see me in" had a busted clutch. Nobody in my family had any money to get it fixed "right away".

Right away in my family meant several months; I knew that I could easily be without a car for four or five months. I couldn't keep a night job for three or four months without my own transportation. I used my girlfriend's car for awhile, but I didn't feel right leaning on her so hard. She didn't seem to mind; she actually appeared to be glad to help, but I didn't like the feeling it gave me, so I let the job go.

Without a job, I was a prisoner on campus during the final stretch run of the basketball season. My vexation was constant, but I endured. The funny thing about it was that my ankle was finally starting to heal, and as the season started to come to an end, my mind began thinking about a comeback. The first thought crept into my mind without my consent and I quickly dismissed it. Being cut from the team had hurt me so bad that my first developed defense mechanism was to promise myself that I would never put myself in that position again. But after that initial thought, I allowed myself to entertain the idea in my heart of hearts.

I say that because I once heard that a man has three hearts. A heart that he shows the world, a heart that he only shows to friends and to the people that he loves, and a heart that only he knows. The heart that only I knew was where I kept my first rekindling thoughts of a comeback. The visible of my exterior was still a collage of hurt, but for the first time since I had been cut from the team my heart beat with a small sense of basketball hope. I felt that what had appeared to be an ending a few months earlier could actually turn out to be a new beginning. I had made up my mind that I would try out for the team again in the fall of 1993. I would prove that the coaches had made a terrible mistake by letting me go in the fall of 1992.

PROMISE FULFILLED

With my secret hope in my heart of hearts, I began to feel more like my old self again and the drive to get away from campus started to wane. Nonetheless, I couldn't resist an opportunity that presented itself to me in the cafeteria in the spring of 1993. There was a white guy going around trying to recruit people to volunteer for an after-school tutoring program for children who lived in the Jordan Park housing project. Just from the term housing project, I knew that most, if not all, of the kids involved in the tutoring program would be Black children.

I knew that I would be able to relate to those kids better than most people who attended Eckerd because I knew what they were going through trying to make it in that environment. I felt so fortunate to have escaped my own childhood situation that I wanted to be of some help to someone else. I decided to go to Jordan Park to help; I was also going to fulfill a promise that I had made to myself a few years back. It was a promise that I couldn't wait to keep.

During my high school years, I had made up my mind that I would go out of my way to help another Black male child avoid some of the pain that I felt as a child. I made the commitment to myself that I would do that the first opportunity that I got. I had actually attempted to form a mentor relationship with a Black male child in Bradenton the summer after my senior year in high school, but the relationship deteriorated when I had to leave to go to college. Some years later I would see that kid on the wrong path and I would wonder if I could have helped to change his life.

It hurt me to see him in his doped up green Chevy Impala slangin' drugs in the hood. I knew that he was headed straight for a felony charge, a courtroom, and the penal system … or even worse, an early grave. He was my brother, not through blood, but by circumstance; he grew up without his parents just like I did. But that's another story to be a told at another time, the Jordan Park opportunity was upon me.

I knew that there was a strong chance that I would find a child at the Jordan Park community center that was silently crying out for help from anybody willing to listen, just as I had done as a child. I figured that I was now in a position to be there for another Black male child as somebody who could help, so I viewed the tutoring as an intermediate step to my real goal of permanently and positively impacting the life of another Black male child.

The first day that I arrived at the community center where the tutoring was to take place, I knew that I had made the right decision. I saw that there were many kids who could have benefited from having a mentor, but there was one kid who just jumped out at me as the one that I could help the most. I found out that he was eleven years old, he was smart, and had crazy hoop skills for his age. His name was David.

He was kind of a shy kid, but definitely well respected in his peer group. After a few conversations with him, I found out that he lived with his mother, his brother, and his sister. Every conversation that I had with him confirmed my decision to try to add some positive value to his life. I just wanted to be able to offer some guidance in the situations that I thought he might encounter as a result of his situation of being a male child growing up Black and poor in America. He was facing triple jeopardy in a world where double jeopardy was hell.

In a way that an eleven-year-old could understand (an eleven-year-old in Jordan Park was equivalent to a twenty-one-year-old in street knowledge), I explained to him what I was interested in doing and asked him what he thought about the idea. He said that he was cool with it, so my next step was to ask his mother how she felt about it.

One day after a tutoring session, I went to their apartment to see what his mother had to say about the situation. I talked with her for a couple of hours that night and she thought that it was a wonderful idea. She was extremely happy that I wanted to do such a thing and it seemed that my proposed gesture of help had been something that she had prayed for because she kept thanking the Lord. She said that what I wanted to do was a blessing for her and her son, but in my eyes, it was I who was blessed.

I was blessed that she trusted me to be true to my word by granting me the permission to interact with her son. I knew that by helping David, I would be helping myself rise above my own constricting pain that I experienced growing up. I was a child who had traveled down many dark roads alone, accompanied only by the stars in the heavenly sky and by the tears that rolled down my cheeks.

I remembered the nights that I had to walk to my grandmother's house from the ballpark as a ten-year-old. David was already a year older than I was when I did that, so I knew that he had already traveled some dark roads of his own. Be that as it was, I knew that there would be many more dark roads from then until he graduated from high school. I knew that I would not always be able to be there for him, but I did feel confident in my ability to minimize the amount of times that he felt alone when he traveled those dark roads.

The possibilities contained in my new relationship with David gave me a deep feeling of fulfillment. That feeling helped me a great deal as summer approached. The combination of my growing desire to pursue my hoop dreams and the fact that I would finish up with a very decent academic performance for the 1992-93 school year only added to my sense of accomplishment. It was safe to say that I was feeling a lot better at the end of the year than I was at the beginning of the year. My grades for the Spring Semester of 1992-93, including my Winter Term course, were:

Ethics in the NCAA: A

Latin American Area Studies: B

Principles of Macroeconomics: B

Statistical Methods: B

Computers and Management Info Systems: A

I had finished up my sophomore year in college with a 3.52 cumulative GPA. Academically, I was off to a much stronger start after two years of college than I had gotten off to during my first two years of high school. My mind started racing with the possibilities of what I could do if I really pushed to achieve.

After that year, I made up my mind that I was going to aggressively pursue my studies with everything that I had no matter what happened with basketball. I realized that I got a lot of intrinsic satisfaction from performing well academically. I was also learning a lot; I was learning things that gave me a better understanding of the world around me. I was ready to assert my academic prowess and to show the world that I was as smart as anybody else who attended Eckerd College. I could have easily broke out into, "I'm Coming Out", Diana Ross's 1980 classic.

I was certain that I could do it on the academic stage with the best of the best if I applied myself. I was certain because I had already done it. I had proven to myself that I could do it in both elementary and middle school, and now I had done it in two out of my four semesters in college. I was totally convinced about my chances for academic success, but I wasn't as confident about making a comeback on the basketball court. Although I had overcome adversity on the court in high school, I just didn't know if I could do it again on the collegiate level.

My supreme confidence was completely shattered when my coach told me that he was going to have to let me go. I felt like a champion boxer who had been knocked-out by a punch that he never saw coming in his last fight. And even though I felt that that situation would have never happened if my ankle had been a hundred percent, I was still hurt by the fact that it did. Nevertheless, I knew that I had to try again; I would succeed or fail on my own terms. I was unwilling to let a bum ankle and one man's opinion haunt me for the rest of my life.

I didn't know what the outcome was going to be, but I knew in order to have peace in my life that I had to face down adversity and deal with it. That was the reality of the situation. I was confronted with a proposition best summed up in the words of Alex Haley. "Either you deal with what is reality, or you can be sure that the reality is going to deal with you".

Faced with that proposition, I went back to what worked well for me when my back was against the ropes as a basketball player at Southeast ... good old fashioned hard work. It was my only chance and it was my best chance. I was going to work to be a part of a program that now looked upon me as an outsider.

I arranged to work on campus for the summer so that I would have constant access to the campus weight-room and the basketball gym. I planned to spend hours in both places, so I didn't want to be too far away from either location. I also planned to work a week as a coach at the Manatee Christian Basketball Camp that I had first attended heading into my freshman year at Southeast High School. My summer was going to include a lot of basketball.

Right away, I worked to see if I could get David into the camp. It wasn't a very expensive basketball camp, but when you live in the ghetto even the inexpensive isn't financially feasible. You live in a constant state of: "money too tight to mention". I knew that from first hand experience, but I had learned from my grandmother that a strong desire to get something accomplished could lead you to the almighty dollar if you weren't too proud to ask people for help.

The first scent of the cash led me to my former high school coach. I told him about David and his situation and he graciously agreed to work it out so that he would be able to attend at no cost. My coach's help in that situation helped me to forgive and forget about his uninvited intrusion into my personal life two years earlier. It was a nice gesture on his part, but it was still in alignment with what I had thought two years ago—niggers and basketballs was one thing, but niggers and white girls was quite a different thing. I had never had any problems with him and the former, only the latter caused problems.

With the camp fee handled, I talked to my uncle and his wife about room and board. They agreed that both David and I could stay at their house during that week of basketball camp. So we were all set for that camp, but I also wanted David to attend an annual basketball camp held at Eckerd.

I knew that that was going to be a little more difficult camp to get him into because it was much more expensive than the camp in Bradenton. The kids were paying for room and board at the college as well as the instruction that they would receive from the basketball camp. I talked to my college coach—the man who had crushed my dreams over a value meal at McDonald's—about the dollar and cents of the matter. He suggested that I talk with a man in Campus Ministries to see if they had any programs that would cover the camp cost for David. I took his advice and I was glad that I did. Campus Ministries agreed to cover the cost and David was in just like that.

I felt real good that I was able to help open up some opportunities for him because that's what I had set out to do. I wanted to help him have as many opportunities as possible. He was a good kid who deserved a fair chance to make it in life. A lot of the kids that lived in Jordan Park were good kids who deserved a fair chance to make it in life; but the reality was that many of them would never get that chance. They were trapped in a vicious cycle that started over the day the doctor smacked them on their backsides and the Lord gave the word to let them take their first breath in this world.

I was satisfied with my efforts to help David gain access to a couple of opportunities that I thought he might enjoy, so I concentrated my efforts and focused my energies on becoming a better basketball player. Everyday I put in time working on something that would make me a better basketball player. I ran, I jumped, I shot, I lifted weights, and I thought.

I thought about what would help me make the team and what would keep me off the team. The biggest thing in my mind that would keep my off the team was my ankle, but that had become a non-issue over the course of the year that I was out of basketball. So in my mind the odds were clearly in my favor that I would once again suit up in a college basketball uniform.

I just happened to be in the right place at the right time to get in on some very competitive summer basketball as a starting point guard. I found myself playing in a summer Pro-Am league, which reinforced my confidence. I took advantage of the opportunity and really thrived during that summer of play. Members of the Eckerd coaching staff caught a couple of those games. I tried not to put too much stock in the coaches seeing me play well because I knew that summer league basketball was an entirely different brand of basketball than what Eckerd liked to play.

The summer league games enforced NBA rules like illegal defenses and a 24-second shot clock. That made the games more of a fast paced style of basketball that allowed for individual creativity and talent. At the same time, if you were a defensive liability it would bring that out in the open as well. At Eckerd, the philosophy of the coach—he had been there forever, at least since the 1960's—was more of a slow paced game with very little room for individual creativity. In hindsight, Eckerd wasn't the best place for me to go to pursue my basketball dreams if for no other reason than its let's watch the paint dry before we shoot the ball style; but it was my only option to play with Floyd, so I took it. Now I had to make the best of the situation.

That summer I did everything in my power to get better, I was like the little engine that could when it tried to climb the hill, and I picked up steam everyday. As the summer progressed, I went from I think I can, I think I can to I know I can, I know I can. I was not going to be denied that was all to it. As far as I was concerned, the matter was no longer open for discussion. My veins carried the force that Dr. Du Bois talked about in 1910 when he said: "There is in this world no such force as the force of a man determined to rise". My heart of hearts beat with the promise of maximum effort everyday.

I was going to make it an indisputable gross injustice to the world if I didn't make the team. That was my goal. I wasn't going to ask to be on the team or crawl back begging to be taken back; I was going to, through my play and my commitment, demand that the plans of the 1993-94 Eckerd College Men's Basketball program be made to include me.

I was a Black male who had already spent a lot of my time on this earth fighting to be included in this world on my own terms. I had often rejected those terms that might have been imposed on me by others who were less competent to assess my ability, my potential, or my humanity. But this time my resolve to rise above the would-be limitations placed upon me by naysayers was deeper than I had ever known. It extended beyond the boundaries of the basketball court. I was ready to stake my claim in the classroom as well. I was galvanized in my God-given Blackness, my God-given ability, and my God-given potential. I wasn't going to let any man take away what He gave.

I stood alone against the world. My will, my confidence, and my faith were all compressed into a force of one that was ready to guard against any possible attack on my agenda. Unlike high school, I didn't need Floyd to bolster my confidence in my abilities. Unlike a few months earlier, I didn't need the comforting and soothing presence of my girlfriend to take me away to new and different experiences. I wanted to be in the familiar mode of defiance that I had known since I was a small child. On the surface my mindset could have easily been interpreted as a mere reaction to me being cut from the basketball team, but it was much bigger than that and it permeated throughout my essence.

For me, it was really about how easily I would allow others to decide the fate of my existence for me. The question just articulated itself best in the context of basketball given the circumstances during that time. That piercing question in my mind was: Are you going to let that man, prone to the same error in judgment as any other man, tell you that you are not a basketball player anymore?

My answer always came back the same. I would decide when I would no longer be a basketball player based upon my own thoughts, feelings, and abilities. That was my attitude about basketball, and my attitude about life. I knew that God held the rights to my life and the happenings within it, but to no other human was I willing to concede those rights; my life was all I had, and I would not spend it in acquiescence to any man. My choices about my life would not be taken freely by man or bought cheap by currency.

The victory in that last statement does not lie in whether you keep or lose the rights and choices in your life. It lies in the fact that you never stop fighting to retain them at all cost or stop fighting to get them back if they are ever taken away from you. No matter what else happens, the battle is won as long as your spirit is never broken and you never surrender. The only time that life should be able to find a man on his knees is when he's praying; other than that, he should be standing on the two feet that God gave him ready to confront any situation that is placed before him. It's like Bob Marley said: "Get up, Stand up, stand up for your right …don't give up the fight".

HIT THE HIGHWAY

School resumed that fall of 1993, and I was prepared for a battle for my life. I was ready to oppose anyone who depended on that same breath of air, that same drop of water, or that same morsel of food that I needed to sustain my own flesh. If the phrase "survival of the fittest" was an axiom, then I was out to prove my fitness. I chiseled and shaped that energy and emotion into a double edge sword that I intended to use to attack on the court and in the classroom.

I was feeling quite confident on the first day of the tryout/conditioning program that Eckerd used to determine who would be a part of their 1993-1994 team. I had worked hard and I was a better player than I had ever been. Even the conditioning program that had a reputation for being very tough was not able to deter my determination or enthusiasm. I did the sprints without complaint and I did the endurance roadwork without gripe. During the days where we actually played basketball, I gave it all I had. At the end of the day, the old adage about hard work paying off held true. I was on the team ... once again a college basketball player. I was happy, but I wasn't surprised. I expected to accomplish what I set out to do.

Unfortunately my close friend—the white boy who I had gone around and around with as a freshman about being able to get a 4.00 GPA—met the same fate as I did a year earlier. I knew the depth of his hurt; I had to share in his pain as if it were my own. My initial dream when I started college was to play hoops with Floyd, but after my freshman season it had expanded to include the other three guys who had become the brothers that I never had. But the dream of our own version of fabulous five wasn't to be.

My friend from Ft. Lauderdale was cut along with me the year before and never came out again, and now my other friend had been cut. That left Floyd, my friend from St. Pete, and me; but even that trio would be reduced before we got too far along in the 1993-94 season.

That reduction came when I was hit with an unexpected blow. Right at the outset of the season the team was scheduled to hit the road for the first few games. I can't remember where the games were supposed to be played, but I do remember that the same coach who broke my heart a year earlier almost doing the same thing again. I say that because Floyd and I were excited that we would be back together again on the hardwood. We were excited about the practices, the trips, and the games. Our basketball experiences together had always included those three things. We thought that they were just a part of being on a basketball team, but I guess my coach had other ideas of what being on the team meant.

He called me into his office and told me that he wasn't going to be able to take me on the trip. I was like yeah right—you trippin'. But he wasn't, he was as serious as a heart attack. Once again, he had blindsided me with a left hook that I never saw coming. I was on my back again, looking up at the ceiling in a fight that I thought that I had won. The good thing about the situation was that I wasn't knocked silly; unlike the last time, I kept all my senses. It was a very different situation than what had taken place a year earlier at the McDonald's restaurant. I had merely been knocked down by his words; my will had grown too strong to be knocked out.

The first go round at the McDonald's, I didn't have any reason to suspect that me being let go was a terribly unfair situation. I didn't necessarily agree with being cut for the 1992-93 season because I felt that my injury would heal and I would be back to my old self, yet I couldn't argue the fact that I wasn't the same player. But not being taken on the trip was a totally different situation.

I was easily a better player than I had ever been. Aside from that fact, I don't feel that I am exaggerating when I say that I could have easily been the best point guard on the team during that time. But even beyond that, because I know that different people would have their own reasons for disputing that proclamation (at the same time there are those who would also agree with me). Speculation about that is neither here nor there, because the situation was much different for one glaring reason and one glaring reason alone.

There was a point guard that would make the trip that wasn't half the player that I was. I don't mean to put anybody down, but the simple truth was that the guy was not a legitimate basketball player. He was less than my equal in every phase of the game of basketball. I didn't know what to make of such a decision. How could they take him on the trip and not me? That was a question that I couldn't answer with any type of basketball logic. There was just no way that anybody in their right mind could have compared the two of us as basketball players. There was just absolutely no way!

I had set out to make it an indisputable gross injustice to the world if I didn't make the team, and I think that many, if not most, would have seen it that way if I hadn't made the team. I think that the coaches were aware of that and I was glad about that fact, but now they were turning right around by taking this kid with far less ability than I had in any basketball category on the trip and leaving me behind. I knew it wasn't ability and it couldn't have been attitude. I handled being cut from the team with class and dignity that no one could have questioned. I never said one bad thing about their decision to let me go. I just dealt with it.

I could have easily joined in with my supporters who criticized the decision of 1992 to cut me, but I didn't. I couldn't because I knew that I wasn't on my game with my hurt ankle. I was a leader on the court and off the court. I didn't drink, I didn't smoke, I made good grades, I didn't get into any trouble, and I showed the coaching staff respect. Perhaps I had given them too much respect, considering the blatant disrespect that they were showing me.

I was no Marcellus, but I could tell that there was something rotten in the state of Denmark! And I was the victim of a most foul and unjust act. The player that did indeed make the act most foul and unjust was a white player with a rich father. The player's father was also a head basketball coach at a junior college. I deduced the rich part on my own because his son drove around the Eckerd campus in a Porche.

There I was poor and Black, with no father in the coaching ranks to intervene on my behalf. There he was rich and white, with a father who had a professional relationship with the head coach of the Eckerd team. Neither my superior ability nor my better leadership was able to save me from the injustice. The white and the rich had won the day. If you are Black or familiar with the overriding history of race and economics in America, then you will not be surprised in the least that the rich white kid was chosen. You already know that being poor and Black equals double jeopardy in this world. There was nothing that I could do other than stay behind and contemplate my fate.

I knew that I could not acquiesce to the injustice, but I also understood that I was stuck between a rock and a hard place. I could quit and go against my desire to not give in to any human force that sought to deal with me in an unfair and unjust manner. I could stay a partial member of a team that had already tipped its hand on where I stood in the pecking order. I could hope against hope that I would get the one chance that I waited for since that night when I was the freshman who stole the show at McArthur Center.

I went back and forth the whole time that the team was away on the trip, but my mind was instantly made up upon the team's return. I think the visual sight of the coach at the next practice combined with the fact that I knew that I had been so terribly wronged clinched it for me. The whole resuming of business as usual was too much for me to stand. The coaching staff all behaved as if no great injustice had just been perpetrated. I saw that I was expected to behave in the same fashion, and that was something I just could not do. I took the silence of the assistants as their consent to the whole deal. Betrayal through silence made me sick.

I could not be a part of such a system that expected me to bow down to such a deed. I didn't need to be a part of anything bad enough to be robbed of my manhood. I write that because I agree with the words that H. Rap Brown wrote in his 1969 book, *Die Nigger Die*. Brown wrote: "Being a man is the continuing battle for one's life. One loses a little bit of manhood with every stale compromise to the authority of any power in which one does not believe."

My "stale compromise" would have been found in me allowing them to treat me the way that they wanted to treat me (fairly or unfairly) in exchange for them letting me be a part of their team. I thought about how Floyd and I had dreamed of playing hoop together for years and I wanted to be on that team so bad. I just couldn't bring myself to accept such a situation. That day was my last; I requested a brief meeting with the coach after that practice and informed him of my decision to quit the team.

Unlike the times before, it was I who requested the meeting with him. There were no long talks, no tears, and no loss of senses. It was one man letting another man know what the limitation of his endurance was in an eye to eye conversation. I could take no more.

I had endured all that I would endure under the system that never fully embraced me. I would no longer ask for its affection, acceptance, or approval; I didn't need what it was offering. In my heart, I knew that what I brought to the table was good enough to offer to other schools that would be glad to have me. In my junior year, I decided that I would transfer to another school to play basketball. That meant that I would not actually be able to play at a new school until what would have been my senior year at Eckerd.

I told the people who I was close to that I would probably be transferring at the end of the 1993-94 school year. Although I presented it to them as something that wasn't an absolute certainty, I had my mind made up before I decided to quit the team that if at all possible I would definitely transfer out of Eckerd.

I came to the conclusion to transfer to another school for three reasons. The first reason was that I still had a deep love for basketball and a strong desire to play. The second reason was that I did not want my coach or any other man forcing me out of the game that I had grown to love—especially under terms that I saw as unfair. And finally, I had to go in order to have peace within myself. I knew that if I let the situation end like that that I would have never been comfortable with myself for not giving my hoop dreams all I had to give.

I would have spent years asking myself what if, or second-guessing myself about the possibilities. I just didn't want to live with those questions. So I went right back to the hard work routine that I had followed over the summer, this time preparing to be in a different uniform at the start of the 1994-95 school year. It was a whole year away, but I knew that in order to pull it off I would have to be better than I had ever been.

From time to time, I tried to convince my other two friends who were no longer on the team that they should transfer as well, some days they really thought about it and other days they dismissed the idea. We were all hurting from not being able to be a part of something that we had spent the majority of our teen-age years doing, but we handled the pain differently.

Those two spearheaded their pain with anger; at that time, their anger bordered on hatred. They hated the basketball program and they hated the coaching staff. They made sure that those things were well known before they graduated. They wore the opposing team's jersey to an Eckerd home game, they wrote a scathing editorial to the school newspaper about the coach that was printed, and they mercilessly heckled the coach from the stands during home games.

I understood their pain and I figured that in some ways that it was good that they were not letting the questionable ethics of some of the coach's decisions go without bringing some issues to the surface. Still, I couldn't see myself doing the things that they did; it just wasn't my style. As a matter of fact, I didn't go to the games at all and I rarely talked about basketball outside of my transfer decision.

I would have loved it if they decided to transfer with me, but we were at different stages. They both wanted to play hoops, but they also smelled their college degrees right around the corner and decided that putting their degrees off was too much of a price to pay. I respected their decisions and finally agreed that it may have been the best move for them. But for me, I knew that the degree wasn't going anywhere and I knew that I would make sure that I didn't suffer from an academic standpoint as a result of my decision to transfer.

To get around the issues of whether all of my college credits would transfer and all of that rigmarole I decided that I would either do one of two things because I had two years of athletic eligibility. I would either come back to Eckerd after one year of play or two years of play to pick up my degree that I would be leaving on the table. At my new school, I planned to take courses in psychology to pick up a minor if I stayed one year and a major if I stayed two years. In my mind that game plan would prevent me from wasting time academically, while pursuing athletics.

I told a few of my professors about my academic plans, but they didn't see it the same way that I saw it. They said that if I was willing to go to school for an extended period of time, then I should pursue a graduate degree and forget about hoops. I understood their logic and appreciated the fact that they appeared to be genuinely concerned about me, but I knew that I had to do it my way because it was my life and I had to live with myself for as long as I was alive. I was going to play college basketball again and I was going to end up with multiple undergraduate degrees. In order to do college my way, I was going to have to hit the highway, that was all to it.

It was all so ironic, just as the Eckerd College coaching staff and I were agreeing on our joint venture to make me a pariah in the hoops world, I was gaining a lot of recognition for my work with David and my academic prowess. Despite all of my basketball ups and downs, David and I became better and better friends. A man who worked for the college interviewed me after I went to Campus Ministries to request funds so that David could attend the Eckerd summer basketball camp. I didn't really have a complete grasp of what the interview was for at the time, but the by-product of that interview turned up after the fall semester of 1993. It appeared as an article in the 1992-93 Eckerd College President's Report and Honor Roll of Donors. The layout placed a huge picture that David and I took that summer in the gymnasium right in the middle of the page. The following is the article that appeared right beside the picture of the two of us:

> Quincy Smith, 20, came to an important realization not long ago that many people don't reach until they are much older than the Bradenton Junior, if they reach it all: namely, that 'no man is island', and no one is a totally self-made person. The realization has meant a lot to him, to a group of school children in St. Petersburg, and to one 11-year-old among those children who's become a close friend of Smith over the past several months.

> 'I was in the Eckerd dining hall one day last spring', Smith recalls, 'and someone was going from table to table trying to recruit tutors for a school attended by kids from Jordan Park housing project. I'd never done anything like that before, but it occurred to me that a lot of people have helped me [Smith is a dean's list business major with an interest in international affairs], so I decided I'd try to be of help to someone else.'

> Right from the start, Smith enjoyed the experience, 'Just being there was satisfying, I felt like I was giving something back. We helped with all the usual stuff—spelling, math, grammar. A lot of these kids lack motivation. They're able to look up to stars like Michael Jordan, and at the other end of the spectrum they see drug dealers with all the material things. But they don't have a lot of successful—and realistic—role models, and they have a hard time seeing the value of an education. They'd come up in ask, 'You go to college? What's it like? Is it real hard?'

> Almost from the start, Smith noticed David Pierce, an 11-year-old who was getting ready to head this fall for the sixth grade at Riviera Middle School. 'He was obviously smart and interested. He didn't really need much in the way of tutoring, but I felt that I might be helpful to him as a friend.'
>
> The two spent much of the summer together, a basketball player himself, Smith arranged for David to take part in Eckerd's basketball camp, where he got to know a number of Eckerd's players, and then another camp down in Bradenton run by Smith's former high school coach. 'David came down to stay with my family for a week.'
>
> 'I don't hang out with him just because of tutoring or basketball,' Smith says. 'He's just a great kid, and I want to do anything I can to help him have a good future. Eckerd has broadened my perspective so much. I'd like to see him enjoy the same kind of benefits that I have.'

I was really surprised when I saw the article and the big picture of the two of us in the report. After the article, a lot of people came to me to tell me that they thought that I was doing a great thing. Somewhat modest, I appreciated their positive feedback, but I was more appreciative of the fact that I was able to help David in a meaningful way that I thought would make a difference. I wanted to continue to help him, so that he could reach a point where he understood more things around him and realized his potential. I wanted him to truly understand his ability to overcome it all. That was the point that I was quickly approaching at that time in my life.

I realized that my education at Eckerd was a major catalyst in my acceleration toward that point. If education was the horse that would carry me forward toward my hopes and dreams, then I was the determined jockey positioned low in the saddle with heels to the side and whip firmly in hand forever urging the steed to greater speeds.

THE JOYS OF LEARNING

I was true to my commitment that I made to myself at the end of my sophomore year. I pursued my academics with all that I had during my junior year. Unlike the year before, my basketball setback had no negative effects on my coursework. If anything, it only served to motivate me to really want to excel. In my mind, there were no politics in the classroom that could treat me unfairly. If I clearly demonstrated a supreme mastery of the covered material and performed my coursework better than the other students, then I knew what the outcome would be. In light of how I viewed my basketball situation, I welcomed the unbiased challenge.

Despite my tumultuous childhood, I hadn't missed the requisite skills that a student needed to succeed in college. Unfortunately, many of the kids that grew up the way that I did missed out on the basic building blocks of the three R's. My great desire in elementary and middle school to show white people that I was just as smart (if not smarter) as they were kept me on course in gaining the knowledge that I needed. In high school, my God-given intelligence and the TLC of a Godsend of a teacher carried me through.

My first year of college was more about me striking out against my white friend. He was just the latest in the line of people who tried to define my abilities for me. All of my previous years of academic success involved me using energy from an outside source to help me succeed, but my second year in college marked a turning point for me.

My second year was my first real beginning of experiencing the joys of learning for their own sake. Those joys intensified during my third year of college. I was using my courses to probe my environment and to cultivate my intellect. My motivation for doing that came from the pure joy that I received from me feeling myself change as a person. My newfound joys of learning made my junior year in college my best year ever from an academic standpoint. I made straight A's the whole year through. My report card for the year read as follows:

The Managerial Enterprise: A

Principles of Microeconomics: A

Introduction to Psychology: A

Cultural Environment of International Business: A

Principles of Marketing: A

Psychology of Male/Female Relationships: A

Personnel Management: A

Introduction to Business Finance: A

Organizational Behavior and Leadership: A

International Marketing: A

For the first time in my life, the word student completely overshadowed the word athlete in the moniker of student-athlete that I used to define myself. I had taken a great deal of pride in being called a student-athlete for so many years, but deep down I had always favored the word athlete. My decision to quit the basketball team had stripped me of my official claim on the word athlete, but my intense training sessions gave me de facto claim to the term. However, it didn't matter to me. I was so enthralled with being a student that I could have cared less about being called anything else. I wanted to learn and I did.

My mind turned me every which way but loose. It was truly awakened to the joys of learning for the first time in my life and it seemed to go on for hours in bold defiance of sleep or rest. Previous areas of my thought process that had resembled a desert began to bloom with new information. I felt different parts of my brain being transformed into oases of fresh ideas. The new information and fresh ideas kept me on a relentless pursuit of knowledge. There were three courses in particular that I had enrolled in during that 1993-94 school year that I really enjoyed for their stimulating effects: The Cultural Environment of International Business, The Managerial Enterprise, and Organizational Behavior and Leadership.

The Cultural Environment of International Business really opened my eyes to my ignorance about the world. I realized that not only was there a world that I had not thoroughly explored within my own country, but I was also ignorant in regards to the many worlds that existed outside U.S. borders. Growing up Black and in the ghetto forced me to look at the world and at life from a Black and poor perspective. The only exception to Black that I knew was a few Mexican migrant workers that I had been exposed to during my Palmetto years.

In high school, my Black world expanded into the larger mainstream white world. My high school expansion into the mainstream made me functional—and quite proficient—on an everyday level. But the things that I was learning and being exposed to in college were different. Through my coursework, I was acquiring the tools to compete with the best and the brightest that the white world within the U.S. borders had to offer.

When I enrolled in The Cultural Environment of International Business, I wanted to extend my ability to compete into the international arena. I didn't want any restrictions on my thoughts, opinions, or views. I wasn't satisfied to escape the boundaries of the ghetto, to only be confined to the boundaries of the United States. Despite popular opinion in America, I learned that the United States was not the world and that the world was not the United States. The world was a place of many different thoughts, believes, customs, and cultures.

In addition to the desire to know about other cultures outside of the United States, I discovered that I was somewhat naturally drawn to the people from different countries. Eckerd was a small school that could boast of a vibrant international student population, and it seemed to me that I was able to connect with a number of the international students with little or no effort. Sometimes there were slight language barriers between us, and our cultural norms were different; but somehow my Black experience found more acceptance and comfort with those people than it did with many whites from the U.S.

At times, I found myself very much involved in discussions with groups of international students on many different topics. The discussions were never planned; oftentimes, they just popped up around a campus bench or at the student mailboxes. The topics were so broad that it is hard for me to remember all of them, but I will tell you what I remember the most about those conversations was the respect and sincerity that was exchanged between us.

The exchange of those two things always created a very warm and encouraging feeling inside of me that boosted my confidence in humanity. After awhile, I began to talk with many different people from many different countries and I was always impressed with our dialogues. Although none of them ever said it aloud, it was something about their voices, their eyes, and their body language that seemed to say: I might make a mistake with the language or the culture and say or do something to offend you; but please accept my humblest apologies in advance because such a thing would be the furthest thing from my truest intentions—my brother.

As a reciprocal courtesy, I made an effort to give off the same type of vibe that I received. That was the type of atmosphere that was created when we interacted with one another. And it was good because mistakes that sprang from noble intentions were easy to forgive and forget. Later in my life, I would wonder if some of the things that I felt in communicating with foreign students were the same things that made Black people like Dr. Ralph Bunche and the Rev. Jesse Jackson successful in negotiating agreements in the international arena where whites were unsuccessful.

I think that the lack of noble intentions, historically speaking, on the part of the white man is the primary reasons why so many Black people have such a hard time forgiving Mr. Charlie and Uncle Sam. It is not that we haven't searched for the magnanimity of the white man; it's just that we can't find it existing anywhere in mainstream history in a pure form when the matter pertained to the Black race as a whole. Maybe John Brown, but that's it.

My course in The Managerial Enterprise was a real defining course for me as an individual. Like The Cultural Environment of International Business, it also expanded my world. The class grade was made up entirely of presentations based on real business cases from different corporations.

The goal of the class was to hone your ability to analyze and present material while demonstrating a firm grasp of the business fundamentals that you had learned up to that point. Your ability to meet the goals of the class was supposed to show up in your future recommendations for the company that you were assigned to study.

The course was an upper level course that required many management prerequisites before you were allowed to enroll. Little direction was offered on the front end by the professor as to how you should analyze the information, present the information, or what the basis should be for your future recommendation. On the back end—after you analyzed, presented, and made recommendations—you were held accountable.

Your grade reflected that accountability because it was determined by how well you did in those three areas. It was a very daunting task for many of the students and there was always the dreadful fear of making that one mistake that would hurt your chances of getting the grade that you wanted.

To make the matter more interesting, all of the students were placed on teams consisting of four or five students. Our class was made up of four teams. That type of structuring of the class may have been infeasible for another college or university, but Eckerd was a college that prided itself on the fact that it offered smaller class sizes than most colleges and universities.

My team was in totally unfamiliar territory with the requirements of the class. The professor explained the structure of the class, and our silence was taken as consent to the minimum instruction/maximum accountability theory. At least that was the case in class, but when we met outside of class there was genuine panic and fear that made the first meetings tense. Out of the tenseness, new skills that I wasn't fully aware that I possessed emerged to make me the undisputed leader of my group and quite arguably the student leader of the whole class.

My ability to analyze and make sound business recommendations was something new to me, but even more impressive to me was my ability to present the information in a powerful manner that left very little room for disagreement. I know that in writing that last sentence, I am incurring the risk of sounding extremely arrogant; but I am simply recounting how the events of that class transpired.

I knew that I was smart, but I was genuinely surprised with my ability to handle the complex assignments. Oftentimes during my group's presentations, it appeared that the professor and I had gotten together before class to see how much we could agree with each other.

From my group's first presentation to our last presentation, I was given the primary responsibilities to guide our group's efforts in the right direction. I was also chosen to present our findings and recommendations to the rest of the class. I built the frame of fundamentals of what we should analyze and recommend, while the other group members filled in that frame with the various details. I loved that arrangement because I loved the creating of the vision and the challenge of the live presentation of the information, but I hated dealing with the details. That is still a part of my preferred style today.

The third class that had a tremendous impact on me during the 1993-1994 school year was my Organizational Behavior and Leadership class. That class had an even bigger impact on me than both The Cultural Environment of International Business and The Managerial Enterprise. I had been a leader in my peer group as a small child and I had been a leader on the basketball court, but I had never been involved in a setting that actually asked me to study the topic of leadership.

The course was designed to cover leadership theories and practices as they pertained to the business world. But it was broader than that for me because I knew that effective and sound leadership principles could not be constrained to any one forum. The subject matter of that course forced me to look at the entire world around me and to analyze my life experiences up until that point.

The course required a lot of writing assignments about the different leadership topics that were analyzed, and my experiences as a Black male permeated all of my writings that I turned in for that class. Those writings forced me deep inside of myself and completely outside of myself at the same time. I went deep inside of myself to ask deep penetrating questions about my own life and the lives of those who I had grown up with as a child, only to have a part of me to stand on the sideline as a non-participant in the ordeal.

It seemed to me that I was constantly watching myself as an impartial observer and analyzing the metamorphosis that my education was forcing me to undergo. Watching and analyzing myself as two different people was a strange phenomenon. Here's a quote from one of those writing assignments that I turned in for that class. I wrote the following about the differences, yet the sameness, between my friends and I that were becoming blatantly obvious to me whenever I visited Bradenton:

> Eckerd College has allowed my mind to escape some of the situations that I may have experienced somewhere else. The friends that I mentioned earlier do not benefit from this opportunity. Their environment is not conducive to pacifying their hostility. My interaction with them is nothing phenomenal. I can totally identify with their situation and understand their mindset. At the same time, I sense that the separation between us is the result of my education; but then another part of me realizes that there is no real separation. They are me and I am them; we are just at different points on the same continuum of education.

That's the way I felt about my friends that I left in Bradenton. I felt different and the same all at the same time. Many of them had already decided to assuage their capitalist migraine by becoming channels in the distribution of cocaine. They were all the same cats that I grew up with, the same cats that I talked with about being something when we grew up. One of them wanted to be a pilot. I thought that it was a strange thing to want to be, but I always listened. Another one wanted to be an electrical engineer; I didn't know what that was, but I still listened. Now that they wanted to run the dope game in Bradenton, I did the same thing that I always did. I listened.

In addition to the heavy emphasis on writing assignments as a determinant of class grade, there was also a heavy emphasis on the spoken word and how you participated in class discussions. I wasn't the shy type who needed to be prodded into discussions in general, but that was even truer if the discussion was on a topic that I found interesting. The fact that the class participation was fifteen percent or more (can't remember exactly) of the grade was inconsequential to me, but it was sufficient enough to motivate those who otherwise might have been less inclined to voice their opinions during the class discussions.

With those folks being somewhat forced to participate, our class discussions usually included all that were present; and that type of participation usually produced a variety of different opinions on the topic of discussion during any given class session. However, with all of those factors being what they were, my voice still rang out more than average and my opinions seemed to hit the discussion with a little more impact than others. That was true even when my opinion was in the minority opinion group.

One day during one of those very lively discussions that were commonplace for the course, a guest member of our class said something about me that I didn't really quite know how to take at first. The guest was an ASPEC member, which was an acronym that stood for Academy of Senior Professionals at Eckerd College. Eckerd answered the question of what is ASPEC with the following reply:

> It is a membership organization of persons who are recognized by their peers as leaders in their professional lives and in community service, have exhibited broad intellectual interests, and who wish to continue to engage in creative educational, social, and cultural growth. It supports Eckerd College and its various programs through the contribution of time and talent.

The comment that the ASPEC member made after I voiced one of my opinions was: "Quincy looks like just a basketball player until he opens his mouth". In the context of what he was saying, he went on to say how much he respected my opinions. Although he went on to clarify his comments by saying he respected and admired my views; initially, I was bothered by his words.

I wasn't bothered by the fact that he said that I looked like a basketball player. Most of the time after that class I went to the gym to either lift weights or to work on my basketball skills (I didn't want one day to pass without me working toward transferring to another school to play hoops), so I was dressed like a basketball player. I was glad that he appreciated my words, but I couldn't help but to wonder what he would have thought about me if I had not chosen to open my mouth. I concluded, based on what he said, that would have left me "just a basketball player" … whatever that meant.

If I hadn't verbally expressed what was on my mind, would his designation of "just a basketball player" have excluded me from the respect that my words had established with him? I wondered how much of a role of the fact that I was Black played in me looking like "just a basketball player". I knew that I was the same inside regardless of whether I spoke or not. I did not like the fact that I was judged merely by words that I could have easily chosen not to speak. I also felt uneasy about being judged strictly on appearance because I knew that my Black skin would render me a raw deal in the majority of the first impressions that I would make in my life. I knew that from hearing power door locks on vehicles as I passed by parked cars in parking lots. I knew that from being followed around in stores when I had money in my pocket with intent to buy—not steal—what I wanted.

The ASPEC member's words troubled me because even though he meant for his remarks to be complimentary, they reinforced the fact that people are susceptible to forming opinions of others without knowing anything about a person other than what they can see.

In my case, I knew that all too often the first thing that people would see with me was my Black skin. I knew that many would associate all of the lies that America has told about Black people as a whole with me as an individual. But his comments also made me realize something else—something in which I could find some solace.

I took comfort in the fact that my choice to speak or not to speak could have a tremendous impact on the way I was perceived by others. I will always be grateful to the ASPEC member, because his comments were a catalyst to me learning a valuable lesson. I decided from that day forward that as long as I had a voice that I would speak.

In my mind, I concluded that I could not control what people thought about me when they looked at me. I felt that it was a shame that my clothes or my skin color might play a part in others perception of me before they ever knew anything about me. But I was encouraged by the fact that I could change or significantly influence those with preconceived notions with my choice to speak and with the words that I spoke.

In some situations, I realized that my voice would be the only weapon that I had to wield against the forces that might otherwise succeed in oppressing me. However, as I grew older and moved into the stage from which I am writing these words, I have worked toward adding an addendum to my choice to speak. I would caution anyone else that decides to speak to do the same by hearkening unto the words of Jesus in the book of Matthew chapter 12 verses 34-37.

> O generation of vipers, how can ye being evil, speak
> good things? for out of the abundance of the heart the
> mouth speaketh. A good man out of the good treasure
> of the heart bringeth forth good things: and an evil man

out of the evil treasure bringeth forth evil things. **But I say unto you, That every idle word that man shall speak, they shall give account thereof in the day of judgement. For by thy words thou shalt be justified, and by thy words thou should be condemned**.

So before you decide to speak … recognize that the power of life and death is present in the tongue (Proverbs chapter 18 verse 21).

THE NEW PHOENIX

The summer of 1994 was finally upon me. I stood firm in my decision to leave Eckerd and forego my senior year and the completing of my education in the timeliest manner. I had spent much of the final months of the semester trying to find a school that might fit my situation that would be willing to give me an opportunity to tryout. I didn't feel like I needed a lot of schools on my list because I felt that I had worked hard and the only thing that I needed was an opportunity to show what I could do on the court.

Getting that opportunity was my number one priority for the summer and I was determined to make it happen; but in the meantime, I had more practical matters to deal with like getting settled with summer housing and a summer job.

My quandary was soon solved. My girlfriend decided that she was going to get an apartment off campus for the summer months and she had no problem with me moving in with her. So the housing was settled. The employment issue had been settled as well, but it had been contingent upon me being able to find housing in the area.

During the last months of the semester, I applied for an internship at a leading area newspaper and was offered an opportunity to participate in their summer internship program. I was really excited about the program. It paid more money than I had ever made on an hourly basis. I can't remember what the exact figure was, but it was somewhere in the $8.00/hr range. At the time that was a considerable amount over the minimum wage and more than enough for me to cover any summer expenses that might arise. As a matter of fact, those paychecks allowed me to do some things that weren't necessary at all. My education was broadening my horizons, but I still had a lot of the "chasing pawns" mentality in me.

My uncle decided that he did not want to fix the clutch on my last car, the one that I didn't want the police to see me driving, so he gave me his black Oldsmobile Delta 88. I was thrilled because I had been in love with that car since way back when he drove me to Bradenton Middle School every morning. The Delta, as we called it, had lost some luster since its glory days; but it was still a bad ride in the eye of certain beholders. I just happened to be one of those who still saw its fading beauty. But the combination of new money and ambition made me want to restore its past glory.

The money that I was making at my internship burned my hands and I quickly threw a fresh coat of black paint on the Delta. One of my homeboys from Bradenton hooked me up with a box speaker set that I plugged into an amplifier/EQ that I picked up from the flea market. The speaker set didn't sound right in the trunk, so in an effort to get the premium sound I put it in the back seat; thereby creating the world's largest two-seater.

I wasn't quite satisfied with the improvements that I had made to the car, when another friend of mine from Bradenton told me that he could get me a set of rims for fifty dollars. I was like cool, let's do it. I should have known that nothing good could come from that deal, but I was dying to sit behind the wheel of the Delta, lean to the side, and watch the faces of the people in the street as I bent a corner. I wanted to do my best Too $hort imitation and "let 'em count my spokes". I was in college, working as an intern for a leading area newspaper, but the biggest part of me was ghetto and I got a big thrill from picturing such a scene.

The day that I had my rims put on, the Delta was looking ghetto fabulous. I had a summer league basketball game right around the corner from the Jordan Park housing projects where David lived. I was in ghetto heaven because that was the perfect set for me to roll my ride in an area where it would be appreciated. It was ten minutes from Eckerd, but it might as well had been ten million miles away because it was two very different worlds. I pulled up to the gym in style—ghetto style. I backed my car into a parking space just to get the extra exposure that going past the space and backing in brings. My ride was pimped-out and I was on cloud nine.

I was booming my stereo with the songs that pumped out the biggest bass because I wanted the people outside of the car to hear me coming from as far away as possible. On the inside of the car, I played connect the dots with my EQ as I leaned hard to the left like I was a pimp. I stopped at the stop signs like I was waiting for a long train to pass, only to creep forward again at floss pace. You couldn't tell me that I wasn't doing it!

After the game, I was feeling even better about myself than I was before the game. We had won the game and I had scored a lot of points to boot. It was a very good day for the kid! I swaggered out of the gym to get back into my ride to cruise against that time of day that puts a black car at its peak splendor against a dusk backdrop. But the "yeah I'm the man smirk" that was glued to my face quickly disappeared when I got outside and saw my car sitting dropped to the ground like a low rider.

When I got up close, I heard the air coming from the spokes on the leaky rims that my homeboy did me a favor in selling to me for fifty bucks—some favor. I had pulled up to the gym so cool and nonchalantly, but now I was running around without a minute to lose. I was racing against the fact that I only had enough air in the tires to support immediate action. There was no time to hesitate. I was also racing against the shop closing before I could get there to have someone find out what the problem was and what I could do about it.

Luckily, I won both of the races. I made it to the shop on some tires that barely hugged the rims, but I had lost all my cool points that I got from my ghetto fabulous entrance. I don't know if anybody was laughing or not, but looking back it had to be a funny sight to see; especially if you had seen me flossin' on the way to the game.

Needless to say the rims were damaged and were on the back porch where they were stolen from for a reason. The shop put the Delta's old rims back on, and my boy got over on me for fifty until I saw him again. But in my ghetto state of mind, having the experience of riding gloriously through the hood in the Delta was priceless—even if it were for only thirty minutes.

My ghetto state of mind was always just a toggle away from being the active state of mind that I was working from, but by that point in my life I had developed other states of mind that I used in different settings where ghetto wasn't appropriate. My new intern job was such a setting, so I toggled into my professional educated mode. I think I had the educated part down just a little bit better than the professional part, but I was smart enough to blend in on the professionalism point so that I wouldn't look too conspicuous. Any lack of professionalism on my part was due more to my limited exposure to a professional atmosphere than any other factor. As the summer progressed, my professionalism improved as I watched and imitated.

Whatever I may have lacked in professionalism seemed to be overshadowed by the perspective that I brought to our roundtable discussions in various meetings for interns only. We didn't have many of those discussions, but we had enough for me to distinguish myself amongst my peers.

The discussions were facilitated by the Intern Coordinator and consisted of interns from a wide array of different colleges and universities. Many of the schools represented by the different interns were top schools from around the country. It was a good place to test one's intellect and see how one stacked up against his or her peers.

Initially, I participated in the discussions to make sure that I wasn't relegated to a lower standing in the group. The way I grew up put a lot of emphasis on being respected and I wanted to be respected in the group. Not worshipped or revered, just respected. I wasn't trying to grandstand or anything like that; my goal was to demonstrate that I deserved to be a part of a group that some would have looked upon as an elite cluster. Still, I would be lying if I wrote that affirmative action didn't have anything to do with my motivation for wanting to prove that I did in fact belong.

I had been exposed to the different arguments for and against affirmative action in college (The term *affirmative action* was first used by President John F. Kennedy in a 1961 executive order designed to encourage contractors on projects financed with federal funds to racially integrate their workforces). Personally, I agreed with the words that Lyndon B. Johnson spoke in a 1965 speech at Howard University when he stated:

> You do not take a person who, for years, has been hobbled by chains and liberate him, bring him up to the starting line of a race and say, 'you are free to compete with all the others,' and still justly believe that you have been completely fair.

I didn't know if my selection had anything to do with affirmative action or not; and to be honest, I didn't care if it did or not. Once selected, my goal was to prove that I belonged in such a touted group. In my heart, I was pretty confident that I belonged; but I wanted everybody else to be confident that I belonged as well. I didn't want anybody going home at the end of the day wondering why I was chosen.

My desire not to be relegated to a lower position in the group and my drive to dispel any doubts as to my qualifications was the initial reason that I began to participate in our roundtable discussions, but my motivation changed midway through the internship. I started to really enjoy the conversations. It was really interesting to hear the different viewpoints that different people had on the various topics of discussion.

The conversations made me realize that if you could get different people together and talking openly and honestly, then you had the potential to change things. I don't know if I got that notion because we were all so naïve and ambitious about the impact that we could have on the world or because I thought it was actually possible for a few people to change the world. My hope for the future leads me toward the latter.

While I was at Eckerd College, I read something once by Margaret Mead, a U.S. anthropologist. It said: "Never doubt that a small group of thoughtful, committed citizens can change the world; indeed, it's the only thing that ever has."

I pondered the concept when I first read it because I wasn't sure if I believed it or not. I only decided to give its veracity the benefit of the doubt after concluding that the circumstances had to be right for that small group to triumph. There were times during our round-table discussions that I believed that the circumstances were right and that we could be that small group to make a big difference.

The commitment and passion toward making a difference that could be heard in the voices of the interns was essential in making me realize the possibilities of positive change. A lot of times in that room where we had our discussions, the commitment and passion that I heard made me feel that we were all of one accord. I felt as if we were all bounded together in the belief that we could and we would change the world into something better than what it was. That was a great feeling for me because it allowed me to transcend the limits that the world tried to impose upon my Blackness and enabled me to experience a greater humanity.

The respect that I thought that I would have to wrestle away from unwilling hands was extended to me as a common courtesy.

The walls that separated society-at-large seemed as if they vanished into thin air.

The group seemed to be of one like mind, but that's where the likeness ended. The collection of young minds included individuals from both sexes and many different races. I'm sure that there were many more unobservable differences as well. However, as we broke down the walls, the problems that plagued the world didn't seem that difficult to solve.

Now that I have become more knowledgeable in the area of world history, I know that we were on the right track, especially in the area of breaking down walls. There's a particular quote that I read in a *Letter from Nelson Mandela to Mrs. Manorama Bhalla, Secretary of the Indian Council for Cultural Relations, New Dehli* that talked about the damaging effect of walls. Mr. Mandela wrote the letter on August 3, 1980 as a response to receiving the 1979 "Jawaharlal Nehru Award for International Understanding". The first Black president of South Africa, in quoting Jawaharlal Nehru—the first prime minister of independent India—wrote the following concerning walls:

> Walls are dangerous companions, they may occasionally protect from outside evil and keep out an unwelcome intruder. But they also make you a prisoner and a slave, and you purchase your so-called purity and immunity at the cost of freedom. And the most terrible of walls are the walls that grow up in the mind which prevent you from discarding an evil tradition simply because it is old, and from accepting a new thought because it is novel.

If it were up to me, our intern period would have had many more roundtable discussions than we had; but the newspaper hired interns for at least two reasons. The first reason was that an internship program was an excellent recruiting tool to attract talent and potential for the newspaper. And the second reason was that there was real work for us to do.

My real work assignment placed me in the circulation department. It was ironic that it was called circulation, because it took me out of circulation with the rest of the interns. I was sent to help manage a district during a time period that was referred to as papertime operations.

Papertime operations took place at designated places throughout the newspaper's distribution area. Those places were called substation districts, and they were where newspaper employees—known as carriers—were paid to insert, bag, and deliver newspapers within their designated routes. I was sent in to help the district manager manage this hectic period, so most of the time I was filling in as the assistant district manager. The odd thing was that that period usually began in the substation somewhere around 1:30 or 2:00 AM (12:30 AM for the Sunday paper). With redeliveries to missed or unsatisfied customers, that period could extend to 11:00 AM (1:00 PM for the Sunday paper). I never opened and did redeliveries on the same day unless something was seriously wrong. Still, I worked enough hours to make me appreciate my days off.

My body was on a totally different schedule than the majority of the rest of the population, not to mention the rest of the interns. I didn't really mind it, because it gave me the afternoons and early evenings free. If you were a basketball player, then that was the time that you needed to be free.

I spent most of the summer playing in various basketball leagues, but my main goal was to get on somebody's university or college court to try out and get a scholarship so that I could transfer from Eckerd. With the way that things were going in the summer leagues and the way that I was playing, I figured that I wouldn't have any problem accomplishing that goal.

My opportunity to prove my theory arrived over one weekend during that summer, when I visited the University of Alabama at Huntsville. It wasn't a visit where they rolled out the red carpet or anything even close to that. It was basically me talking with the coach a couple of times on the telephone and explaining my situation. He told me that he was going to have a look at some guys; and that if I arranged my own transportation that he would put me up with a dorm room for a couple of nights. That was all that I needed to hear; I was all over that opportunity like a team down by two in a full-court press in a national championship game with less than a minute to play.

I took some of that cool cash that I was making at the newspaper and rented a car. I didn't have a lot of confidence that the ten-year-old Delta could handle such a trip without mishap and I didn't want to have to fill the gas tank every time I turned a corner.

Besides those two reasons, I didn't have a strong desire to be on any Alabama road in a car that might break down.

On what I considered the biggest trip of my life, my homeboy Floyd was right there beside me to offer me his support and to help with the driving. Floyd was my mellow, my ace like that! He always had my back, and it was real. You know a lot of people say they got your back, but when you need them you can't find them or they just flat out tell you a lie or make up an excuse of why they can't do it for you. Floyd wasn't like that. He was true blue and down for me. When most people were telling me what a mistake I was making, my man was telling me: I see it like you see it, so I'm ridin' shotgun.

We had known each other since 1984, and ten years later we were still kicking it strong. There we were on our way to Alabama during the summer of 1994 in a rental. We had a couple days worth of gear, some makeshift directions written down from my phone conversations with a coach that I didn't know, some money for gas and food, and my hoop dreams. Although my mother never had any sons other than me, I considered Floyd to be my brother. So once again, just like high school, my brother was by my side helping me to fight for my basketball life.

On our way to Alabama, we got lost momentarily somewhere in Georgia and stopped at a store in the hood to ask for some directions. It was one of those kinds of stores that you can only find in the hood. It had malt liquor ads on the window, substandard lighting, and a small crowd gathered outside like it was the hangout spot. I mean it was so typical that it wasn't even strange to us. Albeit we were in another state, but it might as well have been around the corner because we had seen stores that could have been the exact replica of that store in Florida.

I was glad that I had stopped to refuel in Valdosta, Ga. because if I would have bought gas at the station where we stopped to get directions, then I would have paid a slightly higher price than what seemed to be the going rate round them there parts. I guess it was just like Florida in that respect too.

All the ghetto or hood stores that had gas pumps in Bradenton and St. Pete were always priced slightly higher than the gas pumps that were not in the so-called hood or ghetto. One would think that stations located in the poorer sections of town would have cheaper gas, but based on my experience it was the exact opposite. I guess Langston Hughes was right on the money when he said the ghetto is "the section where a nickel costs a dime." Well, I kept my dime in my pocket and got back on the road toward Huntsville.

We made it to Huntsville on time, because I had calculated what I called "get lost time" into the travel plans. Considering the fact that neither of us had ever driven more than the fifty or so miles that separated Bradenton from St. Pete, we didn't use nearly as much of that time as I thought we would. I guess we were sort of lucky. I was hoping to be equally as lucky in the try-outs that lay before me later that afternoon and the next morning. I say that because basketball had taught me that sometimes it was better to be lucky than good. I knew that I was good, but I also knew that the race wasn't always to the swift and the battle wasn't always to the strong. Nevertheless, I went out both days and gave it all that I had to give. I left it out on the court.

After the second day of try-outs, I sat outside of the coach's office like a man being tried for a serious crime sitting on a courtroom bench waiting for the jury to come back with the verdict. As he called me into his office, I could feel a moment of truth upon me. I hoped for the best, but I was prepared for the worst … I got neither.

He told me that he admired the fact that I was a hard worker. He said that he could tell that I worked hard by watching me play and by looking at my body. He said that he could tell that I spent a lot of time in the weight-room working on my strength and conditioning. He also said that I was quick, a good defender, and that I had excellent ball handling skills. He said that I was welcome to come to Huntsville and try-out for his team in the fall, but he couldn't promise a spot or a scholarship. He said that I would probably be able to put together a real solid financial package with my grades, a federal Pell grant, and some work study money.

I was encouraged by what he said about the money because money was always an issue for me. From what he described to me, I knew that my financial situation would be no worse in Huntsville than my situation at Eckerd. My money situation did not change in dollar amount after my basketball mishaps at Eckerd; it just came from other areas of the school's scholarship fund. Still, Eckerd was so expensive (over $20,000 a year) that most of the Black players that I talked with had some kind of loan of some sort. We never asked the white players because we knew that most of their parents had the means to fill any financial shortages left by their scholarship packages.

My first package, as a freshman in 1991, looked something like this in the award letter that I received:

Eckerd College Basketball Grant & Other Grants
Florida Tuition Voucher & assistance grants: $13,400
College Loans: $ 3000
Total: $16,400

The total cost of that 1991-92 school year was about $16,100 ($300 was mine to keep through the work study program). Nearly four years later, my package was about $15,000 strong in different grants and my loan amount was around $5,000 strong. The cost for the 1994-95 school year was somewhere in that $20,000 area. I knew that even as an out-of-state resident that I could have gotten an affordable package at Huntsville because it was so much less expensive than Eckerd. There was no way that I would have had to take out a loan for $5,000 at Huntsville, but that was all secondary.

The issue was all about basketball for me. I would have been right back in the same situation that I was in at Eckerd. I would have been fighting for some marginal existence and participation in the basketball world. If the Huntsville coach would have said those words to me after my freshman or sophomore year at Eckerd, I would have grabbed them with both hands and held onto them like a prized possession because I would have had a little bit of time on my side. But I wasn't a freshman or sophomore any more.

Academically, I had completed my junior year and was a rising senior. Athletically, I still had two more years of eligibility. In either case academically or athletically, it wasn't a lot of time to enter into a situation where I had to fight for marginal existence and participation. It was a situation where I had some hope, but the odds were against me. I was looking for some dead even odds or better. A situation that said I had the chance to be a starting point guard right off the bat.

Floyd and I talked about the words that the coach spoke to me as we gathered up our stuff from the dorm room. We analyzed the situation inside and out. Finally, we both agreed that I was in a better position than if I had never made the trip. At least now, I had another option. However, it wasn't an option that I could really get that excited about, the only time that it made me feel good was when I really thought about how much I didn't want to go back to Eckerd in the fall. It was nice to know that I didn't have to go back.

My excitement was quelled even more when we drove to get something to eat before we left town and I saw a sign for Pulaski, Tennessee. I really didn't realize how close to the Tennessee border we were until I saw that sign. I remembered reading somewhere that Pulaski was the town where the Klu Klux Klan got their start shortly after the issuance of the Emancipation Proclamation. I just looked out over the beautiful landscape with its scenic hills and imagined the terror that must have been experienced by my people back in the day in the area that I was now driving in near Pulaski, Tennessee.

I looked at the trees and wondered to myself if any brothers or sisters had ever swung from the trees that were around me. I meant "swung" in the sense of the words sang by the incomparable, Ms. Billie Holiday, in her 1939 classic "Strange Fruit":

Southern trees bear strange fruit,

Blood on the leaves and blood at the root,

Black bodies swinging in the southern breeze,

Strange fruit hanging from the poplar trees.

I wondered if the trees that I saw had produced any strange fruit. I thought to myself … *if only trees could talk.* Of course they didn't talk, but if they could? Would they have testified, in 1994, to the words that Ida B. Wells-Barnett wrote in 1892? She wrote the following words in a pamphlet called *Southern Horrors: Lynch Law in All Its Phases.*

> … the dark and bloody record of the South shows 728 Afro-Americans lynched during the past 8 years. Not 50 of these were for political causes; the rest were for all manner of accusations from that of rape of white woman, to the case of the boy Will Lewis who was hanged at Tullahoma, Tenn., last year for being drunk and 'sassy' to white folks. These statistics compiled by the Chicago 'Tribune' were given the first of this year (1892). Since then, not less than one hundred and fifty have been known to have met violent death at the hands of cruel bloodthirsty mobs during the past nine months.

Before heading home, Floyd and I ate at a restaurant called *Quincy's*. For me, that was ironic. I hadn't run across my name very much in my life, not outside of the Quincy Jones scenario. I had been called Quincy Jones so many times that I could have easily changed my name to Quincy Jones without the majority of the people that I knew ever noticing. The famous African-American arranger, producer, composer, entertainment industry executive, etc. definitely had a lock on the name Quincy. It seemed that the Lord said in a statement—after Jones was born—that all people named "Quincy" from that point forward would be Black males and measured against Quincy Delight Jones Jr.

I didn't really mind my last name always being mistaken for Jones. I was happy that my mother gave me the first name of the man they called "The Dude". I was also glad that I never had any real attachment to my last name the way that many of the kids that I grew up around did. Those kids—a lot of grown-ups too—always tried to assert some strength or some other noble characteristic from being a Williams, a Johnson, a Smith, a Jones, a Jackson, a Washington, or some other last name that was common among Black people. I guess their logic was that the more Black people who had their last name the better.

I had a common last name, but I never tried to jump bad because of it. Maybe that was because I didn't really have a sense of family associated with my last name; there were only a few people in my immediate family who had the same last name as I did. Whatever the reason, once I heard Malcolm X's scathing indictment that began with the question of: "Who are you?"; I was forever grateful that I had never rejoiced in the fact of bearing the slaveholder's name of Smith—a name that Malcolm mentioned specifically. He asked:

> Who are you? You don't know. Don't tell me Negro, that's nothing!
>
> What were you before the white man named you a Negro? And where were you? And what did you have?
>
> What was yours? What language did you speak then? What was your name?
>
> It couldn't have been Smith, or Jones, or Bunche, or Powell; that wasn't your name! They don't have those

kinds of names where you and I came from!

No, what was your name! And why don't you now know what your name was then?

Where did it go? Where did you lose it? Who took it? And how did he take it? What tongue did you speak? How did the man take your tongue?

Where is your history? How did the man wipe out your history?

Those are some questions that we rarely deal with these days, but they are just as relevant today as they were when Malcolm asked them. Until our children learn the answers to those questions before they learn that George Washington chopped down a cherry tree, we will always find a reason to be happy about being a Williams, a Smith, a Jones, or some other slaveholder's name.

Floyd and I talked some more about my options and the pros and cons of the whole matter while we ate as much as we could from *Quincy's* buffet bar, then we got in the car in headed home. As we got farther and farther away from Huntsville and closer and closer to Florida, I felt better and better about the trip.

I didn't feel better because I wanted to go fight for some marginal participation in the basketball program at the University of Alabama at Huntsville, but more so because I had fought for some control over my life. Through hard work and effort I had created a choice that had not been there before my trip. I wasn't letting other people dictate to me what my life would be and not be—at least not without a fight. I knew that I had a fighting spirit that was not easily conquered. And that felt good.

When I got back to Florida, I felt good enough to turn up the heat in my search for even more options. Earlier in the year, I had called my old AAU coach from high school. He was the coach that had chosen to start me on his team ahead of much better known names prior to my senior year at Southeast. He was also the one that had dropped a bug in my ear about the Huntsville opportunity. He was an assistant coach at a community college and I asked him to keep his ears open about any possibilities that I might be able to take advantage of during the summer.

My former AAU coach was a cool white man as far as I could tell, but I never made any more one hundred percent firm opinions about white men after my high school coach tipped his hand when it came to my white girlfriend. After my incident with him, I realized that it was a very strong possibility that a lot of white men in America would reveal their true prejudices about Black men if you dated their daughter. I imagine that a white man that will sincerely accept you dating his daughter will sincerely accept you as a human being.

In any event, when I got back from Huntsville, I called my old AAU coach and gave him some feedback on how I thought things went in Huntsville. I asked him if he had heard of any more potential opportunities. I was interested in basketball, not his daughter.

To my surprise, he told me that he had an old friend who was recently hired on as the coach of a small NAIA school in Tennessee called Tennessee Wesleyan. I told him that I had never heard of it, but that I was interested. I asked him if he would call his old friend, put in a few good words about me. He said that he would and that he would have the coach to give me a call.

In the next couple of days, I got a telephone call from the coach from Tennessee Wesleyan. He said that based on what he heard about my basketball skills and classroom performance that he would be able to award me a scholarship package that was half-athletic and half-academic if my grades were up to par. I thought to myself ... *this is too good to be true already, but let me hit him with my prospects of being a starter.* In the most serious voice I could speak, I asked him what chance I had of being a starter. I knew that it was a bold question considering my circumstances, but I had to know.

He came up with the perfect answer, when he said that my chance was just as good as anybody else's because he was brand new and none of the returning guys were his guys. That's all I needed to hear, I knew that I would be heading for Tennessee for the fall semester of 1994 with an opportunity to become the starting point guard for an all-expense paid school year with no loans. All of sudden life seemed very good to me. However, there was one exception ... my girlfriend.

She knew that I wanted to transfer in order to play basketball. She realized all along that I might actually end up succeeding in my endeavor. But now that the reality was right there in our faces, she was sad and sullen. Decisions had to be made.

She had graduated from Eckerd during the spring of 1994 and had not decided if she would stay in St. Pete for a little while or go back to her home state of Connecticut. Naturally, her decision was impacted by my situation. Was I going to be in St. Pete or was I going to be somewhere else? That had been the question throughout the whole summer. Now that my situation was settled, she had all the pieces of the puzzle in place to make her decision. We didn't talk about it for a few days, and then she decided that she would go back home to Connecticut and drop me off in Tennessee on the way. Over the next month or so, she asked few questions and I gave even fewer answers.

The summer was coming to a close and my internship at the newspaper was winding down. I had learned so much in such a short period of time. I was truly thankful for the experience. I was pleasantly surprised when they asked me if I would like to continue to work for the newspaper through what they thought would be my senior year at Eckerd.

I hadn't really thought about informing my direct supervisors or the Intern Coordinator of my plans to attend school in Tennessee for the 1994-1995 school year. I didn't see the importance of it one way or the other if my internship was over at the end of the summer. But now all that had changed, I was compelled to give them the reason why I would have to turn down their gracious offer to continue working at their company.

I was glad that I did because honesty really paid in that situation. They wished me the best and offered me a scholarship for $2,500 for my upcoming school year at Tennessee Wesleyan. Of course it was contingent upon my GPA remaining above a certain level. I was speechless, but the big grin on my face took the place of my voice in conveying my acceptance.

A few days later, I tried to explain to those wonderful people that my expenses were already paid up for the 1994-1995 school year, but they would hear none of it and said that I would simply have to find a way to use the money toward my education. They said that I should spend it on books and the like. My voice was able to say thank-you that time around, but once again the big grin that broke out on my face played a major role in conveying my gratitude. I was going to school, I was going to have an opportunity to be a starting point guard, and I was going to be receiving two $1,250 checks over the course of the two semesters to top it all off.

I was on cloud 8. I would have been on cloud 9, but I did feel a little sad about having to separate from my girlfriend. We agreed that we would just take things as they came ... whatever that meant. We were going to face the new uncertainty surrounding our relationship with no promises made, so none could be broken ... just one day at time. All that kind of talk made me somewhat sad, but the sheer exhilaration of being on the brink of an opportunity that I had worked so hard towards and prayed so hard for was too much to be contained and my spirit felt happy and triumphant.

I felt like Rocky drinking eggs, catching that chicken, and running up those steps. I felt that way, even as my girlfriend and I kissed each other and said goodbye. I felt like the new phoenix rising from the ashes of the old!

TENNESSEE

Upon arrival, my mind was like a tabula rasa. I had no real expectations of the state of Tennessee, of Tennessee Wesleyan College (TWC), or the basketball program. In looking back, I would surely have to write that that was probably a good thing. I am sure that if I had had any expectations I would have been somewhat disappointed.

The town of Athens was a small town sort of in between Chattanooga and Knoxville. I could tell immediately that it was a much different kind of place than I had ever known in Florida. It was a small place where small things were still the big news of the day. The campus was small and badly in need of renovations. It caused me to immediately upgrade my opinion of the facilities at Eckerd. The basketball gym looked more like a high school gym than a college gymnasium.

Although my first impression was less than stellar, I didn't let it have an impact on me. The town's size and the school's facilities were inconsequential to me; I was not concerned with anything other than achieving the goals that I had set out to achieve when I left Florida.

Academically, I opted to pursue a course of study completely unrelated to my business major at Eckerd. I decided to take psychology courses and courses that would help me toward my international business degree when I went back to Eckerd. I had made up my mind that I would go back to Eckerd, but I hadn't decided if it would be after one year at TWC or two years at TWC. If things were really good—I mean really good— I would stay two years; but if things were just all right, I would leave after one year.

If I chose to stay two years, then I would graduate from TWC with a psychology degree with one year to pick up a double major in management and international business at Eckerd. If I chose to stay one year, then I would leave TWC with a minor in psychology and return to Eckerd the following year to double major in management and international business. Regardless of the amount of years I chose to attend TWC, I was completely set on making straight A's every semester that I was enrolled at their college.

Athletically, my first and foremost goal was to become the team's starting point guard. I wanted to play a lot of minutes and the best way that I could ensure that I had an opportunity to play was to be out there on the court during the opening tip and earn major minutes. I figured that if I was on the court, then the rest would take care of itself. I wanted to prove to myself that I could get the job done on a collegiate level as a starting point guard. If I happened to prove others wrong in the process, then so be it.

Two interesting things happened in my first week of school that I hadn't really thought about. The first one was the fact that I ran into a cat from Bradenton. I knew him pretty well, but we never hung out or anything like that. He was just a dude that I knew growing up in Bradenton, but I was glad he was there. I had never even considered seeing anybody that I knew in the Volunteer State. Nonetheless, when I saw him I thought to myself boy you look like a home-cooked meal that included some of my grandma's collard greens … that was always a good thing.

The second thing that happened was like a wake-up call that said *boy you here to play basketball, but this is still Tennessee*. It happened when a few of the handful of the Black students attending TWC were walking to the cafeteria for dinner. A truck rolled by on the street that we were about to cross when a man yelled out for us niggers to go home, while spitting out of his window. Thankfully, the wind blew the spit away from our group. Perhaps God decided that "us niggers" had been spit on enough that day in Tennessee.

I just watched the truck roll away and thought to myself—*oh boy here we go with this garbage already*. The three second interchange served to solidify many of the stereotypes about Tennessee that had made the trip with me from Florida … I didn't pack them in any suitcases, but they were packed away in the back of my mind.

Although I didn't like the racial slur, I didn't let it bother me too much because I had goals to achieve. Everything outside of those goals took a back seat ... including being called a nigger in Tennessee. Besides, it didn't feel too much different than being called a nigger in Florida. I was kind of glad that it had happened so quickly, just so the first time would hurry up and be over and done. It was going to take more than the word nigger and some spit to knock me off task. I was completely focused on what I wanted to accomplish and nothing could distract me.

The fruits of my focus began to show up immediately when we played informal pick-up games. I quickly set myself apart from the other two point guards that were competing for the same starting job that I was determined to call my own. First, I saw the respect in their eyes, when they faced up to me in a defensive position realizing that I was a lot better than they had originally thought. Next, I saw it in the coach's eyes when he started to give me the look that coaches give to their preferred players.

Yessir! I yelled inside my heart, I was making my mark early and staking my claim quickly just like I knew that I had to with the time frame that I was up against. I had a lot that I wanted to accomplish and I knew how much time I had to get it done. I had to make up for the time that I had lost on the court at Eckerd.

I was the frontrunner for the starting job when we headed into our conditioning program, but it was still far from a done deal. I just took it all in stride and did my best to meet the challenge.

The conditioning program was a lot easier for me because it wasn't all that much more difficult than what I had put myself through in preparing for my opportunity. I had once heard or read somewhere that luck was where preparation met opportunity. My summer workouts were my preparation toward making myself lucky when I finally did get my opportunity. I had it all planned out. Nobody could accuse me of the adage that said failing to plan was planning to fail.

The coach was trying to add his inspirational spin on what we were doing by making us do the conditioning program of the Utah Jazz and passing out a folder that had a copy of their workout routines inside. The outside of the folder had a message written on it. The message was more inspiring to me than the fact that we were doing the same conditioning program of the Jazz. I had been a Laker fan since the first time I saw Magic throw a no-look pass to a streaking teammate for a dunk.

Nevertheless, the fact that it wasn't the conditioning program of the Lakers wasn't the problem; the problem was the coach running the conditioning program. I was surprised that he didn't have the conditioning program of a drill sergeant. He was constantly yelling every five seconds. I couldn't figure out why you would yell so much during a conditioning program. Was he conditioning us to play basketball or was he conditioning us to be yelled at? In any event, I preferred the message on the front of the folder instead of the yelling. I don't know who wrote the message, but I do remember it read something like this:

> Every morning in Africa the fastest lion wakes up realizing that if he wants to eat that day that he will have to run faster than the slowest gazelle. That same morning in Africa the slowest gazelle wakes up realizing that if he wants to live another day that he will have to run faster than the fastest lion. Either way, whether you are the lion or the gazelle ... in the mornings in Africa, you wake up running.

After the conditioning programs, the real on-court battles began for who would be a part of the starting five that would line up for the opening tip of the opening game. I approached every minute of practice like it was going to be that minute that would determine if I got the nod for the starting point guard position. I was intense and motivated. The coach scheduled two scrimmage games against two different teams right before the start of the season that seemed to carry more weight than everything else that we had done up until that point. The scrimmages were sort of like a final test that was designed to separate the fake from the real before the real games.

I didn't worry about it too much, because I felt that I could play with whoever was on the court. I know that may sound brash, but it wasn't. It was necessary. That's the kind of confidence and belief in yourself that you need to succeed in athletics. Your level of success is oftentimes—not all of the time—directly proportional with your belief in yourself. Muhammad Ali said it well in a speech given at Dacca, Bangladesh on February 19, 1978 when he said: "To be a great champion you must believe you are the best. If you're not pretend you are."

In my mind, I didn't have to pretend, because I believed that I was the best point guard in the gym at both of the scrimmages as soon as I stepped into each building. Notice that I said in my mind, I didn't say it with my mouth. I am glad that I didn't say it with my mouth. I'm glad because since that time, I've read the wisdom from the book of Proverbs that the Lord gave to Solomon. In Proverbs chapter 27 verse 2 it was written: "Let another man praise thee, and not thine own mouth; a stranger, and not thine own lips." I was lucky in that instance because my behavior exceeded my knowledge. I held my own tongue like I should have, but it wasn't because I knew the verse from Proverbs like I do now.

I wish that my whole life had been a situation where I was lucky enough to have had my behavior exceed my knowledge. If I only knew then, what I know now ... I could have been a contender.

Lucky for me, my adherence to the wise words of Solomon during the preseason not only kept me in contention for the starting point guard position, but it helped me to become the starting point guard for Tennessee Wesleyan at the beginning of the season. It was all just like I had planned. It was a very joyous achievement for me.

I had fought so hard and what seemed to be so long for an opportunity to be a starting point guard on a college team. I had fought a good fight and won. I didn't care if it was a small NAIA school; I didn't care about anything. I was proud of myself, and that was a great feeling. I felt like I was the kind of person who wouldn't let the world decide my fate. My internal locus of control was strong. I felt like I was the person in charge of my life. I felt that my individual destiny was more in my own hands than someone else's hands.

I didn't feel like a person was asking too much by requesting to control how he or she spent his or her days. At that time in my life, I wanted to spend my days being on a college basketball team. At Eckerd, I allowed another man to take my control away from me. At TWC, I had taken that control back.

Still, I knew that if I wanted to keep that control that I would have to keep fighting for it every day of my life. In a very real sense, the fact that I was now a starting point guard represented a victory for me on a much bigger scale than just the basketball court. I learned that if someone took something from me that I could take it back. I learned that the spirit that was within me would not allow me to do anything less.

I am glad that I got such a big sense of fulfillment from earning the starting job, because the feeling would not last for very long. As an individual, everything was going fine for me during the first two games of the season. I know for sure that we lost the first game, but I'm not sure if we won or lost the second game. I played well in both games and everything was going according to plan on the basketball court. After that my memories of the actual games and specifics about those games fails me, and I don't think that is because I have a bad memory. As the season began to wear on, I began to block it all out. We weren't too far along in the season when I discovered that I had a real strong personality conflict with the coach.

The conflict had emerged during conditioning and before the season started, but I was too focused on becoming the starting point guard to let it bother me. Now that I was the starting point guard, the personality conflict that we had was front and center. The coach liked to yell and lead by intimidation. The problem with that was that I did not particularly liked to be yelled at every minute of a game or practice and I wasn't easily intimidated. It wasn't in my personality to hide my feelings about the issue.

I never verbally disrespected his authority or did anything counter to his basketball wishes. I didn't attempt to retaliate against him because he gave me an opportunity that no one else would give, but I never responded to his style the way that I think that he wanted me to respond. My behavior was cool, but my spirit was defiant. It wasn't basketball related as far as I was concerned; I didn't like the way that he treated me as human being. I thought that the way that he treated our entire team was very dehumanizing.

He used profanity to get every point across, he yelled more than he talked, and he physically threatened some of the guys on the team. There was an actual incident where he struck a player. Now it all came out in the wash like it was an accident, but it sure didn't look like an accident.

Maybe it was a legitimate accident, but when a person had a temper like our coach had it was very hard for me to give him the benefit of the doubt in that type of accident. Once he kicked the entire ball rack over in the middle of practice as he began to tell one of the players how bad of a player he was. It wasn't me that he was talking about, but I felt just like he was talking to me. He would rant and rave and scream and shout the whole practice about this or that and take all the joy that I had ever experienced playing basketball away. Under his leadership, I literally began to not like playing basketball.

Sometimes his antagonizing would start before practice even began. One of the things that I missed when I didn't play at Eckerd was the stretch circle that we sat in before practice began. T.W.C had the same type of stretch circle and I really enjoyed being able to sit in that circle. I never really stretched, but the circle provided another opportunity to interact with different people on the team in a way that gave you a sense of being a part of a team. In the circle, we were just twelve guys bonded together by the game and the desire to win. That was unless Sgt. Yell-a-lot was around.

Coach usually picked on somebody in the circle about something. I guess he thought it was funny to everybody else that he wasn't picking on at the time. I think some people laughed because they were afraid not to laugh. I don't know what his reasons were for doing that to people.

Despite running all the way there, I was usually about five or ten minutes late to practice because I had a French class that ended exactly at the time practice started. Well, I guess one particular day, either he must have been more bothered than usual about my tardiness or he just didn't have anybody else to pick on at the time; so he started with me about my French class. He said: "Maybe we can't win any games because my starting point guard is too busy learning French to get to practice on time."

He was on one of his priority tangents about how we would probably be winning more games if some of the team members had their priorities in order. He used my coming late to practice twice a week as an example of a misplaced priority. Usually I just let him rant and rave, but this time he made the conversation interactive by telling me to say something in French, which I did. It wasn't much, but it was more than he could say so he backed off that road. He then asked me why I was taking the class if I wasn't going to France. I know he wasn't prepared for my answer.

I told him that I had an interest in international business and that I had heard that some of the countries in Africa spoke French. I added on that I might be interested in going to Africa one day and speaking a little French might help. It seemed to me that he hated the fact that I could answer all of his questions in an intelligent way because it limited his ability to ridicule me. I was talking about things that made being five minutes late to practice seem small—especially since I never missed anything in that five minutes. The more that he seemed to hate my answers the more my defiant spirit dared him to ask me another question. He couldn't stand it, and I loved every minute of it. Nobody laughed with him that day.

That day was a victory for the troops and for me, because his intimidation had not prevailed. I had won our little battle, but I knew that he would ultimately win the war between me and him because it was his team and he had the power. Power is a hard thing to beat with anything other than its own reflection. Power must be matched by power. You have to put a mirror to its face and give it something to look at that looks just like it does. Power only respects power; nothing else.

There was no way that I was in a position to match his power. The fact that he had the power over that team forced me to undergo a very difficult process. Somewhere around the eighth game of the season, which is about a third of a college season, I was pulled from the starting line-up. I didn't really mind that much because I knew that it was coming when I realized that I would never be able to perform up to my maximum ability under his coaching style. His style brought out too many negative feelings in me to allow my body to do what it had always done. My mind/body connection was completely severed. His personality was so strong that it completely overshadowed the game.

The game wasn't natural to me anymore; he had spoiled it for me when he took away the joy that I got from playing and competing. It was very much like working in a job where the boss was always yelling and threatening you all of the time. His tactics didn't break me down; they just made me not want to play for him anymore. I held out strong and made up for my loss on the court by sticking to my game plan in the classroom.

I stayed cool, calm, and collected; but I would be telling you a bold face lie if I said that the things that were happening on the basketball court didn't hurt me when I laid my head down on my pillow at night.

On a lot of those nights, I talked to my girlfriend on long distance telephone calls. I never thought that I would feel the need to hear her voice as I did. We had left each other with no promises, so that none would be broken; but the way that I felt during those conversations, I wished that I would have promised her my undying love forever because I missed her that much. I guess I had depended on her much more than I ever knew. I think the time that she was away from me was the first time that I really realized how much I loved her. So I did what I should have done in the beginning, I asked her to come and be by my side in Tennessee for the last semester. I poured my love all over her on the phone and through letters until love lifted her on its back and brought her to me.

We got an apartment off campus that we could afford through her working and my refund money that I received from my leftover scholarship money. I was attending school on three scholarships (basketball, academic, and the scholarship from the newspaper), so it was almost like I got a paycheck for going to school. Before she came I thought that us being back together was going to be making the best out of a bad situation for me, but it really didn't turn out that way. It just turned out to be very hard. We had nothing left to give to each other at the end of the day. We were both too busy.

She really hated Tennessee; it just wasn't the place for her. And then once she started to work and take a couple of classes at a local community college, we never had anytime for each other. I was always practicing or traveling with the team, doing schoolwork, or performing work-study at the library. Our relationship contained none of the stuff that we exchanged over the phone or that we wrote in letters. It just contained a lot of hard cold life that demanded a lot of our time if we wanted to accomplish our goals.

I could have chosen not to do work-study at the library, but it helped a little with the bills and I knew that it would give me some more money in my pocket when we went back to Florida. By that time, I had made up my mind that I would not be returning to TWC.

I definitely need the extra money to take back to Florida, but little did I know that working in the library would give me so much more than a few extra dollars to take back to Florida. I discovered a book in that library that helped my spirit to rebound from my basketball problems and my life problems.

When I found the book, I was dealing with much more than basketball and life in Tennessee with my girlfriend. My past was also running up behind me in the form of a card that I received from my mom. It was from a correctional facility. My mom was incarcerated ... again.

The letter didn't really crush me; over the years, I had developed coping strategies that prevented me from being too deeply hurt by the issues going on in my mom's life. Still, it didn't make things any easier. I don't no if any child wants to see or think about his or her mom being in jail.

The jailhouse letter made me realize that I loved my mom. After all that had happened between us ... and after all that had not happened between us, I still loved my mom. It hurt me to know that she was locked behind a set of bars like a caged animal. I knew that she hadn't changed much since I was a kid. She was a kid when she had me, she behaved like a kid when I was growing up, and she hadn't changed much since that time. Now that I was an adult, she was in her third childhood.

Prior to the letter, I hadn't really thought about my mom much since I'd been in Tennessee. I didn't think about her that much for prolonged period of times because thoughts of her brought on too much emotion. Thoughts of her always made me sad and mad. The stress of just trying to live my own life was all that I could handle at times; I just couldn't bear the additional load that her life problems would have placed on my shoulders.

KNOWLEDGE OF SELF

onsidering all that was not right in my life, my soul really needed to find the book that I found working in Tennessee Wesleyan's library. The book was called *My Soul Looks Back, 'Less I Forget.* It was a collection of quotations by people of color edited by an educator from Detroit named Dorothy Winbush Riley. She had the same first name as Grandma Dot; and like Grandma Dot, she changed my life. Ms. Riley's book would turn out to be the second most important book in my life to date; it was second only to the Holy Bible.

The overwhelming majority of the quotations used in this book came from her book. It's a beautiful book to introduce anyone to the wonderful history that we, the children of the African Diaspora, have behind us. The words of wisdom from the past that can be found within its pages can be used to inspire an even more wonderful future. That's not only true for the children of the African Diaspora, but for the entire world. For me personally, it allows me to heed the ancient words of Ptah Hotep:

> Follow in the footsteps of your ancestors for the mind is trained in knowledge. Behold, their words endure in books. Open and read them and follow their wise council. (Ptah Hotep, c. 2340 B.C.)

I found *My Soul Looks Back 'Less We Forget* quite by accident. I was re-stacking books on the bookshelf, a task that I loathed performing. It seemed like such a never-ending task, a task that one could never say he or she was finished performing. It made me feel like Sisyphus.

The day that I found the book, I was placing reference material back on the reference shelf when my eyes caught the title out of the corner of my eye. I pulled it off the shelf and looked in the table of contents to find that the information was organized by many different topics.

Over the course of pursuing my business major at Eckerd, I developed a self schema that made me gravitate toward business whenever there was a choice involved; so I opened the book up to the business section. The first quote that I read was by Pearl Cleage. At the time, I didn't know who Pearl Cleage was, but her words hit me deep in my soul.

> I've watched the talented ones who were supposed to change the world make a lifetime commitment to business as usual for the price of a Rolex watch and a new BMW. (Pearl Cleage, "Introduction", *Catalyst*, Summer 1988)

Her quote hit me deep in my soul for a few different reasons. One reason was that I was at a point in my college career where I really believed that I was going to make money after I graduated and a BMW was one of the first things that I wanted to buy.

The second reason was that I had fought against the world for a long time when it came to race, and I was tired. I would be lying to you if I said that I never looked for a way out of the mental prison created by racism. There were many times when I thought that it would simply be much easier to go with the flow and collect material possessions than it would be to subject myself to the daily torture of trying to be a conscious and sincere Black male trying to make a difference.

The third reason was that I had always had an insatiable appetite when it came to Black information every since I watched *Roots* and discovered some of my mom's literature as a small child. The white or mainstream world didn't seem to have that kind of information and the Black world that I was exposed to didn't show me where I could find that kind of information. So for me, finding the book was like walking along a lonely road, tripping over a missing piece of my soul, and hitting my head on the tree of knowledge. It was a great fall.

I read over the book and saw quotations from many people that I had never heard of before. I remember running into a few quotes from Kwame Nkrumah and thinking: *who is this guy and why have I never heard of him*? I looked him up and found out that he was a former Prime Minister of the country of Ghana on the continent of Africa. As a matter of fact, I learned that Nkrumah was the first Prime Minister and President of independent Ghana between 1957 and 1966. The book led me on several other voyages in search of more knowledge. I realized that although I was a Dean's List student with nearly four years of college under my belt that I wasn't really that educated at all.

My formal education had left out essential and relevant information that I should have been exposed to a long time ago. I believe that my revelation of my educational predicament was the exact reason that Malcolm said what he said in a January 18, 1965 interview for *Young Socialist*. El Hajj Malik El-Shabazz (Malcolm's name adopted from Sunni Islam) said:

> Just because you have colleges and universities doesn't mean that you have education. The colleges and universities in the American educational system are skillfully used to mis-educate.

So there I stood, so-called educated, but in truth I was ignorant. I was a young Black male who knew so little about the Black people that came before me. As I turned through the pages, I saw names that I had never even heard of or saw before opening that book. The names were underneath quotes that I had never heard before opening that book.

In the moments that I stood there looking over the words of my elders and ancestors, I did what Dr. Maya Angelou had written in her 1969 autobiography, *I Know Why the Caged Bird Sings*. "I had gone from being ignorant of being ignorant to being aware of being aware." Before finding *My Soul Looks Back 'Less We Forget*, I was ignorant of my ignorance and unaware of my unawareness—a state of being that leaves you at the mercy of anyone that has the desire to exploit or take advantage of you.

I believe that if I could have checked that book out of the library that night I would have read it into the early morning. But that didn't happen because it was a reference book and it wasn't available to be checked out. I had to read it whenever I had time on my work-study shift at the library. That was the only time that my busy schedule allowed me to go to library.

The librarians who gave me my assignments believed in an honest day's work for an honest day's pay, so I only had time to read whenever I could find a break here or there. Nonetheless, I knew exactly where to turn to when an outside project was being discussed by some of the Black students on campus.

A few of the students wanted to do something for Black History month. I knew where to turn because the book allowed me to celebrate Black History month much more than just during the month of February. I celebrated it during every break on each shift that I worked in the library.

Tennessee Wesleyan College only had a handful of African-American students, and although the percentage of African-American students attending T.W.C was probably directly proportional with the percentage of African-American students attending Eckerd College; the actual number of African-Americans at T.W.C. was much fewer because T.W.C was smaller than Eckerd. There were no more than fourteen or fifteen Black students attending T.W.C during that spring semester of 1995, and six of those students were a part of the Men's Basketball program.

It seemed to me that all but a couple of the Black students were members of a student club called the AASU (African-American Student Union). I think the club was bigger when the school had a football team, but that was two or three years before I got there. By the time that I arrived, the club had dwindled to a modest twelve or thirteen with no official leadership. It seemed much more like a group of people who rallied around one another for friendship and support more than a group bound by an agenda.

I believe that our small presence on the campus was the main reason that many of the members of the AASU wanted so badly to do something for Black History month. They seemed to be searching for a way to say we are here too, and we have not come empty-handed; we have brought some gifts to share as well. In that sense, it seemed to be a microcosm of what Dr. Du Bois wrote about in *The Souls of Black Folk* in 1903, when he wrote:

> ... [I]n order that some day on American soil two world-races may give each to each those characteristics both so sadly lack. We the darker ones come even now not

altogether empty-handed: there are to-day no truer
exponents of the pure human spirit of the Declaration of
Independence than the American Negroes; there is no
true American music but the wild sweet melodies of the
Negro slave; the American fairy tales and folk-lore are
Indian and African; and, all in all, we black men seem
the sole oasis of simple faith and reverence in a dusty
desert of dollars and smartness.

I am not sure where the whole idea of the AASU doing something
for Black History month first came from or if I was even present when
it was first brought up, but I do know that it wasn't my idea. I had not
even thought about such a thing. I heard about it when someone told
me that AASU was going to have a meeting to discuss whether or not
we were going to do something or not. That was the first and only
time that I ever remember hearing about a meeting in connection
with AASU during my tenure at T.W.C. Prior to that, we all just met
informally in the SAC (student activity center) to talk and socialize.

I went to the meeting with mixed feelings. I was excited and
hesitant at the same time. I was excited because I had hung around
with that group of students throughout the year, but never with
such a clear and expressed singular purpose of promoting something Black. I was nervous and hesitant because I didn't really want
to be a part of something that wasn't organized.

The first order of business in the informal setting was to discuss
whether all the members in attendance (12 students) were interested
in doing something. Everybody agreed and my excitement got the
better of my hesitancy. The next thing was to see who could do what
and determine what type of program we should produce.

We knew that even in such a small group that we had various
talents in our midst. We had natural born singers, comedians, and
thespians in our group of twelve. That mix was supported by a couple of people who were good at organizing and following through.
We decided that we would produce a convocation that was depen-
dent upon those talents for its entertainment portion, while providing a strong message from a convocation speaker. The only question
that remained was who would be the convocation speaker. To my
surprise some of the folks in the group thought that I was the man
best suited to do that part of the program.

I was surprised because in my mind I had not really demonstrated
to them a real aptitude for public speaking. Although I felt comfort-

able in my ability to speak to people, I didn't feel that the short period of time that I had known them was sufficient for them to feel comfortable enough with me to be the convocation speaker. Besides, during the short period of time that we had known each other, I had not exactly emerged as the least controversial brother on campus.

I had had a few discussions with some of the guys who wanted to ask me some questions about why I was in such a serious relationship with a white girl. After those conversations, I knew that some of them didn't necessarily agree with some of my points of view on the whole interracial dating thing. I knew that a couple of the female students wanted to ask me about it too, but they never did. To them, I was a good brother gone bad; I was an ice cream cone that slipped out of your hand and landed in a pile of dirt.

My controversial image wasn't just limited to interracial dating; I always seemed to be at odds in my opinions with somebody about something. However, in the midst of me always being at odds with different people, there was one incident that stuck out in my mind on why they might have chosen to honor the ability that God gave me to speak by asking me to put together and deliver a message.

Over the Christmas/New Year holidays our coach had made it a really restrictive situation as too how much time anybody would have to leave for the holidays because of the games that we still had to play. Because of his decision to do that, it only made sense for the people who lived reasonably close to try to go home for the holidays.

I didn't even think about trying to go back to Florida. But there was a guy on our team from Chattanooga who decided that he would go home for a couple of days and take along two of our teammates. All three of the guys involved were Black. Our coach had already put out a stern warning that there would be no leniency for anybody who was late to practice as result of not returning to campus on time. He punctuated his zero tolerance holiday policy by adding that he would dismiss any truants from the team.

It was just typical of his style to play the strong disciplinarian, with him there were no gray areas, just hard shades of black and white. Well in any event, the three must have gotten separated in Chattanooga and two of them did not make it back in time because of car trouble. True to his word, coach kicked them off the team. He didn't seem to even give it a second thought. He treated the situation like an overdue electric bill payment that had missed the deadline; he turned off the lights without caring who got left in the dark.

If there was anybody on the team that liked the man before he did that, then they definitely reconsidered after his stern punishment. Considering the fact that everybody has car trouble at some point or another, we couldn't understand why he couldn't make the punishment fit the crime. His defense to that—as if he knew what we were thinking—was, "if one of them could make it back, then the other two should have made it back as well." That was a good point; but it all boiled down to the fact that if they hadn't had the car trouble, then they would have made it back on time. Everybody was upset, but they were all just willing to yield to his power, his authority, and his decision. I couldn't do that, because I knew that larger issues were at stake.

I asked him if I could meet with him privately about the situation and he granted my request. I asked him had he ever considered what role basketball played in the lives of the two young men that he wanted to dismiss. I asked him had he ever considered that basketball might have been the only reason that they had to stay on the straight and narrow of going to school instead of pursuing negative means to negative ends. We talked about those two issues at length, and then he asked me why I wanted to see two guys that played the guard position stay on the team when it would impact my playing time. He was alluding to the fact that with those two guys out of the rotation, that he would have no choice but to play me more minutes. I simply looked him in his eyes, and told him that some things were more important than basketball.

A couple of days later he changed their punishment to running sprints until there legs could no longer carry them. I was proud of coach for doing that, I think he respected me a little for bringing it to him like I did without being afraid to challenge him. It wasn't enough to heal the gap between us, but it helped a little. I even started a few more games after that conversation. But those things were insignificant to me in comparison to how I felt seeing my two brothers back at practice. I felt good that they were doing something that made them happy. I felt good that they were doing something that kept them in the classroom and out of trouble. After that I didn't mind the yelling as much ... I still didn't think it was necessary to the degree and frequency that he did it, but at least I knew that coach was a human being capable of treating others like human beings.

That situation was the only real thing that stuck out in my mind that would have made the Black folks on the campus comfortable with the fact that I was capable of being the convocation speaker. Everybody knew that I spoke with coach, and the two guys were reinstated a couple days later. I guess they figured that whatever I said must have been pretty good to persuade coach to change his mind.

Whatever their reason for choosing me, I told them that I would do the speech. I told them that I would work on my speech in the library while they worked on the entertainment portion in the auditorium. I told them that because I knew exactly where I was going to look for help in coming up with my message. I was going to look through the pages of the book that contained the words and wisdom of my ancestors and elders. I knew what I wanted to say, but I would use their words to help me get my points across.

By the time the night of the convocation came around, everybody had done a wonderful job preparing themselves for their particular roles. The audience was primarily made up of the students, staff, and faculty; but there was also a small contingent of folks who were not affiliated with the college. Folks like my girlfriend. I would almost be so bold as to say that the audience was one hundred percent white, but I believe that the two African-American students who were not in the production were in the audience. In addition to those two, a small number of the international students who attended T.W.C were also present. The audience was a sharp contrast to what we were about to present on the stage.

We opened up the program with a prayer that was followed up by a welcoming of those in attendance in their various languages. Since we knew that there would be some international student in attendance, we didn't want to exclude anybody, so during rehearsals we asked a person from every country represented at T.W.C. how one welcomed a person in their native language. They didn't know that we were going to use it in our opening, but I think they appreciated it when we did.

That's the thing that I love about Black people; despite all of the ways that we have been excluded from the feast of the fattened calf, we still don't leave others out. We, probably more than anybody else, really want this country to live up to its lofty ideals.

Our welcome gave way to a skit that the others had put together to demonstrate the strong faith that had always been an integral part of African-American tradition. The skit did a take off on a small southern Black church. It was complete with a big dose of hallelujahs, amens, and hand clapping; we were definitely sanctified! The church scene concluded with a sinner being called to repentance. The preacher's sermon was so powerful that the child had no choice but to "come on home to Jesus".

The sinner that was called to repentance was a young lady from Nashville who had a blessed voice. She had been trained in the church choir, so when she burst into a powerful rendition of the song "*Amazing Graze*"; she took the crowd on a journey that probably made some non-believers in the audience appreciate God's grace. The girl had pipes like Mahalia!

We kept the singing going by having the rest of the cast members join the young lady from Nashville in a rendition of the song written by James Weldon Johnson and his brother Rosamond Johnson in 1900 called "*Lift Every Voice and Sing*". James Weldon Johnson was a Renaissance man much like Paul Robeson. Johnson was a diplomat, poet, novelist, critic, composer, and the first executive director the NAACP. "*Lift Every Voice and Sing*" is now commonly referred to as the Negro National Anthem. At the time that I found out that we would sing the song, I had never heard it. I had never known that there was such a thing as a Negro National Anthem.

In spite of my ignorance, when I heard the words of the song I knew in an instant why it had been given the distinction of being called as it was. It was a beautiful song, a strong song, and a resilient song. It was a song full of faith and full of hope. It was a song just like the people it was written about.

After the singing, it was time for me to deliver my speech. In writing my speech, I had thought long and hard about what I would say and to whom I would say it. Although I knew that the audience would be made up primarily of white folks, I wanted to compose a speech like I was talking to Black folks. I believed that we spent too much time talking to white folks in an effort to get them to help us solve our problems. I felt that way not because I didn't believe that whites were in a position to help, but more so because I felt that they would never take it as far as it needed to go.

I had felt for a long time that Black folks depending on whites to solve our problems was not only useless, but also somewhat silly. Even if white folks were sincerely willing to help, I seriously doubted that they would ever do enough to really make a difference. Self-reliance was and is the best course of action for an individual or a group that wants to bring forth positive change(s) in their life or social conditions. I felt that Black folks were in the best position to handle problems that impacted Black folks. I did not want to say that we could not or should not develop coalitions with other groups of people; I wanted to advocate a position that said that we should assert ourselves in this society in order to gain what is and what has been ours all along. I believed that if our "unalienable Rights" were ever going to be achieved that they were going to have to be brought to fruition by our own Black hands.

At the same time, I was not trying to hate anybody or inspire hate in others. I did not want to hurt or say bad things about white people. I had grown past that point a long time ago in high school. My motivation was not to hurt anybody else, but more so to help Black folks. I didn't believe that, as a Black male, I had to choose one approach over the other when dealing with race. I didn't believe that I had to hate white people in order to love Black people. With all that said, I did understand the temptation that would make Black people hate white people.

I understood the temptation to hate white folks because of some of the things that we, as Black people, have suffered at their hands throughout history. I understood the temptation to hate white folks because we were still suffering at their hands right up to the hour that I delivered that speech (2/28/1995). I overstood the temptation to hate white folks because we were still suffering at their hands as I typed this sentence (2/27/2001). But now, just like when I delivered that speech, I can understand the so-called hate that hate produced without being overcome by it.

Love has conquered the hate that was within me as a youth. The problem is that I don't know how long the love within me can win out. My faith in God tells me that love has greater endurance than hate, but my knowledge of history tells me that white hatred toward Black folks has enough endurance to make it a challenging race.

Lord knows that my spirit is willing to finish the race strong, but my flesh is weak.

These are the words that I delivered to a predominantly white audience at Tennessee Wesleyan College on February 28, 1995—five years and 364 days before I typed this sentence. As I look back on the words, I believe them now, as I believed them then. My words were:

Tonight I have come to deliver a message to a people.

That message is of self-help, self-empowerment, self-improvement, and self-reliance—which leads to community help, community empowerment, community improvement, and community reliance.

Those people are African-American people. We stand on the broad shoulders of the Colored, Negro, and Black people who came before us in this country.

I would not be making any great social revelations if I were to stand up here and spew out statistics on teen-age pregnancy, homicide, crime, drugs, or poverty in the African-American community. Besides it is not my objective to speculate about the causes of these ills. It is my objective to find a solution to these ills.

The first step in this healing process begins within the individual. You must learn to control what you think of yourself and the world around you.

Now many people will say, oh that's easy. I happen to believe differently.

For over 350 years, African-American people have either been no citizen or a second class citizen in this country. We have been regarded as property. We have been regarded as sub-human. We have been regarded as inferior, incompetent, and incapable. Daily the media bombards you with negative images of African-American people.

After prolonged exposure to these stimuli you can no longer think of yourself as a man or a woman—you become a Black man or a Black woman. Everyday you are reminded, rather subtle or blatant, that you are Black and what that has meant in America. It influences your self-concept and distorts the reality of your potential— your potential to be whatever you want to be.

However, to realize your potential you must take control of what you think of yourself and the world around you. Yes you are discriminated against, but by no means are you inferior, incompetent, or incapable. You are the descendant of a once and still proud people. Engulf this mentality into your self-concept. Thinking you can is the first step to becoming. There is a great quote on this topic. Carter G. Woodson, a famous African-American historian, once said:

When you determine what a man shall think you do not have to concern yourself with what he will do. If you make a man feel that he is inferior, you do not have to compel him to accept inferior status, for he will seek it himself. If you make a man think that he is justly an outcast, you do not have to order him to the back door. He will go without being told; and if there is no back door his very nature will demand one. (*The Mis-education of the Negro*, 1933)

I say it is time to think differently. If there is no front door, then demand one and walk through it with high self-esteem and self-respect.

It's a wonderful feeling to like who you are, but the battle is not over. Now you have to function in the world around you.

In today's world it is becoming extremely difficult to succeed without an education. Malcolm X was much more effective in getting his point across on this issue than myself. In his blunt eloquence, he proclaimed "Without an education you are not going anywhere in this world" (Speech given at Militant Labor Forum, 29 May 1964).

He was and is absolutely right.

However, I do think it is critical that you have the right grasp on the word education. You need an education in order to maintain a comfortable economic status. A college degree makes it easier to get a job that provides for that economic status.

The reason economics plays such an important role is very simple. You need a financial base from which to operate on a day to day and month to month basis. If you have to worry where your next meal is coming from or how you are going to pay your rent next month, then you really don't have time to develop your mind. To avoid this is plenty of reason to seek an education. But it isn't enough to learn from a book and earn money.

There is much more to an education. Once you are educated in the true sense of the word your outlook tends to expand. Kwame Nkrumah, former Prime Minister of Ghana, explains it well. He claims:

Education consists not only in the sum of what a man knows, or the skill to which he can put this to his own advantage. A man's education must also be measured in terms of the soundness of his judgement of people and things, and in his power to understand and appreciate the needs of his fellow man and to be of service to them. The educated man should be so sensitive to the conditions around him that he makes it his chief endeavor to improve those conditions for the good of all. (Speech given at the Institute of African Studies, 25 October 1963)

That's what point I'm trying to reach, and that's what point everybody should be striving to reach.

With this in mind, and considering some of the problems within the African-American community, I would think it would be the "chief endeavor" of at least every African-American person to try to improve those conditions. I'm speaking of drugs, violence, single parenthood, teen pregnancy, materialism, and a general lack of love for one another.

Unfortunately, this is not the case. Don't get me wrong, I'm not saying that there are no African-Americans working in the community to improve these situations. What I am saying is there is not nearly enough. To compound the problem, it is often the best qualified for the task who choose to do nothing.

Everyday there is a mass exodus of African-American potential away from the problems in our communities. They leave—never to return—in search of better housing, safer streets, and better schools for their children. I can't say that there is anything wrong with them leaving in search of these things, but not to return is a crime. It's a crime against humanity and a crime against their own people.

In effect, what it creates is a talent drain. All the people with talents and who have used the system to their advantage are not around. They are not around to show another person how to do the same thing. They are not around to let their success represent that it is possible to avoid pitfalls and excel as a doctor, teacher, or an entrepreneur. This is how a community becomes a ghetto, because you have also taken your checkbook with you. What you have left is a place devoid of productive resources.

Now what have you accomplished with your success? Instead of making it easier for the next person who may come from similar circumstances, you have made it harder by not being there.

I'll tell you who is there in your place. Michael Jordan and the neighborhood drug dealer. We are all aware of the chances of being a professional athlete. On the other hand it is pretty easy to become a drug dealer—who also didn't benefit from your help or example. I also say that it is not to your advantage not to share your success with the people who haven't been as lucky as you. For the reason that Dr. W.E.B. Du Bois knew many years ago. He proclaimed that if you do not lift a people up, then they will pull you down. ("The Talented Tenth", *The Negro Problem*, 1903)

Right now, what I am saying to you is that we have the means to change our situation and like the preacher says at the end of his sermon at the church I attend. I urge you not to let this opportunity pass you by.

He speaks of the opportunity to devote your heart to the Lord, which is the most important thing that a person can do in this world. I speak of the opportunity to help your people. Zora Neal Hurston, the famous African-American writer, knows what I am talking about. She reasons: "When you find a man who has lost his way, you don't make fun of him and scorn him and leave him there. You show him the way. If you don't do that you just prove that you are sort of lost yourself" (*Moses, Man of the Mountain*, 1939).

It is time for every person to find their own way, and then it is their responsibility to help another find their way. In order to be successful in doing this, we must adopt a higher moral code. These days people are always claiming you can have one hundred different rights and wrongs. It's right for you to do that and right for me to do this. It's fine to allow for individual differences, but it has to be a common ground.

We know deep down in ourselves the differences between right and wrong. If we are going to improve as individuals and as a race, then it is time to walk the straight and narrow. It is my goal for my people and for myself to be upright in thought and action. So that no man can find just fault in our character or conduct.

Now I grant you that no man who has walked this earth, except the Lord and Savior Jesus Christ, has achieved this perfection. However, I don't think that it would be too detrimental to uphold Jesus as a personal role model and try to walk in the way of his teachings.

We must let the light that is in all of us shine, and help the light in our brothers and sisters to shine, so that we shine as a people. Not to claim that we are better than another group—it would be very unwise to rise above oppression and then become an oppressor.

We want to shine to light up the world. To be an example that all people can respect and admire. Then we as a people can offer the world the light of hope, love, and respect. So that one day we all might be able to come together at that table Dr. King spoke of in 1967. He said: "One day somebody should remind us that, even though there may be political and ideological differences between us, the Vietnamese are our brothers, the Russians are our brothers, the Chinese are our brothers; and one day we've got to sit down at the table of brotherhood" (Sermon given at Ebenezer Baptist Church, New York City, 4 April 1967).

We concluded our program with the entire cast assembling onstage to receive whatever applause or disdain that the audience had in store for us. Only after hearing the sound of applause did we realize that those in attendance had enjoyed the gifts that we gave.

We gave the gifts that Dr. Du Bois spoke of in his 1903 classic. We offered the audience the gift of our spirit, we gave freely the "wild sweet melodies" of our voices, and we displayed the depths of our "faith and reverence". Perhaps Dr. Du Bois—a Fisk University/ Harvard man himself—would have been proud of the events that took place on the night of February 28, 1995 on the small campus of Tennessee Wesleyan College. I'll never know for sure; but if I had to say one way or another, then I would venture to say that he would have been proud indeed.

We closed the show by letting the audience file out to the no profanity instrumental version of a song from one of my favorite rap groups. The group was Outkast and the song was called "Git Up, Git Out". It was taken from their 1994 debut album, Southern playalisticadillacmuzik. The instrumental version gave us the same catchy beat as the regular version, but it only contained one lyrical refrain that kept pumping a message that we would have wanted Black folks to leave with if they had been in attendance. That lyrical refrain bounced over the laid back beat and delivered the following message to the people who were slowly making their way toward the exit. It said:

You need to git up, git out, and git something.

Don't let the days of your life pass by.

You need to git up, git out, and git something.

Don't spend all your time trying to get high.

You need to git up, git out, and git something.

How will you make it if you never even try?

You need to git up, git out, and git something.

Cause you and I got to do for you and I.

It was a befitting close to a show that was positive and strong from a message standpoint. I can only hope that the audience and the other cast members enjoyed the experience as much as I did. For me it was an epiphany. I felt a deep calmness and sense of purpose standing on that stage as I delivered the words that I spoke that night. I felt that somehow that what I was doing on stage had a lot to do with the reason that God put me on this earth. I didn't really make big deal about it or say very much about it; I just put it away in the back of my mind. I reasoned that if it was something that was a part of my reason for being here that the Lord would lead me—one way or another—to do it. I had to walk by faith, not by sight. I had to trust that if He wanted it to be so it would be so. I had no choice because my human eyes just could not see a clear path that would lead me to doing what I did on stage that night.

In retrospect, I know that I took the right approach concerning the epiphany I experienced. Looking back over the six years or so that has passed since that night, there is no way that I could have known what path my life would travel from then until now. It has been a rocky ride where at times I tried to walk according to the word of God and at other times I have simply followed after the footsteps of the world and my own worldly desires and lusts. But after such an up and down journey; I feel confident in telling you that if the Lord has something for you to do that you will indeed do it. Make no mistake about that. Nothing ever returns to God without performing His will or fulfilling its intended purpose—not even one single drop of rain.

I encourage everybody to try to get closer to God and stay close to the word of God, so you will discover your own unique and individual purpose in this world. I suppose Prince had it right in his November 1988 interview, "Spotlight: Prince—What U See Is What U Get", in *Essence* magazine. He said: "When one finds himself, one finds God. You find God and you find yourself."

You are the only one that can fulfill your unique role and purpose. Dr. Benjamin Mays said it well in an article entitled "I Knew

Carter G. Woodson" that appeared in *Negro History Bulletin*, in March of 1981. Dr. Mays said: "Every man is born into this world to do something unique and something distinctive, and if he or she does not do it, it will never be done." By no means do I claim to be as wise as Dr. Mays was, but I am smart enough to know when to agree with his words.

Undoubtedly, you will encounter trials and tribulations in this world en route to fulfilling your unique purpose. The challenge is not to be moved and to hold fast to your faith. As the world places those obstacles in your path, you need to know that you can overcome those obstacles "because He that is in you is greater than he that is in the world." (I John chapter 4 verse 4)

In the next few days after the show many people came up to me and told me that they really enjoyed what I had to say and the way that I delivered my speech. Besides the message, the thing that people seemed to be the most impressed with was the fact that I did not use any index cards or notes to deliver the speech. I memorized the speech word for word, but it wasn't as much a feat to me as it was for some folks. I had the words of the speech written down and I had read them when I was on stage. The words were not on paper, but they were written down. The words were written on my heart and I read them from my heart. When I was standing there on stage, I simply had to give voice to the turning of the pages of my heart. Any man or woman is capable of turning the pages of their own heart if it is something that's truly important to their soul.

BLACK JIVE

fter the AASU program, the basketball season came to an unceremonious end with me somehow starting a few games here or there at the end of the year. By the time the last buzzer sounded, I wasn't really passionate about basketball. I gave it all I had in practice and in the games, but the love of the game didn't drive me the way that it once had. My basketball soul felt like a lover who discovered some infidelity on the part of their partner. It was hurt.

I still loved basketball, but not like I did. I wasn't sure if I just needed some time or if the damage was irreversible. I realized that I wasn't going to be a professional basketball player. I realized that basketball was a career for only a select few; for everybody else, it was just a game.

The contraction of the place in my heart reserved for basketball was quickly filled by the expansion of the place in my heart reserved for helping my people. The speech and the book that I had used to prepare the speech really rekindled a flame that had flickered in my heart since I was a small child. That flicker was now transformed into a blazing fire that burned out of control both day and night.

I didn't really have anybody to talk to about how I felt. The Black folks that I felt I might be able to talk to about it were not intense enough for me. It seemed that many agreed with me on the problems, but they didn't really believe that there were any solutions. I understood where they were coming from, but I couldn't let it die like that. I couldn't let it die with their, "yeah, but what a nigga 'posed to do?" or "that's how it's always been and that's how it will always be".

I was screaming, if there is no current solution; then let's make one! I had a blazing fire inside of me that couldn't be extinguished by the False Evidence that made it Appear Real that nothing could be done. My mind was always awake with the problems that I saw facing our people and the possible solutions to those problems.

Later in life, I found out that a lot of Black folks were afraid to move beyond problem perception when it came to white folks and racism. They engage in circular thought, which means moving from problem perception in a manner that leads them away from problem solution and back to problem perception. With that pattern of thought, one is always able to see the problem, but can't envision the solution. That's why it seems that positive change has taken us so long to achieve; we spend too much time under the influence of circular thought. Linear thought—which posits a philosophy of moving from problem perception toward problem solution—requires too much courage for many to handle.

Why are some Blacks afraid of linear thought? It requires them to begin with the proper cause of the problems that impact our individual lives and collective communities. That proper cause is the white man and the conditions under which he has forced us to live for four hundred years. The physical effects of slavery faded away much quicker than the devastating mental effects. The evidence of the mental effects have been reborn through each generation ... the damage has been unquantifiable. The manifestations of that damage are ubiquitous.

The bottom line is that some of us are afraid to come out and straight-out cite slavery, white racism, and discrimination as the underlying causes of our problems because we are still afraid of the white man. I am not talking fear as in a snake crossing in front of you; I am talking about a deep psychological fear that has been imbedded in the psyche of the collective Black mind. We have all seen what happened to our leaders who were too bold and truthful in their defiance of the white man. The fearful ones subconsciously or consciously ask themselves: who wants to end up dead like them? Well, I tell you what white man, if you don't set this thing right, there is gonna be a day that a new breed will emerge to provide a different answer to that question. In the Garvey whirlwind, the words of Malcolm X will smite this non-repenting land with an unforgiving hand.

If it costs me my life in the morning I will tell you tonight
that the time has come for the Black man to die fighting.
If he is going to die, die fighting. (Malcolm X, c. 1964)

I didn't have any more success in talking to my girlfriend about race issues than I had with the Black folks at T.W.C. I will never truly know if it was because she was white or not. But I do know what always hung us up if we tried to talk about something racial.

At the time, my girlfriend believed that all people were the same and that was all to it. She felt that the past was the past and those people involved in those situations were not her and they were not me. That was easy and convenient for her to say, but it wasn't easy for me to hear. In my mind, those people who were not her had kidnapped, raped, enslaved, exploited, and murdered those people who were not me. Besides, I knew that I would never be able to separate my life and my Black skin from what happened to the Africans who lived and died in this country before me. It will take many generations of work in all things social, economic, and political to reverse the stigma that U.S. slavery has woven into this country's warp and woof.

My "that wasn't me and that wasn't you" girlfriend also believed that hate and prejudice coming from either side was one of the biggest parts of the problem in race relations. Her solution was that she was not going to accept or be a part of it either way. I agreed with her theories on the surface, but I tried to explain that it wasn't that simple and it was deeper than that.

On the surface what she was saying was absolutely correct, but the surface isn't always an accurate measure of depth. If race relations would have started out in America in the way that she wanted them to be during our lives, then the issues that I found myself facing in 1995 would have been either very small or non-existent. But that wasn't the way that it went down. It went down a whole different way and that can't be ignored or buried by the passage of time.

The effects of the past have to be worked out before we can just pick up and say let's make it the right way starting right now. The relics of the past have caused too much pain, too much hurt, too much anger, and too much nihilism. Those issues have to be thoroughly and effectively dealt with before we can start planning new beginnings. I know that there will have to be the kind of new beginning that she was describing at some point if we ever hope to improve how we all view and interact with one another as human beings. But it can't happen overnight and it can't happen without some serious dialogues that lead to some serious changes.

I am still firmly convinced that we are a part of the same family—every time I see a child's face I can see the oneness of humanity. But we have to deal with the issues first, and therein lies the problem.

White people don't want to deal with the issues first. They just want the horrible stain of their barbaric treatment of Black people to evaporate from history. The general attitude of many white people suggests that we should all just agree to wake up one day and forget that slavery ever happened. Some feel that we—Black folks—won't let *IT* go because we are looking for a handout or because we want to make excuses. They can't understand why we can't just move beyond the past or why we can't just let bygones be bygones.

One of the best responses that I have seen dealing with the after-math of the pain that slavery has left upon the Black race can be found in words written by Richard Wright. In his 1941 book, *12 Million Black Voices*, Wright wrote:

> … years are a long time for millions of folk like us to be held in such subjection, so long a time that perhaps scores of years will have to pass before we shall be able to express what slavery has done to us, for our person-alities are still numb from its long shocks; and as the numbness leaves our souls, we shall yet have to feel and give utterance to the full pain that we shall inherit.

You see white people, we just can't forget about *IT*.

My girlfriend and I never made it far enough in our few race discussions to allow for me to "give utterance to the full pain" that I inherited, so we always stayed on that surface level where we could both agree. That was the level that maintained that every-body was the same and asserted the position that believed that hate and prejudice was unacceptable no matter which side from whence it came. I must say that even that level was further than a lot of people have achieved, even at this late stage of the game. For that, I tip my hat toward what we shared. But I needed to be able to go deeper. Our relationship just never developed enough to go to the depths where I felt my deepest emotions regarding race. Perhaps it was through no individual fault of ours, just the collective fault of all of us. Nevertheless, I gave the conversation a rest with her just as I did with the Black students at T.W.C.

I gave the conversation a rest with everybody, but I felt like 2-Pac on his 1995 *Me Against the World* album on the song *"So Many Tears"*. He said: "inside my mind I couldn't find a place to rest".

My mind was constantly turning over with the plight of the Black man in this country—a plight that was mine whether I chose to recognize it or not. The problems were not going away, so my thoughts wouldn't go away. I didn't have anybody to talk to who felt as strong as I felt about it; but I had to get the thoughts out, because if I didn't get them out, it felt like that flame within me was going to consume my soul.

I took advantage of an opportunity to get the thoughts out in a Social Psychology class that I was taking at the time. I figured that if I couldn't talk to anybody about my feelings that I would have to write about them; maybe that's why I'm writing this book now.

I know that I have always felt compelled to write about being a Black male in America. My Black friends from Eckerd College frequently commented that I was always writing about "Black jive" to make sure that I always got an A in my coursework. But the truth was that I couldn't write about anything else but "Black jive". I never did it to get a high grade in a class; I did it because it was in me. There was never any jive in any thing that I ever wrote about being Black, because being Black was no jive. The things that were inside of me either had to be born or I had to die.

The "Black jive" that they called my writings were and had always been my life. (I suspect it always will be.) It was my reality. I had to deal with my life and my realities before I wrote about other people's lives and their realities. Perhaps my friends would have accused James Baldwin of always writing about "Black jive" too. Baldwin said:

> I had not written about being a Negro at such length because I expect that to be my only subject, but only because it was the gate I had to unlock before I could hope to write about anything else. (James Baldwin, c.1984)

The Social Psychology professor gave a writing assignment with an accompanying presentation that would account for a large percentage of our final grade. The great thing about the assignment was that it could be on any topic that we chose to write about, as long as it was related to Social Psychology.

In the book that we were using, Social Psychology was defined as "the scientific study of the way that individuals think, feel, and behave in social situations." The definition was so broad that I knew that I was definitely safe in pouring out some of my thoughts concerning my plight of being a Black male in America.

I decided to focus the paper on an aspect of the plight that I knew would allow me to find adequate research material. After all, it was assigned as a research paper, so research had to be done. Considering the length of the paper, I hope that you do not mind me reproducing it in this book. I feel that that's the best way to preserve the integrity of my mood and sentiment at the time.

The cover page of my paper was direct and to the point, and the content of the paper was my answer to the question I asked on the cover. It was the spring of 1995, and I had no idea that a few years later I would be wishing with all my heart that I would have been fortunate enough to go to an all Black male school. The future would force me to ask myself would I have become a better Black man sooner if I had.

The Black Male-
An Endangered Species?
Are All-Black Male Schools the Answer?

The Black man is fast becoming an endangered species in the United States. America has proven itself a place of near insurmountable odds for this group. We (I am a Black male) are, as a group, the most vulnerable in this society. Betty Greathouse and Sandra Sparling, two African-American female educators, declare: "From conception to death, the African-American male is at dire risk in the United States. The sources of such risks are reflective of ills that plague the entire social system" (p. 132). Statistics show that Black male infants (the terms Black and African-American will be used interchangeably in this paper) have a mortality rate twice that of white infants. This is just the beginning of our problems. The chance that we will grow up in a home with no father is comparable to a flip of a coin.

Black women head 56% of all Black families, and this figure rises dramatically in inner-city neighborhoods (Farrell, p. 80). This has a profound impact on the development of the African-American male child. The lack of a father figure at home places the child in a hole of which he may never be able to climb out. I believe that women are very capable of raising a male child, but I also believe that it is a duty of a man to teach that male child to become a man. In Africa, males must go through rites of passage ceremonies into manhood; other men conduct the ceremonies.

In America, there is an absence of Black men that are willing or able to perform these tasks. Unfortunately, there is a vicious cycle that repeats itself in African-American fatherhood. If you were raised in a home where there was no father, then more often than not you are not going to be a live-in father to your own child. For a Black male child with no father, there's no role model.

Our hero, more times than not, is not another man with the same last name, unless our last name happens to be Jordan, Johnson, or Murphy. We identify with the Black men that we see. Through television, Michael Jordan, Magic Johnson, and Eddie Murphy are more visible for most Black male children than their fathers. David Evans, a senior admissions officer at Harvard, offers support to this point. He says, "... most African-American male children do not often meet black role models in their daily lives. They must look beyond their daily lives. They must look beyond their immediate surroundings for exemplary black men to emulate. Lacking in-the-flesh role models, many look to TV for black heroes" (p10).

I am not trying to say that these men should not be heroes, because Black people have come a long way in the sports and entertainment industries. Their accomplishments are something that we (Black people) fought long and hard for, and we should be proud of them. However, the status that these individuals have reached is rare and unobtainable for most people.

The young Black males who look up to these men all think that they could be the next one. I am not the kind of person to tell anyone that they can't become something, but it is simply impossible for everyone to be a professional athlete or entertainer. Yet, in pursuit of these aspirations many young Black male children underestimate the value of an education. Evans claims: "... the glamour of millionaire boxers, ballplayers, musicians, comedians appear so close, so tangible that, to naïve young boys, it seems only a dribble or a dance step away. In the hot glare of surrealism, schoolwork and prudent personal behavior can become irrelevant" (p10).

In light of this, what happens to the ones that never make it? Professional athletes and entertainers aren't the only Black men who make money. The other role model for young Black males consists of the many visible drug dealers in Black inner-city communities. So at one end of the spectrum you have high profile athletes, and at the other end you have dealers. Where is the in-between? Where are the businessmen? Where are the lawyers? Where are the educators? Where are the people who make up this Black middle class that I hear so much about; does it really exist?

Contrary to what I see in the ghetto, there is a Black middle class in America. In the past two decades, the middle-class (families earning more than $50,000 a year) has increased at a rate of 46%. White families have increased at a rate of 35% (Economist p17). So I ask myself—what's the problem?

Well, for those Blacks that have reached this middle-class status there really isn't a problem. They have gotten their piece of the American dream. The problem stems from their perspective. A great number of them don't contribute anything back to the places that they made it from. A disproportionate number of times the place where they made it from is the ghetto. In effect, what you have is a talent drain.

It is similar to what happens to third world countries in the international arena. The most talented individuals in third world countries often go to more advanced countries to search for better opportunities. Both they and their new country are beneficiaries, but their parent country suffers. This is what happens in the Black community.

The Economist reports: "A third of American blacks are now middle-class. They have taken advantage of fair housing legislation and moved to the suburbs, looking for better schools, safer streets, better services" (p17). This exodus takes its toll on the Black community. What you have left is a community devoid of its most talented resources. The Black communities of yesterday have evolved into the ghettoes of today.

Let's examine the people who make up those ghettoes. Professional Black athletes and entertainers don't live there, and neither does our middle class. So who lives there? Colin Powell. I really don't think so. What do you have left? A community that doesn't file tax returns—a society within a society.

The ghetto operates under a whole different set of rules. The Economist admits: "What is regarded as pathological in most communities—unemployment, unwed childbearing, welfare dependency, drug-taking, violent crime—is regarded as normal in the ghetto" (p17). Ill-fated young Black males grow up in this environment. Without the example of the middle-class Black male and confronted with the rarity of success in the sports or entertainment industry, where does the young Black male turn?

Young Black males that don't live in the suburbs with their parents or whose father isn't Air Jordan, can turn to the neighborhood drug dealer. In America the drug game and other types of crime are interrelated. A majority of the crime is of a violent nature. The triad of drugs, crime, and violence is where we lose most of our young Black males. The leading cause of death among Black males between the ages of 15 and 24 is homicide. Most of these homicides are Black on Black, where the victim and the perpetrator are Black males.

The young Black males that escape the homicide statistic can't seem to escape incarceration. Black males constitute a mere 12% of the U.S. male population, but make up nearly 50% of the U.S. male prison population. These statistics must be a joke, surely no one group could be this afflicted. It isn't a joke, and it definitely isn't funny. But the question is: do Black male infants have to grow up to fulfill this unimaginable cycle? The answer is no.

I have already discussed the Black middle-class earlier in this paper—a Black middle class who, for the most part, obtained their status through education. Education—unlike the professional sports or entertainment industry—is a viable option for most. Education is also free of the consequences of the drug and crime game. African-American males can use education to disjoin the cycle of statistics alluded to in the preceding paragraphs. Conclusion: Education is the savior for African-American males. This seems logical, but I don't want to bet the farm just quite yet on education. In order to gain a better perspective on education and the Black male child, a further exploration of the issue must be done.

The environment of most young Black males in the inner-city neighborhoods is not one that places a high value on education. Why? Because the people that used that tool to escape poverty and crime are not present in their environments. Remember, those people make up the middle-class; they have all moved to the suburbs. This portrays a very harmful message about education and Blacks. One that basically says if you get an education and excel in school that you are going to become a sell-out—a message to the Black middle class. If the shoe fits, then lace it up!

Kids view success in the classroom as "acting white". They can't relate to being Black and getting an education as two things that can coexist. Black youths in the ghetto adopt an anti-education attitude, in order to maintain their Black identity. Those that don't adopt this attitude often face ridicule and hostility from their peers.

Sophronia Scott Gregory agrees: "The anti-achievement ethic championed by some black youngsters declares formal education useless; those who disagree and study hard face isolation, scorn, and violence" (p44). This attitude really upsets me when I think about all the sacrifices that our ancestors made in order to educate themselves and to provide their children with an opportunity for an education.

We are a people who risked their lives as slaves to learn how to read. We are a people who populated Morehouse College and Howard University in 1867 just two short years after the Emancipation Proclamation was officially enforceable in all states. We are a people who improved our literacy rate from 20% to 70% between reconstruction (the period immediately following the Civil War) 1865-1867 and 1910 (p45). We are a people with strong roots in education and achievement. To excel and to be Black went hand in hand. Kids today don't know about our strong history in education or any other area for that matter. We as Blacks have failed to pass it down to the next generation. We dropped the ball. Who in the hell do we expect to pick it up?

I know that the American school system isn't going to pick it up. The curriculum taught in the American school system is Eurocentric. It provides no other perspectives of history or achievement other than that of the European variety. Black kids can't relate. This makes them apathetic when it comes to learning. Greathouse and Sparling comment: "I've found that children who are centered in their own cultural information are better students, more disciplined, and have greater motivation for schoolwork" (p29). They refer to children who are taught in their own cultural framework as being "culturally grounded". The advantage that white children have in the public school system is tremendous. They are in an environment that uses their culture as the dominant culture. What is the nature of the disadvantage for the Black kids in the classroom?

In some cases they don't learn as well as the other kids, in other cases they don't want to learn, and finally there are some that do actually learn and excel. The kids who don't learn are left behind and labeled as slow. Those who don't want to learn are regarded as troublemakers and rebels. Ironically, even the Black kids who do learn and excel in a Euro-centric educational system are victimized. Greathouse and Sparling report: "These children may learn, but without cultural grounding, the learning will have destroyed their sense of place ... children abandon, in their minds, their own culture in order to become like others culturally ..." (p30). Black children must kill their cultural reference, in order to birth the culture being taught at school. Maybe that is why the Black kids in school say that the "smart" Black kids are "acting white". The white children are also hurt in a system that is only "culturally grounded" in an Euro-centric system.

By not teaching more than one perspective of history the complete story is not told. Instead of history, it becomes his story. No one benefits from this. The children that are not of the dominant culture are not "culturally grounded" and the kids of the dominant culture are mis-educated. In order for kids to be able to appreciate the accomplishments of others, they must first understand their own and then be taught about the accomplishments of others.

When you teach a child about his or her own culture first, then and only then can you teach that child about others. That is the formula for building a monument of diversity that rests on a strong foundation. Without a foundation, you can't build anything that can stand. This is exactly what the American school system tries to do with African-Americans; it leaves us without a foundation.

African-American males can least afford this type of education. I am not saying that the American education system is the only element responsible for the problems of Black males. I hope that I successfully illustrated some others earlier in this paper. However, I am saying that the education system is an element that Blacks can use to remedy the plight of the Black male.

We must realize that we are the only ones who are going to help our situation. No one else cares. And if they do, then it's all talk and no action. There are movements to save everything from the whales to Sequoia trees. Have you heard of the movement to save the young Black male? I haven't. We must reclaim ourselves. The Economist points this out, declaring: "Whatever their personal views, blacks are likely to find themselves relying on their own resources in the next few years. Even liberal whites seem to be reluctant to do more for blacks" (p18).

In view of the situation of the African-American male, I think that the only rational solution is to set up all Black male schools for grades K-8. For anyone who thinks that this measure is a bit drastic, I can only reply to that with "drastic times call for drastic measures". We are in a state of emergency. Provide a better seed and I will plant it. Such schools have been started in Milwaukee, Detroit, and Baltimore. It is too early to tell what the effects of these programs will have, but it has to be a step in the right direction. Perhaps the results of a Dade County (Miami, FL) elementary school are an early indicator for the potential success of these three programs.

The principal of Pine Villa Elementary School, Willie J. Wright, started the program in Dade County. The program consisted of a kindergarten class of 20 Black males and a first grade class with 23 Black males, both classes taught by Black male teachers. The program focused on attendance, academic achievement, a partnership between two boys, gentlemen social graces, and appropriate behavior for school life.

The Black male kindergarten class scored 7-11% higher on standard tests of sounds and letters and their mathematics scores were 8-9% higher than their coeducational counterparts. 18 out of the 20 also had perfect attendance. The 23 first graders math scores were 5-7% higher than their coeducational peers and their reading comprehension was 5% higher. More importantly, the kids were taught how to disagree. Wright claims, "they had to learn the art of disagreeing without hostility or confrontation" (p16). How far can this lesson go in a group that cites homicide as the leading cause of death between the ages of 15 and 24?

At this point in time, we can't waste any more time waiting on anybody else to solve our problems. The Black male is becoming an endangered species. We must reclaim ourselves as the people that we once were. We have endured much injustice, but we have always survived. It is the duty of every Black man to ensure the survival of another. As the kids were taught in the program at Pine Villa Elementary, you must become your brother's keeper.

Don't get me wrong, I would like for this type of brotherhood to exist among all men, but it doesn't. We can't afford to beg for this type of society any longer. American society has shown the Black male nothing but its ugly side from the time the first slave arrived here almost 400 years ago. As a Black male, I have no choice, but to conclude that all Black male schools are a necessity. This nightmare for the African-American male must end, and we must be responsible for ending it. Each one, reach one, teach one.

Works Cited

Evans, David L. "The Wrong Examples." Newsweek 1 Mar. 1993: 10.

Farrel, Christopher. "An Anguished Cry of 'enough' in America's Killing Fields." Business Week 13 Dec. 1993: 80.

Greathouse, Betty and Saundra Sparling. "African-American Male-Only Schools: Is That The Solution?" Childhood Education Spring 1993: 131-133.

Gregory, Sophfronia Scott. "The Hidden Hurdle." Time 16 Mar. 1992: 44-47.

"The Other America." The Economist 10 July 1993: 17-18.

Wright, Willie J. "The Endangered Black Male Child." Educational Leadership Dec.- Jan. 1991: 14-17

That was the paper that I turned in to fulfill my research assignment. I knew that my research would confirm what I already knew; life in the ghetto could be as hard as steel and the chances of making it out seemed to be perpetually stuck somewhere between slim and none for a lot of folks. I wanted to highlight the group that I belonged to; the group where my voice could rang out as somewhat of an expert. In my mind, I had more credibility than most of the people that I cited as references. For the most part, they merely studied what they wrote about by reading about it or observing others; I lived what I was writing about. I had been a Black male every second of my fragile life. No amount of training or course study could duplicate that.

For my class presentation, I had to make my audience see and feel the urgency of why I felt that we needed all-Black male schools. I knew that I was a member of one of the most volatile groups in the country. I recognized the fact that Black men in the United States were as different and diverse as any other group of people living in America. I also recognized that we were visible at every level of society. But I knew from my own experiences that there was one segment of America's Black male population that had to be America's worst nightmare. The way that I saw it, that segment was young Black males who just didn't care. However, at the same time, I knew that those individuals were victims too, even though they often grew up to victimize others. I had to make my classmates see and feel that principle.

I knew that the brothers who were selling drugs and committing violent crimes were not born into the world with a penchant for destructive behavior. I also knew that mainstream American media loved to tell a different story in their newspapers and through their television news cameras. Let them tell it, we all came out of the womb ready to rape the nurse and rob the doctor. The thing that bothered me most was that those same media people never seemed to have time to report on the conditions that produced the violent or deviant behavior. That's why the mainstream image of the young Black male was so one-sided.

I knew that from personal experience. I could not began to tell you how many times that I have had to walk through parking lots listening to the serenade of automatic door locks locking as I walked toward my own car. I suppose it never crossed the minds of those folks that I was only interested in getting into my own car ... not theirs. I wanted to use my presentation to tell a version that the mainstream media didn't seem to have time to cover.

My mission for my presentation was twofold. First, I had to show my audience, which was ninety-nine percent white, the seriousness of the situation with young brothers in the hood. I had to show them how easy it was for something negative to jump off. Second, I had to explain to them how a person gets to that point where they really don't care about consequences. At the same time, I had to provide support for the idea that all-Black male schools for grades K-8 could improve the situation.

In order to accomplish the first task, I played the opening scene to the 1993 movie, *Menace II Society*, directed by Allen and Albert Hughes (The Hughes brothers). During the scene that I played, Caine (Tyrin Turner) and O-Dog (Larenz Tate) went into a Korean store to buy a 40-oz malt liquor; but they ended up robbing the joint and killing the two Koreans store owners. It was a violent scene, but it definitely got everybody's attention. It was the perfect scene to demonstrate how easily and how quickly something could jump off or go down.

In order to accomplish the second task, I talked a lot from my own personal experiences. I broke down the stages that a lot of young Black males growing up in the hood find themselves face to face with at different points in their lives. I think that for some of the white students in that class, it was the first time that they had ever really sat down and really thought about some of the issues that I brought up in my presentation. I say that because the question and answer session went on a lot longer than normal. I didn't mind the questions; I was happy that they were interested enough to ask so many. The instructor seemed interested as well; she let the questions go on until the end of the class.

A couple of weeks after my presentation, my instructor told me that she thought that my presentation was really powerful. She asked me if I would come in as a guest speaker to talk with her Education majors about my views on educating minority students. She wanted me to emphasize how important the role of a teacher was to the success of minority students. I told her that I would be more than happy to do that if she thought it was a good idea. She reassured me that she thought it was an excellent idea, so I agreed to visit her class during the month of April.

I thought a long time and asked myself: "what would I want to say to a group of future educators?" I knew that I wanted to address the self-fulfilling prophecy involved in the school systems. I thought that was extremely important because I knew that a student's performance was correlated to the teacher's level of expectation. It's sad, but I believe that there are still teachers today standing in front of Black children who feel that Blacks are inferior. Many of them are subconsciously passing that message on to some of our youth and wondering why they have difficulty learning.

I definitely wanted to address the need for diversity in the curriculum. A Black child needs to know that he or she has a place in this world and the specific group to which they belong has contributed to the world.

And last but not least, I wanted them to realize that it would be their responsibility as teachers to have as much of a positive influence as possible on every child that they came in contact with in the classroom. I wanted them to accept the challenge of trying to prevent as many kids as possible from slipping through the cracks.

Once again, to help me with the task at hand, I went straight to Ms. Riley's book of quotations from people of color to search for a couple of quotes to help me drive home my points. I found two quotes that I decided to use. I used one to support my views about the effects of self-fulfilling prophecies. I used the second one to support my views on how important it was for Black children to be taught about their own culture and history as opposed to only being exposed to the Euro-centric version of history. Here are those quotes:

> If you want to teach a child to be good, don't tell him how bad he is. Tell him how good he can be. (Kwasi Geiggar, in *Jet*, 10 December 1990)

> If you can show me how I can cling to that which is real to me while teaching me a way into the larger society, then I will not only drop my defenses and my hostility, but I will sing your praises and I will make the desert bear fruit. (Ralph Ellison, "What These Children Are Like", *Going to the Territory*, 1986)

For my final point relating to how important it was for them, as future educators, to have as much of a positive influence as possible on as many kids as possible, I used my own life as an example. I told them how instrumental my high school SAT prep teacher had been in making sure that I would have a chance to go to college and how much she believed in my potential. I told them how she was a white female who had a tremendous impact on the life of the young Black male that they saw standing before them.

I wanted them to know that the gift that great teachers possessed was powerful enough to overcome racial barriers and gender differences. I told them all about myself and my experience with a wonderful educator because I wanted them to believe that they could actually make a difference, even if it was one child at a time. I told them to believe in that, because I was that one child to that one teacher during one school year (Just in case I never got around to saying it, I want to say it now … Thank-you Mrs. Valcarcel for being a great teacher).

I left that classroom feeling real good. I felt that I had actually connected with many of the students in the class. I felt that I had done some small amount of good. My professor had her Education students write about how they perceived the presentation and gave me copies of what they wrote. Their responses made me feel even better. Here are a couple of samples from some of the students' written responses.

> He let us have a feel for how easy it could be to treat students differently. I feel that now, as a teacher, I would be very careful to help and treat my students fair. I will also try to motivate my students as much as possible and hopefully I'll have a lot of students with the outlook and dedication that Quincy has. The quotes that he shared with us were very strong and true. He motivated me and I needed that. (A future educator)

> Quincy and I have much in common. He is a black male and I am a female. Both are minorities. Being a future educator I must realize, just as Quincy said, that it is up to me to let every child that I come in contact with know that they are just as good as everyone else. I hope that I will always be mindful of the children that have fallen through the cracks. I appreciate Quincy speaking very openly and honestly about his feelings. I feel that he has helped each of us in very different ways. (A future educator)

There were more kind words written by the other students in addition to those that I just shared; they all expressed their appreciation and gratitude for the different things from our discussion that had motivated or inspired them. I was glad I had an opportunity to inspire or motivate those folks as future educators; but I also realized that those folks, through their openness and willingness to accept the message that I was trying to convey, had also inspired and motivated me. It was a good feeling. I felt like there was actually a chance to change things. It was the same feeling that I got when I was an intern at the newspaper back in Florida and all the interns gathered in a room for roundtable discussions to solve the world's problems. It gave me hope. Considering how I was feeling about all the Black jive, hope was a lot to have.

WEARY

The school year was almost over and I was counting the days until I would be back in Florida. I decided to give one of the area managers that I had worked with at the newspaper a call to see if I could return as an intern during the summer. He said that he was very glad that I had telephoned him because they were going to be working on a project that he felt that I could help get off the ground. I told him when I expected to be back in town and we set a date where we could get together to discuss the particulars. So just like that I had a good job lined up for the summer. I was glad that I had not burned that bridge because I was sure that it would be enough money to get me through the summer.

With my summer employment plans secure and my plans for my trip back to Florida already made, the only thing I had to do was close out the last few days of the school year and my experience at Tennessee Wesleyan would be in the rear-view mirror of my life.

I was satisfied with what I had accomplished at T.W.C. I was even satisfied with my basketball experience. It was definitely true that I had not accomplished all that I had hoped for when I decided to transfer in an effort to pursue my hoop dreams, but it was equally true that I had achieved a victory in of itself just by going after what I wanted. I could have stayed at Eckerd and just accepted a fate determined by men who were blind to justice, but I didn't. I fought for something that I wanted, and my victory was achieved in the fight.

In some cases in life, the decision to fight is actually more important than if you win or lose. It is better for "The Man in the Arena" to fail than it is for the man to not have entered the arena at all.

I could live with what happened with hoops at T.W.C, but I don't think that I would have been able to be what I wanted to be if I accepted the lie that the Eckerd coaches were trying to make me believe. They tried to tell me that the rich white guy who drove around campus in a Porche—whose father just happened to be a basketball coach with a professional relationship with the Eckerd basketball staff—was a better basketball player than me. And they expected me to believe that and accept that!

I may have been poor and Black, but I wasn't dumb and I wasn't a mark. Still, it was bigger than basketball; it was more about the principle of the matter. Was I going to allow people to treat me so unfairly without standing up for myself? My answer was no. I had to leave! If I hadn't, then I would have never been able to look at those men in their face in the manner that a man is supposed to be able to look another man in the face.

It would have only been natural for them to feel that they could treat me as they saw fit. It would have been my fault; my acquiescence would have been my consent. I would have never been able to feel good about myself for allowing a period of my life to go by without standing up for myself and fighting when life was standing in my face so brazenly trying to discount my own input into my own individual destiny. My locus of control was mine.

It was all for the best, because I found something at Tennessee Wesleyan that I had struggled to find all my life. I found an overflowing source of the knowledge of self that had eluded me my entire life. *My Soul Looks Back, 'Less I Forget* was that source.

I knew that there was more to being Black than what they were teaching in classrooms. I knew that my feelings were not the first feelings of their kind among our people, but I had never really found sufficient material to show me that my ancestors and elders had already felt the feelings that I was feeling. More importantly, I never knew that they had triumphed over those feelings.

Many of them triumphed through the giving of their own lives. They died so that I would not have to face the feelings that they had to face on the same unequal terms that they had to face them on during their life. In many respects, I was a free man who walked around as a slave before I discovered the people who paved the road for my feet to travel. I was a slave because I was lacking the knowledge of my past and the terrific history that we had behind us as a people. Some of my ancestors were related to Jesus Christ—they had the same Father, and like Him some of them gave their lives for me. I thank the Lord for all of them. Hallelujah!

The words of my ancestors that lie between the pages of Ms. Riley's book sometimes reinforced thoughts and feelings that had been with me for a long time. At other times, they produced new thoughts and feelings that I never really experienced up to that point in my life. My mind was a constant bed of activity examining the race issue from as many angles as I could find, and I never seemed to be able to exhaust all the angles. Something always happened, almost on a daily basis, to produce a different angle than I examined the previous day.

Most of the angles from which I examined the impact of my Blackness on my life placed me in a battle mode where I had to fight against the white or mainstream world around me. It was a battle that I didn't hesitate to engage in; it was a battle that I embraced. I was happiest when I was actively fighting back against the image of inferiority of Black folks that America had so carefully planted in the world's mind through four hundred years of slavery, lynching, segregation, second-class citizenship, discrimination, and prejudice against its African people.

I was always ready to man the front line in the battle against their four-hundred-year-project to keep my people down, but that constant readiness took its toll on me. The world and its constant attack on my Blackness would not give me a place to rest. I was a prisoner with no way out because I refused to pretend that I didn't see what the world had tried to do to me.

My mind was the most common battlefield for the battles that I was fighting and it seemed to always be engaged in the fracas. James Baldwin described the ordeal the best in his 1961 classic *Nobody Knows My Name* when he wrote: "I was free only in battle, never free to rest—and he who finds no way to rest cannot long survive the battle." For the battle, I was always ready and willing, but it had made me tired and weary.

The turnings of my mind during the last part of the year at T.W.C gave me no place to rest and my breakdown in the battle came when my Sociology professor gave a mandatory assignment that dealt with race. Based on what I have told you up until this point about some of the things that I did at T.W.C, a person would probably conclude that that type of assignment on race would not pose any problems for me. Since I had voluntarily tackled the subject so many times on my own, I understand how a person would draw that conclusion. But in the case of that particular assignment, they would have been wrong. They would have been wrong because I was seeking refuge from the combat.

I was wounded and I needed desperately to crawl away from the battlefield. I needed to let my battered soul recover from the inevitable wounds that one receives when they are constantly fighting for their right to be a full and complete human being in a world that is determined to prevent them from ever taking full possession of such a thing. My professor was a nice enough lady that she would have excused me from the assignment had she been able to see my wounds, but she couldn't see them. No one could see them. I couldn't even see them, but I knew that they were there because I could feel them being made anew each day. My wounds were internal wounds that were bleeding from the outside in.

The assignment was based on an article that dealt with a form of racism known as regressive racism. The article claimed that folks had a tendency to revert back to racist attitudes and actions when things got intense or situations became too serious. It gave examples of how normal every day people had reverted back to stereotypes and other forms of racism whenever it got too hot in the kitchen or when scarce resources were at stake. It was a depressing thought in of itself. It seemed that there was no real hope to get past the deep racial feelings that most Americans carried somewhere inside of them. It was an assignment that I just couldn't deal with at the time. The following is what I wrote in response to that assignment given by the professor.

Regressive Racism

Sometimes, I sit down and wonder. I wonder how we, as human beings, have reached this point. We live in a world that is so far from anything positive. It has gotten to the point where no one really wants to say how bad it really is in America. We like to pretend that problems don't exist.

We pretend that we don't see that homeless person we just stepped over on the street. We pretend that we don't hear the cries of battered women across the country. We pretend that the powers that be do not hold racist and sexist views—views that say I won't hire you because you are a spic, a nigger, or a chink and views that say I won't pay you what you are worth because you are a woman. We pretend that people don't go hungry while we throw food away. These are just some of the pretend games that we play in the United States. There are many more, but there is one more in particular. We pretend that there is not a severe race problem in this country.

At this point in my life, I would consider myself a successful person by many standards. I also think that my success up to this point has had a high price tag. For me, success in the world at large has primarily been in a white culture dominated world. This success at times has been a failure. It has made me realize that being a Black male in this world is dangerous.

It's dangerous either way, whether the peril lies in words of white praise or white looks of disapproval. Through the words of praise you realize that you are held out to be an exception. You are regarded as Black, but something must have been special about your individual genetic coding because you are not like the rest. Through the eyes of disapproval, white stares penetrate your soul in an effort to convey a message that no matter how successful you become you will still be regarded as a nigger. The words of praise and the looks of disapproval create a very stressful atmosphere in the mind of Black males. These words I write from experience.

Not one single day goes by that I am not aware that I am a Black male in a land full of danger. My mind is always aware of a situation or a potential situation. Through years of developing coping strategies, I have many faces and many voices in my wardrobe. This is very dangerous because it is very easy to forget which is your real face and real voice. I wonder is it possible to have a real face and a real voice in such a masquerade. The constant turning of the mind is enough to drive me crazy.

It is no surprise to me that many upper middle class Blacks in the country suffer from hypertension. They try to say that they are genetically prone to such illnesses. I say that it is because of all the pressure and stress that they experience due to their success and the coping strategies that they have to develop. The fact that Black Africans have among the world's lowest hypertension rates tends to support my view. I know that diet comes into play in that comparison, but I know that stress levels do as well. I really do feel that my constant awareness of the issue of race is detrimental to my physical well being. That is why I am really hesitant to deal with this article on regressive racism.

It seems to me that this question of race will never be solved. People will always harbor prejudice opinions somewhere in their mind about people of other races. Like the article portrays, no matter how well intended an individual might be, all that it takes is an insult and boom! People are right back to square one of being a racist. I can't deal with that right now.

That was my response to the assignment given; I had avoided the real intent of the assignment. I avoided it because the level from which I would have dealt with it under "normal" circumstances was too wounded for me to access. I would have preferred to keep pushing forward with the believe that people were capable of overcoming all of the obstacles that kept us from realizing that we were all part of the same human family. I would have preferred to keep the dream of Dr. King alive with my response, but my faith in the dream of Dr. King and in mankind was in critical condition. I felt that there would always be enough white folks to pick at the scab of the wounds of racism with racist attitudes and racist actions until there was fresh blood flowing from the sores of America's flesh once again. I felt that there would always be Blacks who were tired of turning the other cheek and forgiving seven times seventy.

I was tired of trying to hold fast to the idea of one human family. In trying to stick to the idea of one human family, I felt like I was against what appeared to be insurmountable odds. If racism and America were to coexist, then I was ready to get down with the get down. I was ready to give as good as I got. I was ready to trade an insult for an insult, a tooth for a tooth, and an eye for an eye—even if it made the whole world blind. That's what Mahatma Gandhi said about it: "an eye for an eye makes the whole world blind", but I didn't care about that on the day the assignment was given. I was digging the words of James Weldon Johnson, when he said:

> There comes a time when the most persistent integrationist becomes an isolationist, when he curses the white

world and consigns it to hell. This tendency is strong
because it springs from a deep-seated natural desire—a
desire for respite from the unremitting grueling struggle; for a place in which refuge might be sought.

I didn't want to keep hope alive. I wanted to be left alone to seek
refuge in order to fulfill a "deep-seated natural desire—a desire for
respite from the unremitting grueling struggle".

I can't remember any one event or major incident that put me in
the frame of mind that I was in when the professor gave the assignment. I was just tired of the small day to day hassles of being a Black
male in America. If it is hard for anyone to understand that concept,
then allow me to try to offer some clarity.

I once read something about the reason why Nelson Mandela
decided to join the ANC in their efforts to liberate South Africa
and to eradicate apartheid. He wrote that he was motivated by "no
epiphany, no singular revelation, no moment of truth, but a steady
accumulations of a thousand slights."

My need to seek refuge just added to the reasons that I was
so happy when the school year finally ended and I was free to
return to Florida. My girlfriend was overjoyed too. Our relationship had seen its share of problems over the past five months,
and we were both convinced that Florida would provide the remedy to whatever was wrong with our situation. I also knew that
I would soon be reunited with the friends that I left behind. I
looked upon those guys as the brothers that I never had. I was
eager to get back to David as well; he was just a year away from
starting high school and I wanted to be around for that. I was
ready to see my grandmother and taste some of her collard greens
that I knew she would be making for me. I wanted to get back to
all the important people that I had left in Florida; it was just good
to be going home.

On the way back to Florida, we got caught in the gridlock of
Atlanta's Freaknik traffic. That was quite a sight to see as I looked
out of the window of the driver's side of my girlfriend's car. The
highway looked like a sea of Black folks in a sea of tight rides. The
scene made me think of a line that rang out from the chorus of an
Oukast song called *"Players Ball"* that said:

All the players came from far and wide,

wearin' afros and braids,

pushin' them gangsta rides.

I soaked up the scene as we moved at a snail's pace through Atlanta. It was cool to get stuck in the Freaknik traffic, but I was glad to be back up to regular driving speeds after the creep and crawl. For most of our remaining drive, I just thought about how I felt about the last nine months of my life in Tennessee.

I had made my peace with the basketball issues in my life. Although I wished things had gone better for me with basketball, I was satisfied with what I accomplished with hoops. I had made the choice of what I wanted out of basketball based on what I felt was right for me and my life. I had made the choice based on the strengths and talents that the Lord gave me. It was time to let it go and get on with whatever lay ahead for me. I realized that I wasn't going to be a professional basketball player. My eyes could finally see that it was just a game for me; it wasn't my life. It had helped me achieve some of my goals, and I was thankful for that.

Basketball wasn't life, but sometimes it imitated life. I wanted to control as many choices about my own life as possible. My choosing to end it in Tennessee—as opposed to being forced to end it at Eckerd—was something that I could reconcile in my heart and soul. Courage is the virtue that allows the practice of all the others. I was proud of myself for having the courage to attempt a change that many called foolish. At best it was life lived, at worst I was a courageous fool. I knew that I would be better able to live with being a courageous fool than a cowardly genius.

Off the court, I had accomplished more than I set out to accomplish. A large part of that had to do with the inspiration that I received from the words of my ancestors that I found in Dorothy Riley's book. I had found something that it felt like I was born to do. Throughout my life, I discovered that the Lord had blessed me with many talents and I knew that I was good at a lot of things, but none of them made me feel like I was born to do them. When I spoke at the Black History Month convocation, I felt that I was born to do that. I didn't expect to find such an experience at Tennessee Wesleyan.

Conversely, I fully expected to achieve the results in the classroom that I achieved during the school year. By the time the dust had settled and the year was done, I had earned an A in every course that I took at T.W.C. My transcript from the 1994-95 school year read as follows:

Biological Concepts: A

Masterpieces of World Literature: A

Elementary French I: A

Developmental Psychology: A

Experimental Psychology: A

International Trade and Finance: A

Personalities of Russian Revolution: A

Social Psychology: A

Physiological Psychology and Learning: A

It was the second consecutive full school year where I had earned all A's for my coursework. I was really proud of the fact that I could say that I had made straight A's in nineteen consecutive classes over a two-year period and thirty A's out of a total of thirty-six courses over my four years in college. The only thought that bothered me when it came to my grades was the feeling I felt that made me wish that I had only applied myself earlier. I was confident that I could have made an A in every class that I had taken if I had only set my mind to do it. I knew that I could've done it because Dr. Benjamin Mays told me that I could do it. He said: "You have the ability, now apply yourself."

EVIDENCE OF
THINGS NOT SEEN

The feeling of accomplishment at T.W.C carried me right into my summer internship with the newspaper. My contact in the Home Delivery dept. informed me that my duties would be totally different this time around in comparison to what I did last summer. This time around they needed me to design a software package to automate the record keeping of the department's expenses. I wasn't really sure if I could do that, but I was sure that I needed that summer income. That's why I told him that I could handle it.

They wanted the automation to be done in a Quatro spreadsheet format, so I found a copy of the manual for the program and got busy downloading the information from the manual to my brain before people started asking me questions that I couldn't answer. Fortunately for me, my assignment changed somewhat in mid-stream.

It did not change because I was failing at the project. It was quite the opposite. My success in the project caused me to be pulled into a different assignment. I was already dealing with expenses for the city operation, so I was pulled in when the top people in the Home Delivery dept. needed those numbers turned into projections.

The team needed the projections for a proposal that was being put together in an effort to consolidate the entire operations of five separate city districts and the partial operations of three additional separate city districts into one distribution center. I understood the basic concepts, and when I was missing a piece of information I found the right person with the right answer. The quest to find the right person with the right answer led me to many different people, and that's how I received the best on the job training I had ever had.

I was learning about all the things that I sat through in my college classes. I was learning about capital gains on the sale of property, acceptable methods for deriving future projections according to GAAP, and the art of the business presentation. I found that the business presentation wasn't much different than what I had done in my Managerial Enterprise course during my 1993-93 fall semester at Eckerd. It was the same formula: preparation on the pre-work and confident presentation of the end results. I was up for the challenge.

In fact, many of the people that I had to present to were some of the same people that I had consulted in gathering my information. All of my sources and references were right at the table if anything went awry. I was confident that the presentation would go well and it did. It went even better than I expected. I had a blast and my numbers and presentation were solid. I became so busy that I was told to pass most of my automation project on to another intern.

I was feeling good about what I was doing and my excitement was too much to contain when the Intern Coordinator organized a two-minute video spot for every intern to explain what he or she was working on for the summer. I didn't have an office when she came around to tape my segment, so I borrowed the corner office of the top manager in the Home Delivery department. He wasn't in at the time and I had to go into his office frequently to review budget numbers, so it was no big deal to me that I used his office to let everyone know what I was working on for the summer.

I sat in his high-back chair and beamed all over the camera about my part in putting together a proposal that would "revolutionize the way that we did business in the city". After the taping, I didn't really think too much about it until the segments of all the interns were shown at an intern luncheon at the end of the summer.

Different department managers and supervisors were on hand to show their appreciation for the contributions made by their intern(s). Some other company representatives who had a special interest in the intern program were on hand as well. The room was quite full for the occasion. I was sitting around a huge table listening to the coordinator speak when I realized that she was planning on showing that tape at this luncheon. I was like uh-oh! There was a chance that the Home Delivery manager would have my head for profiling in his chair. But it was too late to wish that I had done something other than what I did, so I played it cool the way that

Marie-Antoinette did in 1793 on her way to the guillotine. She said: "Courage! I have shown it for years; think you I shall lose it at the moment when my sufferings are to end?"

The Intern Coordinator popped in the tape and it finally reached my segment. All the other interns on the tape prior to my segment were in little cubicles or open office spaces. Oh, but not me, there I was sitting in the big boss's swivel chair beaming from ear to ear. I told the whole room that I couldn't go into too much detail, but I was part of a team that was working on a project that would revolutionize the way we did business in the city if approved. The coordinator paused the tape to ask me if I had gotten a promotion that she didn't know about. Someone else from the peanut gallery yelled out that I looked awfully comfortable in that big chair.

Some of the other folks in the room teased me about my "revolutionize the way we did business" comment, but it all turned out to be in good fun. I definitely got a kick out of seeing myself like that. Looking back I can see that all of that energy was more a result of naïve exuberance than anything else.

Somebody in the Home Delivery shop must have enjoyed my naïve exuberance because they asked me to stay on and work with them during my final school year. I suppose there was more work to be done in revolutionizing the way that we did business in the city.

I was really happy about continuing to work during the school year because my girlfriend and I didn't make it through the summer living together and I had to pay the rent on my own every month. We just couldn't get along under one roof anymore. We eventually decided to stay a couple, but she moved out to go live with one of her friends. Under that arrangement the apartment was all mine, but so were all the bills. It was cool though, because I had enough money coming in with the job from the newspaper to tie up all the loose ends until my lease ran out. After the lease expired, I figured it would be cheaper for me to move back on campus for the second semester of school.

My fifth year in college felt weird to me; it was almost like time was out of joint and I wasn't supposed to be on the campus at Eckerd anymore. The guys that I came in with had all graduated and moved on to graduate school or professional life. I missed their presence because they were the biggest part of what I liked most about Eckerd College. Needless to say, I was in a little funk about school when classes began in the fall of 1995.

My melancholy caused me to really think about my life. It forced me to ask myself what I wanted out of life. I searched my mind to find the answer.

I told myself that the thing that I wanted most out of life was what I saw few people possessing. I wanted control over how I spent my time. I was working in a very professional environment where productivity was important and I was going to school enrolled in the maximum number of courses. I was a very busy man. I didn't mind being busy, but I did mind the fact that I wasn't busy doing the things that I wanted to do.

I understood the fact that I was a student and that I would have to put in my time like the many people before me, but as far as I could tell the whole concept of putting in time was not an exclusive thing for college students. The way that I saw it, there didn't seem to be a set time when you could stop putting in your time and start spending more of your life doing the things that you considered important.

I looked around my job, I read articles in the media, and I looked around at the people that I encountered in my daily experiences; I concluded that a lot of people were rushing through life doing things that were really not all that important to them. Many of the things that they were doing were important to them from the financial point of view, but not from the point of view of self-actualization.

I saw people on my job that hated their jobs and their bosses, but they needed their paychecks. The need for that paycheck made them spend forty-hours a week or more of their life doing something that they did not want to be doing and working with people with whom they didn't want to be working.

I read articles that suggested that many parents were not spending enough time with their children because of their busy schedules. I read articles that spoke about the divorce rate that said that couples were getting divorced as a result of not having enough time to spend with one another. On the highways, I saw people rushing in their cars to the jobs and to the bosses that they did not like. If that was my fate on the highway of life, then I was looking for a sign that pointed to an exit ramp before it was too late. I did not want to live like that, but I didn't see how I was going to avoid it—at least not entirely.

I reasoned that the only reason that people were willing to lead lifestyles like that was because they needed the money. I started to realize that if I had money, then I would be exempt from being forced into a life where I was obligated to spend the majority of my time doing things that I did not want to do. It was the first time that I had really thought about money outside of my desires for material things.

I had always known about the connection of money and material things. I had made that connection during my days at Stewart Elementary. Even as a small child, I saw all the material things that the rich white kids had as a result of their parents having so much money. In comparison, I saw the material things that my friends and I did not have because our parents didn't have any money.

As a college senior, I saw getting money as the key to buying something much more valuable than material things. It became a means to purchasing the time to do what I wanted to do in my life. I realized that it was that—not the actual money—that made a person rich in life (health considerations aside). But I didn't confuse the situation; I knew that money could buy the time and a whole lot more.

I just couldn't see how a person who did not have money could possibly be in control of how they spent their time. I didn't see how a person could be independent enough to have the freedom to choose how they spent their time without the dollars to finance that independence. Alice Walker broke it down the best in her 1983 book, *In Search of our Mothers' Gardens,* when she said: "Without money of one's own in a capitalistic society, there is no such thing as independence."

My mind was in deep thought about how I was going to get my hands on some cash; not for the sake of cash for material things, but for the sake of being able to control how I spent my time in my life. The way I saw it was very simple. It was my life and I should be in control of it, not other people. They had a life of their own that they could control, but I didn't want them controlling my life and I knew that money could stop them from doing so.

I knew that there weren't any quick fixes for me to get the money that I wanted—no NBA, no future in entertainment, and no winning lottery ticket. After making up my mind in that area, I thought that the next best thing was to try to get on the path that would allow me to make the most money in the least amount of time. I was knee deep in my business & international business majors, so I limited my choices to that arena.

I reasoned that I would have the most opportunities in an area where I had the most education. I had a broad education that could have taken me into a variety of areas such as finance, human resources, management, or sales. I had read information from different sources that reported the expected starting salary range in the different fields for someone with my educational background. I was surprised to see how much that expected salary range went up for business majors that went on to graduate school to earn their M.B.A. I was even more surprised to find that the salary ranges went up even further for M.B.A. graduates that earned their degrees from top business schools.

Armed with that information, I rationalized that a top graduate school would be the quickest way for me to make the most money. There was only one problem with that plan. Top graduate schools were expensive and I didn't have any money. I had to laugh about that … I was going to have to spend some money that I didn't have in order to get access to making the money that I wanted.

I looked for ways around that little problem and I thought that I had come up with the perfect solution when I found a fellowship program for minority students offered by an organization called the Consortium for Graduate Study in Management. It was a group of institutions founded in 1966 that wanted to ensure that talented minorities developed the business skills necessary to compete for entry-level positions in American businesses.

I wished that I had started out trying to do my very best from the beginning, but I figured that I had just as good a chance as anybody. I mean a 3.77 GPA wasn't anything to sneeze at. The only thing that concerned me was the fact that my mentoring professor at Eckerd informed me that most top MBA schools preferred at least a couple of years work experience. I wondered why I liked him so much; he was always telling me things that I did not want to hear.

I checked on the average age of the Consortium fellowship recipient and it seemed that my mentor was right. The average age was a few years older than the twenty-two years that I had lived. As a matter of fact I believe that it was much closer to my current age of twenty-seven-years-old. Still, I had to apply. I was counting on stunning them so much with my sheer brilliance that perhaps they would forget about my age.

I sent in my application complete with my transcripts, GMAT scores, written essays, and two letters of references. One of my references came from a professor and the other came from the top manager in the Home Delivery department of the newspaper where I was still working. It all looked pretty good to me at the time, although I looked back at the essays recently and they were absolutely terrible.

With all my paperwork completed, the only thing left for me to do to fulfill the requirements of the selection process was to interview with a past Consortium graduate. The closest graduate to my location was a fellow who worked in Orlando, Florida.

A month later, I was driving to Orlando to meet a man by the name of Mr. Bland. He was a Black male in his thirties. I made the drive to Orlando early one morning to interview at his office. I remember my first impression of the brother when I saw him. I was really impressed with the fact that he seemed to carry a certain amount of weight around his office. People were calling him Mr. This and Mr. That; people were telling him that they would have various documents on his desk by certain times. I thought to myself that he was a fella that really had it going on. If that was what being a Consortium graduate did for you, then I wanted to get down with the program.

The interview was going fine, as he asked me many of the same questions that I had been asked in other situations. Where did I see myself in five years, what were my goals, and how did I plan on achieving my goals? I think I did fine answering all of those types of questions, but I am not so sure how I did when the interview took an informal turn. He asked me why I wore my earring to the interview.

I didn't get defensive, but I thought to myself ... *oh boy, here we go with that!* As a result of having some experience in working in Corporate America for the last five years, now I can totally understand where he was trying to take me with that question. But back then I was still too ghetto in too many areas to understand. I had limited experience in a professional environment through my internship at the newspaper, but hindsight would prove it to be just that ... limited. I was twenty-two years old with limited professional experience and I know now that my answer showed as much.

I told the Consortium Graduate that wearing an earring was a part of who I was and that I wasn't going to try to change who I was in order to get a job. I told him that if people were going to judge me harshly because I had an earring in my ear, then so be it. I went on to further inform him that anybody who judged me based on my earring would miss out on what I could potentially bring to his or her organization by making an erroneous assumption. He said that he understood my answer, but he pressed his position and tried to clarify his point. He told me that an earring did not really define who I was and he tried to convince me that I could still be who I was without the earring.

I couldn't hear what he was saying; the ignorance of youth had clogged up my ears. The more he talked, the more resolute I became in my position of not changing my cultural practice of wearing an earring to please white folks. That's what I heard him asking me to do.

Almost every Black man that I knew had his ear pierced. All the Black men that I thought were cool had their ear pierced. The players and hustlers on Laura Street had earrings when I was a kid, many of my sports heroes had earrings, and all my friends from back home wore earrings. As far as I was concerned, wearing an earring was a part of who I was. I tried to explain to him that an earring fit into all the parts of my life and didn't have anything to do with whether I was qualified to do the job or not. I don't think that he and I ever agreed on the matter and he decided to continue with the formal aspects of the interview.

I wish that I could see that man again to thank-him for what he was trying to tell me then. *Back then* I saw myself as somewhat selling-out if I had to change something that I felt was a part of my cultural identity in order to conform to white folks business standards. I didn't judge him if he felt that he had to sell-out in order to please white folks, but I told myself that I wasn't going to do it.

I can see *now* that I wouldn't have been selling-out at all, but that's because I am five years older and ten times smarter. I say that with conviction, but I know that a young Black male who observed me at my job today might feel the same way about me and my opinion as I felt about the Consortium Graduate five years ago.

It's all so ironic because I see some of the younger brothers who work in the entry level positions at my job today who are trying to prove the same point that I was trying to prove five years ago. They are trying to prove a point that says that they don't have to change what they consider to be a part of their cultural identity in order to conform to white folks business standards.

Some of them wear their hip-hop clothes and the baggy styles that is a norm—if not a must—in hip-hop culture. Their body language is more reflective of the hip-hop body language than it is reflective of a professional environment. I want to go up in explain to them how they are setting themselves up to be stereotyped and not considered for various opportunities for promotions.

I want to tell them that it doesn't matter whether people's perceptions are right or wrong; it isn't worth it to put themselves in that type of situation. I want to tell them that I have some of the same clothes in my closet at home, but I wouldn't let the white folks at work know that at the stage of my career where I needed all the help that I could get in order to advance. I want to tell them all of those things and eventually I will; but I know that if they are anything like I was, then they are going to see my message as selling-out just like I saw it five years ago.

I want to tell them that if they want to be able to express who they are culturally do it the way that Russell Simmons does it. Own the places where you work, then you can wear what you want; but if you are still working for $12.00 an hour at another man's job, then you need to conform (while you are at work) to the dominant culture where you are working. If you ever want to do it the way Russell Simmons does it, then you definitely are going to need some cash to pull it off. Simmons pulled it all of so smooth that he owns the company that makes his clothes. Now that's a Phat business model ... or should I say a Phat Farm business model.

I want to tell the young cats at my job that I am not copying the white man's dress and advocating a yeoman's work ethic because I am a sell-out. I'm copying his dress and working hard because I know that in order to win the war of gaining control of my life that I will have to lose a few battles along the way. Wearing an earring or dressing hip-hop at a job that has a different business culture is a battle that you can afford to lose when your ultimate goal is gaining financial independence from the money that you earn.

It is not only about the money, it's also about experience. The more experience that you get in the business world the better chance you have to take that experience and start your own business. If you are not at a point in your life where you can operate from a position of power, then you have to fit-in until you are ready to make your power move. You have to go along to get along.

You don't do that because you are a sell-out; you do that so that you can have full access to opportunities that may help you achieve your goals quicker. Play the game until you can control the game ... and you need money to control the game. Don't think of it as a sell-out, think of it as maximizing your opportunity to buy-out.

It is no more of selling-out than the slaves who played the master's game so that the master might be willing to let them keep a little bit of their wages so that one day they might be able to buy their freedom. It makes more sense today than it did then because there are laws to make sure that the master pays you and you get to keep more of the money you make. The smarter and more prudent you are, the more money you can make to pursue your economic freedom in this fierce capitalistic society.

Political justice and social justice have taken us a long way in this country; in some cases they have taken us as far as they can take us. In those cases, the pursuit of economic justice and economic equality has to be prioritized ahead of political and social justice. Economic justice can buy political and social justice at wholesale prices.

I think that the recognition and application of this concept is critical if we hope to accelerate our overall ability to create proactive programs to empower the next generation. Black dollars will create better individual households, lead to better neighborhoods and schools, and ultimately lead to a more competitive Black community. We are going to need resources; the access to resources requires cash. In America, money pays tha cost to be tha boss. For this reason, we have to maximize our pursuit of capital to finance the next leg of the struggle.

I think that those were some of the things that the brother who interviewed me wanted to tell me, but it was probably too risky for him to blow his cover on a person who he really didn't know all that well. I think that he wanted to tell me that the chances were real strong that I would get eaten alive without even realizing it in Corporate America with the way that I was thinking on the earring issue.

I see some of the young brothers getting eaten alive today at my job without even realizing it. Whether it's right or wrong, for the sake of what they view as "keeping it real", many of the young Black men at my job today will not be looked upon as legitimate promotional candidates and will be passed over when it comes to financial promotions and other opportunities.

Knowing what I know now about Corporate America, I am almost sure that I would have been viewed the same way if I had continued to insist on wearing my earring to interviews, but we will never know. Although I did not agree with what the brother that I interviewed with for the Consortium fellowship was saying to me at the time, he said enough to make it my last interview where I wore an earring.

Hopefully, I have written enough to make some young brother change his game plan. Attack your career goals the same way that M.J. attacks the basket, but don't get called for a charge. Be smart and be a true player that plays the game, don't let the game play you. You might just end up like Mike. He's an owner now. Madison Avenue didn't pay him all that money just because he was so good in basketball; they paid it to him because he went along with the program. It has helped make him rich enough to break the rules and make the rules all over again—just call them the Jordan rules.

I wouldn't get the results from the Consortium application until the end of the school year and I didn't really have a solid back-up plan, so I spent the majority of the 1995-96 spring semester hoping for the best until I finally got the results in late April. The results informed me that I was not selected for a Consortium fellowship at that time and that I was welcome to submit a new application for the following school year. At first I was really upset about the whole thing because I felt that I could have easily handled graduate school. I just needed someone to finance it for me.

The rejection awakened those old fears of me not being able to make enough money to have the type of control over my life that I wanted to have. But I couldn't feel down for too long, because graduation was finally right around the corner.

I didn't have the drive to hit the books during my last year at Eckerd that I had the previous three school years. I failed to get straight A's both semesters, but I was still respectable. My transcript for the 1995-96 school year read as follows:

Abnormal Psychology: B

Intermediate Spanish I : B

Judaeo-Christian Seminar: A

The Living Theater: B

Sr. Seminar: Issues in Management: A

Business Policy/Strategic Management: A

Intermediate Spanish II: A

Ecotheology: A

Introduction to Anthropology: A

Multinational Corporate Strategy: B

I finished up my college career with an overall 3.75 GPA and I was set to graduate with Honors with a Bachelor of Arts degree from Eckerd College on May 19, 1996. I would leave the "right climate for learning" with a double major in Business Management and International Business, with a minor in Psychology thrown in for GP.

College had taken me on a long journey and that journey culminated with a triumphant walk across the stage to pick up my degrees. I had more relatives at the ceremony than one would expect from someone who grew up bouncing from place to place. But then again that may have been the reason why, I had a couple of people from a little bit of everywhere. My mom came to see the child that she had had twenty-three years ago walk across the stage to join the ranks of America's college educated. We weren't close, but she was the woman that birthed me. And of course Grandma Dot came and gushed over the fact that her grandson graduated with Honors.

Before my big day, I had heard through Grandma Dot that even my long lost dad was going to make an appearance for the special occasion. She also later relayed a message that something came up for him at the last minute and he couldn't make it. That was cool because I didn't know if he expected us to be like a dad and son thing and I didn't want to hurt anybody's feelings.

Although my dad didn't make it, his side of the family was well represented. My Aunt Linda was there, my cousins, and Grandma Mary with her only legitimate daughter-in-law. They now both shared the same first and last name. The newest Mrs. Mary McNeal had married Grandma Mary's most successful son, the accountant with the master's degree. I guess he always had to have a Mary McNeal in his life. I understood his thinking. After knowing my paternal grandmother, I didn't think that anyone could ever have enough Mary McNeals. I was happy to share my happiness with all that came to see me graduate, but the deepest part of my happiness was too private to share. I thought about all of the obstacles that I had to overcome in order to get a college degree in my hand. I thought about all of the private pain that had to be conquered just to keep on fighting and pushing toward the moment in my life upon which I stood on my graduation day. The joy of the moment and sense of accomplishment that I felt was like a temporary reprieve from all the past pain and my soul rejoiced in triumphant jubilation.

My soul was dancing and my spirit was high when my grand-mother's daughter-in-law asked me what I thought I would be doing five years from now. She had a video camera aimed directly at my face ready to immortalize the moment VHS style. I never saw the tape, but I remember what I said.

I told her, as I looked directly into the camera, that I wasn't sure what I would be doing five years from now; but I believed that it would be something great (Mama Cleo's prophecy ran through my mind). I didn't tell her that because I was arrogant, I told her that because when she asked the question I really believed deep down in my soul that the Lord would have me doing something great five years from that moment.

Today is March 19, 2001. Only time will tell what I will be doing two months from now on May 19, 2001. When I made that statement on May 19, 1996, my faith was waxed strong in the fact that the Lord would bless whatever I was doing. I had overwhelming evidence in the fact that He had already delivered me over my past obstacles to allow me to be standing there looking into a video camera with a college degree in my hand. I felt that my life had to be ordered by God. There were too many things that should have happened to me that didn't.

Who would have ever thought I would end up graduating from college with Honors coming from the background from whence I came? When answering that question, you have to exclude my grandmothers; they had insider information. It seemed to me that they talked directly with God or He talked directly to them. I was glad that I was my grandmothers' grandchild. I knew that they had both prayed long and hard for me.

Nevertheless, I did not make that statement that I would be doing "something great" out of arrogance; I made the statement based on faith. And what is faith other than "the substance of things hoped for, the evidence of things not seen"? (Hebrews chapter 11 verse 1) I was standing on faith. My grandmothers' taught me that when you stood on faith, you may slip, but you would never fall. I made the statement because like the old Negro spiritual that my ancestors and elders sang, I didn't feel "No Ways Tired". I had come too far from where I started from. Nobody told me that the road would be easy, but I didn't believe that He had brought me that far to leave me.

INDEX

A

AAS. *See* Afro-American Society
AASU. *See* African-American
    Student Union
Abolitionist cause, 40
Academic achievement. *See*
    Intellectual potential
Academy of Senior Professionals
    at Eckerd College (ASPEC),
    378–379
Accusations, 183
Achebe, Chinua, 135
Achievement, 111, 152–153, 160,
    176–177, 313–314, 357–358, 369,
    376, 443, 450
    in writing, 185
    See also Athletic talent;
    Intellectual potential
Acting grown up, 50
Acting "ugly," 31
Action, time for, 237
Ad Hominem fallacy, 350–351
Adidas, 89
"Advice to Young Writers," 313
Affirmative action, 384
Africa
    colonialism in, 204
    contributions to antiquity,
    81–82
    cool progenitors from, 260
    and learning French, 403
    possible war with a nation of,
    199
    rhythm of, 125–135
    view of death, 3
Africa in History, 82

African culture, 128–130, 400
African pride, 133, 292, 414
    seeds of planted, 131
African proverbs, 25
African roots, 338
African Studies, Institute of, 279
African-American Child
    Conference, 156
African-American Student Union
    (AASU), 410–411
African-American Women in
    Literature, 283–284
African-Americans, proposed
    reparations for, 198
Africans, low hypertension rates
    of, 447
Afrika Bambaattaa, 262
Afro-American Society (AAS),
    330–333
Afro-American Studies
    Department, Harvard
    University, 46
Alcohol
    abstinence from, 30
    mother's use of, 29
Ali, Muhammad, 155, 400
*All God's Children Need Traveling
    Shoes*, 130
All-American basketball players,
    211–212, 233, 275
Allen, Richard, 340–341
The Almighty
    keeping our faith grounded in,
    19
    most worthy to be praised, 12
The almighty dollar, worship of, 17
Amateur Athletic Union (AAU)
    teams, 227–228
The American Dream, 45

America's wars, Black men serving in, 339
America's wilderness, Black people in, 18
Anderson, Marian, 45, 93–94
Angelou, Maya, 128–130, 261, 331, 344, 350, 409
Anger, 153, 254, 331
   bordering on hatred, 367
Ankle injury, 310–311, 314, 325
Anti-police, lyrics of N.W.A., 307
Antiquity, African contributions to, 81–82
Anxiety, 180–181
Appeal to the Coloured Citizens of the World, 340
Arcadia Desoto team, 243
Arguments, 290
Aristotle, 350
Art, 19
Ashe, Arthur, 49
Assaults, becoming impervious to, 156
Athletic talent
   developing, 44, 106, 117
   discovering, 43–44
Atonement, America's, 18
Aunt Gene, 40–41, 69, 165, 187
Aunt Linda, 70, 77, 167, 464
Authority, 29, 59
Auto sound system, 318
The Autobiography of an Ex-Colored Man, 262, 287
The Autobiography of Malcolm X, 135, 344
The Autobiography of W.E.B. Du Bois: A Soliloquy on Viewing My Life from the Last Decade of Its First Century, 18

Avery, Shug, 73

B
Baldwin, James, 74, 81, 104, 429, 445
"The Ballot or the Bullet," 264, 341
Baraka, Imamu Amiri, 135, 313
Barbershop talk, 335–346
Bar-Kays jam, 73
Baseball playing, 117–121, 123–124
Basketball camps, 167–170, 227–228
Basketball coaches, 219–220, 231, 276, 399
Basketball playing, 121–122, 161, 171–174, 186–187, 209–212, 274, 309–314, 325, 390, 425, 443
   being a crowd favorite, 248–251, 289
   being a team player, 210
   dribbling skill, 239, 246
   getting dropped from, 352
   getting injured, 310–311, 314
   importance of, 328
   making a comeback in, 353
   mental rehearsal in, 248–249
   mojo of, 348
   quitting the team, 366
   scholarships for, 211, 227
   slipping up, 177–178
   succeeding, 233–251
   working hard at, 178–179
Battle, of being a Black man, 199
Battle, Mo, 324
Bealsville, Florida, 25–26, 30, 32, 50
"Beating their stringy heads," 137–141
Beauty, 19
   cultural standards of, 135
Bebop, 306

Bee-in-the-classroom episode, 222–223

Bennett, Lerone, Jr., 346

Benson, Janice Hale, 156, 313

Benson, Kent, 168

Berton, Pierre, 205

Bethune, Mary McLeod, 76

Bethune-Cookman College, 76

Betting it up, 281–292

The Bible, 17, 407
  reinforcing slavery, 133
  studying, 186
  See also individual books of

Big man on campus, 171–174

Bird's Bar, 92

Birth saga, 2, 313

Birthdays, 21

Births, premature, 9, 313

Black, symbolic associations with, 93, 133–134

"Black and Blue," 302

Black athletes, 41, 44–46, 117, 257
  youngsters seeking to emulate, 44–46, 117
  See also individual athletes

Black Boy, 185

Black children
  challenging, 46, 97, 226, 328
  confusing academic success with "acting white," 434
  importance of a teacher for, 439

Black churches, 4, 415

The Black Collegian Online, 313

Black conscious mind, 267

Black contributions to the United States, centuries' worth of, 339–340

Black culture, 18, 98
  aspirations promoted by, 45–46

teaching in public schools, 65, 434

Black grandmothers, 192, 465–466

Black hair styles, 134, 259, 335

Black History month, 410–411, 450

Black jive, 240, 425–441

Black literature, 145

Black men, 59, 182
  calling each other "baby," 259
  crack-up cocktail of, 189
  endangered species in the U.S., 430
  feeling of self-worth, 94
  fulfilling wedding vows, 38–39
  going off the deep end, 307
  grueling and unremitting battle of, 199, 449
  as martyrs, 265, 338
  rage of, 152
  serving in America's wars, 339
  standing in the face of prejudice, 240
  voices of trumping the voices of all other groups, 331

Black music, 18, 261, 306
  getting hooked on, 262
  profiting white people, 261

Black on Black violence, 57–58, 92, 113

Black people
  achieving economic success, 19
  in America's wilderness, 18
  brainwashed by whites, 130
  collective castration of, 130
  core values of, 17
  depending on God, 16
  gifted with second-sight, 193
  during the Great Depression, 15–16

image of being inferior, 445
injustices suffered by, 80, 125–128
lack of opportunities afforded to, 15, 89–90
looking out for each other, 16, 103, 414–415
love and compassion among, 55
maintaining a united front, 49
meekness of, 34
needing to help themselves, 435–436
observing, 337
realizations needed by, 131–132, 135–136, 426
regarded as property, 132–133
relationship with their music, 306
rights of, 132–133, 300, 339, 416
roots in education, 434
skin color among, 134
stealing hope, 45
stolen from Africa by whites, 338
traditions of, 3, 20
trouble with forgiveness, 374
"two-ness" felt by, 194–195, 197, 346
yoke of oppression carried by, 14
See also The less fortunate
Black Reconstruction, 264
Black soul, 106, 286
not bleaching, 203
Black sounds, & White girls, 209–224
Black student population, 234–235, 253
Black unity, quest for, 346

Black world
backlash from, 202
being watched by, 217
growing up in, 195
playing Black cards in, 218
Blackburn Elementary School, 69
Blackness, 338
basking in, 335
feeling ashamed of, 98, 133–134
feeling good about, 106, 236, 259–260
God-given, 361
impact of, 445
limits imposed by the world, 385
Bleaching the Negro Soul, refusal of, 203
Blindness, 15
Blood
given by Blacks, 341
thicker than water, 191
The blues, 306
listening to, 71
significance of, 130
See also R&B (Rhythm and Blues)
Bobos, 63–68
Boogie. See Julius
Born to Rebel, 226
Boycott of South Carolina, 47
Boys in school. See Frog; Julius; Peewee; Vietnamese boy in school (Sonny); Watkins, Floyd; Williams, Michael Jermaine
Boyz N the Hood, 188
Bradenton, Florida, 30, 37–38, 42, 69, 77, 123–124, 147, 293, 316, 398
newspaper coverage in, 242, 248–251

Bradenton Middle School, 148–154,
172, 236
receiving awards in, 160
Brainwashing, of Black people by
whites, 130–131, 134
Bravery, 105–106
Brilliance, stunning, 458
Brooks, Charles (Granddaddy
Charles), 3
Brothers, caring for, 422, 436–437
Brown, Claude, 145, 259–260, 304
Brown, H. Rap, 366
Brown, James, 326
*Brown v. the Board of Education of
Topeka*, 268
Buick, 32, 34
Bunche, Ralph, 374
"Burial insurance," 80
Business recommendations,
making sound, 375

C
Café/poolroom, 27, 30, 43, 47, 49–50
dialogue in, 28–29
Cain and Abel, 133
Calvin Klein, 89
Campus Ministries, 359
Car phones, 318
Carmichael, Stokley, 138
Carrie. *See* Great Great-Grandma
Carrie
Carrington, John, 128
Catalyst, 408
Cee, Granddaddy. *See* Knighten,
Ceola
Ceremonies, rites of passage, 431
The Challenge of Blackness, 346
Challenging Black children, 46
Character, events shaping, 179

Charles, Granddaddy. *See* Brooks,
Charles
Chasing pawns, 324, 382
Chess playing, 141
Chevy Impala, 355
Children, Black, challenging, 46, 97
Chris, 51–52
Christianity
importance of, 186
influence on world affairs, 345
view of interracial dating or
marriage, 204
whites' version of, 344
Christmas tournaments, 212
Chua-Eoan, Howard, 302
Church, attending, 71–73
Cleage, Pearl, 408
Cleo. *See* Mama Cleo
Clothes
being judged by, 89, 319
buying new, 187–188
stolen, 209
See also Jewelry
Coaches
basketball, 219–220, 231, 255–
258, 326
pressure from, 255–258, 394
respect for, 257, 402
Cocaine. *See* Crack cocaine
Coexistence, peaceful, 345
Cohen, Adam, 305
College campus
racism on, 286–287
switching to another, 368
College education, 281
developing desire for, 225
getting advice on, 220–221,
273–274

improving chances of getting, 227

scholarships for, 237, 277

Colonialism, 204

The Color Purple, 36

Colored people's time (CPT), 287

Commerce, triangle of, 128

Community policing, 24–25

Competition, true, 179

Compromise, rejecting, 259–265, 366

Confederate flag, 47–49

Confidence, 59, 111, 155–159, 169, 233, 250, 277, 319, 325, 400

the Floyd Watkins School of, 313

losing, 178, 184

Conquerors, writing history, 96

Consortium for Graduate Study in Management, 458–460

Constitution, not referring to those of African descent, 132–133

Convictions, spiritual, 16–17

Coolness, 260

Core values of Black people, 17

Counting, learning, 63–64

Courage, 455

Cousin Kary, 27, 47, 51–52, 57, 60–63, 84–87

Cousins, 27

CPT. *See* Colored people's time

Crack cocaine, 144–146, 165, 189–191, 320, 377

crippling entire families, 191

Crackers. *See* White people

Cracking up, 175–192

The Crack-Up, 218

Crime

escaping, 434

people not born to, 438

pitfall of, 46

within police departments, 297

Crisis, 158

Cross-Race Identification Bias, 286

Crying, 188–189

The Cultural Environment of International Business, 372–374

Curiosity, 75

Cush (in Bible), 98

Cussing. *See* Profanity

D

Dade County, 436

Danae, birth of, 9–12

Dancing, 71, 261, 465

Dandridge, Dorothy, 45

Danger, on the strip, 55

Dapper Dan Roundball Classic, 230

Dating. *See* Interracial dating and marriage

David and Goliath, 9–11, 181, 251

See also Pierce, David

Davidson, Basil, 82

Death, 165–167

African view of, 3

Declaration of Independence, 411

not referring to those of African descent, 132–133

Demeanor, learning about, 319

Denby, 304–305

Dennis, 92–93

'The Desert Fathers, 345

"The Destiny of the Colored American," 342

Destruction, science for, 19

Deuteronomy 8:3, 20

Diallo, Amadou, 299–305

N.Y.P.D. shooting of, 301

Dialogue, in the poolroom, 28–29
Diana, story of, 9–12
Diaspora, of the African, 129
Die Nigger Die, 366
"Dirty Street," 23
Disco, 306
Diversity, 25, 97
Dog, scared by, 33–34
Dollar, worshiping the almighty, 17
Donell, 83–86, 89
"Don't Stop 'Til You Get Enough," 84
Dorsett, Tony, 45
Dot. *See* Grandma Dot
Douglass, Fredrick, 297–299, 304, 332–333, 340–342
Dred Scott case of 1857, 132–133
Drugs
  abstinence from, 30
  dealing, 420, 438
  mother's use of, 29
  pitfall of, 46
Drum playing, 138
Du Bois, W.E.B., 18, 141, 158, 193–194, 202, 206–207, 264, 281, 340–341, 361, 410, 420, 422
Duffs Smorgasbord, 104–105
The Dukes of Hazzard, 47, 49
Dustin, story of, 10

E
Eastwood, Clint, 83
Eating out, 104
Ebenezer Baptist Church, 422
Ebony magazine, 336
Eckerd College, 274–275, 281–292, 306, 309, 322, 328–330, 335, 355, 360–361, 365, 464
  African-American students at, 329–330
  Director of Multicultural Affairs, 285–286
  reflections on, 377
  tryout/conditioning programs at, 363
Economic opportunity, 19
The Economist, 431–432
Education, 49
  beyond college, 409
  of the heart, 36
  ignoring Black culture in, 65
  as the key to breaking out, 279, 370, 433
  See also Mis-education
Egyptians, ancient civilizations of, 82
Ellington, Duke, 29
Ellison, Ralph, 64–65, 440
El-Shabazz, El Jajj Malik. *See* Malcolm X
Emancipation Proclamation, 391
Emotions
  helpless, 295
  maladjusted, 282
  vulnerable, 217
  whirlwind, 254
English classes, 185
Enlightenment, 184
Entertainment, 33
  influence of, 45
Envy, of white children, 91
Erving, Julius, 327–328
Escape, 173
Essence magazine, 198, 423
Ethiopia, 98
Eurocentric value system, 131, 197
Eurocentric version of history, 96, 435

European people
  foundations of, 82
  stealing Black people's moves,
    261
Evans, David L., 431–432, 437
Evers, Medgar, 338
Eviction, 163–170
Evidence, of things not seen,
    453–466
Extended kinship, 40–41

F
Faces
  placing, 29
  See also Saying it in my face
Fairness, 182, 365
Faith, 19–20, 76, 169, 181
  the substance of things hoped
    for, 174, 466
Fallacies of logic, 350–352
Family & friends, 143–161, 256
  crack cocaine crippling, 191
  crimes of, 189–191
"Famine days," 103–104
Farrel, Christopher, 437
Father
  anger with, 272
  feelings toward, 77–78, 271
Fear
  acronym spelling, 228, 426
  moving beyond, 232
Fever, in infancy, 5–6
Fighting, 139–141, 153–154, 157,
    231–232, 235–236, 263, 393, 401,
    444–445
Films, market morality in, 18
The Fire Next Time, 74
Fitzgerald, F. Scott, 218

Florida
  Bealsville, 25–26, 30, 32, 43–44,
    50
  Bradenton, 30, 37–38, 42, 69, 77,
    123–124, 147, 242, 293, 316, 398
  Palmetto, 23, 30, 32, 37–38, 41,
    43, 50, 69, 87–88, 92, 101–102,
    123–124, 231
  Plant City, 25, 27, 30, 32, 35, 43,
    50, 60, 63, 68, 89, 165, 173, 192,
    272–273, 319
  Sarasota, 2, 165, 242, 293
  weather in, 176
Florida State University, 277
"Foday in the morning," 32
Ford, Phil, 212
Fortune. *See* The less fortunate
Founding fathers, not interested
  in those of African descent,
    132–133
Franklin, C.L., 127
Free lunches, 90–91, 102–103
Friends & family, 143–161
Friendship, 150
Frog, 56–59, 92–93, 152
Fruit workers, seasonal, 32–33
Funk, 306
The Furious Five, 262

G
Gandhi, Mahatma, 345, 448
"Gangsta Cops," 305
"Gangsta rap," 262
Garland, Phyl, 306
Garvey, Marcus, 131
Gates, Henry Louis, Jr., 46, 129
Gaye, Marvin, 234
Geiggar, Kwasi, 440
Genesis 9:24-25, 133

Genesis 10, 98

"Geronimo!", 105–106

Gestapo tactics, of the police, 296–297, 299–305

Gheri-curls, 134

Ghetto fabulous, 294, 382

Ghetto mentality, 323–324, 383

Ghetto stores, 388

Giftedness, 269

"Gimme 5," 101–111

    See also High-five jive

Gimme a Break, 92

Girls, 209, 213–214, 394–396

    See also Dating; Interracial dating and marriage; White girls

"Git Up, Git Out," 422–423

God, 2–3

    getting closer to, 423

    gratefulness toward, 356

    greatness of, 9

    holding the rights to my life, 362

    intervention by, 6–8, 11

    as invincible, 268

    learning about, 168

    as love, 196, 268

    plan of, 8

    praising, 34

    praying for help from, 181, 278, 465–466

    of Right, 341

    running to, 192

    seeking first the kingdom of, 20

    sense given us by, 269

    sufficient in all adversity, 75–76

    See also The Almighty; The Lord

God's child, feeling secure as, 174

Godsends, 31, 150, 371

Going to the Territory, 64, 440

Gooding, Cuba, Jr., 188

GQ magazine, 200

Granddaddy Cee. See Knighten, Ceola

Granddaddy Charles. See Brooks, Charles

Grandma Cleo (Mama Cleo), 3–6, 8, 165, 465

Grandma Dot, 1–2, 23–24, 30–41, 47, 69, 72, 79–80, 87, 101–102, 113–116, 145, 151–152, 160, 165, 173, 187, 407

    coming to college graduation, 464

    heartstring of, 192

    injury to, 49–50

    resolve to care for, 116, 123

    support from, 121, 191, 317

Grandma Mary, 69–70, 77, 117, 121, 149, 165, 167, 173, 175, 187, 219, 271, 464

Grandmaster Flash, 262

The Great Depression, Black people during, 15–16

Great Great-Grandma Carrie, 87

Greathouse, Betty, 430, 437

Greatness, 6

Greek civilization, foundations of, 82

Gregory, Sophronia Scott, 434, 437

Griot, role in different West African societies, 4

H

4-H Public Speaking Program, 108

Hair styles, Black, 134, 259, 335

Haley, Alex, 126, 344, 358

Ham (in Bible), 98, 133
The "Hard Road," 23–24
Harlem, 126, 145
Harvard University, Afro-
    American Studies Department,
    46
Hatred
    an antipode of love, 196
    anger bordering on, 367
Heads, stringy, 137–141
Healing power, 75
Healthcare, 49
Heart
    of a champion, 244
    of hearts, 347–353
    turning the pages of, 424
The Heart of a Woman, 261, 331, 344
Heartstrings, 192
Hebrews 11:1, 466
Hell, consigning all white people
    to, 267
Helplessness, 295
Henry, Patrick, 65, 264
Here I Stand, 342
Heroin, 145–146
High Jump competition, 111
High-five jive, 240
Highway of life, 456
    hitting, 363–370
Hindsight, 193–207
Hip injury, 5–6
Hip-Hop culture, 262, 461
History
    Eurocentric version of, 96
    written by the conquerors, 96
Hitting the highway, 363–370
Holiday, Billie, 391
"Holy Ghost," 73
The Holy Ghost, 69–76

"catching," 74, 222
    having power over people,
    73–74
Hope, 174
    Black people stealing, 45
Hotep, Ptah, 407
Howard University, 434
Hughes, Allen and Albert, 438
Hughes, Langston, 388
Human family, 448
Humanity, 236, 413
    not preceding, 200
Hunger, 49, 103–104, 163–164, 183
Hurston, Zora Neale, 265, 284, 421
Hurting. *See* Pain of living
Hypertension rates, low, of
    Africans, 447

I

"I Heard It Through the Grapevine,"
    234
"I Knew Carter G. Woodson,"
    423–424
I Know Why the Caged Bird Sings,
    350, 409
Ibgo tribe, 48
Identification Bias, Cross-Race, 286
"I'm Coming Out," 358
Incredible Hulk, 38
Individuality, not preceding, 200
Inflation, 20
Injury, ankle, 310–311, 314, 325
Institute of African Studies, 279,
    419
Insurance man episode, 79–82
    punishment for, 79–80
Intellectual potential
    discovering, 44
    failing to fulfill, 184, 269

fulfilling, 44, 99, 176–177, 311–312, 357–358, 372

God given, 108, 361, 371, 412, 450

indifference over grades, 122–123, 219

International students, discussions with, 373–374

Internship programs, 315, 381, 384, 386, 395, 453–454

Interracial dating and marriage, 201–206, 215–216, 270, 330–333, 412

Intimidation, 404

Invisible Man, 64, 90

Irony, 267–278

Izzod, 89

J

Jackson, Jesse, 374

Jackson, Michael, 45, 83–84, 113, 160, 463

Jackson Five, 84, 86, 122

"Jawaharlal Nehru Award for International Understanding," 386

Jazz, 306

Jesus Christ, 20, 265, 343, 379
   as best friend, 150
   claiming victory through, 169
   coming home to, 415
   having ancestors related to, 444
   as the Son of God, 278, 344

"Jesus on the Mainline," 4

Jet magazine, 440

Jewelry, 459–463

Jim Crow, 340

Jive, Black, 425–441

Jobs, 316

newspaper, 226, 381, 453

shoe store, 352

I John 4:4, 424

Johnson, Jack, 45

Johnson, James Weldon, 262, 287, 415, 448

Johnson, Lyndon B., 384

Johnson, Magic, 46, 107, 399, 431

Jones, Quincy, 392

Jordache, 89

Jordan, Michael, 46, 200, 319, 369, 420, 431

Jordan Park housing project, 355–356, 360, 369

The joys of learning, 371–380

Jukeboxes, 28

Julius, 43

Jungle Fever, 330

Justice, 137–138

K

Kaffir Boy, 279

Kary. *See* Cousin Kary

Keeping it all together, 182

Kennedy, John F., 384

Kindergarten, 43

King, Martin Luther, Jr., 97, 206, 226, 265, 338, 422, 448

King Middle School, 125, 138, 143, 148, 152–153, 235

Kingdom of God, seeking first, 20

Kinky hair, 134

Kinship, extended, 40–41

Kinte, Kunte, 139–140

Klymaxx, 148

Knighten, Ceola (Granddaddy Cee), 30–34, 36–37, 39, 43, 47, 87, 102, 114–115, 154–155, 182

Knowledge, 19, 313

highest form of, 313
of self, 376–377, 407–424, 444
as "spendable currency," 350
Kool Herc, 262
Kool Moe Dee, 263
Kool-Aid, 323
KRS-One, 263, 297
Ku Klux Klan, 391

L

Lakeland Civic Center, 84
Lakeland Kathleen team, 237–239
Laughter, 35, 62, 257
Laura St. Bar, 28–30
food served at, 53
Laura Street, 27, 43, 47–62, 83–84,
107, 165, 175, 261, 319
Learning, the joys of, 371–380
Learning counting, 63–64
Lee, General, 47
Lee, Spike, 126, 330
The less fortunate, 34
*Letter from Nelson Mandela to Mrs.
Manorama Bhalla, Secretary of
the Indian Council for Cultural
Relations, New Dehli*, 386
"Letter to Roland A. Barton," 158
Life
defining, 18–19, 281, 456
of diminishing chances, 221
highway of, 456
letting others make decisions
about, 362
unfairness of, 182
*The Life Experience and Gospel Labors
of Richard Allen*, 341
"Lift Every Voice and Sing," 415
Lightning Bolt, 89
Linda. *See* Aunt Linda

Linear thinking, 426
Little white lies, 77–82
Living by the Wind, 36
Locke, Alaine, 16
Logic, 349–352
Logical fallacies, 350–352
Ad Hominem, 350–351
Post Hoc, 351
Straw Man, 351
Lonely teardrops, 113–124
Long, Nia, 188
Looking, without touching, 31
The Lord
devoting your heart to, 421
getting on knees to, 192
getting strength from, 179
intervention by, 8
praying to, 13–14, 181, 356
Losing, 232
Louis, Joe, 45
Love, 18, 62, 115, 166, 182, 216,
267–268, 270
being a sucker for, 215
colorblind, 329
God as, 196
of money, 19
opposite of hate, 196, 416
Luck, 389
Lunch ticket, shame over, 90–91
Lying, 77–82
Lynn, 70–71, 167

M

Makes Me Wanna Holler, 324
Malcolm X, 48, 126, 131, 134–135,
198, 203, 206, 264–265, 338,
340–341, 344, 392–393, 409, 418,
426–427
renunciation of racism, 206

trip to Mecca, 205

Malcolm X, 126

Malone, Moses, 106

Mama Carrie. *See* Great Great-
Grandma Carrie

Mama Cleo. *See* Grandma Cleo

"The Man in the Arena," 443

The Managerial Enterprise, 372,
374–376, 454

Manasota Industrial Council
program, 315

Manatee Christian Basketball
Camp, 167, 186
working as a coach at, 359

Manatee Civic Center, 274

Manatee County teams, 220, 228

Manatee Elementary School, 69, 77

Manchild in the PROMISED LAND,
145, 260, 304

Mandela, Nelson, 386

"Manifest Destiny," 18

Marie-Antoinette, 455

Marijuana, 29, 60–62, 143–144
selling, 54
trying, 60–61

Market morality, 17–18

Marley, Bob, 362

Marriage. *See* Interracial dating
and marriage

Martha B. King Middle School. *See*
King Middle School

Mary. *See* Grandma Mary

Masculinity, 51

Masquerade, 447

Materialism
falling prey to, 35
threat from, 17

Mathabane, Mark, 279

Matthew 6:33, 20

Matthew 12:34-37, 379

Matthew 16:26, 17

Mays, Benjamin, 226, 423–424, 451

McCall, Nathan, 324

McCourtie, Cheryl, 198

McDonald's, 146–147, 173, 326–327,
359, 364

McDonald's All-American game,
230

Me Against the World album, 429

Mead, Margaret, 385

Mecca, Malcolm X's trip to, 205

Media attention, 242, 245, 248–251,
438

Meekness, 34

"Meeting In The Ladies Room," 148

Mel, Melle, 307

Melanin, 129

Menace II Society, 438

Mental poisoning. *See*
Brainwashing

Mental rehearsal, 248–249

Mental segregation, 268

Message, 417–423
imperative to deliver, 412, 414

Metropolitan Opera, 93

Mexican playmates, 106

Mfume, Kweisi, 48

"Michael Jordan in His Own
Orbit," 200

Mickey Dees. *See* McDonald's

"Middle Passage," 127, 129

"Migos," 106

Migratory living, 41

Militant Labor Forum, 418

Millennium, opening of the new, 7

The mind
ability to learn, 319
changing, 115

greatest weapon of any Black
against oppression, 107–108,
135–136
a tabula rasa, 397
See also Brainwashing
Ministers, exploitative, 18
Miracle Hold Church, 37
Misbehaving in public places, 31
Mis-education, 87–99, 409
The Mis-Education of the Negro,
98–99, 418
Mojo, of basketball playing, 348
Money, 176, 187, 189, 321, 457–461
love of, 19
ways of getting, 54
See also Pay received
Montgomery Bus Boycott, 97
Moral fiber, testing the endurance
of, 81
Morehouse College, 434
Moring, Mark, 248
Morrison, Toni, 284
Moses, parting the Red Sea, 332
Moses, Man of the Mountain, 421
Mother, 29
coming to college graduation,
464
living with, 37–38
in prison, 406
problems with drugs, 62, 271
troubled relationship with, 27,
60, 272
"Move on Up a Little Higher," 17
Moving frequently, 37, 39, 66, 125,
151, 163–164, 182–183
advantage in, 154
Mr. Charles, 204
Murder, allowed, 304–305
Murphy, Eddie, 431

Music is My Mistress, 29
Music videos
market morality in, 18
See also Jukeboxes
The MVP trophy contest, 163–170
My Bondage and My Freedom, 297
My Soul Looks Back, 'Less I Forget,
407, 409, 444

N
NAACP, 18, 47, 49
Names, from slaveholders, 393
"Nappy" hair, 134
*Narratives of Sojourner Truth, A
Northern Slave,* 40
National Council of Negro
Women, 76
Native Americans, slaughtered in
the USA, 18
NBA, 41
Neatness, 319
Needs, all provided for, 20
Negro History Bulletin, 424
Negro National Anthem, 415
The Negro Problem, 420
Negro spirituals, 306
The New Negro, 16
The New Phoenix, 381–396
New Year's Eve, church attendance
on, 7
Newspaper jobs, 226, 381, 386–387,
395
papertime operations, 386
"Niggas." *See* Black people
Nihilism, pitfall of, 46
Nike, 89
Nimrod, 98
Nin, Anais, 150
Nkrumah, Kwame, 201, 279, 409, 419

Nobody Knows My Name, 445
Normalcy, 2, 282
North Star, 342
Norwood, Dorothy, 75
Not compromising, 259–265
Notes of a Native Son, 104
N.W.A., 235, 262, 306
  anti-police lyrics of, 307
N.Y.P.D., shooting of Amadou
  Diallo, 301

O
Observing Black people, 337
Obstacles, overcoming, 424
Ocean Pacific (OP), 89
Off the Wall (album), 84
Ol' time religion, 13–21
Oldsmobile Delta 88, 147–148, 382
"Ole Rickety Bridge," 75
OP. *See* Ocean Pacific
Opportunities, redistribution of,
  201
Opportunities afforded to Black
  people
  economic, 19
  lack of, 15
Oppression, yoke of carried by
  Black people, 14
Orange groves, 23–36
Orange Ridge Elementary School,
  42
Organization of Afro-American
  Unity, 135
Organizational Behavior and
  Leadership, 372, 376–377
Outkast, 422, 449
The Outlaw Josey Wales, 83
Overcoming obstacles, 424
Overpass Apartments, 23–25

Overseers, 297–299
Owens, Jessie, 45

P
Pain of living, 173–174, 283, 348
  conquering, 465
  trusting someone with, 271
Palmetto, Florida, 23, 30, 32, 37–38,
  41, 43, 50, 69, 87–88, 92, 101–102,
  123–124, 231
Palmetto Youth Center, 102, 111
Papertime operations, 386–387
Parenting, 25, 456
Passage, rites of, 431
The past, values from, 16–17
Paternal grandfather, 166–167
Paternal great-grandfather, 15–16
Paternal great-grandmother, 15–16,
  116
Pawns, chasing, 324, 382
Pay received, 226, 458
Peaceful coexistence, 345
Peewee, 56–59, 92–93, 152
Pell grants, 389
Philippians 4:13, 169
Phoenix, The New, 381–396
Phones, car, 318
Physical punishment, 31
Physician, 2–3, 9
  as a career goal, 327–328
Pierce, David, 356–357, 360, 369–370
Pine Villa Elementary School, 436
Pitfalls facing Black children, 46
Plan of God, 8
Plant City, Florida, 25, 27, 30, 32, 35,
  43, 50, 60, 63, 68, 89, 165, 173, 192,
  272–273, 319
Plato, 350
"Play cousins," 27

"Play That Funky Music," 33
"Players Ball," 449
Playing, ability to, 309–314
"Please, Please, Please," 326
Pledge of Allegiance, 43
    hatred toward, 137
Police, 288, 294–297
    anti-police lyrics of N.W.A., 307
    Gestapo tactics of, 296, 299–305
    need for adequate internal
    supervision, 302
Policing, by the community, 24–25
Poolroom/café, 27, 30, 43
    dialogue in, 28–29
    skill in playing pool, 84
Possum, eating, 26
Post Hoc fallacy, 351
Poverty, 49
    constant companionship of, 14
    escaping, 105, 433
    lessons of, 35–36
Powell, Colin, 291
Power
    for healing, 75
    over words, 158
    projecting through words,
    28–29
Prayer, 3, 9, 19, 74–75, 93, 183
    a multi-purpose cure, 14
    serious business for Black
    people, 13
Prayer meetings, 14–15
Prejudice, 93–94
    putting into words, 109–111
Premature births, 9, 313
Pressure, full-court, 238
Prince, music of, 144, 423
Prine Elementary School, 39
Pro-Am league, 360

Profanity, 50, 402
    punishment for using, 24, 71
Professionalism, 384
Progenitors from Africa, cool, 260
The promise, fulfilled, 355–362
Promise of Power, 201
Promises, cashing in on, 53
The prophecy, 1–12, 206, 465
"The Prophet and Dry Bones in the
    Valley," 127
Prospects for Freedom in 1965, 48
Proverbs 18:21, 380
Proverbs 22:6, 72
Proverbs 27:2, 401
Psalm 139:1-13, 6–8
Psychological profiling, 135
Ptah Hotep, 407
Public Enemy, 263
Public places, misbehaving in, 31
Public speaking, 411
Pull poles, 33
Punishment, physical, 31

Q
Questions no one asked, 269–270

R
Rabbit, taste of, 26
Raccoon, eating, 26
Race Matters, 17, 303
Race relations, trying for a more
    positive attitude toward,
    255–258
Race-based insurance premiums,
    80–81
Races, all human, 203
Racial profiling, 302
Racism
    deliberate, 126

interwoven into the fabric of this country, 95

lurking beneath every other issue, 201

Malcolm X's renunciation of, 206

questions about, 125

regressive, 446–448

in school, 88–89, 95

in white girlfriend's father, 258

Rage, of the Black man, 152, 157

Ragtime, 260, 262, 306

Rain

and the African view of death, 3

unique scent of, 9, 11

Rap artists, 28, 262

Rap music, 260, 285–286, 306–307

See also "Gangsta rap"

R&B (Rhythm and Blues), 306

"Real cousins," 27

Reality, separating life from wishes, 78

Rebellion, 253, 264, 402

Red, 56

Red Lobster, 212

Red Sea, Moses parting, 332

Redistribution, of resources or opportunities, 201

Reefer. *See* Marijuana

Reggae, 306

Regressive racism, 446–448

Relationships, depth of, 85–86

Religion

exclusive domain of Grandma Mary, 71

the ol' time, 13–21

serious business for Black people, 13

trying to comprehend, 72

Renault Alliance, 320, 323, 352

Rent, paying on your own, 455

Rental cars, 387

Reparations, proposed for African-Americans, 198

Repentance, 415

Resources, redistribution of, 201

Respect, 58–60

for coaches, 257

The revolution, 343

beginning with self knowledge, 263

challenge of 21st century, 135–136

The Revolutionary War, 131–132

Rhonda, 70, 167

Rhythms of Africa, 125–135, 260

See also R&B (Rhythm and Blues)

Right, the God of, 341

Riley, Dorothy Winbush, 191, 407, 440, 450

Rite of passage ceremonies, 431

Robbery, 188, 320

Robeson, Paul, 129–130, 340, 342

Robinson, Jackie, 45

Rock and Roll, 306

"Rock With You," 84

Romeo and Juliet, 257

Roots, 126–127, 137, 198, 408

Ross, Diana, 358

Russell, Bill, 41

S

Sacrifice, 15

Sarasota, Florida, 2, 165, 293

newspaper coverage in, 242

Sarasota Booker team, 244–245

Sarasota Cardinal Mooney team, 239–243
Sarasota Memorial Hospital, 4
Sarasota Police Department, 288, 294–297, 306
Sassoon, 89
SAT preparation course, 233, 268
SAT scores earned, 277
Saving some for another, 103
Saying it in my face, 225–232
School days, 37–46, 256
    fighting in, 139–141, 153–154, 157
    grades earned, 218–219
    racism on, 88–89, 95, 148–150
    receiving awards, 160
    reputation among faculty and staff, 224
    segregated classrooms, 268
    See also Big man on campus; individual schools
Science, for destruction, 19
SCU. See Street Crime Unit
Second Wind, 41
Second-sight, Black people gifted with, 193
Segregation, mental, 268
The self, knowledge of, 376–377, 407–424, 444
Self-consciousness, 119–121
Self-empowerment, 417
Self-esteem, 95
Self-help, 417
Self-improvement, 417, 451
Self-reliance, 416–417
Selling, and buying, 18–19
Selling out, 196, 217, 236, 263, 462
Sex, 18, 27–28
Shaky, 56–57

Shame
    in athletics, 119–121
    of being black, 98
    over free lunch ticket, 90–91, 138
Sharecropping, 26
"Ship of Salvation," 166
Shoes, symbolism of, 67–68
Shortness, 245, 382
Simmons, Russell, 459–463
Sin, 79
Singleton, John, 188
Sisyphus, 408
Skin color, 257
    among Black people, 134
    superficiality of, 268
Skin lightening cremes, 134
Slaveholder's names, 393
Slaveholding states, 300
Slavery days, 40, 81, 126–133, 205, 340, 426
    ignorance about, 137
    reparations for, 198
Small-time thinking, 318
Smell of Rain (e-mail), 9
Smith, Dean, 211–212, 230
The Smurfs, 109–110
"So Many Tears," 429
Social Psychology class, 430
Socrates, 350
Sojourner Truth, 40
Solomon, wisdom of, 401
Sonny. See Vietnamese boy in school
The soul
    leaving the body, 327
    losing, 17, 181
    See also Black soul
Soul belief in self, 169

The Souls of Black Folk, 141, 193–194, 202, 206, 341, 410
"Sound of Da Police," 297
Sound system, auto, 318
South Africa, liberation of, 449
South Carolina
    boycott of, 47
    display of Confederate flag in, 47–48
Southeast High School, 167, 171, 186, 207, 209, 214, 220, 229, 231, 234, 249, 256, 273
    team pride at, 243, 246–247
Southern Horrors: Lynch Law in All Its Phases, 391
Southern playalisticadillacmuzik album, 422
Sparling, Sandra, 430, 437
Speaking, without yelling, 31
Specialness, 2
Spelling contest, 44
Spiritual convictions, 16–17, 344
    selling out, 17
Spirituals, Negro, 306
Split-level hi-top fade, 259
Sports, influence of, 45
St. Peter, 3
St. Petersburg Gibbs team, 274
Staying in your place, 253–258
Step Up! program, 315
Stewart Elementary School, 88–91, 95, 99, 107, 109, 114
Stonewall Jackson Elementary School, 63
Storytelling, 35
Straight Outta Compton album, 235
Straw Man fallacy, 351–352
    perpetrators of, 351–352
Street concepts, 63–64

Street Crime Unit (SCU), 301–305
Street life, 50–51
Stringy heads, beating, 137–141
Sub-standard academic achievement, pitfall of, 46
Subway sandwich shop episode, 294–297
Sugar Hill Gang, 262
Suggs Projects, 77–78
Summer school attendance, 224–225
Suncoast Animal Clinic, 117
Superiority, claims of, 155–156
Support
    from friends, 151
    from Grandma Dot, 121
    for playing baseball, 124
Swing, 306

T
"The Talented Tenth," 420
Talk, barbershop, 335–346
Talk That Talk, 129
Taney, Roger B., 132–133
Tangents, going off on, 207
Tate, Larenz, 438
Teachers, important role played by, 440–441
Team Suncoast, 276
Teardrops, lonely, 113–124
Telephone calls home, 160
Tennessee, 397–406
Tennessee Wesleyan College (TWC), 397–398, 401–405, 417, 427, 444
Textbooks, deficiencies of, 94
Thankfulness, 16
Their Eyes Were Watching God, 265
Things Fall Apart, 135

Things not seen, evidence of, 453–466

Thinking
linear, 426
small-time, 318

Thriller, 160

Time, putting a high value on, 322

Time magazine, 46, 302, 305

Time warp, 26

I Timothy 6:10, 19

Tokenism, 97–98

Tongues, speaking in, 75

Tonya, 77–78

Total Release trophy, 168, 187

Toughness, 229

Transatlantic slave trade, 128

Trapnell Elementary School, 44, 47

Trophies, 168–170, 187

"Trouble In My Way," 37

Truth
cold, 83–86
universal, 268

Truth, Sojourner, 40

Turner, Tyrin, 438

12 Million Black Voices, 428

"Two-ness" felt by Blacks, 194–195, 197, 346

2-Pac, 429

U

"Ugly," acting, 31

"Ugly American," 96

Uncle Hennisan, 27

Uncle Willie, 70, 167, 170

United States
centuries' worth of Black contributions to, 339–340
conspiring to create a racist environment, 303
created by and for white people, 131
hatred for, 137
its crimes against the Black community, 305
popular opinion in, 373
racism interwoven into the fabric of, 95

Universal truths, 268

University of Alabama, 387, 393

University of Central Florida, 277

University of Florida, 277

University of North Carolina, 227, 230

University of South Florida (USF), 227

U.S. Highway 301, 23

U.S. Supreme Court, 268

USA Weekend, 49

USF. *See* University of South Florida

V

Valcarcel, Debra, 233, 268–274, 440

Values
of Black people, 17, 35
Eurocentric, 131

Victory
claiming through Christ, 169
shared with teammates, 347

Videos, market morality in, 18

Vietnam War, effect on returned veterans, 114

Vietnamese boy in school (Sonny), 42–43

Violence, 439
Black on Black, 57–58, 92, 113

Visualization, of successful free-throw attempts, 249

Vitale, Dick, 212
The voices of Black men, 332
    trumping the voices of all other
    groups, 331
Voting Rights Act of 1965, 132
VW Bug, 38
VW Rabbit, 278, 293–294, 316, 320

W
Wakeland Elementary School, 116,
    121, 175
Walker, Alice, 36, 73, 457
Walker, David, 340
Walking, without running, 31
Washington, Denzel, 126
Watkins, Floyd, 150–161, 168–174,
    178, 225, 227–229, 233–234, 237,
    244, 247–251, 274–275, 283–286,
    289, 313, 316, 347, 360, 363–364,
    366, 388
Weary, 443–451
Weather, 176
Wedding vows, Black men
    fulfilling, 38–39
Wells-Barnett, Ida B., 391
West, Cornell, 17–18, 303
Whales, Josey. *See* Donell
"What These Children Are Like,"
    440
"Where I Enter," 198
White girls
    & Black sounds, 209–224
    choosing to date them, 201–202,
    214–216, 253–255, 329, 359
    fathers of, 256, 258
    under lock and key, 256
"White is right" mentality, 196
White people, 42, 235
    consigning all to hell, 267

    feelings toward Blacks, 108–11
    hatred for, 137, 165, 416
    mainstream of, 217
    selfishness of, 130, 261
    systematically racist, 126, 292, 426
    thinking all Blacks look alike,
    286
White world
    backlash from, 202
    disapproval from, 195, 254
    never making peace with, 264
    playing White cards in, 218
    version of Christianity, 344
WHO magazine, 76
Wife beating, 39, 144
Wild Cherry, 33
Will, growing stronger, 364
Williams, Doug, 45, 107
Williams, Michael Jermaine
    (Mike), 121–122, 151, 153, 172
Willie. *See* Uncle Willie
Winn Dixie (Quick Check) grocery
    store, 31
Women
    attracting, 51
    how to satisfy, 28
    touching, 52
Woodson, Carter G., 65, 98, 418
Word of God, staying close to, 423
Words
    holding the power of life and
    death, 380
    idle, 380
    power over, 158–159
Work, 163, 175–176, 187
    See also Jobs
"Working Day And Night," 84
World affairs, Christianity's
    influence on, 345

Wright, Betty, impression of, 2
Wright, Richard, 185, 428
Wright, Willie J., 436–437
Writing, 429
    success at, 185

Y

Yahweh people, 138
Yankee Doodle, 65
Young Socialist, 409